JBoss: Developer's Guide

A complete guide to the JBoss ecosystem

Elvadas Nono Woguia

BIRMINGHAM - MUMBAI

JBoss: Developer's Guide

First published: August 2017

Production reference: 1290817

Published by Packt Publishing Ltd.
Livery Place
35 Livery Street
Birmingham
B3 2PB, UK.

ISBN 978-1-78829-619-9

www.packtpub.com

Credits

Author
Elvadas Nono Woguia

Reviewers
Meissa Sakho
Peter Guo Pei
Alain Dang Quang PHAM

Commissioning Editor
Smeet Thakkar

Acquisition Editor
Larissa Pinto

Content Development Editor
Aditi Gour

Technical Editor
Ralph Rosario

Copy Editor
Shaila Kusanale

Project Coordinator
Ritika Manoj

Proofreader
Safis Editing

Indexer
Mariammal Chettiyar

Graphics
Jason Monteiro

Production Coordinator
Shantanu Zagade

About the Author

Elvadas Nono Woguia is a software engineer, consultant, and open source technology enthusiast living in Paris. Elvadas studied computer science at Ecole Polytechnique Yaounde in Cameroon, and also holds a specialized master in IT systems management from Ecole Centrale Paris. He has now been working for 10 years in EMEA IT industry for various companies and customers, and is currently employed by Red Hat as Middleware and PAAS consultant.

Elvadas is a certified Oracle Web Component Developer Expert and a Certified Red Hat Platform As a Service Delivery Specialist. He currently helps Red Hat customers on their open source journey to design modern and scalable architectures, and build, customize, and integrate various middleware and cloud technologies and products around JBoss and Openshift ecosystems.

In his free time, Elvadas loves playing and watching soccer. He shares tech posts with the open source community on his blog on the Red Hat developers website. He cares about humanitarian causes; he founded and worked to bring peace and light among the needy through this charitable organization UrgenceSolidaires.

About the Reviewer

Peter Guo Pei is a Canadian big data and web technology expert. In the recent years, he has also worked on various mobile technologies. He lives in the quiet town of Langley along the US-Canadian border with his fantastic wife and two amazing kids. He studied information science in Fudan University, Shanghai.

He has worked for various IT companies in China, US, and Canada, including Sun Microsystems, Tandem, Wang, Kodak, and Motorola. He has also worked for major retailers.

He loves to travel with his family, and plans to volunteer for Tokyo 2020, be part of this historic event, enjoying Japan's rich history, wonderful people, and exquisite food.

I would like to thank my fantastic wife Yan and my two amazing kids—-my daughter Angel and son Jimmy. You have always been the sunshine of my life.

www.PacktPub.com

For support files and downloads related to your book, please visit www.PacktPub.com.

Did you know that Packt offers eBook versions of every book published, with PDF and ePub files available? You can upgrade to the eBook version at www.PacktPub.com and as a print book customer, you are entitled to a discount on the eBook copy. Get in touch with us at service@packtpub.com for more details.

At www.PacktPub.com, you can also read a collection of free technical articles, sign up for a range of free newsletters and receive exclusive discounts and offers on Packt books and eBooks.

https://www.packtpub.com/mapt

Get the most in-demand software skills with Mapt. Mapt gives you full access to all Packt books and video courses, as well as industry-leading tools to help you plan your personal development and advance your career.

Why subscribe?

- Fully searchable across every book published by Packt
- Copy and paste, print, and bookmark content
- On demand and accessible via a web browser

Customer Feedback

Thanks for purchasing this Packt book. At Packt, quality is at the heart of our editorial process. To help us improve, please leave us an honest review on this book's Amazon page at `https://www.amazon.com/dp/1788296192`.

If you'd like to join our team of regular reviewers, you can e-mail us at `customerreviews@packtpub.com`. We award our regular reviewers with free eBooks and videos in exchange for their valuable feedback. Help us be relentless in improving our products!

Table of Contents

Preface

Introduction

The JBoss ecosystem is very large and dynamic; the JBoss community drives innovation every day to bring the best projects and products to the world. This book does not pretend to cover all possible and imaginable JBoss products in detail, but this book aims to be the best and fastest getting-started guide for Enterprise application development with the JBoss brand.

The book covers five main parts:

Part 1 explores the basics, Users will be presented the global project we will cover progressively during this book, JBoss developer studio.

This part also presents the BeOS Bank project example that will drive the chapters and labs.

`Chapter 1`, *Introduction to the JBoss Ecosystem*, presents the users with the project, that will serve as a guide throughout this book. The chapter also introduces JBoss developer studio's features in order to improve developer productivity.

Part 2 covers web application development and deployment with the JBoss EAP and Undertow.

`Chapter 2`, *Developing and Hosting Scalable Web Applications*, takes a look at developing and hosting scalable web applications using JBoss Application Server. The user will learn how to develop and deploy scalable web applications and monitor their states on JBoss Application Server. Users will also get hands-on JBoss EAP configuration tips to tune the platform to respond to various operational events.

`Chapter 3`, *Custom Web Deployment Using Undertow and Swarm*, explains that Undertow is the default web server included in JBoss Application Server. In the last chapter, users implicitly used the embedded version of Undertow in JBoss AS to host applications; this chapter is about handling custom deployment scenarios by embedding Undertow in Java applications. The user will also learn how to set up highly available deployments and build microservices with Undertow

Part 3 is centered on data management tools in the JBoss ecosystem. It covers data caching with JBoss Data Grid and data refactoring using JBoss data virtualization.

`Chapter 4`, *Storing and Accessing Distributed Data,* deals with data caching in a JBoss ecosystem with JBoss Data Grid/Infinispan; various configuration tips will be experimented through labs and coding sessions. The chapter also shows how to store and retrieve data from local and remote caches, how to develop and deploy cache-based applications, how to listen to cache event, and how to leverage the Advanced Cache API.

`Chapter 5`, *Exposing Data as a Service,* outlines data virtualization with JBoss Data Virtualization tools through illustrated examples; you will discover how to create aggregated, unified, and virtualized views from disparate data sources, how to create source models and virtual models, how to query join data from various sources, and finally, how to expose data views as a service.

Part 4 is about **Enterprise Service Bus** (**ESB**) and messaging. We will discuss JBoss Fuse ESB's features and development guide as the well as JBoss AMQ messaging platform.

`Chapter 6`, *Integrating Applications with JBoss Fuse,* is organized around application and component integration. After a brief presentation of the JBoss Fuse architecture, it progressively teaches how to develop, deploy, and monitor various OSGi integration scenarios on JBoss Fuse Platform, and explore some integration patterns with Apache Camel through illustrated cases.

`Chapter 7`, *Delivers Information Safely and Connects IoT,* discusses how to weakly couple distributed systems using the JBoss AMQ messaging platform. Through practical business cases, users will learn how to set up broker configuration, and how to build and run applications that rely on JBoss AMQ to share data in a safe and reliable way.

Part 5; at the end of the journey, a company is governed by processes and rules; this part covers both business rule and business process application development with JBoss products.

`Chapter 8`, *Making Better Decisions in Your Applications,* introduces artificial intelligence programming using the JBoss ecosystem. JBoss Business Rule Management System (BRMS) and Drools Rule Language (DRL) features are explored to build rule-based applications, decision tables, and complex event handlers.

`Chapter 9`, *Developing Workflows,* takes you through how to develop workflow applications using JBoss Business Process Management Suite. Process/activities modeling tasks/event handling are explained through practical use cases. Human interaction through forms is covered to enable users to design and test real-life advanced business processes.

What you need for this book

- Install JDK 8
- Install Maven 3.5

Who this book is for

If you are a Java developer who wants to have a complete view of the JBoss ecosystem or quickly explore a specific JBoss product, this is the book you want. Integrators and consultants familiar with JBoss who want to integrate several JBoss products within their ongoing project will also find this book useful.

Conventions

In this book, you will find a number of text styles that distinguish between different kinds of information. Here are some examples of these styles and an explanation of their meaning.

Code words in text, database table names, folder names, filenames, file extensions, pathnames, dummy URLs, user input, and Twitter handles are shown as follows: Client applications can then consume data from virtual databases using standard interfaces such as the `ODBC`, `JDBC`, and `REST` protocols.

A block of code is set as follows:

```
$ export EAP_HOME=$HOME/books/jbossdev/installs/jboss-eap-7.0
$ cd $EAP_HOME/bin
$ ./standalone.sh
```

New terms and important words are shown in bold. Words that you see on the screen, for example, in menus or dialog boxes, appear in the text like this: "JBoss is fully **Java Authentication and Authorization Service** (**JAAS**)"

Warnings or important notes appear in a box like this.

Tips and tricks appear like this.

Reader feedback

Feedback from our readers is always welcome. Let us know what you think about this book--what you liked or disliked. Reader feedback is important for us as it helps us develop titles that you will really get the most out of.

To send us general feedback, simply email `feedback@packtpub.com`, and mention the book's title in the subject of your message.

If there is a topic that you have expertise in and you are interested in either writing or contributing to a book, see our author guide at `www.packtpub.com/authors`.

Customer support

Now that you are the proud owner of a Packt book, we have a number of things to help you to get the most from your purchase.

Downloading the example code

You can download the example code files for this book from your account at `http:/ / www. packtpub. com`. If you purchased this book elsewhere, you can visit `http:/ / www. packtpub. com/ support` and register to have the files emailed directly to you. You can download the code files by following these steps:

1. Log in or register to our website using your email address and password.
2. Hover the mouse pointer on the **SUPPORT** tab at the top.
3. Click on **Code Downloads & Errata**.
4. Enter the name of the book in the **Search** box.
5. Select the book for which you're looking to download the code files.
6. Choose from the drop-down menu where you purchased this book from.
7. Click on **Code Download**.

Once the file is downloaded, please make sure that you unzip or extract the folder using the latest version of:

- WinRAR / 7-Zip for Windows
- Zipeg / iZip / UnRarX for Mac
- 7-Zip / PeaZip for Linux

The code bundle for the book is also hosted on GitHub at `https:/ / github. com/ PacktPublishing/ JBoss- Developers- Guide`. We also have other code bundles from our rich catalog of books and videos available at `https:/ / github. com/ PacktPublishing/` . Check them out!

Downloading the color images of this book

We also provide you with a PDF file that has color images of the screenshots/diagrams used in this book. The color images will help you better understand the changes in the output. You can download this file from `https:/ / www. packtpub. com/ sites/ default/ files/ downloads/ JBossDevelopersGuide_ ColorImages. pdf`.

Errata

Although we have taken every care to ensure the accuracy of our content, mistakes do happen. If you find a mistake in one of our books maybe a mistake in the text or the code we would be grateful if you could report this to us. By doing so, you can save other readers from frustration and help us improve subsequent versions of this book. If you find any errata, please report them by visiting `http:/ / www. packtpub. com/ submit- errata`, selecting your book, clicking on the Errata Submission Form link, and entering the details of your errata. Once your errata are verified, your submission will be accepted and the errata will be uploaded to our website or added to any list of existing errata under the Errata section of that title.

To view the previously submitted errata, go to `https:/ / www. packtpub. com/ books/ content/ support` and enter the name of the book in the search field. The required information will appear under the Errata section.

Piracy

Piracy of copyrighted material on the Internet is an ongoing problem across all media. At Packt, we take the protection of our copyright and licenses very seriously. If you come across any illegal copies of our works in any form on the Internet, please provide us with the location address or website name immediately so that we can pursue a remedy.

Please contact us at `copyright@packtpub.com` with a link to the suspected pirated material.

We appreciate your help in protecting our authors and our ability to bring you valuable content.

Questions

If you have a problem with any aspect of this book, you can contact us at `questions@packtpub.com`, and we will do our best to address the problem.

1
Introduction to the JBoss Ecosystem

JBoss initially referred to an application server edited by **JBoss** Inc. The first JBoss version was designed by Marc Fleury; he incorporated the JBoss Company in 1999 with an innovative business model around services, training, and certifications.

JBoss is fully written in Java, and it obtained the **Java 2 Enterprise Edition** version 1.4 certification in 2004. This standardization by SUN Microsystems largely contributed to propel the Jboss application server into large accounts to the point of making it a first choice element while deploying enterprise Java applications.

This situation has naturally fueled the appetite in companies looking for external growth, and it was almost natural that Red Hat Inc. acquired Jboss in 2006 to embrace the service industry.

One decade after, the most important acquisition in history, Red Hat has not only worked to significantly improve the JBoss application server, but has also been designing a strong portfolio of middleware and application development products, which also have the JBoss denomination.

Today, the Red Hat JBoss Middleware portfolio is mainly maintained by the open source community and the Red Hat JBoss division. It covers a set of products to enable developers to have the tools they need to create, integrate, deploy, and manage enterprise applications. Regarding the product delivery strategy, there are two main editions for each product: a community edition driven by the open source Community, and an Enterprise edition taken from the community stream.

The community edition is open source and is available to all for free while the Enterprise edition is accessible through a subscription. With the subscription model, companies, organizations, and individuals with an active subscription are allowed to download and use Red Hat certified and tested enterprise software; the editor, in return, provides them with guidance, support, patches, updates, and services around the product through an online network.

Even if there are two distinct editions, it is truly an open organization; bug fixes, for example, from the community version are reported in the commercial edition and vice versa. Red Hat provides and maintains the tested configuration for each product enterprise version release.

The JBoss ecosystem is very large indeed, from developers tools to application platforms. JBoss products now cover the following categories: applications and web servers, enterprise service buses, messaging, data management platforms, rules, workflow management, services, APIs and many other features.

You may have often wondered what is the best JBoss product to solve a specific problem or need, how to get started with a specific JBoss product, or how to integrate different JBoss products in your IT systems.

Through hands-on labs from the business world, this book presents practical use cases that you can leverage to build your own enterprise services around the JBoss ecosystem. In this chapter, we will cover the following topics:

- Presenting the global project that will serve as a compass throughout the book
- Installing and setting up the JBoss developer studio
- Setting up the integration stack, to start our Jboss development journey
- Creating our first project
- Creating objects using the Forge console

Beos bank project

Beos bank is a financial institution that operates worldwide, and its main locations are in five continents: Mexico, Boston, Chennai, Paris, and Baham. Beos bank provides various digital financial services, including mobile banking and instant payment. It also allows individuals and companies to realize money transfers and cross-border remittances. As a lead developer, the reader will have the responsibility to drive the Beos bank digital transformation using JBoss products. The following projects have been identified to make Beos bank the next billion-dollar company:

- **Money transfer web application**: Users have been complaining about the instability of the current web transfer portal--sometimes servers go down during transfer operations and user data is lost. You have to set up a new architecture to deploy the money transfer application to support new business reorganization. Develop a new transfer application allowing users to send money to a recipient using JSF, and use JBoss EAP to host and cluster the application. Configure and test the session replication between 02 or 03 nodes. Deploy a HA cluster behind an undertow load balancer and check load balancing features; persist transfers data using JPA and JBoss data sources.
- **Banking API Management System**: Use Undertow to build and deploy serverless microservices for staff/user authenticated money transfer requests. Use Undertow to reduce the server park and help Beos bank enter the microservices and container world; this program will also help the bank achieve ISO 50001 certification.
- **Withdraw remittances**: Beos bank has a centralized database to host transfer data; some countries are complaining about the response time to validate a transaction: poor network connections, timeouts, and so on. Use a JBoss data grid cluster to keep in different countries. Use the JBoss data grid Hot Rod client to validate user remittances.
- **Cash and currency management**: Beos bank would like to be agile enough to quickly adapt to new regulation policies and would like the transfer fees and commissions to depend on both the sender and receiver countries. Coding this rule, use the BRMS decision table to compute transfer fees based on country and ranges. Use the Virtual Data Model from Yahoo and partners to convert currency rates, and use JBoss Data Virtualization to refactor the price catalog from different countries.

- **Fraud detection system**: Some illegal transactions have been identified; use BRMS rules, Complex Event processing, and a real-time decision server to detect frauds and illegal transactions. Use the Virtual Data Model from Yahoo and partners to convert currencies.
- **Invoices and accounting**: Use the JBoss Fuse OSGi flow to process/send bills, and use JBoss Fuse to send a file to regulatory institutions.
- **Promotions and coupons**: Use JBoss AMQ to notify the partner working on loyalty cards, and use JBoss AMQ to communicate with a mission critical-bank approval system with no message lost. Configure Active MQ to support various runtime and production incidents.
- **Customer relationship management**: Users are complaining about some Beos bank processes in some countries. Design the incriminated Beos bank business processes with JBoss BPM and improve the process.

In all the book, we will be relying on `System.out.println(String out)` to print some output on the console when needed; for more advanced ouputs you can refer to `String.format` method to format the output before printing it to the console.

To understand all the coding stuff related to this project, we will work with a brilliant project called JBoss Developer Studio.

JBoss Developer Studio

JBoss Developer Studio (**JBDS**) is a development environment created on top of Eclipse and is currently developed by the Red Hat JBoss division. Some companies such as Exadel, the Eclipse foundation, and open source individuals are also working on the JBoss Developer Studio project. JBDS empowers users with a set of plugins, called JBoss Tools; it supports multiple programming models, frameworks, and technologies, including Maven, SVN, and Git.

JBoss Developer Studio is modular like Eclipse and supports development with multiple JVM versions. At the time of writing this book, the last JBDS release version is 10.3.0. JBDS is available as other Jboss products on the Red Hat developer portal--`developers.redhat.com`; you need a social account (GitHub, Stack Overflow, Linkedin, Twitter, Facebook, Google, or Microsoft) and credentials to download the software.

Installation

JBoss Developer studio installation requires the following configuration:

- 4 GB RAM (minimum 2 GB RAM)
- 2 GB hard disk space
- JDK 8 to run, but it can deploy applications using lower versions

Download `devstudio-10.3.0.GA-installer-standalone.jar` and begin the installation using the following command:

```
java -jar devstudio-10.3.0.GA-incstaller-standalone.jar
```

This installation needs JRE 8 to proceed; once launched, the GUI installer starts an installation workflow where you will have to click on the **Next** button to move to the next step:

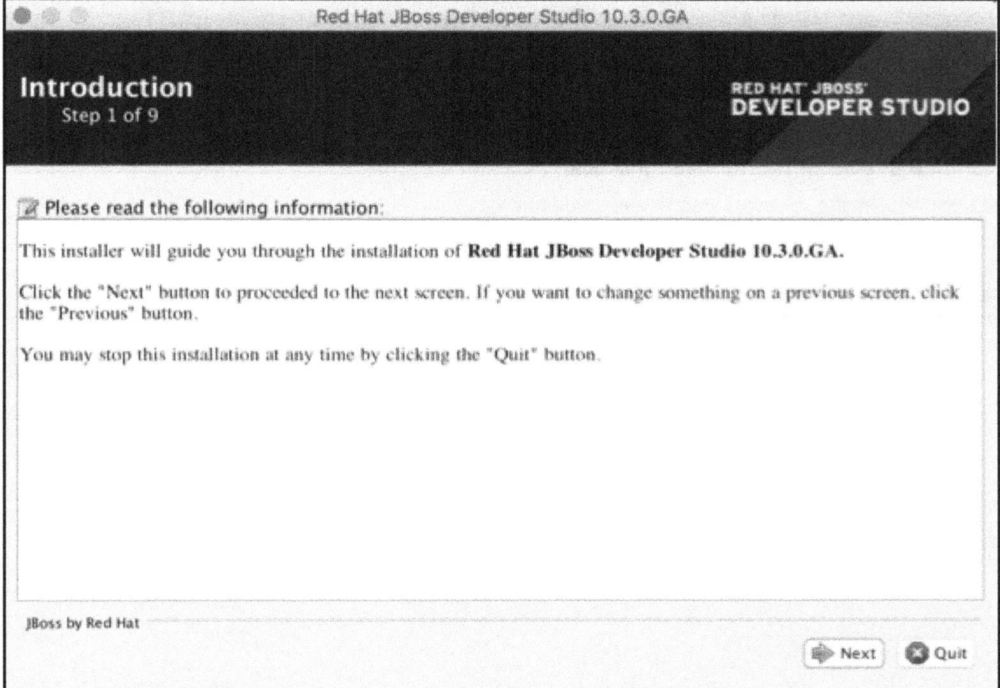

The installation wizard has nine steps, which are easy to follow:

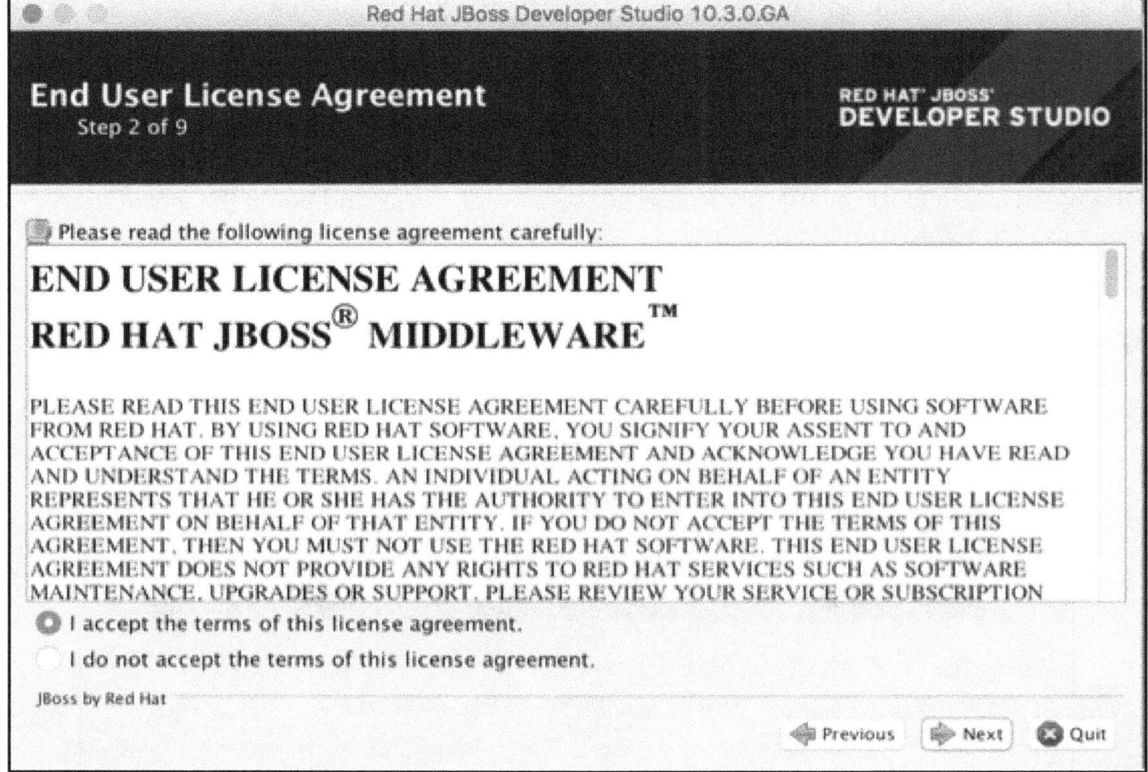

Read and accept the terms of the license agreement:

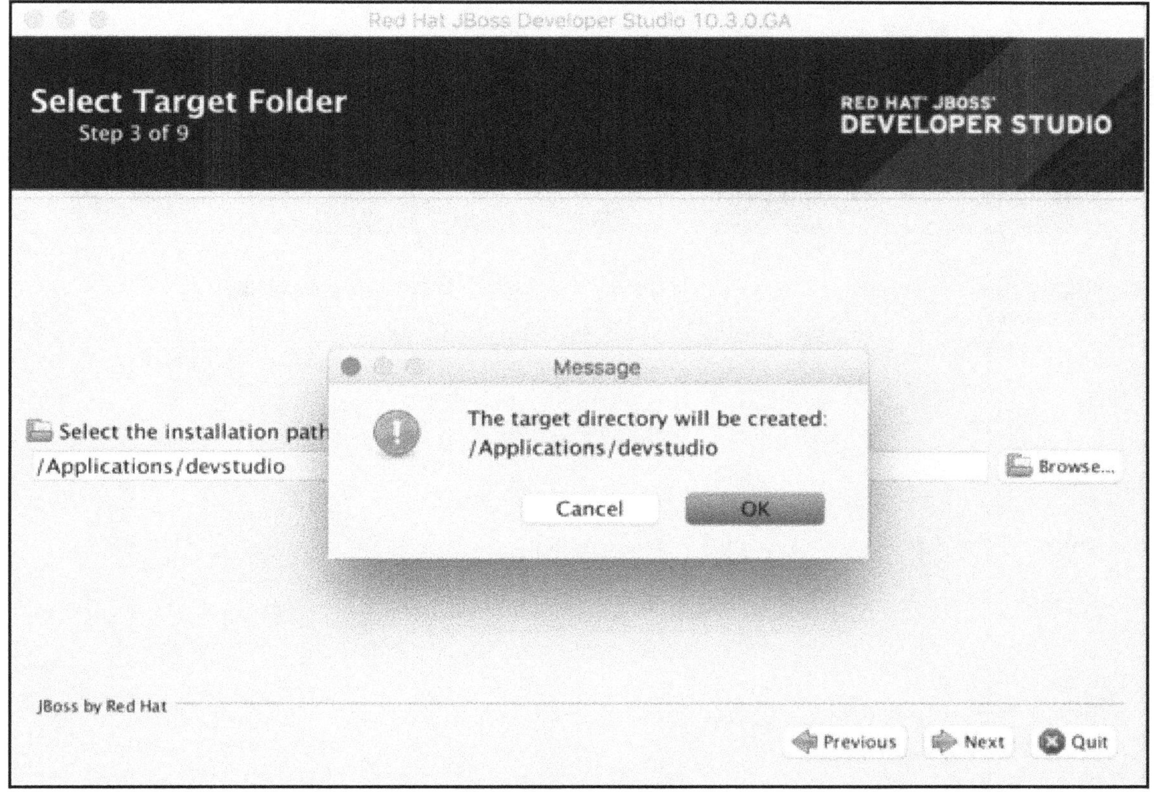

Installation is done by default in `/Applications/devstudio`; you can change this directory to use a custom one:

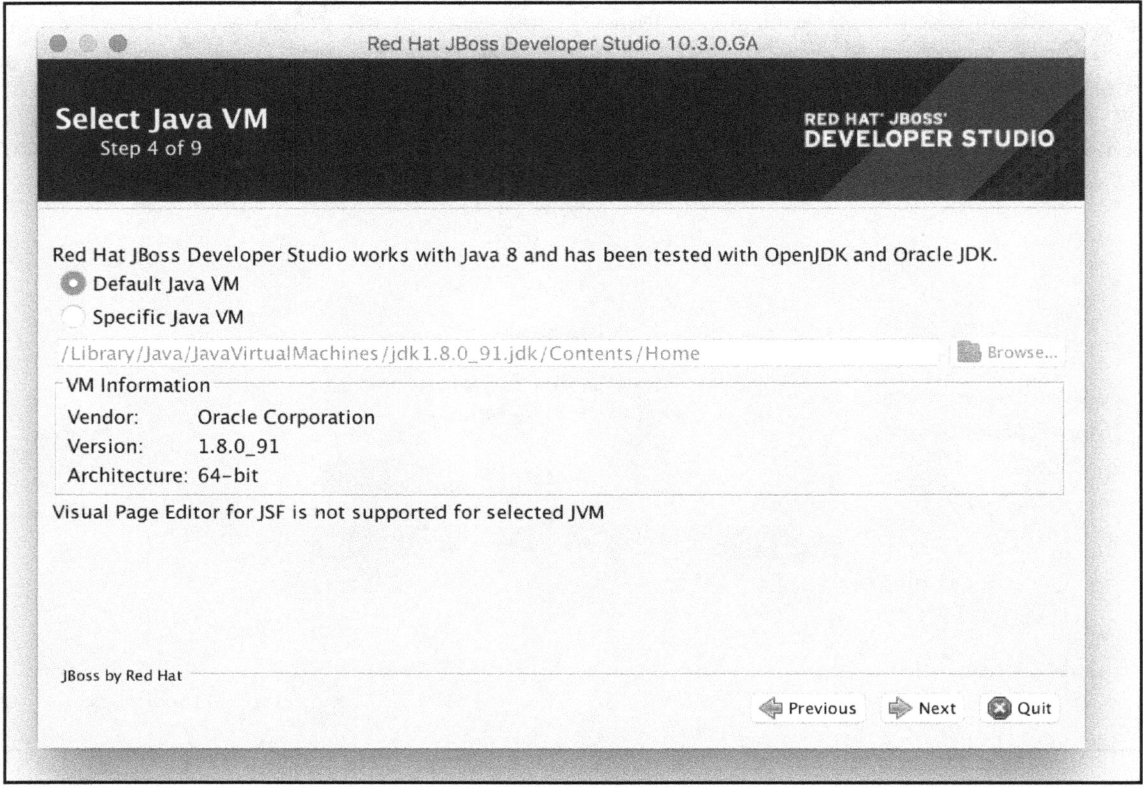

Select the default Java 8 Virtual machine and click on **Next** button:

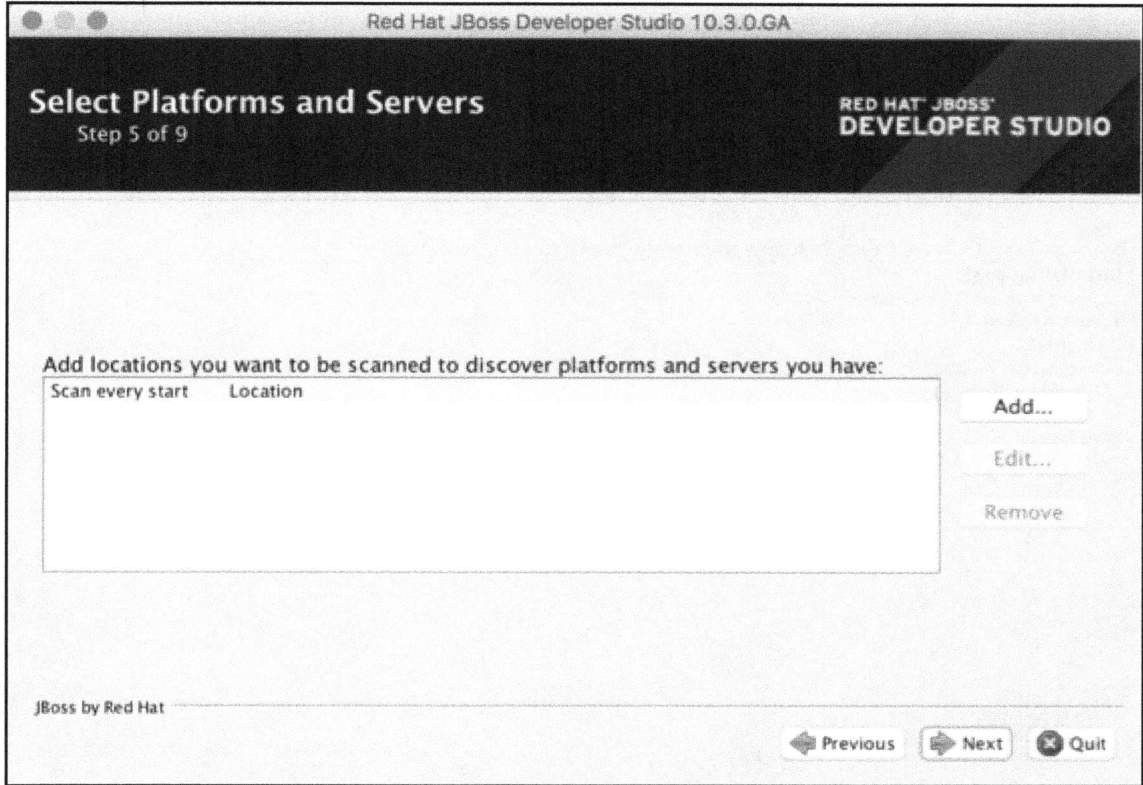

JBDS can scan specific directories to reference your existing JBoss servers.

We will not add a specific location for now; we will just move on to the next steps:

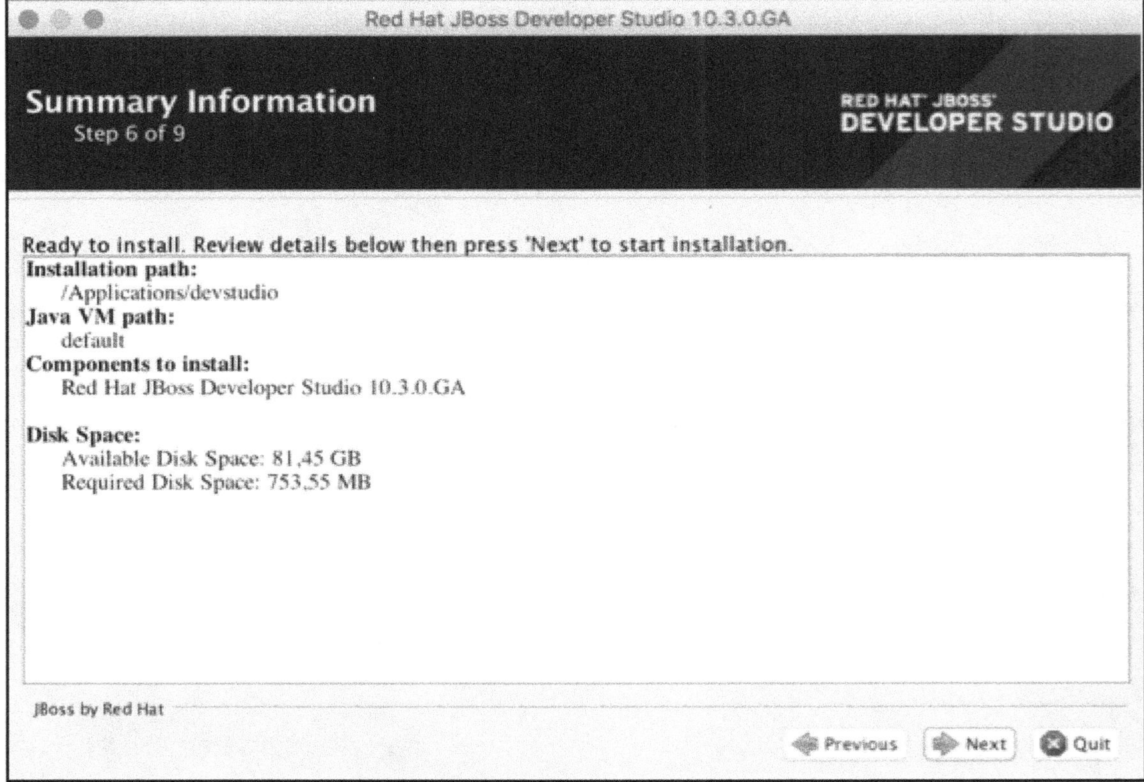

The installer displays the installation path, the component to be installed, as well as the available and required space on your computer. Click on the **Next** button to proceed with the installation:

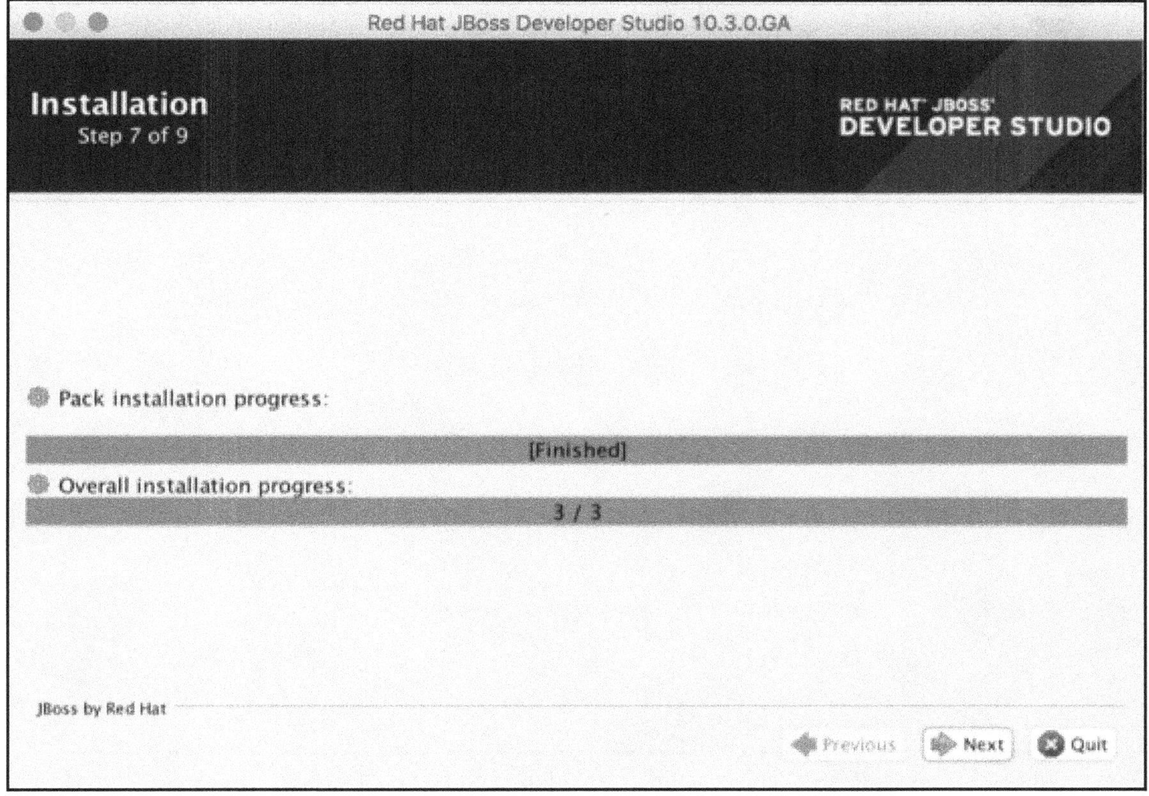

In step 7/9 details of each installed component are printed on screen. Wait for the overall installation process to complete:

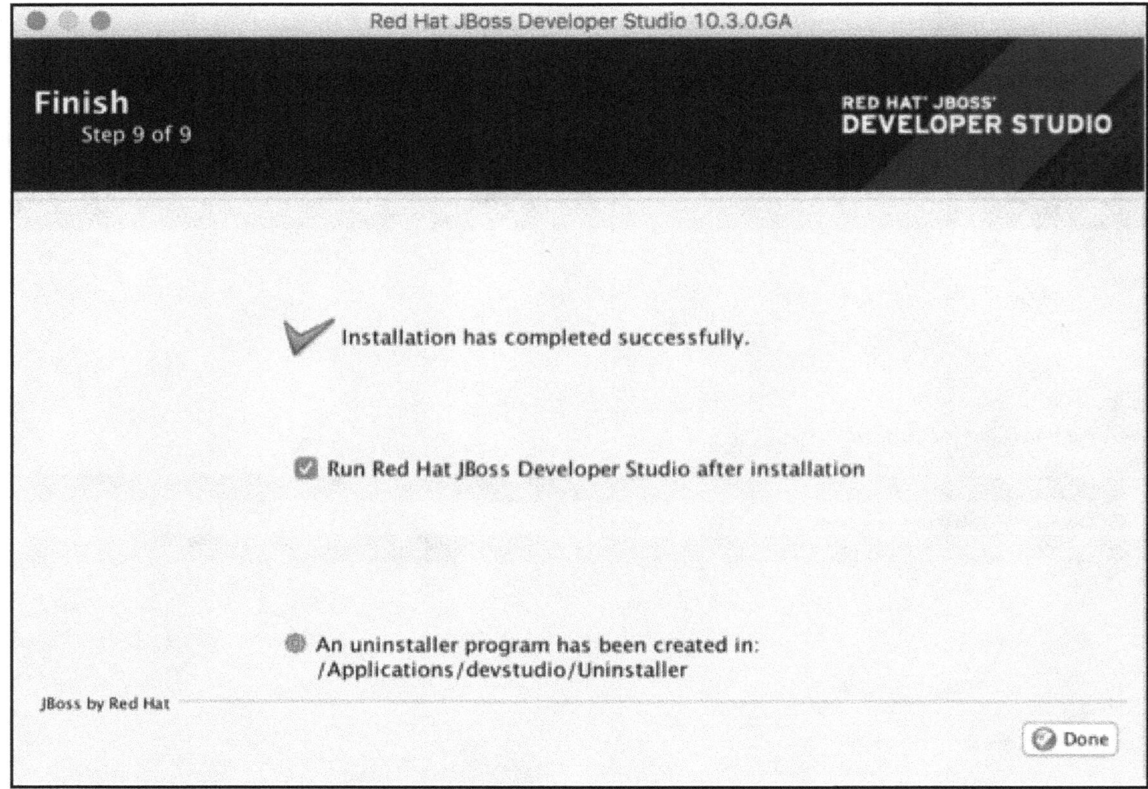

Click on **Done** to finish, with the **Run Red Hat JBoss Developer after installation** option checked. Select a fresh workspace to reach the welcome view.

We will use the `$HOME/jbdevgWorkspace` folder for our installation throughout this book:

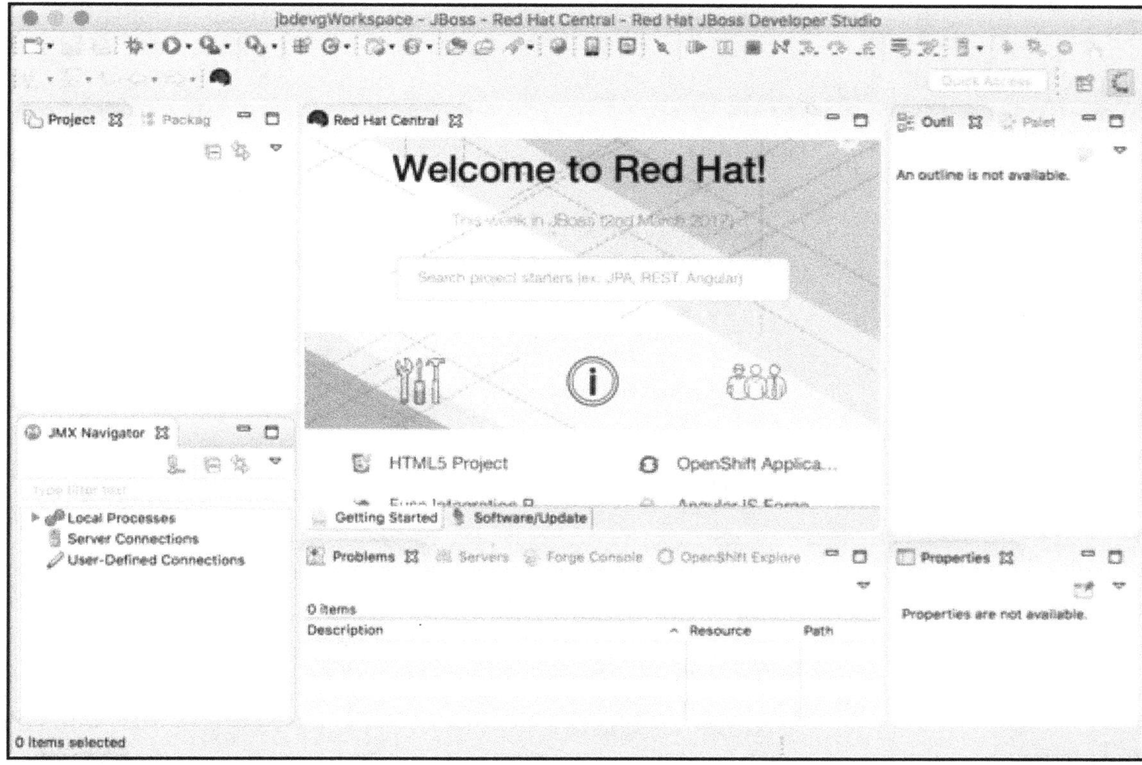

This completes the JBDS installation. Once the JBDS installation is complete, you need to ensure that all the development plugins are also installed. While working with JBoss, the integration stack provides a set of plugins and features to ease the development process; let's install the JBoss integration stack plugin.

Integration Stack

By default, JBoss Tools is installed along with JBDS; this is not the case for the JBoss Integration Stack, which provides users with a toolset to integrate applications. It works with Apache Camel, JBoss Data virtualization, and various others features related to Integration.

The most simple way to install the JBoss Integration Stack is from the **Red Hat central** view:

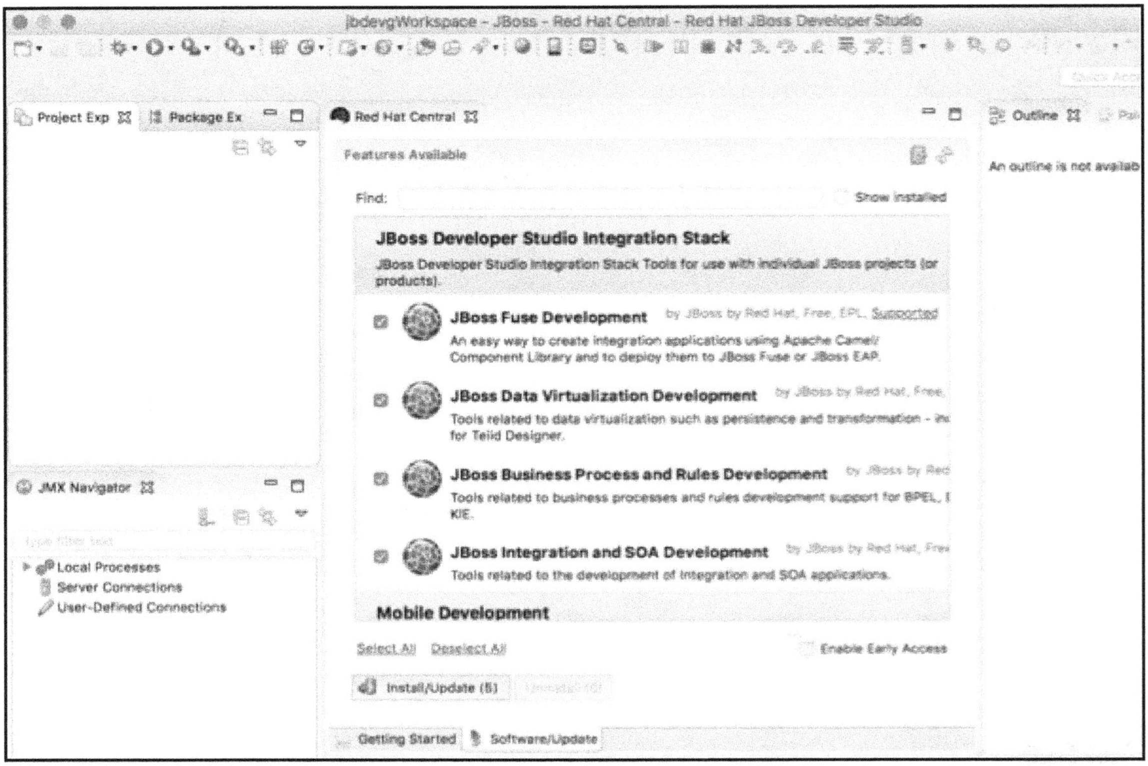

Check the listed options:

- JBoss Fuse Development
- JBoss Data Virtualization Development
- JBoss Business Process and Rule Development
- JBoss Integration and SOA Development

Integration stack plugins can also be installed from a ZIP file at `http://tools.jboss.org/downloads/devstudio_is/`.

Click on the **install/update** button and complete the installation steps. Each plugin has its own working problem to solve, and the user manual, as far as possible, refers to the official documentation of the plugin. In the current section, we install both the JBoss Developer Studio and the Integration stack plugin. We are now ready to create projects and work on them within the IDE. JBDS has an integrated console, called the Forge console, to perform some tasks quickly. In the next section, we will perform various project tasks using this console.

The Forge console

The Forge console provides an integrated command-line interface in the IDE. The Forge console command actions automatically synchronize the workspace views. Forge brings out a powerful command line interface to interact with the IDE. Forge is also available as an Eclipse wizard for users who really don't want to remember the commands. We will perform various Forge console tasks on a new Java project called Name `bank-forge-demo`.

Working with the Forge CLI

In order to interact with the Forge CLI, the console needs to be started. In the quickview, search for Forge console; click on the green button to start the Forge CLI:

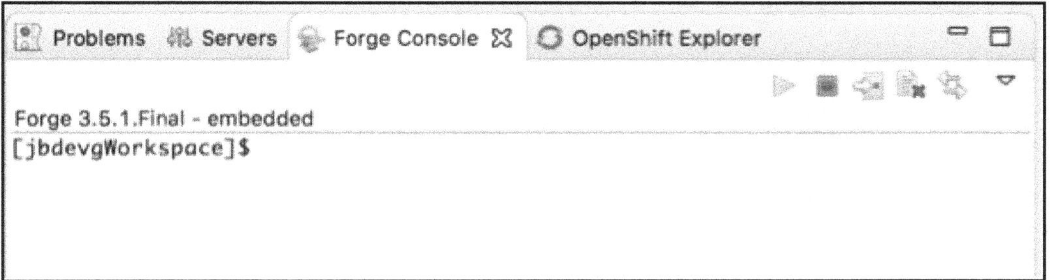

The command line starts, and a shell is opened on the current workspace directory. You can now enter various commands to create projects, and to interact with the project model and objects. Now, let's see how to create a project using the Forge console.

Creating Maven projects

Use the command `list` to see the commands available and the `man` command to get help on a specific command's usage. Forge commands work both interactively and with options. To create a new project, use the `project-new` command, and provide answers to the interactive questions asked.

```
[jbdevgWorkspace]$ project-new beosbank-forge-demo
***INFO*** Required inputs not satisfied, entering interactive mode
* Project name: beosbank-forge-demo
? Top level package [org.beosbank.forge.demo]: com.beosbank.forge.demo
? Version [1.0.0-SNAPSHOT] HIT ENTER to pick the default version
? Final name: beosbank-forge-demo
? Project location [/Users/enonowog/jbdevgWorkspace]:
? Use Target Location Root? (If specified, it won't create a subdirectory
inside the specified Project location) [y/N]: N
[0] (x) war
[1] ( ) jar
[2] ( ) parent
[3] ( ) forge-addon
[4] ( ) resource-jar
[5] ( ) ear
[6] ( ) from-archetype
[7] ( ) generic
Press <ENTER> to confirm, or <CTRL>+C to cancel.* Project type: [0-7] 1
[0] (x) Maven
Press <ENTER> to confirm, or <CTRL>+C to cancel.* Build system: [0] 0
[0] ( ) JAVA_EE_7
[1] ( ) JAVA_EE_6
[2] ( ) NONE
Press <ENTER> to confirm, or <CTRL>+C to cancel.
? Stack (The technology stack to be used in this project): [0-2] 2
***SUCCESS*** Project named 'beosbank-forge-demo' has been created.
```

The project is created with the specified input options and is available in the workspace immediately:

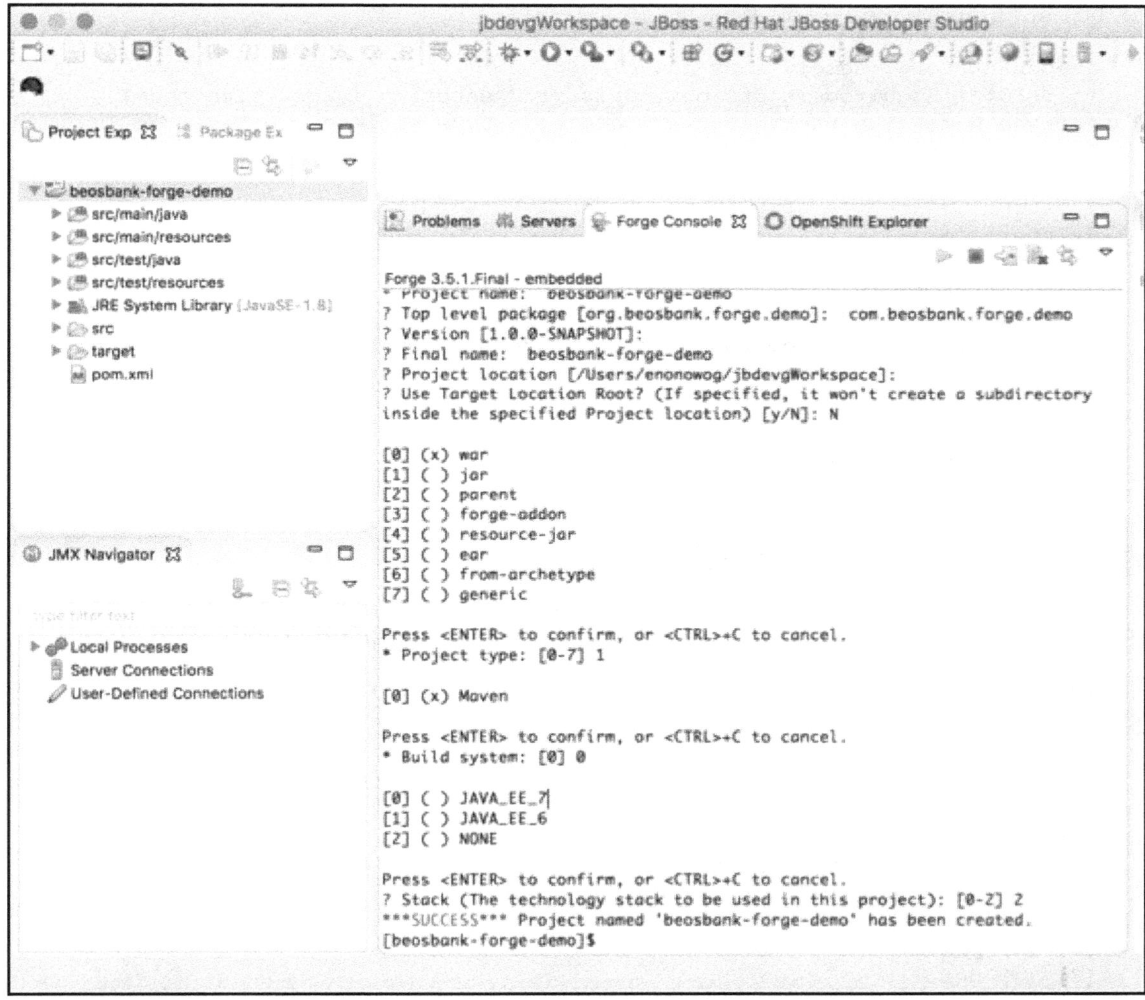

By default, the Forge CLI relies on your system's command-line font configuration. After creating a project, the next step may be to add a class; let's see how to create Java class in the project source folder using the Forge console.

Creating a Java class

Use the `java-new-class` command to add a non-final `HelloJBossWorld` class to the `beosbank-forge-demo` project:

```
[beosbank-forge-demo]$ java-new-class
***INFO*** Required inputs not satisfied, entering interactive mode?
Package Name (The package name where this type will be created)
[com.beosbank.forge.demo]: HIT ENTER
* Type Name (The type name): HelloJBossWorld
? Extends (The type used in the extends keyword):
? Interfaces []:
? Is Final? [y/N]: N
? Is Abstract? [y/N]: N
? Is Serializable? [y/N]: Y
***SUCCESS*** Class com.beosbank.forge.demo.HelloJBossWorld was created
[HelloJBossWorld.java]$
```

The new class is empty; you may wonder how to add attributes and methods to this newly created class using the Forge console.

Adding attributes to classes

To add a private name property with getters and setters to the `HelloJBossWorld` class, use the `java-new-field` Forge command. This command is applied to the selected classes:

```
[HelloJBossWorld.java]$ java-new-field
***INFO*** Required inputs not satisfied, entering interactive mode
[0] (x) com.beosbank.forge.demo.HelloJBossWorld
Press <ENTER> to confirm, or <CTRL>+C to cancel.
* Target Class (The class where the field will be created): [0] 0
* Field Name (The field name to be created in this class): name
* Field Type (The type intended to be used for this field) [String]:
[0] ( ) public
[1] ( ) protected
[2] (x) private
[3] ( ) default
Press <ENTER> to confirm, or <CTRL>+C to cancel.
? Access Type (The access type): [0-3] 2
? Generate Getter (Generate accessor method) [Y/n]: Y
? Generate Setter (Generate mutator method) [Y/n]: Y
? Update toString (Updates the toString method by adding the field) [Y/n]:Y
***SUCCESS*** Field name created
```

We now have a mini project set up with a single class. Forge commands are not only used to create a project's objects but can also serve as gateways to interact with project builder tools such as maven.

Building projects with Forge

Using the Forge CLI, you can run maven goals on your project. The forge `build` command can be used to run maven goals on the created project:

```
[HelloJBossWorld.java]$ build
[INFO] Scanning for projects...[INFO]
[INFO] ------------------------------------------------------------------------
[INFO] Building beosbank-forge-demo 1.0.0-SNAPSHOT
[INFO] ------------------------------------------------------------------------
----
[INFO]
[INFO] --- maven-clean-plugin:2.5:clean (default-clean) @ beosbank-forge-
demo ---
[INFO] Installing /Users/enonowog/jbdevgWorkspace/beosbank-forge-
demo/target/beosbank-forge-demo.jar to
/Users/enonowog/.m2/repository/com/beosbank/forge/demo/beosbank-forge-
demo/1.0.0-SNAPSHOT/beosbank-forge-demo-1.0.0-SNAPSHOT.jar
[INFO] Installing /Users/enonowog/jbdevgWorkspace/beosbank-forge-
demo/pom.xml to
/Users/enonowog/.m2/repository/com/beosbank/forge/demo/beosbank-forge-
demo/1.0.0-SNAPSHOT/beosbank-forge-demo-1.0.0-SNAPSHOT.pom
[INFO] ------------------------------------------------------------------------
----
[INFO] BUILD SUCCESS
[INFO] ------------------------------------------------------------------------
----
[INFO] Total time: 8.509 s
[INFO] Finished at: 2017-03-10T14:12:56+01:00
[INFO] Final Memory: 193M/496M
[INFO] ------------------------------------------------------------------------
----
***SUCCESS*** Build Success
[HelloJBossWorld.java]$
```

So, the Forge console can be used to invoke maven commands on the project. The Forge console is a powerful tool on which you can rely to be more productive in your development tasks. It comes in complements to various shortcuts available in Eclipse and JBoss Developer Studio.

Summary

At the end of your first journey, you completed your first steps in the JBoss ecosystem with brilliance. You are now more familiar with what the JBoss ecosystem is about. You discovered the JBoss Developer Studio Development and integration platform, how to install plugins such as the JBoss integration stack to gain in productivity, and how to use the Forge command line to perform various tasks in your workspace very quickly. The global project was also introduced, and we hope you are ready to drive the Beos bank digital transformation with JBoss products.

In `Chapter 2`, *Developing and Hosting Scalable,* Web Applications you will be working with JBoss Doctor and a BeosBank Project Manager to streamline and secure the Beosbank money transfer web portal.

All the labs and source code presented in this book can be downloaded from GitHub at `https://github.com/jbossdevguidebook/chapters`

2
Developing and Hosting Scalable Web Applications

The JBoss Application Server is the oldest and the most popular product of the JBoss family. The community version was renamed to **WildFly** in 2013, and Red Hat began making the binaries for the **Enterprise Application Platform** (**EAP**) available for download for the developers.

This table shows the relation links between the community and commercial editions for the last three releases:

Community edition	**Enterprise edition**
JBoss AS 7.4.0.Final	JBoss EAP 6.3
JBoss AS 7.5.0.Final	JBoss EAP 6.4
WildFly 10	JBoss EAP 7.0.0

JBoss EAP 7.0 is a certified Java EE 7 application server and supports both Java SE8 and Java EE7 specifications. After installing JBoss EAP, we will discover its features and architecture through practical samples. The reader will get familiar with simple administration and configuration tips to leverage a development server. In this chapter, we will go through the following:

- How to set up a JBoss EAP installation both in the standalone and domain modes
- How to create and manage JBoss resources such as server group, server instances, datasources, and security domain
- Introducing and progressively using the JBoss CLI to interact with the server
- Developing and deploying a clustered application with session replication

- Application deployments with the JBoss-as maven plugin, modules, and datasource deployments in the source code
- Setting up a security domain to implement a custom authentication policy in a web application
- Setting up a HAProxy load balancer in front of two JBoss EAP backend systems to experiment with high availability and failover processes
- Java EE API integration within JBoss EAP through a practical JPA sample

Installation and configuration are the first steps developers will face while working with JBoss EAP applications.

Installation and configuration

For the next steps, we will work with JBoss EAP 7.0. We will also assume that you have a working JDK 8 installed. In the following section, we will interchangeably use WildFly, the **JBoss Application Server** (**JBoss AS**), and JBoss EAP to refer to the same notion. JBoss AS can be started in the standalone or domain modes.
The simplest way to install EAP 7.0 is to pick the ZIP archive on `Red Hat customer portal` and unzip it on your computer in a specific location. Here's the command to do that:

```
$ unzip jboss-eap-7.0.0.zip -d $HOME/books/jbossdev/installs
```

Start the server using the following commands:

```
$ export EAP_HOME=$HOME/books/jbossdev/installs/jboss-eap-7.0
$ cd $EAP_HOME/bin
$ ./standalone.sh
```

The JBoss Application Server can start services concurrently, only when needed, or on demand; making the initial boot process faster, non-critical services are started in a passive mode until first use:

```
15:25:24,571 INFO [org.jboss.as] (Controller Boot Thread) WFLYSRV0060: Http
management interface listening on
http://127.0.0.1:9990/management15:25:24,572 INFO [org.jboss.as]
(Controller Boot Thread) WFLYSRV0051: Admin console listening on
http://127.0.0.1:999015:25:24,572 INFO [org.jboss.as] (Controller Boot
Thread) WFLYSRV0025: JBoss EAP 7.0.0.GA (WildFly Core 2.1.2.Final-redhat-1)
started in 3212ms - Started 267 of 553 services (371 services are lazy,
passive or on-demand)
```

Applications are available by default on port 8080 at `http://127.0.0.1:8080`. The Web Administration console is available by default at `http://127.0.0.1:9990/console`. Graceful shutdowns are supported; this is important in an application development configuration where it is necessary to make numerous restart operations. Just press *CTRL+C* to stop your instance:

```
^C
15:33:02,986 INFO [org.jboss.as.server] (Thread-2) WFLYSRV0220: Server
shutdown has been requested....
JBoss EAP 7.0.0.GA (WildFly Core 2.1.2.Final-redhat-1) stopped in 15ms
```

These are the simple steps to start and stop JBoss EAP in standalone mode. In the following sections, we will deep dive into the EAP architectural components users need to master in order to deploy and manage highly-scalable web applications.

Architecture and features

According to an `IDC study` on the business value of Red Hat JBoss EAP in 2014, it appears that JBoss EAP:

- Increased the number of business applications developed per year by 70%
- Reduced the time per application developed by 35% per week
- Reduced the instances of unplanned downtime per Year by 80%
- Reduced the time to resolve planned downtime incidents (hours)

This is certainly due to the JBoss architecture which seems to be mostly acclaimed because of the following characteristics:

- JBoss EAP is a modular and lightweight application server
- An EAP server is a collection of modules or extensions
- An extension defines one or more subsystems
- A subsystem is a set of capabilities added to the server by an extension
- A server is started with one profile
- A profile is a collection of subsystems available to the server running the profile

In configuration files, extensions are referenced as follows:

```
<extension module="org.jboss.as.jmx"/>
<extension module="org.jboss.as.jpa"/>
<extension module="org.jboss.as.jsf"/>
```

Subsystems configuration and settings are specific to the profile to which they relate:

```
<subsystem xmlns="urn:jboss:domain:jmx:1.3">
   <expose-resolved-model/>
   <expose-expression-model/>
   <remoting-connector/>
</subsystem>
<subsystem xmlns="urn:jboss:domain:jpa:1.1">
  <jpa default-datasource="" default-extended-persistence-
inheritance="DEEP"/>
</subsystem>
<subsystem xmlns="urn:jboss:domain:jsf:1.0"/>
```

By default, the EAP comes with four predefined profiles:

- **default**: The default profile embeds the most frequently used subsystems, including logs, ejb3, security, and weld
- **ha**: The ha profile extends the default profile subsystem list with clustering capabilities offered by the JGroups subsystem
- **full**: This is similar to the default profile, but it notably adds the messaging (HornetQ) subsystem (as well as a few other subsystems)
- **full-ha**: This is the same as full profile, but it includes clustering features from the JGroups subsystem

The server can be started using two different modes: standalone or domain mode. The standalone mode is ideal for running a single server instance with a single server. As soon as you have a collection of server instances and want to be able to manage all the instances from a single location, the domain mode is recommended.
In a domain mode topology, server configuration is centralized in the `domain.xml` file; on the contrary, in the standalone mode, each standalone instance has its `standalone.xml` configuration file.

Practical JBoss

In the following section, we will start the BeOSBank digitalization. Let me introduce you to the client who is responsible for maintaining BeOSBank's development environments: Doctor JBoss. You have a business meeting with the client; listen and improve the way he and his team are managing their environments today:

Doctor JBoss: Hi Mr, nice to meet you.

Client: How are you today? Nice to meet you too.

Doctor JBoss: Let me introduce my assistant (you). We are working in the same team and are glad to have this meeting with you.

You: Nice to meet you.

Client: We have a lot of problems with our development environments; we are running many release cycles, and since we are migrating to the new web portal in the next few months, we are still maintaining the old portal bug fix branch concurrently. We have the same issue when a configuration parameter is changing; we have to apply the modification manually on each server. We have a lot of silo servers; when we have to deploy one application, we have to manually do it on each server; the process is very time consuming, and we would like to improve this.

Doctor JBoss: Hmmm, I am seeing, so you are still running in standalone mode? I have good news for you; from EAP 6, you have a domain mode that helps you manage server configuration from a single location.

Client: How is it possible? We are running EAP 7, and we worked with a guy from NullConsultantAgency to set up this architecture, but he said the domain is not good for us since we have different applications to manage and different Dev environments to support in parallel.

Doctor JBoss: How many applications and environments are you running in parallel?

Client: For the pilot, we want to focus on the money transfer portal app only. We have two silo servers running two different versions of our web portal. When one server goes down, the version hosted on this server is not available anymore; we want to add two new machines to support two concurrent branches for the new portal app in the same configuration. This situation will probably change, and we will have more and more environments to support various development requests.

You: So here's your current deployment topology?

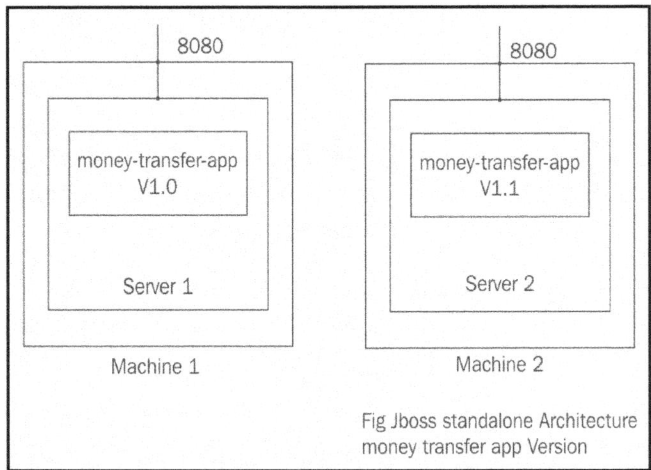

JBoss standalone architecture money-transfer-app version 1.x

Doctor JBoss: Do not worry, with my assistant, we will design a new architecture to support a single administration dashboard, running old and new versions of the money transfer concurrently, and the most important one: high availability of the server instances.

Client: What is high availability?

Doctor JBoss: This means you will not have a single point of failure in your configuration anymore; if one machine is down, you will still have another active node for each version of the application.

Client: Good, so I need to purchase six new machines right?

Doctor JBoss: Not really! The current material configuration is enough to add more server instances. We will play with port offset to have more than one server instance per machine. You will save a lot of money, and you do not have to buy two more machines to deploy the new versions. The new version will be handled by new server instances on both the machines.

Client: That's cool, so I need zero new machines.

Doctor JBoss: We will add a small machine for a domain controller; this is the host on which you will perform all your administrative tasks. The domain controller will interact with host controllers to manage all the configuration.

You: Drawing :

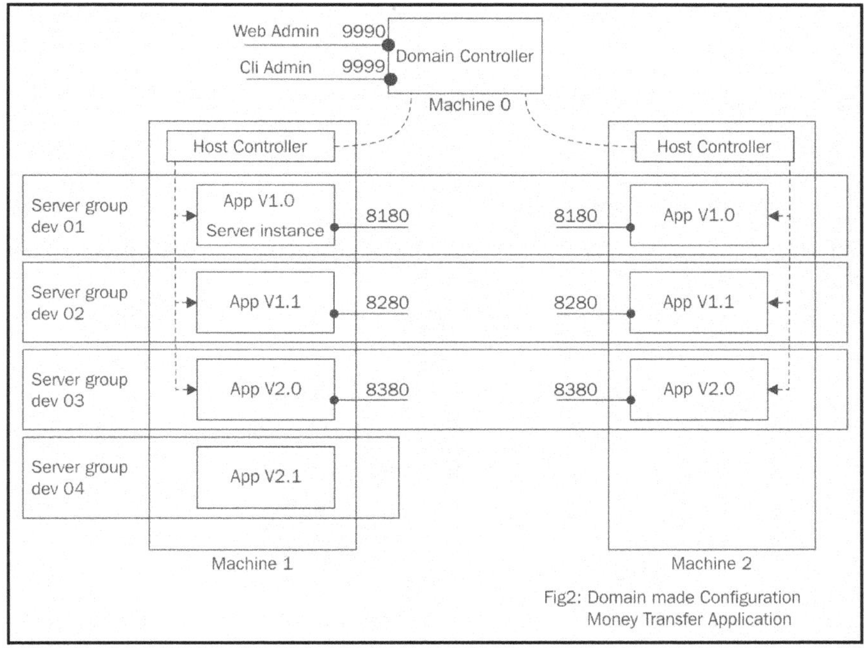

JBoss domain architecture money-transfer-app version 1.x and 2

Client: What is a host controller?

Doctor JBoss: The host controller is a process running on each machine of your domain; it will be responsible for starting and stopping the server instances. It cooperates with the domain controller to maintain the domain configuration policy on the host its managed.

Client: What about the server group?

Doctor JBoss: The server group is a deployment unit; literally, it is a collection of server instances running the same configuration and deployments. Any update on the group configuration affects all the members of the group.

Client: Nice stuff, but how do we implement this? Can you make a small PoC for my `money-transfer-webapp`?

Doctor JBoss: My colleague will take the floor and show you.

Lab - setting up a simple JBoss EAP domain

The purpose of this lab is to create an EAP domain with the following specifications:

- One domain controller on host0
- One host controller on a machine host1 with four EAP instances: `node11`, `node12`, `node13`, and `node14`
- One host controller on a machine host2 with three EAP instances: `node21`, `node22`, and `node23`
- Host controller host0 should be run as the master controller
- Hosts `host1` and `host2` are slaves connecting to host0
- Servers `node11` and `node21` are members of the `dev01` server group (`name=dev01-server-group`) running the `money-transfer-webapp-v1.0`
- Server instances `node12` and `node22` belong to the `dev02` server group (`name=dev02-server-group`) running the `money-transfer-webapp-v1.1`
- Server instances `node13` and `node23` belong to the `dev03` server group (`name=dev03-server-group`) running the `money-transfer-webapp-v2.0`
- Server instances `node14` is the only member of the `dev04` server group (`name=dev04-server-group`)
- In real-life machines, `host1` and `host2` are mostly in different physical/virtual locations, but for the purpose of this lab, we will simulate them on the same localhost using a single EAP 7 installation and different configuration folders for each machine:

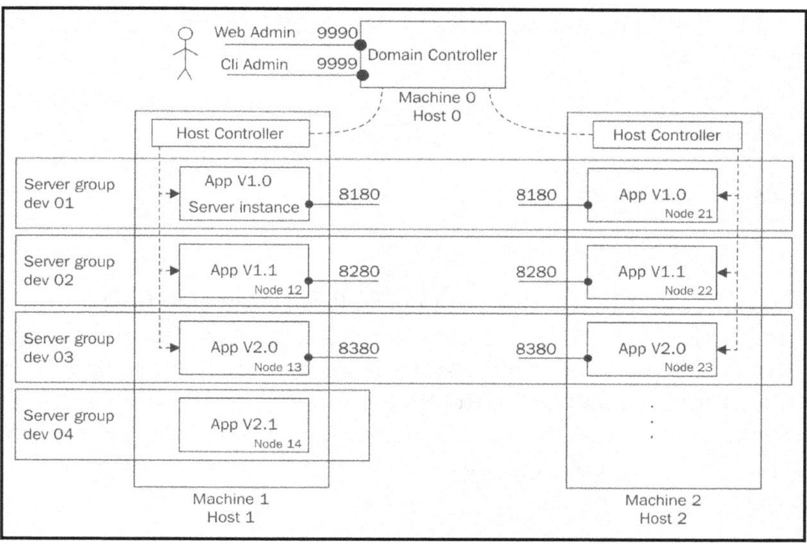

JBoss domain nodes

JBoss EAP 7 installation

To set up the BeOSBank EAP domain with three hosts, we will use various configuration techniques:

- XML file modifications
- CLI commands
- GUI updates

The first step to create our domain is to set up the infra; we will use single installation binaries and different configuration subfolders to simulate remote hosts:

```
$ unzip jboss-eap-7.0.0.zip -d $HOME/books/jbossdev/BeosBankDevDomain
```

Then, we will create virtual hosts and initialize the domain configuration folder with the existing templates:

```
$ export EAP_DOMAIN =$HOME/books/jbossdev/BeosBankDevDomain
$ cd $EAP_DOMAIN
$ mkdir host0 host1 host2
$ cp -r jboss-eap-7.0/domain host0/
$ cp -r jboss-eap-7.0/domain host1/
$ cp -r jboss-eap-7.0/domain host2/
```

In real life, you would have a separate installation binary for each host, but we will use the same installation binaries shared by the three hosts for this lab. The configuration files to be used for each host will be specified in the startup command. This is a best practice that allows you to run multiple instances of the EAP in the domain mode on the same machine from common binaries. It also allows you to upgrade to a newer version of EAP without affecting or overwriting your configuration files.

Configuring authentication

In the domain mode configuration, authentication can be defined at various levels:

- Providing authentication credentials to manage the domain
- Providing authentication credentials to restrict communications with the domain controller only to authenticated hosts.
- Applications user authentication

In this section, we will handle both management users and host to domain authentications. Application authentication and security is handled later in the chapter.

Creating a management to manage your EAP domain

```
$ cd $EAP_DOMAIN/jboss-eap-7.0/bin
./add-user.sh -dc $EAP_DOMAIN/host0/domain/configuration
```

Here, the `add-user` script is used to add a management user only to the `host0/domain/configuration/mgmt-users.properties` file.

The – `dc` option specifies the domain configuration folder (here, we alter the `host0`: domain controller folder).
Choose the following options:

```
Management User (mgmt-users.properties)
userName: admin
userPassword : Admin01#
GroupList : Empty, the user will be added by default to the ManagementRealm
```

The second authentication to set up is regarding the host to domain controller communications.

Configuring host authentication

Host authentication is used when a host controller tries to connect to a domain controller. Host authentication can also be configured using a technical user account.

Create a management user, `slave/Slave01#`, on all the hosts to authorized communications between the host and the controller:

```
$cd $EAP_DOMAIN/jboss-eap-7.0/bin
./add-user.sh -dc $EAP_DOMAIN/host0/domain/configuration
Quel type d'utilisateur souhaitez-vous ajouter ?
a) Management User (mgmt-users.properties)
b) Application User (application-users.properties)
(a): a
Saisir les informations sur le nouvel utilisateur
Utiliser le domaine 'ManagementRealm' selon les fichiers de propriétés
existants.
Nom d'utilisateur : slave
Les recommandations de mot de passe sont énumérés ci-dessous. Pour modifier
ces restrictions, modifier le fichier de configuration add-user.properties.
- Le mot de passe doit être différent du nom d'utilisateur- Le mot de passe
doit correspondre à une des valeurs limitées suivantes {root, admin,
administrator}
- Le mot de passe doit contenir au moins 8 caractères, 1 caractère(s)
alphabétique(s), 1 chiffre (s), 1 symbole(s) non alpha-numériques
Mot de passe :
Saisir mot de passe à nouveau :
Quels groupes souhaitez-vous impartir à cet utilisateur ? (Veuillez saisir
une liste séparée par des virgules, ou laisser vide)[ ]:
L'utilisateur 'slave' va être ajouté pour le domaine 'ManagementRealm'
Est-ce correct ? oui/non? oui
```

```
Utilisateur 'slave' ajouté au fichier
'/Users/enonowog/books/jbossdev/BeosBankDevDomain/host0/domain/configuratio
n/mgmt-users.properties'
Utilisateur 'slave' ajouté aux groupes dans le fichier
'/Users/enonowog/books/jbossdev/BeosBankDevDomain/host0/domain/configuratio
n/mgmt-groups.properties'
Est-ce que ce nouvel utilisateur va être utilisé pour qu'un processus AS
puisse se connecter à un autre processus AS, comme par exemple
pour qu'un contrôleur d'hôte esclave se connecte au master ou pour une
connexion distante de serveur à serveur pour les appels EJB.
oui/non ? oui
Pour représenter l'utilisateur, ajouter ce qui suit à la définition des
identités du serveur <secret value="U2xhdmUwMSM=" />
```

Use the following commands to create the same user on host1 and host2 `slave/Slave01#`:

```
./add-user.sh -dc $EAP_DOMAIN/host1/domain/configuration -r ManagementRealm
-u slave -p Slave01# -ro admin,manager

./add-user.sh -dc $EAP_DOMAIN/host2/domain/configuration-r ManagementRealm
-u slave -p Slave01# -ro admin,manager
```

When the add-user scripts complete, an encrypted password is generated in the output. Keep the encrypted password generated at the end of the user creation and replace the default secret value for `host1` and `host2` server identities:
`host1/domain/configuration/host-salve.xml`
`host2/domain/configuration/host-salve.xml`

```
<server-identities>
     <secret value="U2xhdmUwMSM="/>
</server-identities>
```

At this stage, communications between the hosts and controller is authorized but there is still a set of configuration steps to complete before having a fully working domain cluster. In the next section, we will be editing the domain and host interfaces.

Setting up the domain host and interfaces

This section covers the domain controller host configuration; we will update the `host0/domain/host-master.xml` file.

Using your favorite text editor, rename the first line to set a correct hostname (`host0-master`):

```
$ cd host0/domain/configuration/
$ vi host-master.xml
edit host name to be host0-master
<host xmlns="urn:jboss:domain:4.1" name="host0-master">
```

With this modification, the `host0` name is set to `host0-master` and will prevent confusion in the domain configuration dashboard.

Checking the management interfaces

By default, there are two management interfaces available in the configuration file:

- A native interface listening on port `9999`
- An HTTP interface listening on port `9990`

Make sure they are not commented in the domain controller configuration file as the management users will mainly use this interface for administering the cluster:

```
<management-interfaces>
<native-interface security-realm="ManagementRealm">
<socket interface="management"
port="${jboss.management.native.port:9999}"/>
</native-interface>

<http-interface security-realm="ManagementRealm" http-upgrade-
enabled="true">
 <socket interface="management" port="${jboss.management.http.port:9990}"/>

 </http-interface>
       </management-interfaces>
```

Management interfaces are, as their names indicate, for domain management. Users will connect to these interfaces to administer the domain. How about the host connection to the domain controller? How to indicate the `host0` in the principal domain controller in the cluster.

Reviewing the domain controller configuration

To indicate that a host is a domain controller, locate the domain-controller section in the configuration file and make sure its content matches the following structure:

```
<domain-controller>
 <local/>
</domain-controller>
```

The `local` tag indicates that this is a domain controller, and for other hosts to join the domain, you will need to establish a connection to the socket interface of this controller.

This defines interface ports on which the server is listening. A socket interface is used for CLI administration, and an HTTP interface is used for console webapp access--`9990/console`.

Configuring slaves - host-slave.xml

In the previous section, we initialized the domain configuration. In this step, we will set up communications links between the domain controller and the hosts. For each host, edit the `domain/configuration/host-slave.xml` configuration file:

```
$cd host1/domain/configuration/
$ vi host-slave.xml<host xmlns="urn:jboss:domain:4.1" name="host1">
 use the correct name for host2 as well
```

Change the management interface default port to `19999` for host1 and `29999` for host2; `9999` is already used by the domain controller. The HTTP interface is not active by default on the slave host:

```
<native-interface security-realm="ManagementRealm">
 <socket interface="management"
port="${jboss.management.native.port:19999}"/>
</native-interface>
```

Set up the right configuration so that the host can join the domain controller:

```
<domain-controller>
 <remote security-realm="ManagementRealm">
<discovery-options>
    <static-discovery name="primary"
protocol="${jboss.domain.master.protocol:remote}"
host="${jboss.domain.master.address :127.0.0.1}"
port="${jboss.domain.master.port:9999}"/>
 </discovery-options>
 </remote>
```

```
</domain-controller>
```

Define a default value for the controller IP:

```
addresshost="${jboss.domain.master.address :127.0.0.1}" add :127.0.0.1.
```

This can also be set in the command line when the host starts using `Djboss.domain.master.addess=127.0.0.1`. The discovery options can list many controller addresses, and hosts will try to connect to the first active controller listed in this section.
Remove the content of the servers tag; later, we will look at how to create server group and instances:

```
<servers> </servers>
```

Repeat the same step on `host2` with port `29999`.

Starting the domain

We now have a domain controller ready, and also have an administration user and two hosts with proper settings to interact with the primary domain controller. Let's start the domain controller and the hosts:

```
bin$ ./domain.sh -Djboss.domain.base.dir=../../host0/domain/ --host-
config=host-master.xml
```

Start host1 from one tab of your terminal:

```
./domain.sh -Djboss.domain.base.dir=../../host1/domain/ --host-config=host-
slave.xml
```

From another tab of your terminal, start `host2`:

```
./domain.sh -Djboss.domain.base.dir=../../host2/domain/ --host-config=host-
slave.xml
```

You can see the host registering in domain controller logs:

```
[Host Controller] 11:25:50,519 INFO [org.jboss.as.domain.controller] (Host
Controller Service Threads - 36) WFLYHC0019: Registered remote slave host
"host1", JBoss JBoss EAP 7.0.0[Host Controller] 11:28:06,670 INFO
[org.jboss.as.domain.controller] (Host Controller Service Threads - 37)
WFLYHC0019: Registered remote slave host "host2", JBoss JBoss EAP 7.0.0
```

Let's connect to the domain controller:

```
http://127.0.0.1:9990/console
```

```
    login :admin, Password : Admin01#.
```

You can see **Hosts** that are members of the domain:

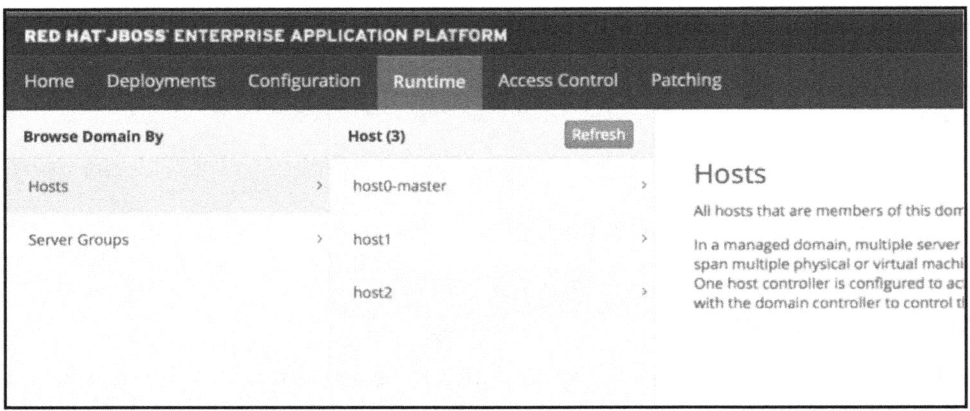

EAP domain console

This concludes the first part of this lab, where we set up a simple domain with one primary domain controller and two slave hosts. In the subsequent steps, we will see how to use the JBoss **Command-Line Interface** (**CLI**) to read and edit the configuration.

Lab - using the JBoss CLI

A JBoss EAP configuration is persisted in XML configuration files. JBoss provides various tools to interact with this configuration:

- You can manually edit the XML file (not the recommended option)
- Alternatively, you can use the web console to update JBoss configuration
- JBoss Command Line Interface tool or CLI for short
- DMR API: Dynamic Model Representation API is a REST API to access JBoss CLI commands

DMR is the JBoss configuration internal representation; it is a flat XML syntax where all the settings appear at the same level.
The CLI allows you to manage and configure EAP instances or domains remotely from a command line, including writing scripts for repetitive tasks.
You can connect to the domain administration console using the CLI:

```
bin$ ./jboss-cli.sh --connect --controller=127.0.0.1:9999
[domain@127.0.0.1:9999 /]
```

The `--controller` option specifies the IP and port to access the domain controller. Use the read-resource command to inspect configuration objects. Here, we display details of the `main-server-group` server group with the `read-resource` command:

```
[domain@127.0.0.1:9999 /] /server-group=main-server-group:read-resource
{
"outcome" => "success",
"result" => {
   "management-subsystem-endpoint" => false,
   "profile" => "full",
   "socket-binding-default-interface" => undefined,
   "socket-binding-group" => "full-sockets",
   "socket-binding-port-offset" => 0,
   "deployment" => undefined,
   "deployment-overlay" => undefined,
   "jvm" => {"default" => undefined},
   "system-property" => undefined
   }
}
[domain@127.0.0.1:9999 /]
```

Creating server groups

Create the `dev01`, `dev02`, and `dev03` server groups for the money transfer web application; use the ha profiles and the associated ha-sockets binding group:

```
[domain@127.0.0.1:9999 /] /server-group=dev01:add(profile=ha,socket-
binding-group=ha-sockets)
{
"outcome" => "success",
"result" => undefined,"server-groups" => undefined
}
[domain@127.0.0.1:9999 /] /server-group=dev02:add(profile=ha,socket-
binding-group=ha-sockets)
[domain@127.0.0.1:9999 /] /server-group=dev03:add(profile=ha,socket-
binding-group=ha-sockets)
```

```
[domain@127.0.0.1:9990 /] /server-group=dev04:add(profile=ha,socket-
binding-group=ha-sockets)
```

The JBoss CLI supports autocompletion; just press the *Tab* key while writing your commands, and you will see the available options depending on your current position.

Creating a server instance

A server instance is created on a host and belongs to one server group. The server exposes various ports to interact with its services.
Since we want to have many server instances on the same host, we will shift the instances port offset. For BeOSBank projects, we take a convention to add **100** to the base offset while moving from one server to another. This means that all the default ports of the associated socket binding will be shifted for a specific instance.

Host1 server creation can be completed with the following command list:

```
[domain@127.0.0.1:9999 /] /host=host1/server-
config=node11:add(group=dev01,socket-binding-port-offset=100)
[domain@127.0.0.1:9999 /] /host=host1/server-
config=node12:add(group=dev02,socket-binding-port-offset=200)
[domain@127.0.0.1:9999 /] /host=host1/server-
config=node13:add(group=dev03,socket-binding-port-offset=300)
[domain@127.0.0.1:9999 /] /host=host1/server-
config=node14:add(group=dev04,socket-binding-port-offset=400)
```

A servers instance on host2 can be created using the same command. Adjust the server names accordingly

Since we are simulating `host1` and `host2` on the same machine, we cannot have the same offset as described on the previous schema (`node11` and `node21` on HTTP port `8180`). We have to continue adding +100; so, `node21` will listen on HTTP port `8580`, `node22 :8680`, and `node23 :8780`):

```
[domain@127.0.0.1:9999/]/host=host2/server-config=node21:add(group=dev01,
socket-binding-port-offset=500)
[domain@127.0.0.1:9999/]/host=host2/server-
config=node22:add(group=dev02,socket-binding-port-offset=600)
[domain@127.0.0.1:9999 /] /host=host2/server-
config=node23:add(group=dev03,socket-binding-port-offset=700)
```

You may have a more verbose result while creating the first server instance on each host:
step-1 => {outcome => `success`}, step-3 => {outcome => `success`}, ...step-256 => {outcome => `success`}

All server nodes are now created. You can start/stop a specific instance or all the instances that belong to a server group:

```
[domain@127.0.0.1:9999 /] /server-group=dev01:start-servers
{
"outcome" => "success",
 "result" => undefined,
  "server-groups" => undefined
}
[domain@127.0.0.1:9999 /] /host=host2/server-config=node22:start
{
"outcome" => "success",
"result" => "STARTING"
}
[domain@127.0.0.1:9999 /]
```

Client: If the domain controller is down, what is the behavior of my instances?
Doctor JBoss: The server instances continue to work perfectly, but administration is not possible on the domain. However, if you had set up a backup domain controller, instances will try to join this one.

You can see the newly created server on the management console by clicking on a specific server group:

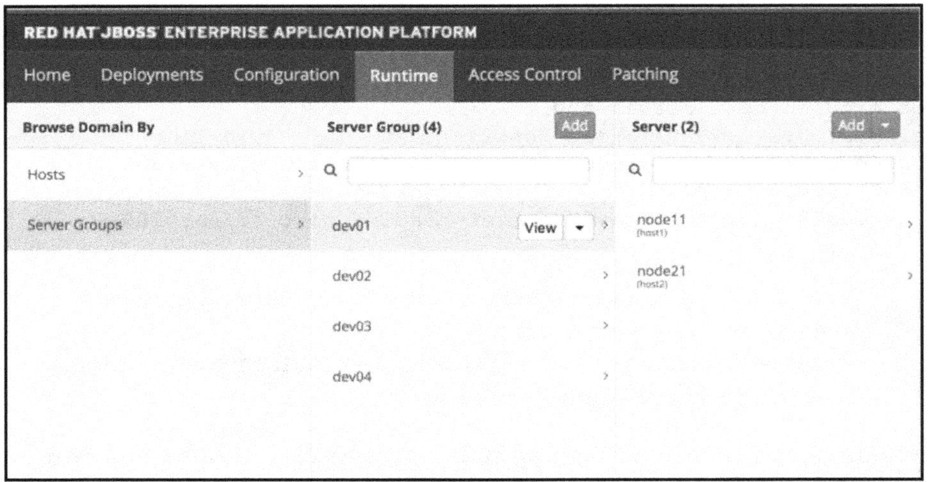

Servers groups and instances

The console is available at `http://127.0.0.1:9990/console`. JBoss remoting port is =`9999`, and HTTP interfaces are on `9990` by default.

Client: Thank you for your demonstration! I am very impatient to see my money transfer application running on this domain; however, I have some important questions: how will these two instances run the application concurrently, and do I have to provide two URLs to my customers?

What is the application behavior when one instance goes down for my critical money transfer application? I do not want to lose any transaction data. Can you show me how it works.

Doctor JBoss: Thank you for your questions. We will show you how to develop and deploy clustered applications using JBoss APIs and the JBoss Application Server. This is the purpose of the next section.

Clustered high available money TransferWebApp

In this section, Doctor JBoss and his assistant have the critical mission to build a proof of concept showing a clustered money transfer web application. The client will rely on this application to improve their money transfer portal.
The customer wants to see failover processes and confirm the transaction data is not lost when a node goes down.
A clustered application is a distributed application running on one or many server instances with the specificity that user data is also replicated on one or more nodes.
Web applications deployed on the JBoss Application Server must explicitly activate the clustering by adding the `<distributable>` tag in their `web.xml` descriptor.
This tag activates clustering on the the JBoss Application Server when the following subsystems are available:

- **Infinispan**: This subsystem provides the replicated cache to store objects: httpsessions and ejbs
- **JGroups**: This provides communication mechanisms used by nodes to discover each other and make exchanges
- **Modcluster**: The subsystem provides capabilities to communicate with the Apache HTTP server when Apache acts as a load balancer

Since user sessions are replicated on various nodes, while hitting the application URL for `node1` or `node2`, the user should see exactly the same content, including dynamic data stored in the session:

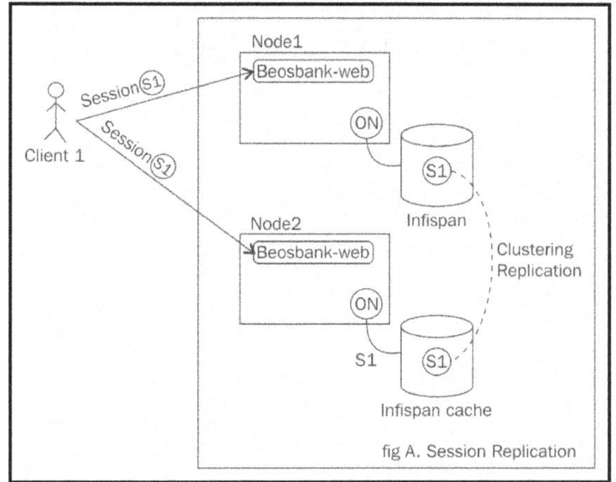

Session replication

If one node goes down, replication is not possible with the failing node; only users connected on the active node will be able to perform their transactions. At the same time, users previously connected on the failing node will face an error unless they have switched to a working node:

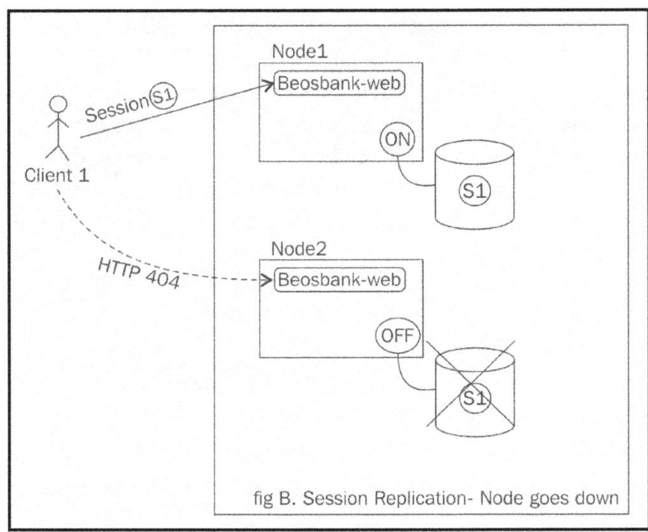

Session replication: a node goes down

To automatically switch clients to working nodes in case of a failure node, load balancers can be used; their main purpose is to listen for incoming client requests and redirect them to one active node. Load balancers also serve as a single entry point, hiding the multiple backend URLs to the final users.

If a user was previously connected to the failing node just before the break, by refreshing its browser or sending a new request, it should be switched by the load balancer to an active node where it resumes its session:

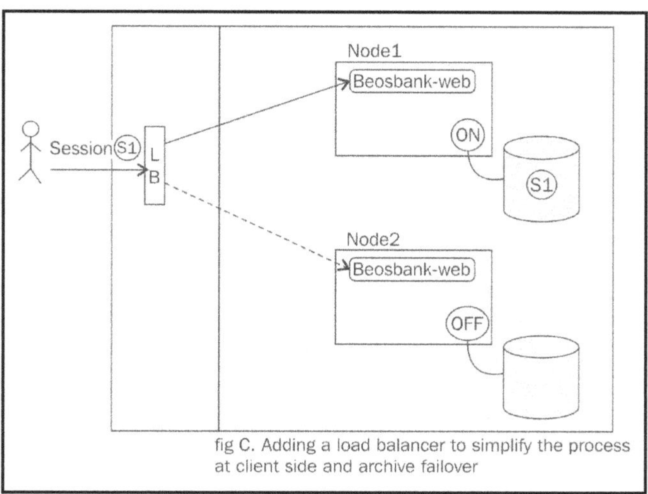

Load balancer in clustered application

Implementing a clustered money transfer web page

The clustered money transfer app is implemented in the `jossdevguidebook/chapters/ch2` subfolder, and two main modules are used to implement the following details:

- Core project `beosbank-core`: This project hosts the model and domain classes. To keep it simple, we have the following entities in the `com.beosbank.jbdevg.jbossas.domain` package:
    - Entity `Customer`: A beosBank customer who can act as a sender or receiver in a money transfer operation.
    - Entity `Address`: Customer address, including country names, in order to handle cross-border remittances. A customer has one and only one address.

- Entity `MoneyTransfer`: This represents a money transfer transaction between one sender and one receiver. The money transfer can have one status listed by the `MoneyTransferStatusEnum`.
  The money transfer entity also has attributes to store various prices, taxes, and currencies to satisfy the transaction.

For all the projects presented in this book, you can check out the code from the GitHub repository at `https://github.com/jbossdevguidebook/chapters`

- Web project `beosbank-web/`: This project holds the web part of the application. It is a JSF2 application including various API dependencies from JBoss maven repositories. The webapp depends on the `beosbank-core` artifact. This web app implements one use case: send a money transfer request to a recipient through three tabs/steps. These steps are implemented with the Primefaces Wizard component. The wizard component allows users to navigate steps back and forth:

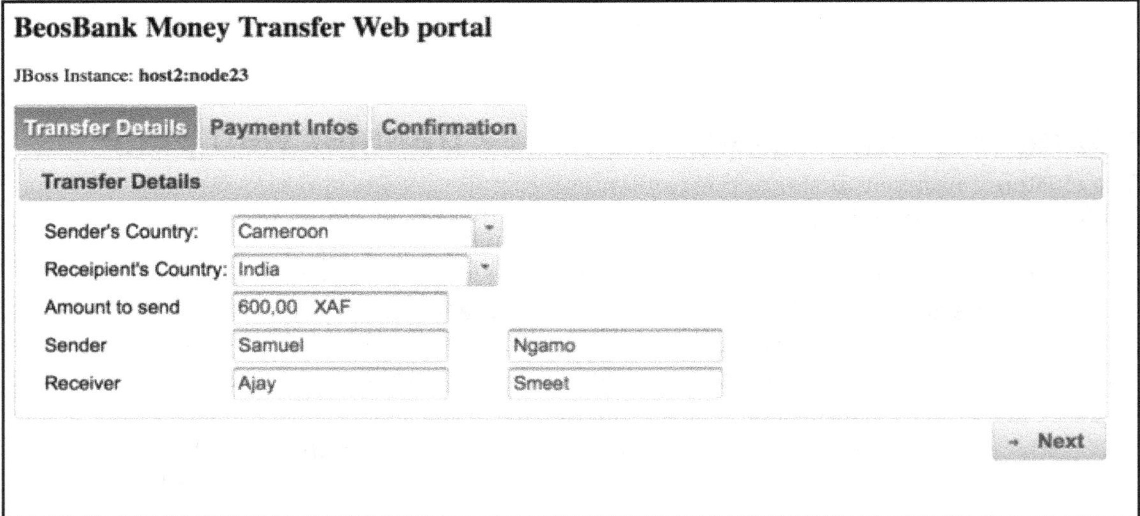

Money transfer web application

The **Transfer details** tab, is used to collect basic information of the money transfer: sender and receiver countries and names, and the amount to send.

The **Payment Infos** tab is designed to collect and/or select payment methods. For the purpose of this lab, the tab has only one field associated to a credit card number.

The **Confirmation** tab is a confirmation page where all the information previously entered by the user is displayed for verification before submitting the money transfer request.

Technically, the view is a JSF page implemented in the `index.xhtml` file. The view is bound to a ManageBean Request Controller named `mtvcBean` of the `MoneyTransferVviewControllerBean` type:

```
@RequestScoped
@ManagedBean(name="mtvcBean")
public class MoneyTransferViewController implements Serializable {
private static final long serialVersionUID = 1L;
private Map<String,String> countries;
private Map<String,String> currencies;
private MoneyTransfer transfer;

@PostConstruct
public void init() {
  //Initialize countries and currencies list
  initCountries();
  initCountriesCurrencies();
  //Load Money Transfer data from session if any
  getMoneyTransferDataFromSessionOrCreateNew();
}

....

//load the money transfer object from the Session
public MoneyTransfer getMoneyTransferDataFromSessionOrCreateNew() {
HttpSession session = getSession();
transfer = (MoneyTransfer)session.getAttribute("transfer");
if(transfer==null){
   transfer=new MoneyTransfer();
   session.setAttribute("transfer",this.transfer);
   }
   return transfer;
  }
}
```

The `MoneyTransferVviewControllerBean` bean as an attribute of the `MoneyTransfer` type to collect user inputs. The transfer injection in the bean is customized to first check whether there is a pending transfer object in the HTTP session; if yes, the session object is used.

During the sending process, a simple test to validate the session replication is to kill the running node when a user completes the second step of the wizard. While recovering his session on the failover node, data entered in the first tab (transfer details) should be available.

When was this bean placed in the session? For the first call, the `getMoneyTransferDataFromSessionOrCreateNew` method will not find any transaction object in the user session; a new object will therefore be created and set as a transaction attribute in the `mtvcBean` bean.

The `mtvcBean` bean and the `httpSession` object have the same reference on transfer objects. Whenever user inputs data, it will update both the transfer object of the `mtcvBean` and the transfer attribute of the `httpSession`:

```
public void setTransfer(MoneyTransfer transfer) {
 this.transfer = transfer;
HttpSession session = getSession();
session.setAttribute("transfer",this.transfer);
 }
```

In your application workflow, you can also set up specific synchronization points to set attributes in the session. For this demo, you can look at the `onReceiverCountryChange` event.
Whenever the sender selects a new value in the drop-down list for the receiver country, the transfer attribute is set on the `httpSession` object.

Once the application is ready, we need to deploy it on server instances

In the following sections, we will see how to deploy the money transfer web application on server group `dev03` (instances `node13` and `node23`), using two techniques.

- JBoss CLI
- JBoss-as maven plugin

JBoss CLI deployment

To deploy an application using the JBoss CLI, first connect to the native domain controller interface, then use the `deploy` method to add a deployment to a server group:

```
bin$ ./jboss-cli.sh --connect --controller=127.0.0.1:9999
[domain@127.0.0.1:9999 /] deploy $WORKSPACE/jbossas/beosbank-web/beosbank-
web.war --server-group dev03

#you can also force deployment and check the result status with
[domain@127.0.0.1:9999 /] /server-group=dev03/deployment=beosbank-
web.war:read-resource
{ "outcome" => "success",
"result" => {
"enabled" => true,
"name" => "beosbank-web.war",
"runtime-name" => "beosbank-web.war"
}
}
[domain@127.0.0.1:9999 /] /server-group=dev03/deployment=beosbank-
web.war:deploy
{
"outcome" => "success",
"result" => undefined,
"server-groups" => {"dev03" => {"host" => {
"host1" => {"node13" => {"response" => {
"outcome" => "success",
"result" => undefined
}}},
"host2" => {"node23" => {"response" => {
"outcome" => "success",
"result" => undefined
}}}
}}}
}
```

Deployment can be performed on a specific server group using the `--server-group` option. Once deploy you can verify the deployment status with the `read-resource` function. JBoss CLI deployment assumes you have a JBoss binary script, What about deployment in continuous delivery pipelines using Java EE standard tools such as Maven?

JBoss as maven plugin

The jboss-as-maven-plugin can be used to manage the application life cycle on the JBoss Application Server: it can deploy, undeploy, and redeploy applications. The jboss-as maven plugin works in the standalone and domain mode. This plugin uses the JBoss remoting protocol to perform deployments.
Update your POM file to use this plugin. In the build plugins list, add the following:

```
<plugin>
<groupId>org.jboss.as.plugins</groupId>
<artifactId>jboss-as-maven-plugin</artifactId>
<version>7.9.Final</version>
 <configuration>
     <hostname>127.0.0.1</hostname>
     <port>9999</port>
     <domain>
         <server-groups>
            <server-group>dev03</server-group>
          </server-groups>
     </domain>
 </configuration>
</plugin>
```

Use the domain controller hostname (default to localhost) and port (default value=`9999`), specify the target deployment server group, and then run the `jboss-as` deploy goal to deploy your application:

```
$mvn jboss-as:deploy
[INFO] ------------------------------------------------------------------
[INFO] Building beosbank-web Transfer Webapp 1.0-SNAPSHOT
[INFO] ------------------------------------------------------------------
[INFO]
[INFO] >>> jboss-as-maven-plugin:7.9.Final:deploy (default-cli) > package @
beosbank-web >>>
.....
[INFO]
[INFO] --- jboss-as-maven-plugin:7.9.Final:deploy (default-cli) @ beosbank-
web ---
mars 19, 2017 5:29:10 PM org.xnio.Xnio <clinit>
INFO: XNIO Version 3.0.7.GA
mars 19, 2017 5:29:10 PM org.xnio.nio.NioXnio <clinit>
INFO: XNIO NIO Implementation Version 3.0.7.GA
mars 19, 2017 5:29:10 PM org.jboss.remoting3.EndpointImpl <clinit>
INFO: JBoss Remoting version 3.2.12.GA
[INFO] ------------------------------------------------------------------
[INFO] BUILD SUCCESS
[INFO] ------------------------------------------------------------------
```

```
[INFO] Total time: 4.668 s
[INFO] Finished at: 2017-03-19T17:29:12+01:00
[INFO] Final Memory: 17M/190M
[INFO] ------------------------------------------------------------------
```

Full documentation of the plugin is available at `https://docs.jboss.org/jbossas/7/plugins/maven/latest/index.html`.

Session replication demo

Once the application is deployed, perform the following steps:

1. Open the application link from `node13` `http://localhost:8380/beosbank-web/`.
2. Fill the money transfer details and click on **Next** to select the payment options:
    - **Sender Country**: **France**
    - **Receiver Country**: **Cameroon**
    - **Amount to send**: **100**
    - **Sender**: **Noe Nono**
    - **Receiver**: **Michele Bertille**

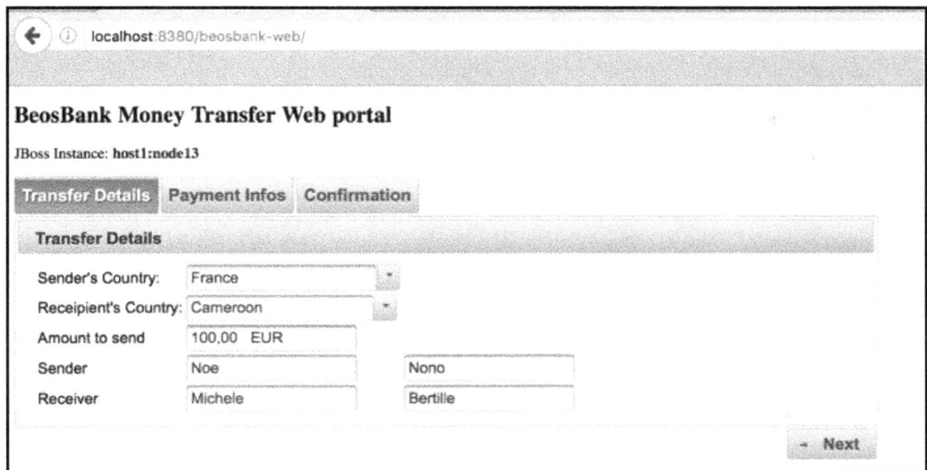

3. Click on the **Next** button to reach the Payment Infos tab:

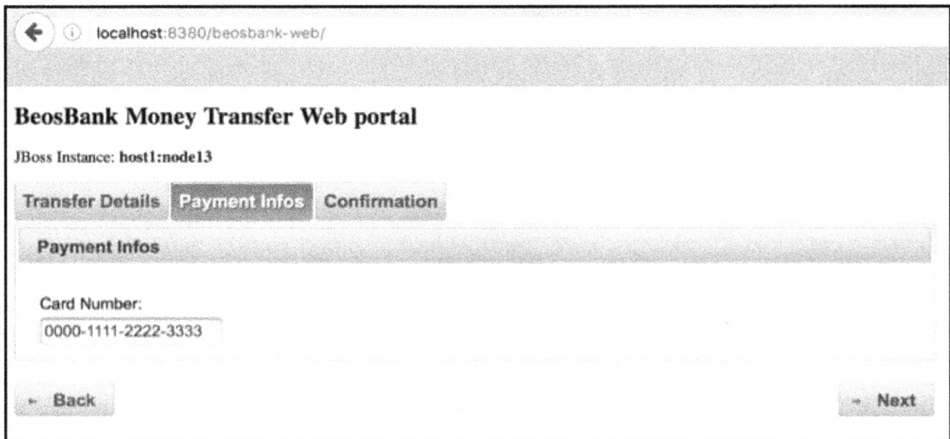

- Fill the credit card number field with the value: **000-1111-2222 3333**
- Click on the **Next** button.
- Try to open the application URL from the second node of the group (**host2:node23**) in another tab of your browser--`http://localhost:8780/beosbank-web/`:

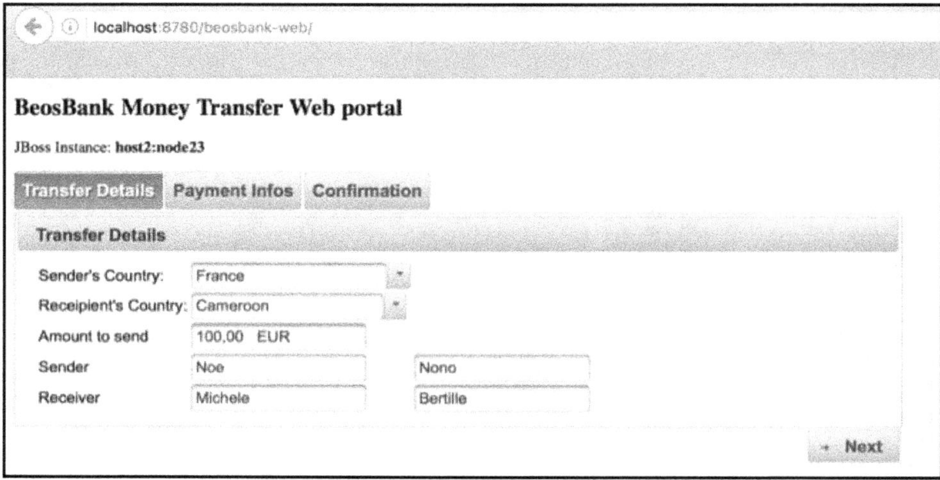

You will automatically arrive on the first tab with data entered from the `node13` session:

- **Sender Country**: **France**
- **Receiver Country**: **Cameroon**
- **Amount to send**: **100**
- **Sender**: **Noe Nono**
- **Receiver**: **Michele Bertille**

The session you started on `node13` session has been replicated on `node23`; if you shut down one node, the caller can still find this data from the other node:

```
[domain@127.0.0.1:9999 /] /host=host1/server=node13:stop
{"outcome" => "success",
"result" => "STOPPING"
}
```

`http://localhost:8380/beosbank-web/` **=> KO**

`http://localhost:8780/beosbank-web/` **=> OK**

With this configuration, in order avoid request failures, the caller has to implement a failover process to automatically switch to a running node when the current node goes down. This approach makes the client code become strongly coupled to the server instance URLs.

Archiving automatic cluster failover

In order to archive automatic failover between instances, the application provider should set up a load balancer in front of his backend nodes.
In a load balancing configuration, clients wanting to access the application pass through a unique intermediate URL, that is, the load balancing URL, which, upon receiving a client request, forwards it to an active node.
There are various ways to implement simple load balancers: HAProxy, Apache httpd, even the JBoss Undertow subsystem can be configured to act as a load balancer. We will look at how to set up load balancing using Undertow in `Chapter 3`, *Custom Web Deployment using Undertow and Swarm.*

For this lab, we are relying on HAProxy for its simplicity and advanced routing features. Install the HAproxy as recommended for your target operating system following the `official docs`:

```
$haproxy -v
HA-Proxy version 1.7.3 2017/02/28
Copyright 2000-2017 Willy Tarreau <willy@haproxy.org>
```

Edit a `haproxy.cfg` configuration file to set up the frontend and backend. Here's the most important part for our example:

```
listen stats
     bind *:9000
     stats enable
     stats hide-version
     stats realm haproxyStatistics
     stats auth haproxy:haproxy
     stats uri /haproxy

frontend haproxy_in
        bind *:9001
        default_backend beosbank_http
        mode http
backend beosbank_http
        mode http
        balance roundrobin
        server node13 127.0.0.1:8380 check
        server node23 127.0.0.1:8780 check
```

The full `haproxy.cfg` file used is in the BeOSbank-web app resource folder for your reference (`beosbank-web/src/main/resources/haproxy.cfg`).
We defined a backend `beosbank_http` with two nodes: `node13` and `node23`. HAProxy frontend is configured to listen on port `9001` and balance load following the round robin algorithm, and provide statistics on port `9000`. Stats are restricted to the `haproxy/haproxy` user only.

Start the HAProxy server with the `-f` option to pass the custom configuration file:

```
$ haproxy -f haproxy.cfg
```

In your web browser, open the HAProxy URL, `http://localhost:9001/beosbank-web/`:

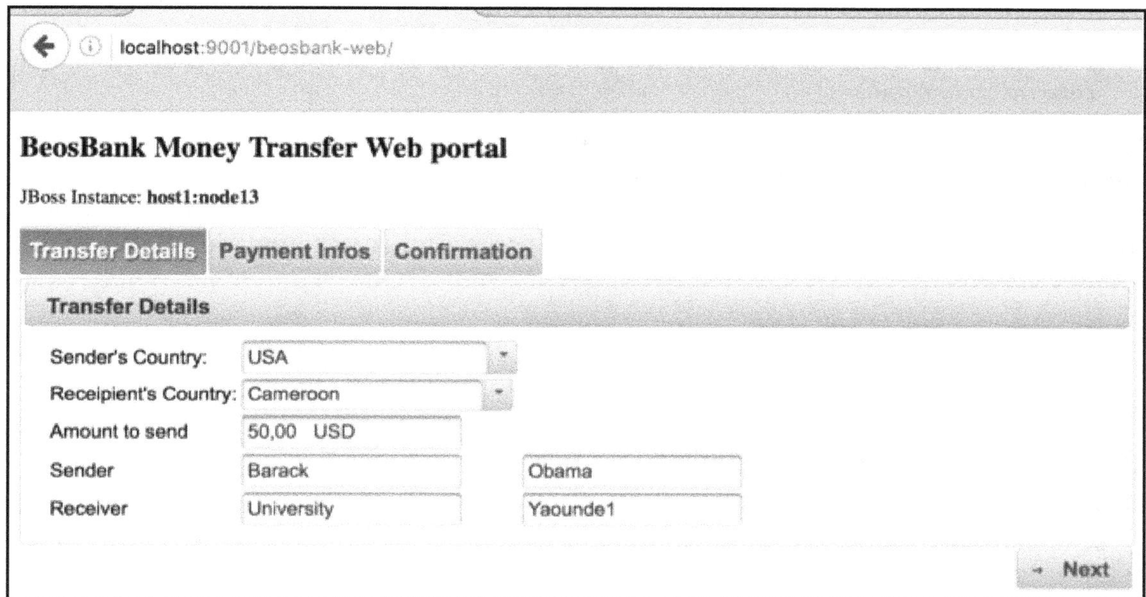

The load balancer forwards the request to `node13`

1. Fill in the Transfer details tabs and Payment Infos tab.
2. Shut down `node13` using the following CLI Command:

```
[domain@127.0.0.1:9999 /] /host=host1/server-config=node13:stop
{
    "outcome" => "success",
     "result" => "STOPPING"
}
```

HAProxy detects that this node is now down and you can see this from the HAProxy console logs:

```
[WARNING] 077/190646 (14290) : Server beosbank_http/node13 is DOWN, reason:
Layer4 connection problem, info: "Connection refused", check duration: 0ms.
1 active and 0 backup servers left. 0 sessions active, 0 requeued, 0
remaining in queue.
```

Now, refresh your browser. You will automatically be redirected to **node23** by HAProxy, and your screens will be similar to the previous one. As the session is replicated on **node23**, the user does not lose his data and will be automatically switched to a working node when the node on which the session was initiated goes down. This is an automatic failover using a load balancer:

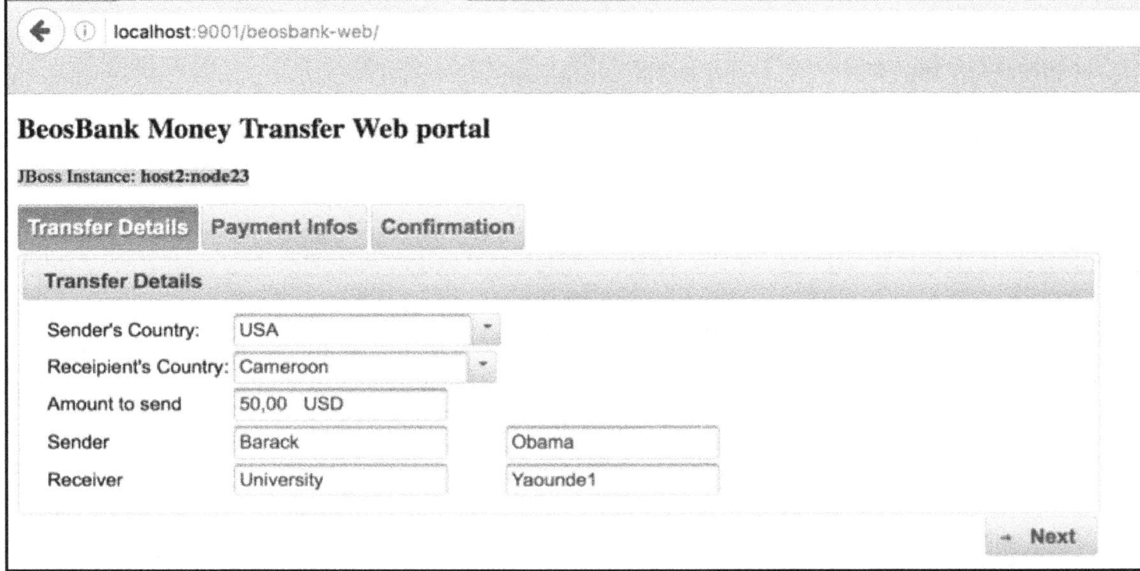

You can also see HAProxy statistics at `http://localhost:9000/haproxy`:

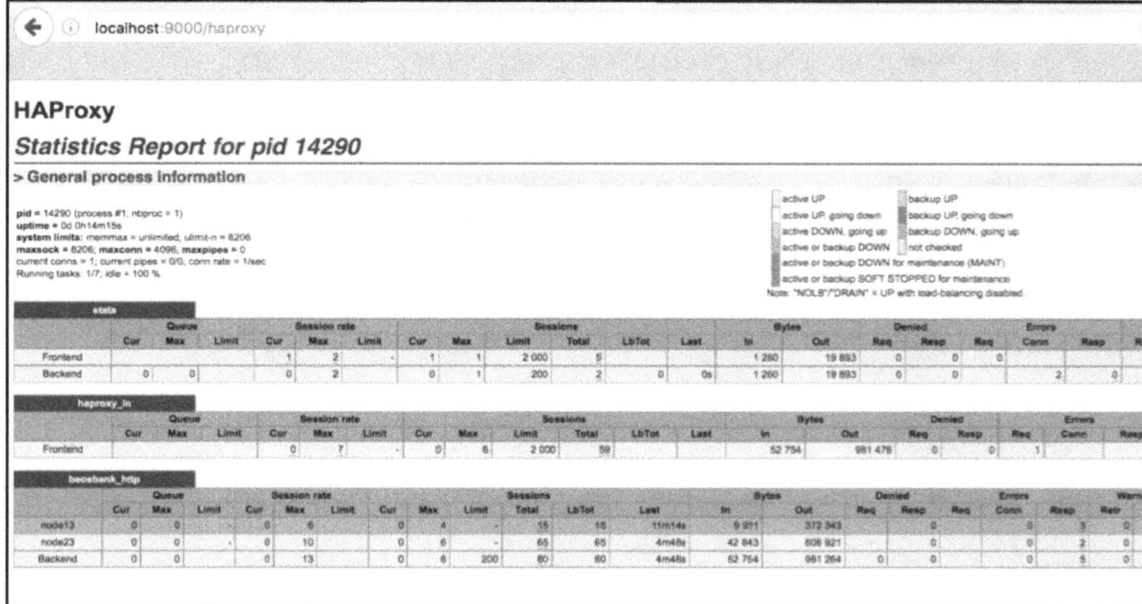

HAProxy statistics

Session distribution on limited nodes and passivation

Client: Hi doctor, if 10,000 concurrent users are connected on the money transfer application, does this mean all the 10,000 sessions are replicated on all the nodes?
DoctorJBoss: User sessions are replicated on one or more nodes; with the JBoss EAP, there are two replication strategies:

- **Full replication mode**, where user sessions are replicated on all the cluster nodes; this configuration is suitable for small clusters with less than six nodes
- In the **distribution mode**, user sessions are replicated on a limited number of nodes in the cluster (two nodes by default), but this value can be customized depending on your application requirements

To reduce memory footprint, developers can also customize session passivation processes: this includes the max active session for an application, the max idle time after which a session should be destroyed by the JBoss Application Server.

Cluster isolation by server groups

Client: I tried to deploy the PoC you provided on another server group (`dev01`), but I am seeing strange logs that the `dev01` and `dev03` server groups are now forming a cluster and exchanging data using JGroups. This does not conform to what you previously said regarding cluster environment isolation by server groups, no?

Deployment was done using the JBoss CLI with the following command:

```
[domain@127.0.0.1:9999 /] /server-group=dev01/deployment=beosbank-
web.war:add
{
"outcome" => "success",
 "result" => undefined,
     "server-groups" => {"dev01" => {"host" => {
            "host1" => {"node11" => {"response" => {
                "outcome" => "success",
                "result" => undefined
             }}},
             "host2" => {"node21" => {"response" => {
                "outcome" => "success",
                "result" => undefined
             }}}
      }}}
}
[domain@127.0.0.1:9999 /] /server-group=dev01/deployment=beosbank-
web.war:deploy
{
 "outcome" => "success",
 "result" => undefined,
 "server-groups" => {"dev01" => {"host" => {
  "host1" => {"node11" => {"response" => {
  "outcome" => "success",
         "result" => undefined
       }}},
       "host2" => {"node21" => {"response" => {
           "outcome" => "success",
           "result" => undefined
       }}}
   }}}
[Server:node21] 21:15:56,629 INFO
[org.infinispan.remoting.transport.jgroups.JGroupsTransport]
```

```
(thread-8,ee,host2:node21) ISPN000094: Received new cluster view for
channel hibernate: [host1:node11|24] (4) [host1:node11, host2:node21,
host2:node23, host1:node13]
[Server:node21] 21:15:56,631 INFO
[org.infinispan.remoting.transport.jgroups.JGroupsTransport]
(thread-8,ee,host2:node21) ISPN000094: Received new cluster view for
channel ejb: [host1:node11|24] (4) [host1:node11, host2:node21,
host2:node23, host1:node13]
```

JBossDoctor: Nice question! Indeed, by default, all the server groups have the same JGROUP configuration, so server instances will build and join a single cluster by default. To archive server group isolation, we need to define a specific JGROUP multicast address and/or an MPING port for each server group.

Creating datasources

Once users complete transactions, data should be kept not only in the session, but in persistent repositories such as databases and files.
The JBoss EAP relies on datasources and various Java specification, such as JDBC and JPA, to access databases.
Before inserting/retrieving data in a table, applications must specify a datasource.
There are various options to create a datasource within the JBoss Application Server; now we'll take a look at the main steps. Datasources are created from drivers, and drivers are implemented by code loaded in modules. In the next section we will see how to create modules, drivers, and datasources from JBoss.

Creating a module

The database provider often releases connectors or libraries to access their product from various platforms; these connectors should be registered as JBoss EAP modules.
In our case, to insert data in a MySQL database, we first have to create a MySQL module with the `mysql-java-connector jar`:

1. Create the module folder.
2. Copy the jar file in the newly created folder.
3. Create the `module.xml` file to index the module
4. Edit the module xml file to reference the jar file and set its dependencies.

```
$cd $EAP_DOMAIN/jboss-eap-7.0/modules/system/layers/base/
$mkdir -p com/mysql/jdbc/main
$cp $HOME/downloadsmysql-connector-java-5.1.41.jar com/mysql/jdbc/main/
$vi com/mysql/jdbc/main/module.xml
```

You can download the jar from the Maven central repository at `https://mvnrepository.com/artifact/mysql/mysql-connector-java`:

```
<module xmlns="urn:jboss:module:1.3" name="com.mysql.jdbc">
<resources>
       <resource-root path="mysql-connector-java-5.1.41.jar"/>
</resources>
   <dependencies>
       <module name="javax.api"/>
       <module name="javax.transaction.api"/>
   </dependencies>
</module>
```

Existing modules can be referenced while creating drivers.

Creating a MySQL driver

In the domain mode, drivers are created on the datasource subsystem; so, we should first select a profile to add a driver, then create the driver on the associated datasource subsystem.
The operation impacts all servers that are configured with the updated profile, as shown in the results of creating the MySQL driver on the ha profile. Remember that the *dev01* and *dev03* server groups, for example, are created with the ha profile:

```
[domain@127.0.0.1:9999 /] /profile=default/subsystem=datasources/jdbc-driver=mysql:add(driver-name=mysql,driver-module-name=com.mysql.jdbc,driver-xa-datasource-class-name=com.mysql.jdbc.jdbc2.optional.MysqlXADataSource)
{
   "outcome" => "success",
   "result" => undefined,
   "server-groups" => undefined
}
```

Here, we create a MySQL driver on the default and ha profiles:

```
[domain@127.0.0.1:9999 /] /profile=ha/subsystem=datasources/jdbc-driver=mysql:add(driver-name=mysql,driver-module-name=com.mysql.jdbc,driver-xa-datasource-class-name=com.mysql.jdbc.jdbc2.optional.MysqlXADataSource)
{
   "outcome" => "success",
   "result" => undefined,
   "server-groups" => {
       "dev01" => {"host" => {
           "host1" => {"node11" => {"response" => {
              "outcome" => "success",
```

```
                "result" => undefined
            }}},
            "host2" => {"node21" => {"response" => {
                "outcome" => "success",
                 "result" => undefined
            }}}
        }},
        "dev03" => {"host" => {
            "host1" => {"node13" => {"response" => {
                "outcome" => "success",
              "result" => undefined
           }}},
            "host2" => {"node23" => {"response" => {
             "outcome" => "success",
                "result" => undefined
            }}}
        }},
        "dev04" => {"host" => {"host1" => {"node14" => {"response" => {
           "outcome" => "success",
         "result" => undefined
      }}}}}
   }
}
```

As an outcome, the command returns the server list impacted by the modification with the status of creating the driver on each specific server.

Datasource

As soon as the driver is present, it can be referenced to create a datasource, as illustrated in the following sample.
The `MoneyTransferDS` datasource is created on the ha Profile with `jndi-name=java:jboss/datasources/MoneyTransferDS`, the MySQL driver we created earlier, and a connections URL, username, and password:

```
[domain@127.0.0.1:9999 /] /profile=ha/subsystem=datasources/data-
source=MoneyTrasnferDS:add(jndi-
name="java:jboss/datasources/MoneyTransferDS",driver-name=mysql,connection-
url="jdbc:mysql://localhost:3306/beosbank-mt", user-name="root",
password="jb0s5!")
{
"outcome" => "success",
   "result" => undefined,
   "server-groups" => {
       "dev01" => {"host" => {
           "host1" => {"node11" => {"response" => {
               "outcome" => "success",
```

```
                "result" => undefined
            }}},
            "host2" => {"node21" => {"response" => {
                "outcome" => "success",
                "result" => undefined
            }}}
        }},
        "dev03" => {"host" => {
            "host1" => {"node13" => {"response" => {
                "outcome" => "success",
                "result" => undefined
            }}},
            "host2" => {"node23" => {"response" => {
                "outcome" => "success",
                "result" => undefined
            }}}
        }},
        "dev04" => {"host" => {"host1" => {"node14" => {"response" => {
            "outcome" => "success",
            "result" => undefined
        }}}}}
    }
}[domain@127.0.0.1:9999 /]
```

The datasource is created and deployed on all the servers defined with the ha profile. The connection string may be different depending on your database management system and version.

With MySQL 5.5.45+, 5.6.26+, and 5.7.6+, the SSL connection must be established by default if an explicit option isn't set. So, if your MySQL version is in this range, update your connection string to set the `useSSL` attribute.

```
[domain@127.0.0.1:9999 /] /profile=ha/subsystem=datasources/data-
source=MoneyTrasnferDS:write-attribute(name=connection-
url,value="jdbc:mysql://localhost:3306/beosbank-mt?useSSL=false")
```

Testing the datasource

At the end of the creation process, you can test the connection to your database from a specific server instance:

```
[domain@127.0.0.1:9999 /]
/host=host1/server=node11/subsystem=datasources/data-
source=MoneyTrasnferDS:test-connection-in-pool
{
"outcome" => "success",
 "result" => [true]
}
```

Ensure that you created the DB using your favorite SQL/Mysql client, otherwise the test will fail. Use the SQL command:
`CREATE SCHEMA beosbank-mt default character set utf8 collate utf8_bin.`

After completing these four steps, you will be ready to run an application that interacts with your datasource. A simple sample will be to persist the `MoneyTransfer` request.

Lab accessing databases with JPA

In the following section, we will review the different steps to plug a data access layer into the Money Transfer web application you built in the previous steps.
As soon as a user clicks on the submit button, we want the application to save a record in the database and return the money transfer request ID.

Referencing a datasource

The first thing to do is to create a `persistence.xml` file in `beosbank-web-jpa/src/main/resources/META-INF`.
This file will be used by JPA to access the database, create/update the schema, and persist entities:

```
<?xml version="1.0" encoding="UTF-8"?>
<persistence xmlns="http://java.sun.com/xml/ns/persistence" version="1.0">
   <persistence-unit name="beosbank-mt-unit">
   <description>BeosBank MoneyTransfer Persistence Unit</description>
   <jta-data-source>java:jboss/datasources/MoneyTransferDS</jta-data-
source>
     <properties>
       <property name="showSql" value="true" />
       <property name="hibernate.hbm2ddl.auto" value="update" />
```

```
</properties>
   </persistence-unit>
</persistence>
```

The `jta-data-source` property is filled with the datasource jndi-name.

Creating entities

In the `com.beosbank.jbdevg.jbossas.domain` package, we will define entities of our application model; this is simply adding JPA annotation to the `Customer`, `Address`, `MoneyTransfer`, and `MoneyTransferStatus` classes:

```
@Entity
@Table(name="T_CUSTOMER")
public class Customer implements Serializable {

       private static final long serialVersionUID = 1L;
       @Id
       @Column(name="ID")
       @GeneratedValue(strategy=GenerationType.IDENTITY)
       private long id;
       @Column(name="FIRSTNAME")
       private String firstName;
       @Column(name="LASTNAME")
       private String lastName;

       @Temporal(TemporalType.DATE)
       @Column(name="BIRTHDATE")
       private Date birthDate;
       @Embedded
       private Address address;
       @OneToMany(mappedBy="sender")
       private List<MoneyTransfer> sentTransfers;

       @OneToMany(mappedBy="receiver")
       private List<MoneyTransfer> receivedTransfers;
       public Customer(){
              address= new Address();
       }
...
}
```

This indicates that the persistence provider must assign primary keys for the entity using a database identity column.

The address is considered as an embeddable property for the customer entity, and thus the address property columns--street, zip code, country, and city mapping--will be added to the `T_CUSTOMER` table:

```
@Entity
@Table(name="T_MONEYTRANSFER")
public class MoneyTransfer implements Serializable {

        private static final long serialVersionUID = 1L;
        @Id
        @Column(name="ID")
        @GeneratedValue(strategy=GenerationType.IDENTITY)
        private long id;
        @ManyToOne(cascade={CascadeType.PERSIST})
        @JoinColumn(name="SENDER_ID")
        private Customer sender;
        @ManyToOne(cascade={CascadeType.PERSIST})
        @JoinColumn(name="RECEIVER_ID")
        private Customer receiver;

        @Enumerated(EnumType.STRING)
        private MoneyTransferStatus status= MoneyTransferStatus.DRAFT;
```

The money transfer status is handled as a string enumeration. The `customer` and `MoneyTransfer` entities have two unidirectional relations; a customer can send 0 to many `MoneyTransferRequests`. A `MoneyTransferRequest` is sent by one and only one customer (sender). A customer is the receiver for 0..N `MoneyTransferRequest`, and a `MoneyTransferRequest` is sent to 1..1 Customer(receiver).
While inserting a money request in the database, we want associated entities (sender and receiver) to be persisted as well, if needed; that's the reason we are cascading the persist operation in the `manyToOne` relation `cascade={CascadeType.PERSIST})`.

Inserting a MoneyTransferRequest

Operations can be performed by an Enterprise Java Bean object:

```
@Stateful
@Named("mtcStatefullEjb")
public class MoneyTransferClusteredStatefullBean implements
IMoneyTransferEjb {

@PersistenceContext(unitName = "beosbank-mt-unit", type =
```

```
PersistenceContextType.EXTENDED)

   private EntityManager entityManager;
       @Override
       public long addMoneyTransfer(MoneyTransfer mt) {
              entityManager.persist(mt);
              return mt.getId();
       }
...
}
```

The data access layer just injects a persistence context and reuses it to query the database. This EJB is injected in the `moneytransferviewcontroller`:

```
//JPA- Inject the DAO EJB service
   @EJB
   IMoneyTransferEjb mtDaoService;

public void sendMoney(){
  transfer.setSendingDate(new Date());
  long ref=mtDaoService.addMoneyTransfer(transfer);
  //Handle result here
...
```

Deploy the `ch2/beosbank-web-jpa` project on the server group `node12`, for example, using either the JBoss CLI or maven `Jboss-as-plugin`:

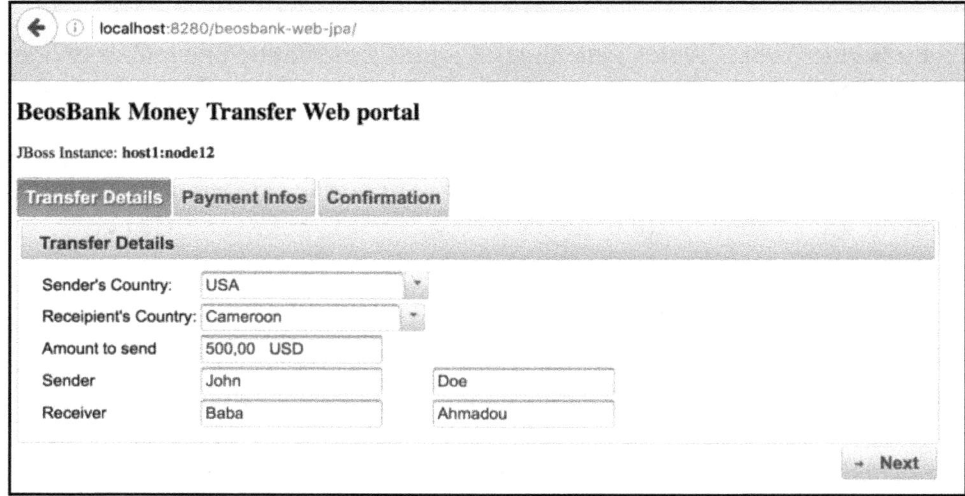

1. Open the project URL and initiate a money transfer transaction.
2. Fill both Transaction and Payment info tabs.
3. Click on the **Send** button to complete your money transfer transaction:

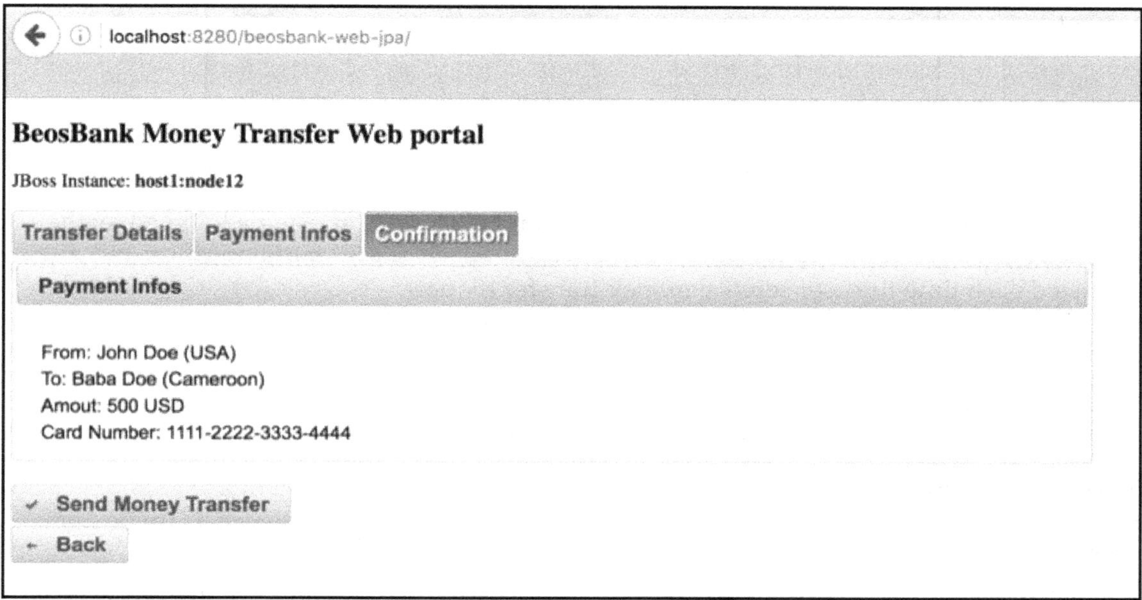

Click on the **Send Money Transfer** button. The `mtvcBean` is invoked:

1. The `mtcStatefullBean` is called
2. The Entity Manager is called
3. The Beosbank datasource is referenced by the Entity Manager
4. The datasource operations used the driver to interact with the DB

The request is saved in the database, and you will receive the following feedback:

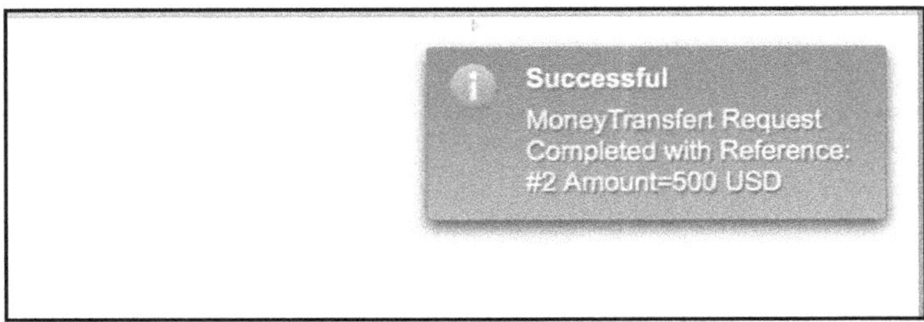

In a normal workflow, the sender will first open an HTTP session using a login page; the sender's `Customer entity` will be loaded once after a successful authentication and not persisted each time the user sends a money transfer request.
You can manually handle transactions while inserting or updating entities using the following:

```
entityManager.getTransaction().begin(); and
entityManager.getTransaction().commit() /rollback()
```

Since we are using the `jta-data-source`, in the `mtcStatefullBean SessionBean`, each method defaults to a `TransactionAttributeType.REQUIRED` and hence its invocation starts a JTA transaction if no JTA transaction is in progress.
If a method is the first called that requires a transaction, it will commit the changes upon completion.

To cluster the Session Bean, use the `org.jboss.ejb3.annotation.Clustered` annotation. All the JPA code is located in the `ch2/beosbank-web-jpa project`

Leveraging the existing features to define security policies

One of the most important features in enterprise web applications is security. Security can takes several paths. In this section, we will see how a web application can restrict access to only authorized users.

Client: Hello doctor, for now, everybody has access to my money transfer web application. I would like to authorize only registered and authorized users who have an identifier and password in the `Account` table.
JBossDoctor: Nice! JBoss is fully **Java Authentication and Authorization Service** (**JAAS**) compliant and defines a set of `login` modules on which users can rely to secure their applications.
Client: What is JAAS?
JBossDoctor: JAAS means Java Authentication and Authorization Service; it is a security API that consists of a set of Java packages designed for user authentication and authorization.
JBoss provides login modules to authenticate/authorize users from LDAP directories, flat files, relational databases, and certificates. By default, a simple configuration is sufficient to set up JAAS authentication in a web application. Some applications may need a specific authentication/verification process. You can perform this by overriding the existing login module classes or by creation of new modules. In this next paragraph, I will show you how to define a database security domain.

Creating a database security domain

To set up authentication in the money-transfer application using the account table, we will leverage the `DatabaseServerLogingModule` provided by JBoss.
The database login module retrieves user IDs, passwords, and roles from a relational database through JDBC. Internally, it relies on two logical tables, Principals and Roles:

```
Table Principals(PrincipalID text, Password text) : storing user identifier and password.
Table Roles(PrincipalID text, Role text, RoleGroup text) : providing users roles and groups.
```

While customizing the database login module, developers have to provide at least the following three parameters:

- `dsJndiName`: The JNDI name of the datasource
- `principalsQuery`: The SQL query to obtain the user password
- `rolesQuery`: The SQL query to obtain the user roles

By default, the following queries are used to retrieve user details:

```
protected String principalsQuery = "select Password from Principals where
PrincipalID=?";
protected String rolesQuery = "select Role, RoleGroup from Roles where
PrincipalID=?";
```

The `principalSquery` retrieves a password for a provided principal identifier while the `rolesQuery` returns the existing role for the user.

Considering the following BeOSBank user account table structure, how can we set up a DB login module?

```
CREATE TABLE `beosbank-mt`.`T_ACCOUNT` (
`ID` bigint(20) NOT NULL AUTO_INCREMENT,
`USERNAME` varchar(30) COLLATE utf8_bin DEFAULT NULL,
`PASSWORD` varchar(30) COLLATE utf8_bin DEFAULT NULL,
`ROLE` varchar(30) COLLATE utf8_bin DEFAULT 'Customer',
PRIMARY KEY (`ID`)
)
```

Here's some data inserted in the `T_ACCOUNT` table:

```
/*!40000 ALTER TABLE `T_ACCOUNT` DISABLE KEYS */;
INSERT INTO `T_ACCOUNT` VALUES
(1,'demo','demo1234','Customer'),
(2,'jboss','jboss','Admin'),
(3,'guest1','guest1',NULL);
```

To define a security policy, we have to create a security domain using CLI commands:

```
/profile=ha/subsystem=security/security-domain=beosbank-web-policy:add
/profile=ha/subsystem=security/security-domain=beosbank-web-
policy/authentication=classic:add(
login-modules=[
                {
     "code" => "org.jboss.security.auth.spi.DatabaseServerLoginModule",
      "flag" => "required",
"module-options" => [
("dsJndiName"=>"java:jboss/datasources/MoneyTransferDS"),
```

```
("principalsQuery"=>"SELECT PASSWORD FROM T_ACCOUNT WHERE USERNAME=?"),
("rolesQuery"=> "SELECT ROLE, 'Roles' FROM T_ACCOUNT WHERE USERNAME=?")
                                        ]
                    }
                    ]
):reload-servers
```

- Add a new security domain for the Beosbank application
- Add a classic authentication that reference the `DatabaseServerLogin` module
- The `org.jboss.security.auth.spi.DatabaseServerLoginModule` code attribute refers to the `module` class we are leveraging.
- To select user roles and groups, use `rolesQuery`= `SELECT ROLE, 'Roles' FROM T_ACCOUNT WHERE USERNAME=?`.

We will pick the `ROLE` column content and return a `ROLES` constant as the associated group. Since we are not managing application groups, all the roles will be mapped to the `ROLES` group:

```
$ ./jboss-cli.sh --file=./createBeosBankSecurityPolicyDefault.cli --connect
{
   "outcome" => "success",
   "result" => undefined,
   "server-groups" => {
       "dev01" => {"host" => {
           "host1" => {"node11" => {"response" => {
"outcome" => "success",
               "result" => undefined,
               "response-headers" => {
                   "operation-requires-reload" => true,
                   "process-state" => "reload-required"
               }
         }}},
          .....
          "result" => undefined,
          "response-headers" => {
              "operation-requires-reload" => true,
              "process-state" => "reload-required"
          }
      }}}}}
   }
}
```

A custom script is available in the GitHub repository to perform the operation in a single `jboss-cli` command: `createBeosBankSecurityPolicyDefault.cli`.

To verify the configuration, try to read the `beosbank-web-policy` authentication attribute:

```
[domain@localhost:9990 /] /profile=ha/subsystem=security/security-
domain=beosbank-web-policy/authentication=classic:read-resource
{
"outcome" => "success",
"result" => {
"login-modules" => [{
"code"=>"org.jboss.security.auth.spi.DatabaseServerLoginModule",
"flag" => "required",
"module" => undefined,
"module-options" => [
("dsJndiName" =>"java:jboss/datasources/MoneyTransferDS"),
("principalsQuery" => "select password from t_account where username=?"),
("rolesQuery" => "select 'Customer', 'Roles'")
]
}],
"login-module" => {"org.jboss.security.auth.spi.DatabaseServerLoginModule"
=> undefined}
}
}
```

The security domain is properly defined as shown in the previous command results; now we can plug it in a web application and check how users are authenticated.

Plugging a security domain in a web application

In order to rely on these security policies to authenticate users, any web application should explicitly declare the newly created security domain in a `WEB-INF/jboss-web.xml` file:

```
<jboss-web>
    <security-domain>beosbank-web-policy</security-domain>
</jboss-web>
```

Once we have a security domain, it is very simple to restrict access to some application resources according to the defined policy. To do this, a developer should customize the application descriptor to set various Java EE security constraints:

```
<?xml version="1.0"?>
<web-app>
<display-name>BeosBank Money Transfer WebApp-JAAS Demo</display-
name><distributable/>
<welcome-file-list>
<welcome-file>index.xhtml</welcome-file>
```

```
</welcome-file-list>
<security-constraint>
<web-resource-collection>
   <web-resource-name>Secured resources</web-resource-name>
   <url-pattern>/faces/secured/*</url-pattern>
</web-resource-collection>
<auth-constraint>
   <role-name>Customer</role-name>
</auth-constraint>
</security-constraint>

<security-role>
  <role-name>Customer</role-name>
</security-role>
<security-role>
  <role-name>Guest</role-name>
</security-role>

<login-config>
       <auth-method>FORM</auth-method>
           <form-login-config>
  <form-login-page>/faces/login.xhtml</form-login-page>
 <form-error-page>/faces/error.xhtml</form-error-page>
          </form-login-config>
   </login-config>
</web-app>
```

The following configuration allows access to any URL under `/faces/protected/` only if the requester has the customer role. Roles referenced in the application should be listed with the `security-role` tag.
As users are connecting using a `login/password` system, we should set up a FORM-based authentication:

```
<form method="post" action="j_security_check">
                  <h:panelGrid columns="2">
<h:outputLabel for="j_username" value="Login: " />
                           <h:inputText id="j_username" />
              <h:outputLabel for="j_password" value="Password:" />
                           <h:inputSecret id="j_password" />
                           <h:commandButton id="login" value="Login" />
                  </h:panelGrid>
                  <h:messages />
         </form>
```

With this authentication method, the container is notified when the `j_security_check` action is posted. It retrieves the `j_username` and `j_password` information and forwards the authentication to the JAAS login module.

Deploying the application and checking the secure pages

The Jboss-as-maven plugin is configured to deploy this application, by default, on the dev01 server group.

Open the `http://localhost:8180/beosbank-web-security/` `Node11` instance:

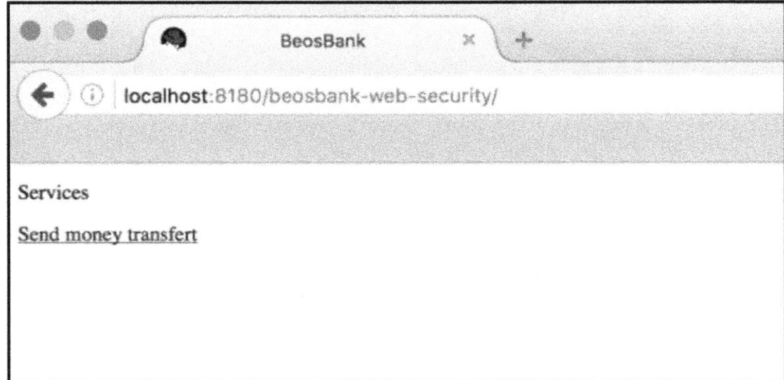

The home page is available to everyone; try to send a money transfer request:

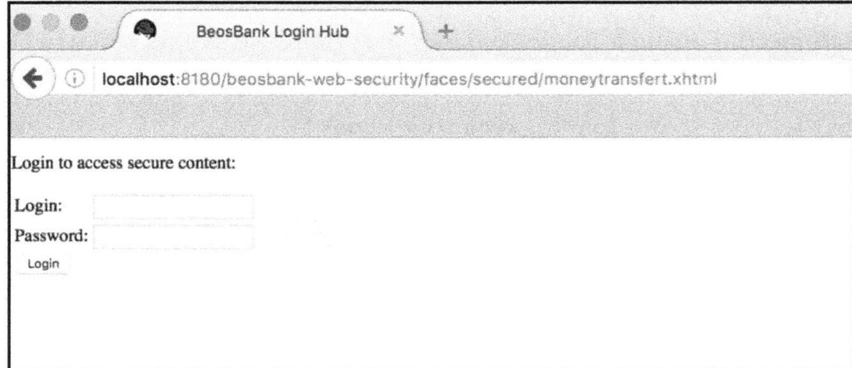

The server detects that you are not authorized to access the resource and redirects the user to the login page.

Try to connect with the `demo/demo1234` user.

The user is connected and automatically redirected to the `moneytransfer` page:

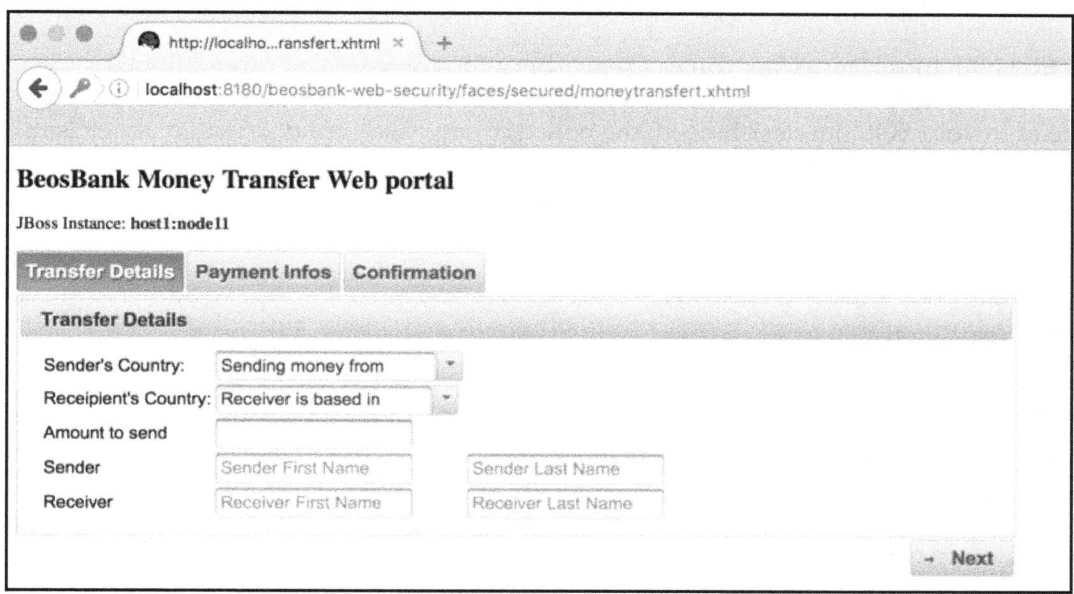

On the contrary, if you try with the `jboss/jboss` user, access is denied since the JBoss user has the `admin` role.

You can find the SQL script to initialize your user repository in the `beosbank-web-security/src/main/resources/sql` folder.

In this section, we used the existing database module with a simplest configuration where the providers customized the queries. JBoss, by default, provides a set of modules but you may face some situations where deep customization is required.

Customizing/overriding security policies

In this section we will

1. Create a custom login module.
2. Deploy the login module on the JBoss EAP.
3. Configure a web application to authenticate users with the new security policy.

Client: Hello JBoss Doctor, as you can see, users and passwords are stored in plain text in my database; how do I manage to be compliant with the internal password encryption policies in your SQL queries? Indeed, the new dummy password encryption policy is to store the password in the `${CRYPT}Base64EncodedValue${CRYPT}` format.
JBossDoctor: If in most cases, the existing login modules are sufficient, you can also write your custom modules that will be loaded by the JBoss EAP at runtime to authenticate your users.
This lab purpose is used to create a custom `beosbank-login-module` to authenticate users with passwords stored as `${CRYPT} Base64EncodedValue${CRYPT}`.

Creating a custom login module

JBoss EAP modules are jar files deployed in `$EAP_HOME/modules/system/layers/base`. Each module is identified by a package hierarchy and an index file--`module.xml`.
The package defines the module name, whereas the `module.xml` file contains the module configuration and dependencies list.

The `beosbank-login-module` project has only one class--`BeosBankLoginModule`--that extends `DatabaseServerLoginModule`.
The `DatabaseServerLoginModule` class is a member of the `org.picketbox/picketbox` Maven dependency.
The `DatabaseServerLoginModule` class has a method to convert `rawpassword` to plain text before verification during the authentication process:

```
protected String convertRawPassword(String rawPassword)
```

By default, this method returns the same raw password; we will override this method to decrypt the `Base64` password value:

```
@Override
protected String convertRawPassword(String rawPassword) {
String plainPassword = null;
System.out.println("======>Password "+rawPassword+" retreived for user
"+getUsername());
if(rawPassword.startsWith($_CRYPT) && rawPassword.endsWith($_CRYPT)){
```

```
String rawPwdEncryptedValue = rawPassword.substring($_CRYPT.length(),
rawPassword.length()-$_CRYPT.length());
         plainPassword= new
String(Base64.getDecoder().decode(rawPwdEncryptedValue.getBytes()));
}
else{
plainPassword=rawPassword;
}
System.out.println("======>Decoded Password "+plainPassword+" for user
"+getUsername());
return plainPassword;
}
```

The new module is ready. Build the `JAR` artifact with Maven and follow the next section to deploy it as a JBoss module.

Deploying the module on JBoss

To deploy the module, we have to build the project and copy the artifact in the expected module's main folder:

```
cd $EAP_DOMAIN/jboss-eap-7.0/modules/system/layers/base
$ mkdir -p com/beosbank/jbdevg/jbossas/jaas/main
$ mvn clean install
$ cp target/beosbank-login-module-1.0-SNAPSHOT.jar $EAP_DOMAIN/jboss-
eap-7.0/modules/system/layers/base/com/beosbank/jbdevg/jbossas/jaas/main
```

Copy the `module.xml` index file to the module -- `main` folder:

```
$ cp module.xml $EAP_DOMAIN/jboss-
eap-7.0/modules/system/layers/base/com/beosbank/jbdevg/jbossas/jaas/main
```

Here is the content of the `module.xml` file. It contains both the default configuration properties, the root resource jar to load, and its dependencies:

```
<module xmlns="urn:jboss:module:1.1"
name="com.beosbank.jbdevg.jbossas.jaas">
   <properties>
     <property name="dsJndiName"
value="java:jboss/datasources/MoneyTransferDS"/>
     <property name="principalsQuery" value="SELECT PASSWORD FROM T_ACCOUNT
WHERE USERNAME=?"/>
     <property name="rolesQuery" value="SELECT ROLE, 'Roles' FROM T_ACCOUNT
WHERE USERNAME=?"/>
   </properties>
   <resources>
       <resource-root path="beosbank-login-module-1.0-SNAPSHOT.jar"/>
```

```
    </resources>
    <dependencies>
        <module name="javax.persistence.api" />
        <module name="javax.resource.api" />
        <module name="javax.security.auth.message.api"/>
        <module name="javax.security.jacc.api"/>
        <module name="javax.servlet.api"/>
        <module name="javax.transaction.api" />
        <module name="javax.xml.bind.api" />
        <module name="javax.xml.stream.api" />
        <module name="org.jboss.logging"/>
       <module name="org.infinispan" />
        <module name="org.picketbox"/>
    </dependencies>
</module>
```

You can define the default values (optional) for the `dsJndiName`, `principalQuery`, and `rolesQuery` parameters. These values can also be overridden later, while creating the security configuration based on this module. The `org.jboss.security.auth.spi.DatabaseServerLoginModule` root class is thrown from the `org.picketbox` module.

Once the module is deployed, the next step is to create a security domain to rely on it.

To create the `beosbank-security-custom` domain, we have to run the `beosbank-web-security/createBeosBankSecurityPolicyCustom.cli` script:

```
./jboss-cli.sh --file=./createBeosBankSecurityPolicyCustom.cli -connect
/profile=ha/subsystem=security/security-domain=beosbank-web-policy-
custom:add
/profile=ha/subsystem=security/security-domain=beosbank-web-policy-
custom/authentication=classic:add(
login-modules=[                                                     {
 "module" => "com.beosbank.jbdevg.jbossas.jaas",
 "code" => "com.beosbank.jbdevg.jbossas.jaas.BeosBankLoginModule",
 "flag" => "required",
 "module-options" => [
("dsJndiName"=>"java:jboss/datasources/MoneyTransferDS"),
("principalsQuery"=>"SELECT PASSWORD FROM T_ACCOUNT WHERE USERNAME=?"),
 ("rolesQuery"=> "SELECT ROLE, 'Roles' FROM T_ACCOUNT WHERE USERNAME=?")
]
    }
          ]
  )
:reload-servers
```

Reload the servers at the end of the operation. Check the result with the `read-resource` command.

The module name is `com.beosbank.jbdevg.jbossas.jaas`

The Main class of our module is `com.beosbank.jbdevg.jbossas.jaas.BeosBankLoginModule`:

```
[domain@localhost:9990 /] /profile=ha/subsystem=security/security-
domain=beosbank-web-policy-custom/authentication=classic:read-resource
{
 "outcome" => "success",
   "result" => {
        "login-modules" => [{
            "code" =>
"com.beosbank.jbdevg.jbossas.jaas.BeosBankLoginModule",
            "flag" => "required",
            "module" => "com.beosbank.jbdevg.jbossas.jaas",
            "module-options" => [
("dsJndiName" => "java:jboss/datasources/MoneyTransferDS"),
("principalsQuery" => "SELECT PASSWORD FROM T_ACCOUNT WHERE USERNAME=?"),
("rolesQuery" => "SELECT ROLE, 'Roles' FROM T_ACCOUNT WHERE USERNAME=?")
            ]
        }],
 "login-module" => {"com.beosbank.jbdevg.jbossas.jaas.BeosBankLoginModule"
=> undefined}
   }
}
[domain@localhost:9990 /]
```

To activate the new policy in the application, we need to change the content of the jboss-web.xml. Update the `jboss-web.xml` in `beosbank-web-security` with the following content to reference the new security policy:

```
<?xml version='1.0' encoding='UTF-8'?>

    <jboss-web>
    <security-domain>beosbank-web-policy-custom</security-domain>
    </jboss-web>
```

Deploy the `beosbank-web-security` application from the Maven command line. The application is configured to be deployed on the dev01 server group by default.
Insert a jdoe/jboss in the `T_Account` table. Jboss in base64 is encoded `amJvc3M=`, so we are storing `${CRYPT}amJvc3M=${CRYPT}` as the password in the database.
The insertion query can be found in the `beosbank-web-security/src/main/resources/sql/InsertJdoeUser.sql` project:

```
INSERT INTO `T_ACCOUNT`(`username`,`password`,`role`)VALUES
('jdoe','${CRYPT}amJvc3M=${CRYPT}','Customer')
```

To verify the appliance of the new security policy, redeploy the application

Open the `http://localhost:8180/beosbank-web-security/` `Node11` instance.
When you click on the send money transfer button, you are automatically redirected to a login page. Enter jdoe credentials: `jdoe/jboss`.
The authentication succeeds, and you are moved to the money transfer creation screen.
At the same time, on the console, you can see the trace sent by the custom logging module class on the server console:

```
[Server:node11] 23:50:58,301 INFO [stdout] (default task-25)
======>Password ${CRYPT}amJvc3M=${CRYPT} retreived for user jdoe
[Server:node11] 23:50:58,301 INFO [stdout] (default task-25) ======>Decoded
Password jboss for user jdoe
```

Logs were just introduced for simplicity and demonstration; in production systems, you don't want to display user credentials like this. You will also need a custom logger instead of printing on the console.

Summary

The JBoss EAP is a certified Java EE application server. In this chapter, we gave the reader a large overview in terms of administration, configuration, application development, and security features. We progressively learned how to set up a JBoss EAP installation, both in the standalone and domain modes. We have been able to verify the facilities offered by a centralized administration in the domain mode for a large installation. We also saw how to reuse JBoss EAP installation binaries for many installations and therefore optimize your migrations and patch installation. We covered how to create and manage JBoss resources and objects--through server groups, server instances, datasources, security domains, and using the JBoss CLI or the administration console.

In terms of application development, we created and deployed a clustered application. We have been able to implement and check session replication in our applications, deploy applications on the EAP using jboss-as maven plugin, install and use modules and datasources in your code, and set up security domains to implement a custom authentication policy in our applications. Most of the middleware products, such as BRMS and Datavirtualization, are running as the top layer on the JBoss EAP. We also saw how to load balance between two JBoss EAP backend systems using HAProxy, and are now more familiar with JBoss EAP Core, especially subsystems. JBoss EAP 7, the Jboss Undertow subsystem, replaced the web subsystem. What are Undertow specifics? How can we handle custom web deployment and move to microservice using Undertow?

3
Custom Web Deployment using Undertow and Swarm

Undertow is the default web server included in the WildFly Application server. *Undertow* replaced the JBoss web server from WildFly 8. In `Chapter 2`, *Developing and Hosting Scalable Web Applications,* users implicitly used the embedded version of Undertow in JBoss AS to host an application. This chapter is about handling custom deployment scenarios by embedding Undertow in Java applications. The user will also learn how to set up highly available deployments and build microservices with Undertow.
This chapters is organized around the following topics:

- Undertow--purpose and architecture
- Undertow request life cycle and error handling.
- Microservices with the Undertow API
- Undertow reverse proxy and load balancing features
- Configuring an Undertow subsystem in WildFly
- Using WildFly-Swarm to package Java EE applications for microservices architecture

Undertow - purpose and architecture

Undertow is a powerful and lightweight web server written in Java, supporting both blocking and non blocking I/O. With a non-blocking programming model, when the client sends a request to a server, most of the time it will be handled asynchronously and in two steps.

An asynchronous call returns immediately, without waiting for the I/O to complete. The completion of the I/O is later communicated to the caller through the triggering of a callback routine that is executed outside the linear control flow of the application.

Undertow relies on NIO to provide a powerful API, enabling users to build high-performance deployments in a composition architecture way. With Undertow, users can build a web server by combining small single-purpose handlers. Undertow supports Servlet 3.1, Websockets (JSR-356), and reverse proxy.

Creating your first Undertow server

The Undertow server is not created like a traditional global container; indeed, the Undertow server is assembled by the embedding applications. The main components of Undertow are *listeners* and *handlers*.
Listeners act as entry points for client requests; all incoming requests go through listeners who are also responsible for opening the connection and creating an `HttpServerExchange` object that will be passed to the handler chain.
Undertow basically provides HTTP, AJP, HTTP/2, and HTTPS listeners; handlers handle the requests and provide responses.

Let's create a simple undertow HTTP server running on port 7070 that always returns BeosBank .

```
import io.undertow.Undertow;
import io.undertow.server.HttpHandler;
import io.undertow.server.HttpServerExchange;
import io.undertow.util.Headers;
public class HelloUndertowServer  {
 public static void main(String[]args){
Undertow server = Undertow.builder()
     .addHttpListener(7070, "localhost")
     .setHandler(new HttpHandler()
{
      @Override
      public void handleRequest(HttpServerExchange exchange) throws
Exception {
   exchange.getResponseHeaders().put(Headers.CONTENT_TYPE, "text/plain");
   exchange.getResponseSender().send("Beos Bank !");
      }
     }).build();
  server.start();
 };
}
```

This code uses the Undertow builder API to create one listener and one handler. The listener accepts HTTP connections on port `7070`, and the handler just uses the sender API to return **Beos Bank !** as output in a non-blocking way. Run the class as a Java application, and open your web browser with `localhost:7070`:

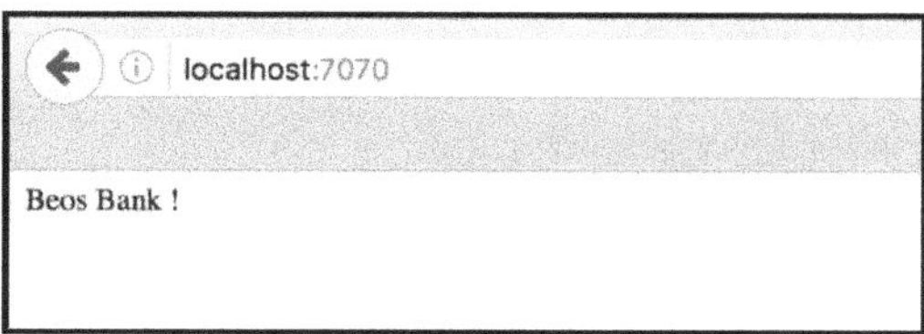

Undertow HelloWorld server

The `io.undertow.server.HttpServerExchange` holds both the Request and Response state: headers and security contexts.
The server remains available until its stop method is called. In the next section, we will see in details how Undertow handles incoming requests.

Undertow request life cycle

In the Undertow programming model, client requests are handled by listeners and handlers:

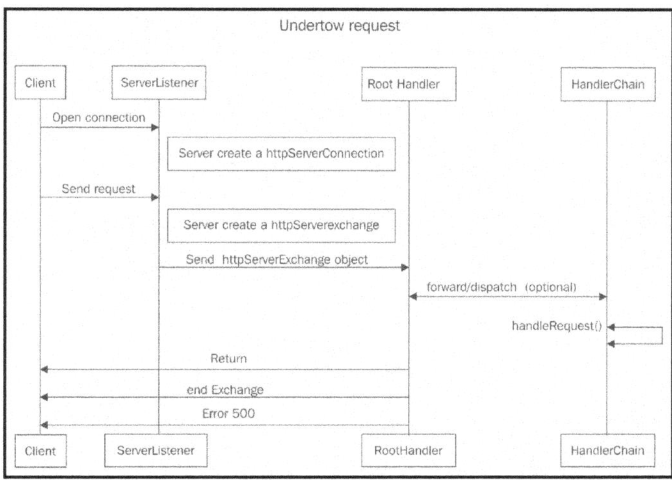

Undertow processing

The listener receives the connection and converts the client request into an `HttpServerExchange` object. This object is sent to the root handler that can delegate execution to another handler or return it.

The return can be done in three different ways: with a 500 error code, a normal return by ending the exchange, or a return without ending the exchange; in the last case, the exchange will be ended. The concrete business logic is provided by handlers; in the next section we will explore Undertow handlers in more detail.

Undertow handlers

Undertow handlers are chained together and each handler in the chain can update the exchange data, return a response, or delegate the request execution to another handler. The root handler is the entry point of the handler chain when the request quits the listener . Undertow provides various built-in handlers to support various request handling behaviors; you can also create your own handlers to perform various tasks. Among built-in provided handlers we can list: path handlers and reverse proxy handlers.

Path handlers

By combining the Undertow `ResourceHandler` and `ResourceManager`, a user can create custom and powerful handlers. With `PathResourceManager`, we can elaborate the `FileServer` with Undertow:

```
public class UndertowHelloDirectoryBrowser  {
public static void main(String[]args){
Undertow server = Undertow.builder()
     .addHttpListener(7071, "localhost")
     .setHandler(io.undertow.Handlers.resource(
       new
PathResourceManager(Paths.get("/Users/enonowog/books/jbdevg/code/jbdevg"),1
0))                        .setDirectoryListingEnabled(true)
).build();
  server.start();
};
}
```

The `io.undertow.Handlers` class has a set of static methods to create custom handlers. While running this code, a user can browse `/Users/enonowog/books/jbdevg/code/jbdevg` directory:

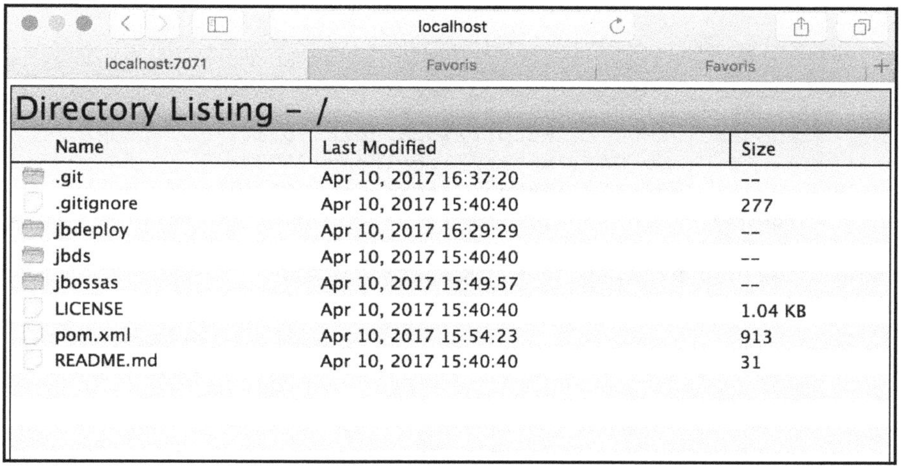

Directory Listing - /

Name	Last Modified	Size
.git	Apr 10, 2017 16:37:20	--
.gitignore	Apr 10, 2017 15:40:40	277
jbdeploy	Apr 10, 2017 16:29:29	--
jbds	Apr 10, 2017 15:40:40	--
jbossas	Apr 10, 2017 15:49:57	--
LICENSE	Apr 10, 2017 15:40:40	1.04 KB
pom.xml	Apr 10, 2017 15:54:23	913
README.md	Apr 10, 2017 15:40:40	31

Undertow FileServer handler

The path handler can be generally used to dispatch execution to a given handler based on a prefix match of the path.

Reverse proxy handler

A reverse proxy handler in Undertow can be used to set up a software reverse proxy. Creating a reverse proxy with the Undertow Builder API is very simple; let's consider two Undertow nodes--`Node1` and `Node2`--built from the `UndertowHelloWorldServer` code template, where each node has an HTTP handler on port `707X` to return `Beos Bank NodeX !` with x= the node index:

```
public class UndertowLoadBalancer {
 public static void main(String[] args) throws URISyntaxException {
  Undertow node1 = Undertow.builder().addHttpListener(7071, "localhost")
.setHandler(new HttpHandler() {
   public void handleRequest(HttpServerExchange exchange) throws Exception
{
    exchange.getResponseSender().send("Beos Bank Node1 !");
   }
  }).build();
  Undertow node2 = Undertow.builder().addHttpListener(7072, "localhost").
```

```
        setHandler(new HttpHandler() {
        public void handleRequest(HttpServerExchange exchange) throws Exception
    {
          exchange.getResponseSender().send("Beos Bank Node2 !");
        }
      }).build();
      node1.start();
      node2.start();
      LoadBalancingProxyClient lbConfig = new LoadBalancingProxyClient();
       lbConfig.addHost(new URI("http://localhost:7071")); //node1
       lbConfig.addHost(new URI("http://localhost:7072")); //node2
       lbConfig.addHost(new URI("http://localhost:7073")); //invalid node
       Undertow lbNode = Undertow.builder().addHttpListener(7070, "localhost")
         .setIoThreads(5)
         .setHandler(new ProxyHandler(lbConfig, 10000,
    ResponseCodeHandler.HANDLE_404))
         .build();
      lbNode.start();
     };
    }
```

When running the `UndertowLoadBalancer` class, the reverse proxy is active at `http://localhost:7070` and balances requests between node1 and node2.

The `UndertowProxyHandler` is built with three parameters: a client proxy that holds the backend server configuration, a timeout limit, and a next handler to use in case no backend is found to handle the request:

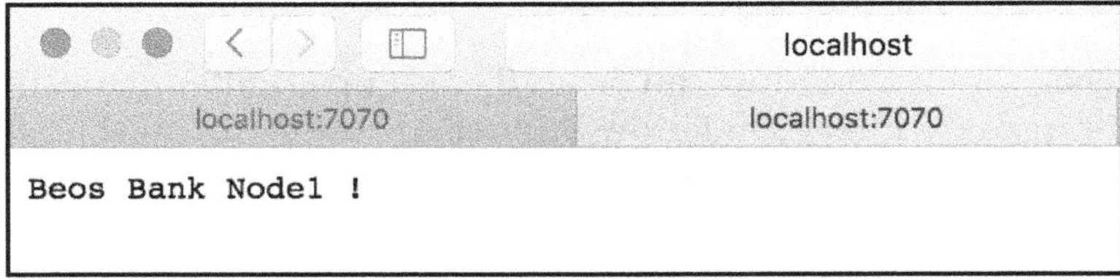

Open another browser tab and hit the proxy url `http://localhost:7070` The request is processed by **Node2**:

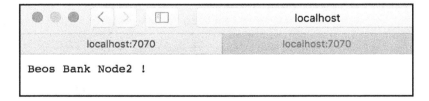

In case one node handler is not responding, the handler chain will forward the request to the working node. You can comment the `node1.start` instruction to verify this behavior.

From all the previously seen examples, we can see that Undertow is very light and therefore can be considered as a good candidate while building microservices. Let's look into how can we rely on Undertow to build microservices in the next section.

Microservices with Undertow

> *Your only limit is your imagination.*

In the earlier sections, we discovered the Undertow architecture and how to quickly build simple web servers, file browsers, and reverse proxy. In the following section, we are interested in how to build complete microservices with the Undertow Builder API, and how to connect Undertow with the open source ecosystem--JPA, CDI, and RESTEasy--to build a simple REST API.

Reading money transfer details

As seen in previous sections, the Undertow API facilitates application development without standard Java EE containers, making it a good candidate for creating microservices. In the following section, we will cover a practical use case on how to create a full microservice to expose money transfer details. The microservice will have access to the money transfer database using JPA.

Client: Hello, JBossDoctor, in our money transfer business, we have a huge demand from partners and back office systems to check money transfer details. These requests come from various application profiles. Money transfer agencies, mobile and tablets use them to verify transaction status and details when final recipients try to recover their money, and internal systems check specific transaction details for various displays and controls. How can we build a simple REST API for this following your Undertow presentation?
JBoss Doctor: The solution is there; with Undertow, you will simplify this business feature. Indeed, Undertow is a RESTEasy extension, on which you can rely to simplify your deployments. By the way, you can interconnect this extension with various Java EE technologies, including CDI, JPA, and the others:

```
package com.beosbank.jbdevg.jbdeploy.undertow.server;
import org.jboss.resteasy.plugins.server.undertow.UndertowJaxrsServer;
import org.jboss.resteasy.spi.ResteasyDeployment;
import io.undertow.Undertow;
```

```
import io.undertow.servlet.Servlets;
import io.undertow.servlet.api.DeploymentInfo;
public class MoneyTransferServer {
 public static void main(String[]args){
 //Get Port
 String host="0.0.0.0";
 int port = Integer.parseInt(System.getProperty("port"));
 //Create the JAXRS Server
 UndertowJaxrsServer server = new UndertowJaxrsServer();
 Undertow.Builder serverBuilder = Undertow.builder().addHttpListener(port,
host);
 server.start(serverBuilder);

 //Create the deployment
 ResteasyDeployment deployment = new ResteasyDeployment();
 deployment.setApplicationClass(MoneyTransferApp.class.getName());
deployment.setInjectorFactoryClass(org.jboss.resteasy.cdi.CdiInjectorFactor
y.class.getName());

 //Configure the deployment info
 DeploymentInfo di = server.undertowDeployment(deployment, "/api");
 di.setClassLoader(MoneyTransferServer.class.getClassLoader())
 .setContextPath("/beosbank-undertow-service")
 .setDeploymentName("BeosBank Services");

 //Add CDI listener
di.addListeners(Servlets.listener(org.jboss.weld.environment.servlet.Listen
er.class));

 //Deploy the API
 server.deploy(di);
 System.out.println("Undertow MoneyTransfer started on "+host+":"+port);
 };
}
```

The `org.jboss.resteasy:resteasy-undertow:jar` extension provides an `UndertowJaxrsServer` class that wraps the Undertow server to facilitate RESTEasy/ JAX-RS deployments.
The `ResteasyDeployment` class is used to initialize and configure the core RESTEasy components. An Undertow deployment needs to set up at least the `applicationClass` which is responsible for defining the JAX-RS resources. In our example, `MoneyTransferApp` just loads the `MoneyTransferRessource`.

```
public class MoneyTransferApp extends Application {
@Override
    public Set<Class<?>> getClasses() {
        Set<Class<?>> resources = new LinkedHashSet<Class<?>>();
```

```
        //add the the money Transfer resource to the application
        resources.add(MoneyTransferResource.class);
        return resources;
    }
}
```

The `MoneyTransferResource` is the class holding JAX-RS annotations to define the URL and paths mapping to access the web service. To perform the expected search, users can rely on JPA; in this case, the JPA service is injected using CDI:

```
@Path("/MoneyTransfer")
@RequestScoped
public class MoneyTransferResource {
 @Inject
 IMoneyTransfetService dao;
    @GET
    @Path("/{id}")
    @Produces(MediaType.APPLICATION_JSON)
    public MoneyTransfer getMoneyTransferById(@PathParam("id") Long id){
        MoneyTransfer mt = dao.getMoneyTransferById(id);
        return mt;
   }
```

To be able to inject dependencies with CDI, `RestEasydeployment` should delegate the object creation process to the `org.jboss.resteasy.cdi.CdiInjectorFactory` CDI Injector Factory class. Each deployment can set a mapping URL using the `undertowDeployment` server. The server classpath, context path, deployment name, and description. To complete the configuration, the CDI `org.jboss.weld.environment.servlet.Listener` weld listener is added to the deployment information.
The server is requested to deploy the created deployment object. The DAO layer is built on top of the `MoneyTransfer`, `Customer`, and `Address` entities from the MoneyTransfer JPA lab from `Chapter 2`, *Developing and Hosting Scalable Web Applications*:

```
@SessionScoped
public class MoneyTransferService implements
IMoneyTransferService,Serializable {
private static final long serialVersionUID = 1L;
    static  EntityManagerFactory emf;
    EntityManager em;

public MoneyTransfer getMoneyTransferById(Long reference) {
  return  em.find(MoneyTransfer.class, reference);
 }

 @PostConstruct
```

```
    public void init(){
     System.out.println("MoneyTransferService.init()");
      if(emf== null || !emf.isOpen()){
       emf=Persistence.createEntityManagerFactory("beosbank-mt-unit");
      }
     em=emf.createEntityManager();
    }
    @PreDestroy
    public void destroy(){
     System.out.println("MoneyTransferService.close()");
     emf.close();
    }
   }
```

A JPA configuration looks like this:

```
<persistence xmlns="http://java.sun.com/xml/ns/persistence" version="1.0">
<persistence-unit name="beosbank-mt-unit" transaction-
type="RESOURCE_LOCAL">  <description>BeosBank MoneyTransfer Persistence
Unit</description>
<provider>org.hibernate.jpa.HibernatePersistenceProvider</provider>
<properties>
   <property name="javax.persistence.jdbc.url"
value="jdbc:mysql://localhost:3306/beosbank-mt?useSSL=false" />
   <property name="javax.persistence.jdbc.user" value="root" />
   <property name="javax.persistence.jdbc.password" value="" />
   <property name="javax.persistence.jdbc.driver"
value="com.mysql.jdbc.Driver" />
   <property name="hibernate.dialect"
value="org.hibernate.dialect.MySQL5InnoDBDialect" />
   <property name="hibernate.format_sql" value="true" />
   <property name="hibernate.show_sql" value="true" />
   <property name="hibernate.hbm2ddl.auto" value="update" />
  </properties>
</persistence-unit>
</persistence>
```

The last step to have a fully working web service is to annotate JPA entities with JAXB annotations provided by the *resteasy-jackson-provider* library.

Labs described in this chapter can be found downloaded at `https://github.com/jbossdevguidebook/chapters/tree/master/ch3/`

Running the application

Applications can be tested using the `maven exec` plugin, as shown:

```
[beosbank-undertow-service]$ mvn clean install exec:java
[INFO] Scanning for projects...
[INFO] -------------------------------------------------------------------
----
[INFO] Building beosbank-undertow-service 1.0-SNAPSHOT
[INFO] -------------------------------------------------------------------
----[INFO] --- exec-maven-plugin:1.6.0:java (default) @ beosbank-undertow-
service ---
avr. 12, 2017 6:34:39 PM org.jboss.weld.environment.servlet.Listener
contextInitializedINFO: WELD-ENV-001007: Initialize Weld using
ServletContextListeneravr. 12, 2017 6:34:39 PM
org.jboss.weld.bootstrap.WeldStartup <clinit>INFO: RESTEASY002225:
Deploying javax.ws.rs.core.Application: class
com.beosbank.jbdevg.jbdeploy.undertow.server.MoneyTransferApp
avr. 12, 2017 6:34:40 PM org.jboss.resteasy.spi.ResteasyDeployment
processApplicationINFO: RESTEASY002200: Adding class resource
com.beosbank.jbdevg.jbdeploy.undertow.rest.MoneyTransferResource from
Application class
com.beosbank.jbdevg.jbdeploy.undertow.server.MoneyTransferAppUndertow
MoneyTransfer started on 0.0.0.0:8080
```

Use `-Dundertow.port=xxxx` to define a custom port:

```
[beosbank-undertow-service]$ mvn exec:java -Dundertow.port=7071
```

You can then retrieve the third transaction details by calling `http://localhost:7071/beosbank-undertow-service/api/MoneyTransfer/3`:

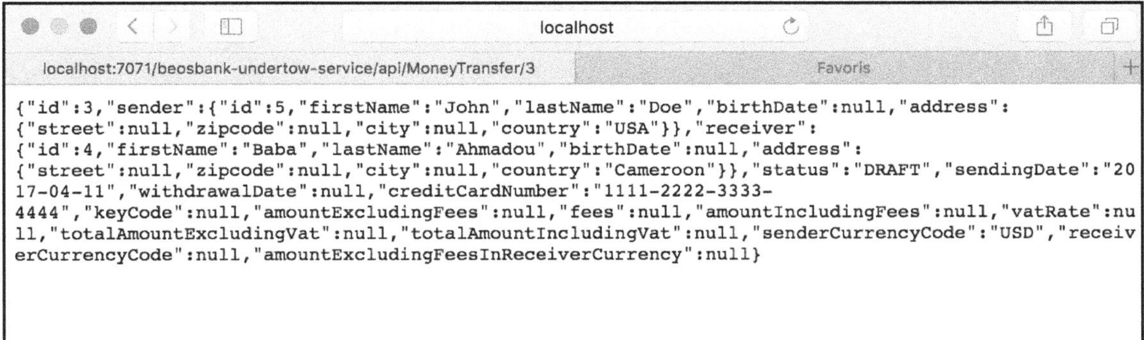
localhost
localhost:7071/beosbank-undertow-service/api/MoneyTransfer/3
Favoris
{"id":3,"sender":{"id":5,"firstName":"John","lastName":"Doe","birthDate":null,"address":{"street":null,"zipcode":null,"city":null,"country":"USA"}},"receiver":{"id":4,"firstName":"Baba","lastName":"Ahmadou","birthDate":null,"address":{"street":null,"zipcode":null,"city":null,"country":"Cameroon"}},"status":"DRAFT","sendingDate":"2017-04-11","withdrawalDate":null,"creditCardNumber":"1111-2222-3333-4444","keyCode":null,"amountExcludingFees":null,"fees":null,"amountIncludingFees":null,"vatRate":null,"totalAmountExcludingVat":null,"totalAmountIncludingVat":null,"senderCurrencyCode":"USD","receiverCurrencyCode":null,"amountExcludingFeesInReceiverCurrency":null}

You can run another instance on port `7072`, and you have the same result--`http://localhost:7072/beosbank-undertow-service/api/MoneyTransfer/3`:

localhost

localhost:7072/beosbank-undertow-service/api/MoneyTransfer/3

Favoris

{"id":3,"sender":{"id":5,"firstName":"John","lastName":"Doe","birthDate":null,"address":{"street":null,"zipcode":null,"city":null,"country":"USA"}},"receiver":{"id":4,"firstName":"Baba","lastName":"Ahmadou","birthDate":null,"address":{"street":null,"zipcode":null,"city":null,"country":"Cameroon"}},"status":"DRAFT","sendingDate":"2017-04-11","withdrawalDate":null,"creditCardNumber":"1111-2222-3333-4444","keyCode":null,"amountExcludingFees":null,"fees":null,"amountIncludingFees":null,"vatRate":null,"totalAmountExcludingVat":null,"totalAmountIncludingVat":null,"senderCurrencyCode":"USD","receiverCurrencyCode":null,"amountExcludingFeesInReceiverCurrency":null}

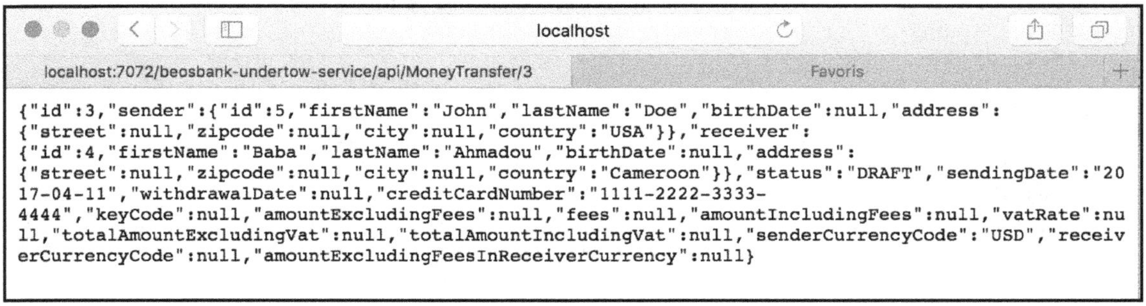

In the previous lab, we saw how to create a reverse proxy programmatically. In the next section, we will see how to edit configuration of the Undertow subsystem embedded in the WildFly application server to act as a load balancer between these two backend server instances.

Load balancing with an Undertow subsystem

Considering the fact that we have two running undertow instances, we will configure a WildFly application server Undertow subsystem to act as a load balancer in the following section.
Start two instances of the `beosbank-undertow-service` project using the following:

```
$mvn exec:java -Dundertow.port=7071
$mvn exec:java -Dundertow.port=7072
```

Download, install, and run a WildFly application server in standalone mode:

```
unzip $HOME/Downloads/wildfly-11.0.0.Alpha1.zip
cd   wildfly-11.0.0.Alpha1/bin
$ ./standalone.sh
```

WildFly is now running and listening on port `9990`; connect to the server using `jboss-cli`, as follows:

```
./jboss-cli.sh --connect
```

For Undertow to act as a static load balancer behind a set of backend systems, we must register remote socket bindings for these backend systems:

```
[standalone@localhost:9990 /] /socket-binding-group=standard-
sockets/remote-destination-outbound-socket-
binding=node1/:add(host=localhost,port=7071)
{"outcome" => "success"}
[standalone@localhost:9990 /] /socket-binding-group=standard-
sockets/remote-destination-outbound-socket-
binding=node2/:add(host=localhost,port=7072)
{"outcome" => "success"}
```

Then, we first need a handler; in this case, the reverse proxy handler is required. Create the reverse proxy handler (`beosbank-rproxy-handler`):

```
[standalone@localhost:9990 /]
/subsystem=undertow/configuration=handler/reverse-proxy=beosbank-rproxy-
handler:add()
{"outcome" => "success"}
```

Add the previously defined remote host to the `beosbank-rproxy-handler` configuration. In this configuration, we will use *lb1* to reference the outbound sockets *node1*, and *lb2* for *node2*, respectively:

```
[standalone@localhost:9990 /]
/subsystem=undertow/configuration=handler/reverse-proxy=beosbank-rproxy-
handler/host=lb1:add(outbound-socket-
binding=node1,scheme=http,path=/beosbank-undertow-service)
{"outcome" => "success"}
[standalone@localhost:9990 /]
/subsystem=undertow/configuration=handler/reverse-proxy=beosbank-rproxy-
handler/host=lb2:add(outbound-socket-
binding=node2,scheme=http,path=/beosbank-undertow-service)
{"outcome" => "success"}
```

Check the whole handler configuration:

```
[standalone@localhost:9990 /]
/subsystem=undertow/configuration=handler/reverse-proxy=beosbank-rproxy-
handler:read-resource(recursive=true)
{
 "outcome" => "success",
 "result" => {
```

```
"cached-connections-per-thread" => 5,
"connection-idle-timeout" => 60L,
"connections-per-thread" => 40,
"max-request-time" => -1,
"max-retries" => 1L,
"problem-server-retry" => 30,
"request-queue-size" => 10,
"session-cookie-names" => "JSESSIONID",
"host" => {
"lb1" => {
"instance-id" => undefined,
"outbound-socket-binding" => "node1",
"path" => "/beosbank-undertow-service",
"scheme" => "http",
"security-realm" => undefined,
"ssl-context" => undefined
},
"lb2" => {
"instance-id" => undefined,
"outbound-socket-binding" => "node2",
"path" => "/beosbank-undertow-service",
"scheme" => "http",
"security-realm" => undefined,
"ssl-context" => undefined
}
}}}
```

Add a mapping URL on the default server, and the default host will be served by the reverse proxy handler:

```
[standalone@localhost:9990 /] /subsystem=undertow/server=default-
server/host=default-host/location=\/mcs01:add(handler=beosbank-rproxy-
handler){"outcome" => "success"}
[standalone@localhost:9990 /]
[standalone@localhost:9990 /] /subsystem=undertow/server=default-
server/host=default-host/location=\/mcs01:read-resource
{ "outcome" => "success",
 "result" => {
 "handler" => "beosbank-rproxy-handler",
 "filter-ref" => undefined
 }
}
```

The `http://localhost:8080/mcs01` URL mapping on the default server will be served by the reverse proxy.

The `http://localhost:8080/mcs01/api/MoneyTransfer/3` URL will either return responses from node1 or node2 in your container's microservices logs:

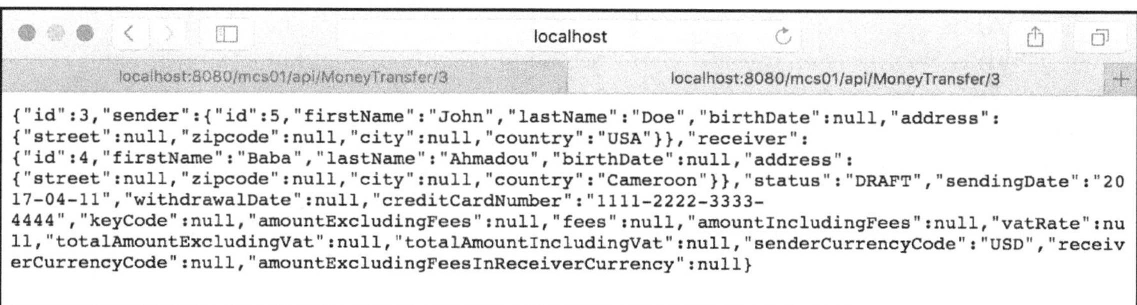
localhost
localhost:8080/mcs01/api/MoneyTransfer/3
localhost:8080/mcs01/api/MoneyTransfer/3
{"id":3,"sender":{"id":5,"firstName":"John","lastName":"Doe","birthDate":null,"address":{"street":null,"zipcode":null,"city":null,"country":"USA"}},"receiver":{"id":4,"firstName":"Baba","lastName":"Ahmadou","birthDate":null,"address":{"street":null,"zipcode":null,"city":null,"country":"Cameroon"}},"status":"DRAFT","sendingDate":"2017-04-11","withdrawalDate":null,"creditCardNumber":"1111-2222-3333-4444","keyCode":null,"amountExcludingFees":null,"fees":null,"amountIncludingFees":null,"vatRate":null,"totalAmountExcludingVat":null,"totalAmountIncludingVat":null,"senderCurrencyCode":"USD","receiverCurrencyCode":null,"amountExcludingFeesInReceiverCurrency":null}

A complete CLI script summarizing the instructions used in this lab to set up the load balancer is available in the Undertow project. Create your load balancer in one step with the following command:

```
$ ./jboss-cli.sh --file=./loadbalancer.cli --connect
```

Undertow can also be used as a dynamic load balancer using server groups and `mod_cluster`. For advanced usage, check the Wildfly model reference at `https://wildscribe.github.io/Wildfly/10.0.0.Final/index.html`.
To run our Undertow components in this labs, we used the `maven exec` plugin; it helps us create the correct classpath and then run the main server class in the same JVM started by Maven, `exec:java` or another JVM, `exec:exec`.
If we want to create a Docker image to run this microservice example, we will either have to run the `maven exec` command in the Docker build file, assuming that our Maven configuration and repository are properly defined in the container, or copy each dependency manually to the container before launching the `java-jar` command.
For some web applications, this can be a perilous task, especially when migrating from monolithic Java EE to microservices. WildFly Swarm proposes an innovative way to package Java EE applications as microservices.

Innovative microservice packaging with WildFly Swarm

WildFly Swarm is a WildFly extension project that aims to facilitate Java EE applications with minimum dependencies in the form of an executable JAR, called `Uberjar` or `flat-jar`. This JAR is deployed on an embedded container derived from the WildFly application server. WildFly Swarm is an initiative around the microprofile that aims to optimize Enterprise Java for a microservices architecture.
To create a `flat-jar` from a web application, you simply have to use the WildFly Swarm `Maven` plugin to package your web application:

```
<plugin>
    <groupId>org.wildfly.swarm</groupId>
    <artifactId>wildfly-swarm-plugin</artifactId>
    <version>${version.wildfly.swarm}</version>
    <executions>
     <execution>
      <goals>
       <goal>package</goal>
      </goals>
     </execution>
    </executions>
  </plugin>
```

The plugin autodetects dependencies (fractions) for your project and includes all the requirements to run the application using `java-jar`. The plugin relies on the `Wildflym-Swarm BOM`:

```
<dependencyManagement>
  <dependencies>
   <dependency>
    <groupId>org.wildfly.swarm</groupId>
    <artifactId>bom</artifactId>
    <version>${version.wildfly.swarm}</version>
    <scope>import</scope>
    <type>pom</type>
   </dependency>
  </dependencies>
</dependencyManagement>
```

Suppose that we want to package the first version of the `beosbank-web` application as a MicroService with WildFly Swarm. Duplicate the project as `ch3/beosbank-web-swam`, add the plugin and the BOM in the project pom file, and then build it using the `Maven install` command:

```
ovpn-117-147:beosbank-web-swarm enonowog$ mvn install
[INFO] Scanning for projects...
[INFO]
[INFO] ------------------------------------------------------------------------
----[INFO] Building beosbank-web-swarm 1.0-SNAPSHOT
[INFO] --- maven-compiler-plugin:3.1:compile (default-compile) @ beosbank-
web-swarm ---
[INFO] Nothing to compile - all classes are up to date
[INFO] --- maven-resources-plugin:2.6:testResources (default-testResources)
@ beosbank-web-swarm ---
[INFO] Using 'UTF-8' encoding to copy filtered resources.
[INFO] skip non existing resourceDirectory
/Users/enonowog/books/jbdevg/code/jbdevg/jbdeploy/beosbank-web-
swarm/src/test/resources
[INFO] --- maven-compiler-plugin:3.1:testCompile (default-testCompile) @
beosbank-web-swarm ---
[INFO] No sources to compile
[INFO] --- maven-surefire-plugin:2.12.4:test (default-test) @ beosbank-web-
swarm ---
[INFO] No tests to run.
[INFO] --- maven-war-plugin:2.2:war (default-war) @ beosbank-web-swarm ---
[INFO] Packaging webapp
[INFO] Assembling webapp [beosbank-web-swarm] in
[/Users/enonowog/books/jbdevg/code/jbdevg/jbdeploy/beosbank-web-
swarm/target/beosbank-web-swarm]
[INFO] Processing war project
[INFO] Copying webapp resources
[/Users/enonowog/books/jbdevg/code/jbdevg/jbdeploy/beosbank-web-
swarm/src/main/webapp]
[INFO] Webapp assembled in [42 msecs]
[INFO] Building war:
/Users/enonowog/books/jbdevg/code/jbdevg/jbdeploy/beosbank-web-
swarm/target/beosbank-web-swarm.war
[INFO] WEB-INF/web.xml already added, skipping
[INFO] --- wildfly-swarm-plugin:2017.4.0:package (default) @ beosbank-web-
swarm ---[INFO] Scanning for needed WildFly Swarm fractions with mode:
when_missing
[INFO] Detected fractions: cdi:2017.4.0, ejb:2017.4.0, jsf:2017.4.0
[INFO] Adding fractions: bean-validation:2017.4.0, cdi-config:2017.4.0,
cdi:2017.4.0, container:2017.4.0, ee:2017.4.0, ejb:2017.4.0, jca:2017.4.0,
jsf:2017.4.0, logging:2017.4.0, security:2017.4.0, transactions:2017.4.0,
undertow:2017.4.0
```

```
Resolving 60 out of 412 artifacts
[INFO] Repackaging .war:
/Users/enonowog/books/jbdevg/code/jbdevg/jbdeploy/beosbank-web-
swarm/target/beosbank-web-swarm.war
[INFO] Repackaged .war:
/Users/enonowog/books/jbdevg/code/jbdevg/jbdeploy/beosbank-web-
swarm/target/beosbank-web-swarm.war
[INFO]
[INFO] --- maven-install-plugin:2.4:install (default-install) @ beosbank-
web-swarm ---
[INFO] Installing
/Users/enonowog/books/jbdevg/code/jbdevg/jbdeploy/beosbank-web-
swarm/target/beosbank-web-swarm-swarm.jar to
/Users/enonowog/.m2/repository/com/beosbank/jbdevg/jbdeploy/beosbank-web-
swarm/1.0-SNAPSHOT/beosbank-web-swarm-1.0-SNAPSHOT-swarm.jar
[INFO] ------------------------------------------------------------------
----
[INFO] BUILD SUCCESS
```

After the compilation process with the `Maven compile` plugin, the `maven-war` plugin is used to package the application as expected for the web project, but just after the war is generated, the `wildfly-swarm-plugin` enters in action, detects the project fractions, and repackages the `beosbank-web-swarm.war` file into a new JAR, `beosbank-web-swarm-swarm.jar`, adding a `-swarm.jar` prefix to the previous war name.
Run the application, as shown:

```
 java -jar target/beosbank-web-swarm-swarm.jar
....
2017-04-14 11:47:52,956 INFO [org.wildfly.swarm.runtime.deployer] (main)
deploying beosbank-web-swarm.war
2017-04-14 11:47:52,979 INFO [org.jboss.as.server.deployment] (MSC service
thread 1-5) WFLYSRV0027: Starting deployment of "beosbank-web-swarm.war"
(runtime-name: "beosbank-web-swarm.war")
....
[org.primefaces.webapp.PostConstructApplicationEventListener]
(ServerService Thread Pool -- 2) Running on PrimeFaces 6.0
2017-04-14 11:47:55,428 INFO [org.wildfly.extension.undertow]
(ServerService Thread Pool -- 2) WFLYUT0021: Registered web context: /
2017-04-14 11:47:55,449 INFO [org.jboss.as.server] (main) WFLYSRV0010:
Deployed "beosbank-web-swarm.war" (runtime-name : "beosbank-web-swarm.war")
2017-04-14 11:47:55,450 INFO [org.wildfly.swarm] (main) WFSWARM99999:
WildFly Swarm is Read
```

The war is deployed and started on a minimal WildFly server, and is accessible via `http://localhost:8080`:

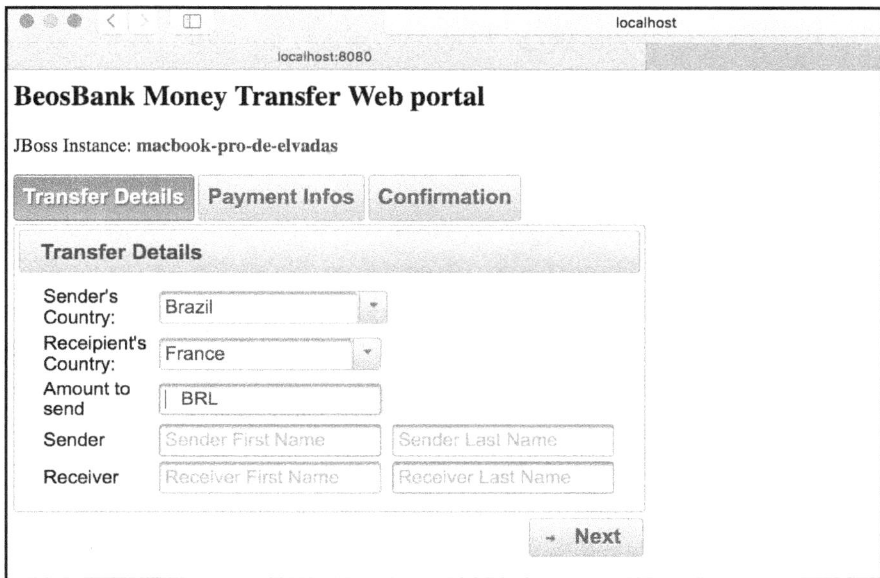

So to build a microservice architecture, Undertow can be used for new projects. While moving from existing Java EE projects to a microservice architecture, Wilfdfly Swarm can be a good fit.

Summary

Undertow is a lightweight and powerful web server written in Java, uses non-blocking IO, and also, users can quickly set up fast applications. Using the Undertow Builder API, users can create custom applications that integrate perfectly with core Java and open source technologies. In the current chapter, we covered Undertow architecture and the API through practical samples; we also saw how to create and deploy a microservice application with Undertow, CDI and JPA. Users can take advantage of the Undertow features from the WildFly application server. An Undertow subsystem can be set up to act as static or dynamic load balancer. Undertow perfectly supports the `mod_cluster` and HTTP2 protocols. Undertow can be a good candidate to start a microservice journey, but for the existing JEE applications, migration to a microprofile can be facilitated by the WildFly-Swarm project.

4
Storing and Accessing Distributed Data

In this chapter, users will learn how to deal with data caching in the JBoss ecosystem using **Infinispan/JBoss Data Grid**. Various configuration tips will be experimented with through labs and coding sessions. The chapter also shows how to store and retrieve data from local and remote cache, how to develop and deploy cache-based applications, how to listen to caches event, and how to leverage the Advanced Cache API to query caches. The topics covered throughout the chapter are as follows:

- JBoss Data Grid/Infinispan architecture
    - Versioning from an upstream Infinispan project to Enterprise versions
    - JBoss Data Grid Library and Client-Server mode
- Working with caches
    - Cache operations
    - Cache monitoring/listeners: synchronous and asynchronous
- Cache Configuration: XML and API
- Advanced Cache API
- Cache visualization
- Data replication across multiple locations
- Accessing remote caches with Hot Rod and REST
- Data security and integrity
- Distributed computing using streams and distributed executors

JBoss Data Grid architecture

Today, data is present everywhere. We are producing and consuming more and more data. At the same time, applications need to access, process, and analyze data faster to deliver a superior user experience. In this context, data caching and in-memory processing have become very interesting options to improve applications' responsiveness. JBoss is present in the data processing and data analytics market through several products, including JBoss Data Grid. JBoss Data Grid is an in-memory, distributed, NoSQL datastore platform; it is the commercial version of the Infinispan project.

Versioning

Infinispan is the community edition on top of which Red Hat builds JBoss Data Grid. The following table shows the relation between Infinispan and Jboss Data Grid versions (the last five releases all the time of writing this chapter):

JBoss Data Grid	Infinispan
JBoss Data Grid 6.5.0	Infinispan 6.3.0
JBoss Data Grid 6.5.1	Infinispan 6.3.1
JBoss Data Grid 6.6.0	Infinispan 6.4.0
JBoss Data Grid 7.0.0	Infinispan 8.3.0
Not yet released at time of writing	Infinispan 9.0.0

In subsequent sections of this book, we will use JBoss Data Grid 7.0.0 and the associated Infinispan version 8.3.0.

Running configuration

JBoss Data Grid can be used to cache various data types from various sources.
While interacting with caches, applications can be located in the same container as the cache they are accessing: this is Library mode. To make an application stateless and decoupled, data can be accessed in a remote cache: this is the Client\Server way. In Library mode, the user application and cache run in the same JVM. JBoss Data Grid can run as a local or clustered cache. In clustered mode, the data can be replicated or distributed.

In Library mode, applications and caches run in the same JVM. An application can directly interact with both the cache public interfaces and the cache manager that is responsible for managing the cache entry's lifecycle:

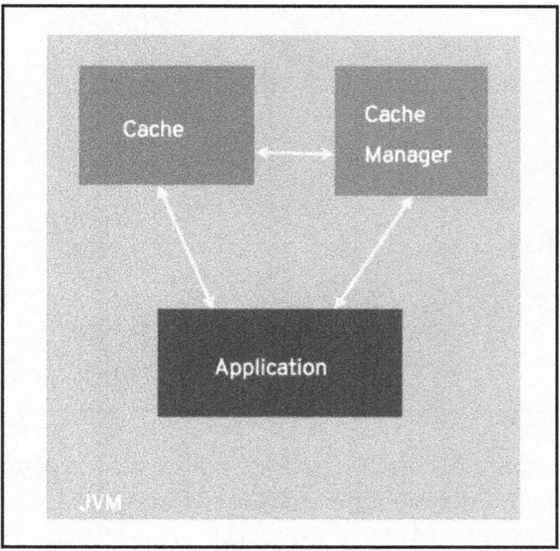

Library mode differs from Client-Server mode; in Client-Server running mode, applications and caches are in separate JVM instances. An application should use a client library to interact with the cache and cache manager:

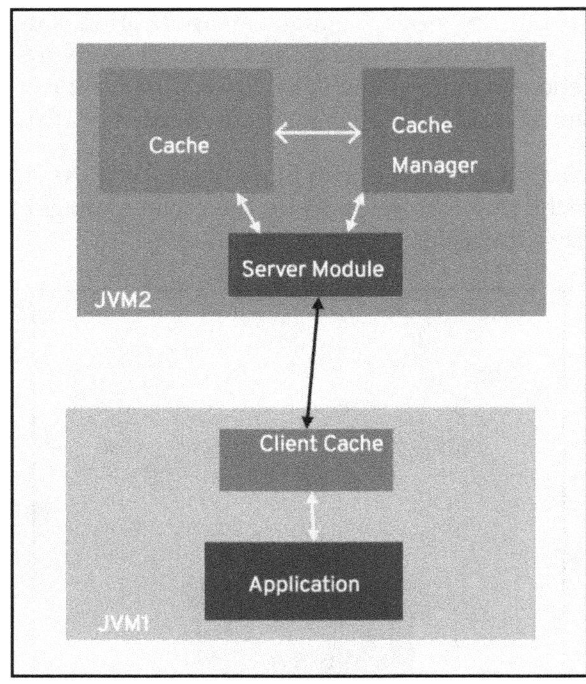

From the **Client Cache**, remote caches are accessible through a set of protocols, including Hot Rod, REST, Memcached, and WebSockets. Once a request is sent by the **Client Cache**, it goes to the appropriate **Server Module**. The module converts the request into a concrete cache operation and stores the result.
JBoss DataGrid provides a transparent API to access caches independently of their locations and startup mode (local/clustered).

In `Chapter 2`, *Developing and Hosting Scalable Web Applications*, you saw how to enable session replication in clustered web applications. JBoss AS uses Infinispan subsystem as an internal caching mechanism and session objects are stored in Infinispan nodes. Applications can add specific Infinispan modules to JBoss AS Server and rely on the custom added modules instead of the built-in JBoss AS uses the Infinispan core libraries to run in Library mode.

Infinispan can also be used as a Java library in any context by referencing the `org.infinispan bom` Maven dependencies:

```
<dependencyManagement>
  <dependencies>
   <dependency>
    <groupId>org.infinispan</groupId>
    <artifactId>infinispan-bom</artifactId>
    <version>${version.infinispan}</version>
   </dependency>
  </dependencies>
 </dependencyManagement>
```

All the time of writing this chapter, `version.infinispan` is:

```
<version.infinispan>8.3.0.Final-redhat-1</version.infinispan>
```

To keep things more practical, after these few introductory words and an overview of the JBoss Datagrid architecture, we will be focusing on practical uses cases with JBoss Datagrid in the next section, entitled Working with caches. Among other things, we will cover cache startup and querying in both Library and Server modes, and also cover cache operations and listeners.

Working with caches

A JBoss Datagrid can be accessed in two ways. In the following section, we will explore cache management with Jboss datagrid in both Library and Client-Server topologies.

Library mode in Java SE

In Java SE, Infinispan can be used as a simple `jar` dependency in your project. Some applications in the BeosBank landscape may want to keep the results of the `MoneyTransfer GetById` operation in an Infinispan/JBoss Data Grid cache to improve their performance.

How can this be implemented using JBoss Datagrid? While calling the web service, applications can receive output similar to the following:

```
<?xml version="1.0" encoding="UTF-8" ?>
<MoneyTransferStream>
<moneytransfer>
  <amountExcludingFees>1500</amountExcludingFees>
<amountExcludingFeesInReceiverCurrency>750000</amountExcludingFeesInReceive
rCurrency>
  <amountIncludingFees/>
  <creditCardNumber>1111-2222-3333-4444</creditCardNumber>
  <fees>25.00</fees>
  <id>3</id>
  <keyCode>TRXa3m</keyCode>
  <receiver>
    <address>
      <city>Douala</city>
      <country>Cameroon</country>
      <street>Bld Liberté</street>
      <zipcode>1103</zipcode>
    </address>
    <birthDate>1984-04-06</birthDate>
    <firstName>Baba</firstName>
    <id>4</id>
    <lastName>Ahmadou</lastName>
  </receiver>
  <receiverCurrencyCode>XAF</receiverCurrencyCode>
  <sender>
    <address>
      <city>Chicago</city>
      <country>USA</country>
      <street>Kenedy Avenue</street>
      <zipcode/>
    </address>
    <birthDate>1950-03-03</birthDate>
    <firstName>John</firstName>
    <id>5</id>
    <lastName>Doe</lastName>
  </sender>
  <senderCurrencyCode>USD</senderCurrencyCode>
  <sendingDate>2017-04-11</sendingDate>
  <status>DRAFT</status>
  <totalAmountExcludingVat>1505</totalAmountExcludingVat>
  <totalAmountIncludingVat>1677.50</totalAmountIncludingVat>
  <vatRate>10</vatRate>
  <withdrawalDate/>
</moneytransfer>
</MoneyTransferStream>
```

This is a `moneyTransfer` serialized object. This stream can be stored in Jboss datagrid, but an object is more suitable for ease of use. Data Grid is aware of the fields and structure of the stored object. Rather then storing serialized objects (that is, XML files), it is better to store objects to take advantage of features such as indexing and distributed processing, which use the content of the object. So, we should first convert this stream to an object (unmarshalling operation). Once the unmarshalling operation is complete, we will retrieve the object's key and store the remaining object in the cache. Various solutions exist to perform the unmarshalling operation; we could rely on BeanIO, for example. To activate Library mode deployment, just add the `infinispan-embedded` dependency to the `POM` file located in `ch4/beosbank-datagrid-labs`:

```
/*
https://github.com/jbossdevguidebook/chapters/tree/master/ch4/beosbank-data
grid-labs
*/

package com.beosbank.jbdevg.jbdatagrid;
import java.io.File;
import java.io.IOException;
import org.beanio.StreamFactory;
import org.beanio.Unmarshaller;
import org.infinispan.Cache;
import org.infinispan.configuration.cache.ConfigurationBuilder;
import org.infinispan.manager.DefaultCacheManager;
import com.beosbank.jbdevg.jbdatagrid.domain.MoneyTransfer;
import com.mchange.io.FileUtils;

public class EmbeddedCacheDemo {
 private static final String INPUT_DIR = "src/main/resources/input/";
String[] inputFileNames = { "data1.xml", "data2.xml", "data3.xml",
"data4.xml", "data5.xml" };
  // Create a Money Transfer Object from XML Message using BeaonIO API
  try {
   StreamFactory factory = StreamFactory.newInstance();
   factory.loadResource("mapping.xml");
   Unmarshaller unmarshaller =
factory.createUnmarshaller("MoneyTransferStream");
   String record;
   ConfigurationBuilder builder = new ConfigurationBuilder();
   Cache<String, Object> cache = new
DefaultCacheManager(builder.build()).getCache();
   //Read Transactions and put in cache
   for (String inputFile : inputFileNames) {
    record = FileUtils.getContentsAsString(new File(INPUT_DIR +
inputFile));
    MoneyTransfer mt = (MoneyTransfer) unmarshaller.unmarshal(record);
```

```
        cache.put(mt.getId() + "", mt);
    }
    //Inspect the cache .
    System.out.println(cache.size());
    System.out.println(cache.getStatus());
    System.out.println(cache.get("3"));
    //Stop the cache
    cache.stop();
    System.out.println(cache.getStatus());
```

Infinispan provides the `ConfigurationBuilder` API to programmatically create cache configuration. Caches are retrieved by their names using `DefaultCacheManager`; this operation starts the cache by default. From cache reference, we can access cache operations:

- `put`: To put a key value pair item in the cache
- `get`: To retrieve an object value from the cache based on the provided key
- `size`: To get the current size of the cache
- `stop`: To stop the cache

The cache interface exposes various others operations to interact with the cache instance. In order to listen to an event occurring in/on the cache, you should register a cache observer. In the next section, we will see how to set up listeners on caches.

Cache Listener

Infinispan provides a mechanism to listen to cache events: item creation, modification, and eviction.
Create a Java class with the `org.infinispan.notifications.Listener` annotation. For each specific event you want to listen to you should have a method annotated with actions from the `org.infinispan.notifications.cachelistener.annotation` package:

```
import org.infinispan.notifications.Listener;
import org.infinispan.notifications.cachelistener.annotation.*;
import org.infinispan.notifications.cachelistener.event.*;
@Listener
public  class DatagridListener {
   @CacheEntryCreated
   public void onCreated(CacheEntryCreatedEvent<String, String> event) {
    if(!event.isPre())
         System.out.printf("Created %s\n", event.getKey());
   }

   @CacheEntryModified
```

```
    public void onModified(CacheEntryModifiedEvent<String, String> event) {
     if(event.isPre())
         System.out.printf("About to modify %s\n", event.getKey());
    }
}
```

The `Listener` method is called twice in the lifecycle: before the related event occurred and after the event has occurs. You can use `even.isPre` to check the timing and react accordingly. Regarding the preceding code, the log will be printed after the cache entry is inserted for the `onCreated` method, and before the cache entry modification (`onModified` event). Use `cache.addListener(new DatagridListener())` to register the listener to your cache instance. Interacting with caches in Server mode has some subtleties that will be presented in the next paragraph.

Client-Server mode

In Client-Server mode, applications and caches do not run in different JVMs. You first need to start a standalone JBoss Data Grid server.
Download, install, and start `jboss-datagrid-7.0.0-server.zip`:

```
$unzip jboss-datagrid-7.0.0-server.zip
$cd jboss-datagrid-7.0.0-server/bin
$./standalone.sh

22:19:47,063 INFO [org.infinispan.server.endpoint] (MSC service thread 1-8)
DGENDPT10000: REST starting
22:19:47,063 INFO [org.infinispan.server.endpoint] (MSC service thread 1-2)
DGENDPT10000: MemcachedServer starting
22:19:47,063 INFO [org.infinispan.server.endpoint] (MSC service thread 1-6)
DGENDPT10000: HotRodServer starting
22:19:47,064 INFO [org.infinispan.server.endpoint] (MSC service thread 1-6)
DGENDPT10001: HotRodServer listening on 127.0.0.1:11222
22:19:47,064 INFO [org.infinispan.server.endpoint] (MSC service thread 1-2)
DGENDPT10001: MemcachedServer listening on 127.0.0.1:11211
```

The Datagrid server starts and, in the console log, you can see ports on which the cache features are exposed. To access this `Remote` cache, applications can use the `HotRod` protocol on `127.0.0.1:11222`. The default `HotRod` port is set to `11222` in the Infinispan `ConfigurationProperties` class (`DEFAULT_HOTROD_PORT = 11222`). Here are the required configuration steps to access a remote cache using the `HotRod` protocol:

- Create a configuration builder
- Add a server host and port to your configuration builder
- Retrieve a `RemotecacheManager` reference for interactions with the cache:

```
/*
https://github.com/jbossdevguidebook/chapters/blob/master/ch4/beosbank-data
grid-labs/src/main/java/com/beosbank/jbdevg/jbdatagrid/RemoteCacheDemo.java
*/
import org.beanio.StreamFactory;
import org.beanio.Unmarshaller;
import org.infinispan.client.hotrod.RemoteCache;
import org.infinispan.client.hotrod.RemoteCacheManager;
import org.infinispan.client.hotrod.configuration.ConfigurationBuilder;
import org.infinispan.client.hotrod.impl.ConfigurationProperties;
import com.beosbank.jbdevg.jbdatagrid.domain.MoneyTransfer;
import com.beosbank.jbdevg.jbdatagrid.listener.DatagridClientListener;
import com.mchange.io.FileUtils;

public class RemoteCacheDemo {

 public static void main(String[] args) {
ConfigurationBuilder builder = new ConfigurationBuilder();
builder.addServer().host("127.0.0.1").port(ConfigurationProperties.DEFAULT_
HOTROD_PORT);
  RemoteCacheManager cacheManager = new
RemoteCacheManager(builder.build());
  RemoteCache<String, Object> cache = cacheManager.getCache();
```

There are specific annotations for remote cache listeners: `@ClientListener` instead of `@Listener` and `@ClientCacheEntryCreated` instead of `@CacheEntryCreated` for an embedded cache:

```
import org.infinispan.client.hotrod.annotation.*;
import org.infinispan.client.hotrod.event.*;

@ClientListener
public  class DatagridClientListener {
   @ClientCacheEntryCreated
   public void onCreated(ClientCacheEntryCreatedEvent<String> event) {
         System.out.printf("Remote# entity created  %s\n", event.getKey());
   }
   @ClientCacheEntryModified
   public void onModified(ClientCacheEntryModifiedEvent<String> event) {
         System.out.printf("Remote# entity updated %s\n", event.getKey())
  }
}
```

The notification event object structure is also more light when interacting with remote caches. While working with caches, you may be wondering whether there's a solution to visualize your instances in real time.

Clustering and visualizing caches

In the BeosBank business, as soon as a user sends a money transfer, the receiver should be able to collect the sent amount from an agency worldwide. The money transfer agency office has a client application which interacts with the global BeosBank IT database to check and validate the information provided by users. To improve this process, we can imagine a set of Data Grid servers in each country/region, where the money transfer that should be paid in the region is cached as soon as the sender validates his request. To route the Money transfer data into the proper caches, we can rely on a JBoss Fuse Enterprise Service Bus application.

This router application will send the money transfer to the target cache so that the remittance application in a different geo has direct access to the money transfer data through `HotRod/Memcached` or the `REST` protocol:

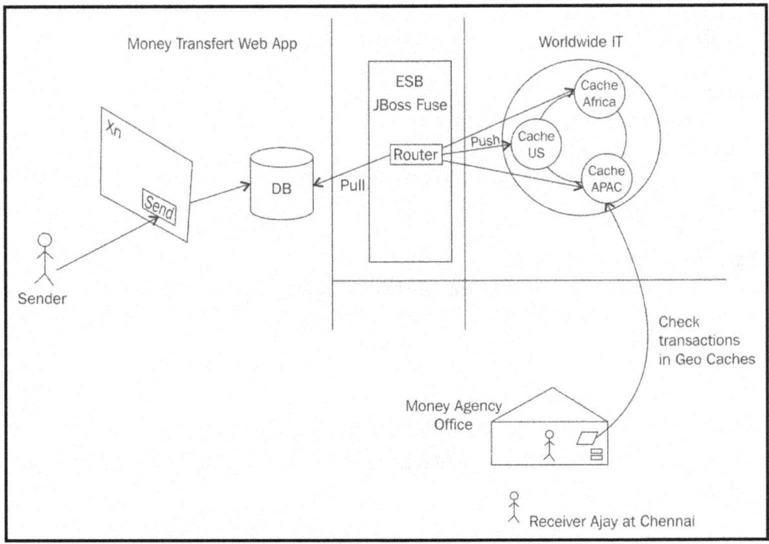

In the following lab, we will build a Datagrid cluster with three regions--Africa, America, and Asia--to simulate the process.
We will also be able to visualize cluster operations using the `Infinispan-visual` project.

Building the Datagrid cluster

To build the Datagrid cluster, we will use a single JBoss Datagrid installation binary and three different configuration folders. Download and install JBoss Datagrid, then create a management user:

```
$unzip jboss-datagrid-7.0.0-server.zip
$cd jboss-datagrid-7.0.0-server/bin
$./add-user.sh -u admin -p Admin01#
```

Replicate the standalone directory to create a specific configuration for each region:

```
$cd jboss-datagrid-7.0.0-server/
$cp -r standalone Africa
$cp -r standalone America
$cp -r standalone Asia
```

Start the three caches on a localhost address. To simulate the process, we need a custom port range for each region. We can achieve this by setting an offset while starting each Datagrid server:

```
$cd jboss-datagrid-7.0.0-server/bin
$ ./standalone.sh -c=clustered.xml -bmanagement=127.0.0.1 -b=127.0.0.1 -
Djboss.node.name=BeosBankCacheAfrica -Djboss.server.base.dir=Africa -
Djboss.socket.binding.port-offset=100

$./standalone.sh -c=clustered.xml -bmanagement=127.0.0.1 -b=127.0.0.1 -
Djboss.node.name=BeosBankCacheAmerica -Djboss.server.base.dir=America -
Djboss.socket.binding.port-offset=200

./standalone.sh -c=clustered.xml -bmanagement=127.0.0.1 -b=127.0.0.1 -
Djboss.node.name=BeosBankCacheAsia -Djboss.server.base.dir=Asia -
Djboss.socket.binding.port-offset=300
```

This operation starts three caches in a single cluster; the `Servers` port including `HotRod` and management interfaces are shifted according to the offset defined at startup:

```
14:00:25,506 INFO [org.infinispan.CLUSTER] (remote-thread--p2-t21)
ISPN000310: Starting cluster-wide rebalance for cache
___hotRodTopologyCache, topology CacheTopology{id=4, rebalanceId=3,
currentCH=ReplicatedConsistentHash{ns = 256, owners =
(2)[BeosBankCacheAfrica: 127, BeosBankCacheAmerica: 129]},
pendingCH=ReplicatedConsistentHash{ns = 256, owners =
(3)[BeosBankCacheAfrica: 84, BeosBankCacheAmerica: 86, BeosBankCacheAsia:
86]}, unionCH=null, actualMembers=[BeosBankCacheAfrica,
BeosBankCacheAmerica, BeosBankCacheAsia],
persistentUUIDs=[3b79c150-1f3a-49d9-917b-c19fb6019acb, 1e11c9df-e260-43b4-
a5b4-594b761cea65, 78a6303f-2102-4dab-802f-783a081894c6]}
```

The `BeosBankCacheAfrica` `HotRodServer` is listening on `127.0.0.1:11322` and `127.0.0.1:11422` for `BeosBankCacheAmerica` and on `127.0.0.1:11522` for `BeosBankCacheAsia`.

Visualizing the cluster

Infinispan includes a custom web app called Infinispan Visualizer, which can help users monitor and display a dynamic visual map of an overview of their cluster. This application can be checked out and deployed on a standalone JBoss application server. It relies on a management user and JMX to collect cache information and display them on a web page:

```
Clone the application
$ git clone https://github.com/infinispan/visual.git
$ cd visual
$ mvn install -DskipTests=true

Deploy the application on a standalone JBoss Application server
$ cp target/infinispan-visualizer.war $JBOSS_HOME/standalone/deployments
Start the server
$./standalone.sh -b 127.0.0.1 -bmanagement=127.0.0.1 -
Dinfinispan.visualizer.jmxUser=admin -
Dinfinispan.visualizer.jmxPass=Admin01# -
Dinfinispan.visualizer.serverList='127.0.0.1:11322;127.0.0.1:11422;127.0.0.
1:11522'
```

Start the server with the Data Grid server list to monitor. If you run the `RemoteCacheClusterDemo`, which tries to add the money transfer to a remote cache, you can visualize the cache updates at `http://localhost:8080/infinispan-visualizer/`. The page displays a list of cache instances with the number of entries in each cache:

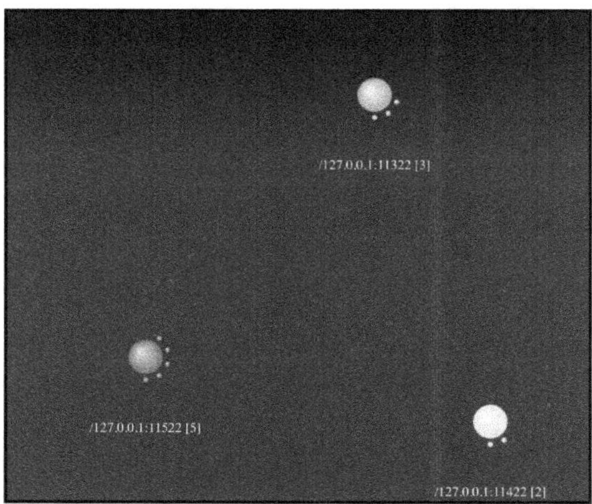

This shows a distributed cluster cache with three nodes. All five entries inserted in `BeosBankAfricaCache` are not present in this cache (`127.0.0.1:11322`); only three of them are stored on this node. On the contrary, there are two entries in `BeosBankAsiaCaches` and five entries in the America node, although the user did not explicitly request insertions in these nodes. This is cache entry distribution. Entries are distributed using a hashing algorithm. For each key value pair, a hash is computed based on the provided key to determine which node will be the primary owner and which other backup nodes will hold the key pair. It may be useful to control entries, distribution for performance for specific business reasons. Infinispan provides an `org.infinispan.distribution.group.Grouper` class on which you can rely to create custom groupings. Entries with the same grouping values will be hosted in the same group.

Replicated and distributed

There are various cache categories: replicated, distributed, and invalidation. In a replicated cache, all entries are replicated in every node; this configuration is suitable for small-size clusters (less than 10 nodes). In a distributed cache, all the entries are not replicated in every node but are distributed based on a key hashcode. Let's create two caches--`beosbank-repl` (replicated cache) and `beosbank-dist` (distributed cache)--using the following configuration in the `$JBOSS_HOME/xxx/configuration/clustered.xml` file:

```
<replicated-cache name="beosbank-repl" mode="ASYNC" start="EAGER"
batching="false" statistics="true"/>

<distributed-cache name="beosbank-dist" owners="2" segments="20"
mode="SYNC" remote-timeout="30000" start="EAGER">
<locking striping="false" acquire-timeout="30000" concurrency-
level="1000"/>
<transaction mode="NONE"/>
 </distributed-cache>
```

In a replicated configuration, items are stored in all the cache instances:

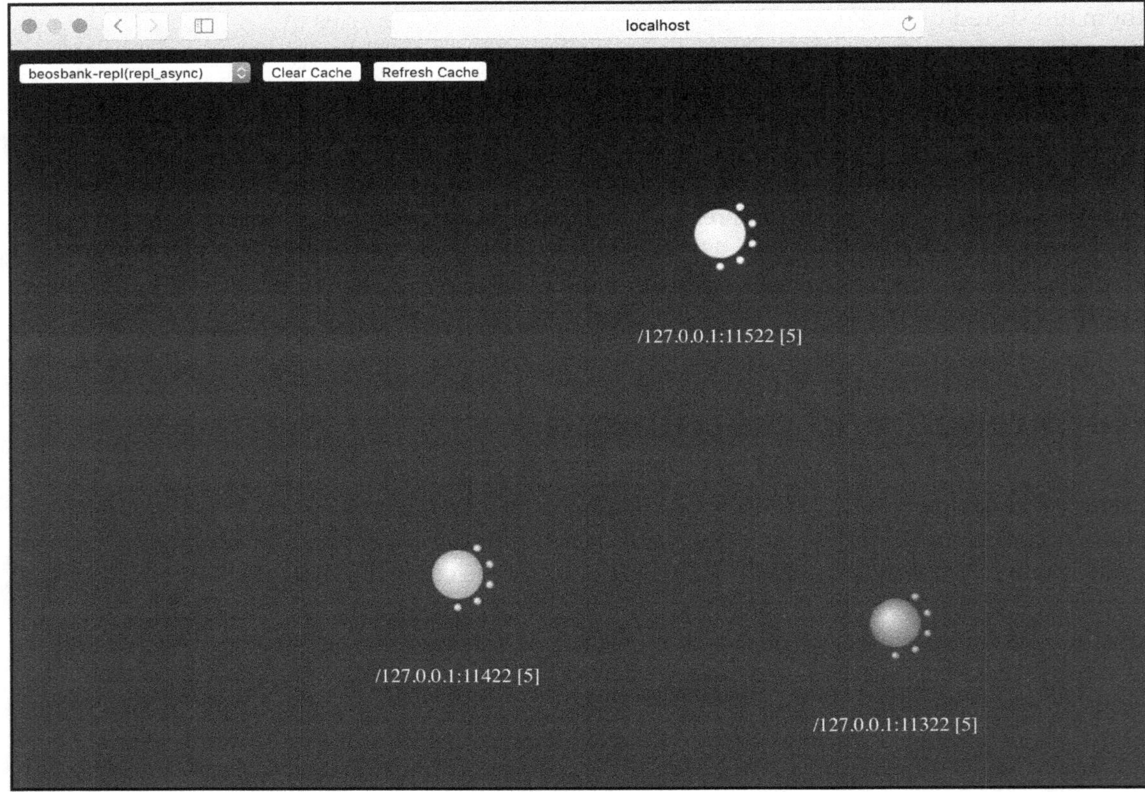

Replication/distribution configuration should be used based on your application specifications. Replication is not suitable when the cache instance number is important. Apart from distribution/replication, there are various advanced mechanisms to maintain cache contents:

- Expiration and Eviction policies.
- Level 1 internal cache. `L1` caches are used to store entries when they are first accessed and prevent unnecessary fetch operations for subsequent usages of the previously accessed entries.
- Grid computing.

In the following section, we will be exploring some advanced features provided by JBoss Datagrid.

Cache advanced usages

Datagrid provides a set of features to facilitate cache usage within applications: REST API, Programmatic, and XML configuration.

REST API

JBoss Datagrid provides users with a REST API to interact with cache objects. This feature is available on the `/rest` context and exposes each cache resource through `SERVER:PORT/rest/${CacheName}`. By default, the `rest-connector` is protected. Edit the `clustered.xml` file to temporarily disable the security configuration on the REST connector:

```
$cd jboss-datagrid-7.0.0-server/Africa
 <rest-connector socket-binding="rest" cache-container="clustered"
security-domain="other" auth-method="BASIC"/>
 <rest-connector socket-binding="rest" cache-container="clustered" />
```

Start the first grid server and connect to the administration console using the JBoss Data Grid CLI:

```
$cd jboss-datagrid-7.0.0-server/bin
$./standalone.sh -c=clustered.xml -bmanagement=127.0.0.1 -b=127.0.0.1 -
Djboss.node.name=BeosBankCacheAfrica -Djboss.server.base.dir=Africa -
Djboss.socket.binding.port-offset=100
./cli.sh --connect --controller=127.0.0.1:10090
```

Create a local-cache named `DEMO` with the default configuration:

```
[standalone@127.0.0.1:10090 /] /subsystem=datagrid-infinispan/cache-
container=clustered/local-cache=DEMO:add(configuration=default)
{"outcome" => "success"}
```

Start the cache:

```
[standalone@127.0.0.1:10090 /] /subsystem=datagrid-infinispan/cache-
container=clustered/local-cache=DEMO:start-cache
{"outcome" => "success"}
```

Put the value (Key1, `"BeosBank Inc."`) in the `DEMO` cache:

```
$ curl -i  -X PUT -d  "BeosBank Inc." http://localhost:8180/rest/DEMO/Key1
HTTP/1.1 200 OK
Content-Length: 0
Connection: keep-alive
```

Read the value:

```
$ curl -i   http://localhost:8180/rest/DEMO/Key1
HTTP/1.1 200 OK
Connection: keep-alive
Content-Type: application/x-www-form-urlencoded
ETag: "application/x-www-form-urlencoded-156134536"
Last-Modified: Thu, 01 Jan 1970 00:00:00 GMT
Transfer-Encoding: chunked
BeosBank Inc.
```

Cache expiration and eviction

In most cases, caches are not supposed to hold information eternally. There are various configuration parameters the user can use to define the life span or eviction policies in a cache. Expiration policies define how long objects can be stored in caches:

```
ConfigurationBuilder builder = new ConfigurationBuilder();
builder
   .expiration()
   .maxIdle(31, TimeUnit.SECONDS)
   .lifespan(51, TimeUnit.SECONDS);
```

Let's consider the following code block from the `ExpirationDemo` class:

```
BeosBankCacheUtils.loadEntries(cache,inputFileNames);
   // Inspect the cache .
   System.out.println(cache.size());
Thread.sleep(2000);
   cache.get(51);
   System.out.println("Cache content after 2 sec");
   printCacheContent(cache);
Thread.sleep(1000);
   System.out.println("Cache content after 3 sec");
   printCacheContent(cache);
Thread.sleep(3000);
   System.out.println("Cache content after 6 sec");
   printCacheContent(cache);
```

The code first loads five entries in the cache, then sleeps for 2 seconds. After this first pause, the application accesses the fifth entry. After 2 seconds, all five entries are still alive (`maxIdle time = 3 sec`), but all the entries except the entry with key=5 expire 1 second later. The entry with ID=5 still remains in the cache because it was accessed just 1 second ago:

```
Created 1
Created 2
Created 3
Created 4
Created 5
5
Cache content after 2 sec
1 = MoneyTransfer [id=1 From: France To:Cameroon  Amount:100 EUR]
2 = MoneyTransfer [id=2 From: USA To:Cameroon  Amount:200 USD]
3 = MoneyTransfer [id=3 From: USA To:Cameroon  Amount:1500 USD]
4 = MoneyTransfer [id=4 From: USA To:Cameroon  Amount:800 USD]
5 = MoneyTransfer [id=5 From: USA To:Cameroon  Amount:1000 USD]
Cache content after 3 sec
5 = MoneyTransfer [id=5 From: USA To:Cameroon  Amount:1000 USD]
Cache content after 6 sec
// Empty
```

Entries created from this configuration builder will expire after 5 seconds. Expiration can also be related to maximum idle times (here, if an entry is idle for 3 seconds, it will also expire). Entries exceeding these time limits are treated as invalid and are removed globally in memory, cache store, if any, and cluster.

Unlike expiration, which causes global data deletion, eviction policies, on the contrary, define how the cache data can be reorganized in memory. When the cache memory size is full, data evicted is not deleted globally, but can be moved from memory to a second cache store such as a filesystem or database, if any persistence context is defined.

Eviction works with the maximum number of entries (`type=EvictionType.COUNT`) or memory size (`type=EvictionType.MEMORY`) the cache can contain. Whenever this eviction criteria is achieved and a `PUT` request is received, the cache manager should remove one or more entries from the memory to insert the new key pair values. Remember that cache eviction is local to the cache, and there are various eviction strategies:

- **NONE**: Never evicted entries, this is the default strategy; eviction should be done manually in this case
- **LRU**: Least Recently Used pattern
- **LIRS**: Low Inter-reference Recency Set; this is an improved version of LRU that uses cache-locality access information to better decide which data to evict

To define a specific expiration or eviction strategy, call a set of methods on your configuration builder object as follows:

```
ConfigurationBuilder builder = new ConfigurationBuilder();
  builder
   .eviction()
   .strategy(EvictionStrategy.LRU)
   .type(EvictionType.COUNT)
   .size(3) ;
```

While running `com.beosbank.jbdevg.jbdatagrid.EvictionDemo`, we have five entry creation notifications, but the cache binds on an LRU eviction policy with a maximum of three entries. The money transfer objects with `Id=1 and Id=2` are the first ones inserted and, therefore, the least recently used. They will be removed from the memory to insert transactions with `id=4 and id=5`:

```
Created 1
Created 2
Created 3
Created 4
Created 5
3  //cache size
//Cache content
//1 and 2 are missing
3 = MoneyTransfer [id=3 From: USA To:Cameroon  Amount:1500 USD]
4 = MoneyTransfer [id=4 From: USA To:Cameroon  Amount:800 USD]
5 = MoneyTransfer [id=5 From: USA To:Cameroon  Amount:1000 USD]
```

Eviction and expiration are mechanisms on which users can play to improve cache performance; configuring an expiration/eviction policy strongly depends on the application's functional and hardware constraints. We saw how to define this configuration using programmatic code; in the next section, we will see how to set up a cache configuration using XML files.

XML configuration

While working with Infinispan/JBoss Datagrid, a cache configuration through Java code is the most simple option if the configuration through Java API is more suitable for simple use case and demonstration purposes. There are various constraints where considering the declarative XML configuration options may be the best option for you. Infinispan/Jboss datagrid aims to reduce at least the configuration part while dealing with the solution. By default, Infinispan will load the `infinispan.xml` configuration file from the application classpath.

The `infinispan.xml` configuration file can be performed using an XML schema. Each Infinispan version is shipped with a specific XML schema. You can find the schema for version 8.2, for example, at the following addresses:

- `http://infinispan.org/schemas/infinispan-config-8.2.xsd`
- `http://docs.jboss.org/infinispan/8.2/configdocs/infinispan-config-8.2.html`

Let's use a custom XML configuration file to create both the replicated and distributed cache instances used in the previous code configuration lab. Create a

`config/beosbank-infinispan.xml` resource file with the following content.

```
<infinispan>
   <cache-container default-cache="local">
      <transport cluster="beosbank-cluster"/>
      <local-cache name="local"/>
      <replicated-cache name="beosbank-repl" mode="SYNC"/>
      <distributed-cache name="beosbank-dist" mode="SYNC">
          <expiration max-idle="3000" lifespan="5000" />
      </distributed-cache>
   </cache-container>
</infinispan>
```

With the preceding configuration, you should have the same result from `ExpirationDemo` and `ExpirationXmlDemo`. The only difference is in cache creation. While using the XML config, the configuration can be loaded using a file reference from the classpath:

```
package com.beosbank.jbdevg.jbdatagrid;
import java.io.IOException;
import org.infinispan.Cache;
import org.infinispan.context.Flag;
import org.infinispan.manager.DefaultCacheManager;
import com.beosbank.jbdevg.jbdatagrid.domain.MoneyTransfer;
import com.beosbank.jbdevg.jbdatagrid.listener.DatagridListener;
public class ExpirationXmlConfiguration {

 public static void main(String[] args) throws IOException,
InterruptedException {
   // Initialize the cache manager
  DefaultCacheManager cacheManager = new
DefaultCacheManager("config/beosbank-infinispan.xml");
       // Obtain the default cache
Cache<Long, MoneyTransfer> cache = cacheManager.getCache("beosbank-dist");
```

There are two ways to set up your cache configuration, either using Java code or XML files; remember that, behind the scenes, the XML configuration invokes the programmatic API.

Now that we have a set of data in caches, we may be interested in how to empower this data and the cache instances; JBoss Datagrid can also be used for grid computing, providing various computational models on cache entries.

Grid computing

JBoss DataGrid is also a computing grid; nodes can be used to perform distributed computing. JBoss Datagrid provides various mechanisms to empower data stored in these nodes:

- Distributed streams that aim to transform a cache entry set into a Java 8 Stream
- Distributed executors that extend the Java Executor stack to schedule tasks on cache instances

Distributed Streams

Data grid can also be used as a grid computing engine to perform various computation tasks on large and distributed datasets. Users can turn all the cache entries of a local, replication, or invalidation cache into a regular Java Stream using the following operations:

```
cache.entrySet().stream()
cache.entrySet().parallelStream()
```

So, instead of iterating on data key values yourself, the underlying `org.infinisap.CacheStream` object handles it, and you just have to provide operations to perform on it.

The primary interest of using streams with an Infinispan cache is Distributed Streams. Distributed Streams allow any operation you can perform on a regular Java 8 stream to also be performed on a distributed cache, assuming that the operations and data are marshallable.

A Distributed Stream is a sort of map reduce algorithm implementation, but Infinispan/Jboss Datagrid adds the possibility to perform various intermediate tasks on each node and a final node termination operation before the final result is sent to the final reduction phase.

Regarding BeosBank, it may be interesting to have a live view of the global amount users are sending between countries. This business information may help build statistical planning on when transactions are mainly sent from country X to country Y, and therefore produce a maintenance window plan for these money transfer routes.

How can we rely on a Distributed cache to compute the ongoing money transfer global amount from the US to Cameroon? In `ch4/beosbank-datagrid-cluster/DistributedCacheStreamDemo` the following code is implemented:

```
//get all transactions from US to Cameroon
 double result = cache.entrySet().stream().
filter(
     mt->
"USA".equalsIgnoreCase(mt.getValue().getSender().getAddress().getCountry())
&&
"Cameroon".equalsIgnoreCase(mt.getValue().getReceiver().getAddress().getCou
ntry())
    ).collect
(Collectors.summarizingDouble(e->e.getValue().getAmountExcludingFees().doub
leValue())).
getSum();
System.out.println("TRX from US to Cameroon  USD "+result);
```

We create a stream from the `entrySet` cache on each node. Intermediate operations include filtering to keep entries with both the US as the sender's country and Cameroon as the receiver's country; then, on each node, a terminal operation is executed to collect the `AmountExcludingFees` field of the serializable `MoneyTransfer` object.

The `collect` operator will create the `Collectors.summarizingDouble` utility method to return the amount for each node; upon receiving the intermediate results from all the nodes, the user thread will perform the `getSum` operation:

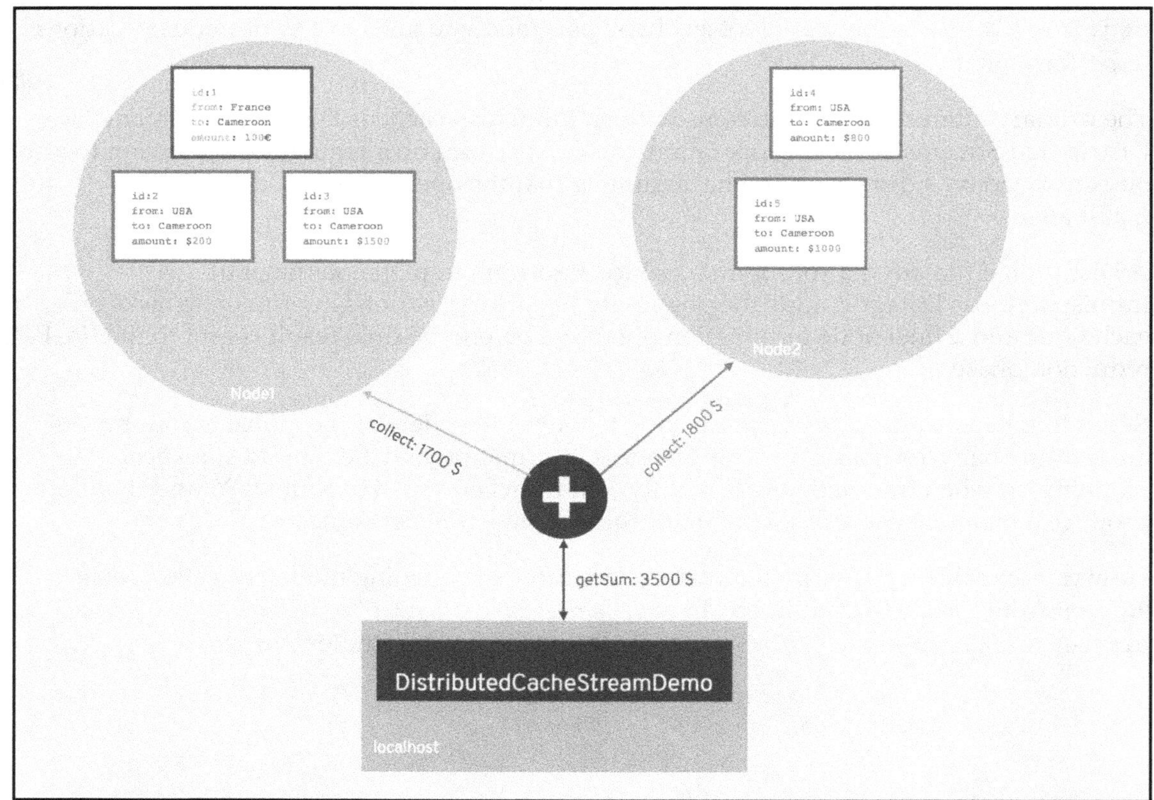

When running the `com.beosbank.jbdevg.jbdatagrid.DistributedCacheStreamDemo` class from the `beosbank-datagrid-cluster` project, we have the following outputs:

```
//Cache insertion listener logs
Created 1
Created 2
```

```
Created 3
Created 4
Created 5

5 //Cache Size
//Cache inspection using foreach
1 = MoneyTransfer [id=1 From: France To:Cameroon  Amount:100 EUR]
2 = MoneyTransfer [id=2 From: USA To:Cameroon  Amount:200 USD]
3 = MoneyTransfer [id=3 From: USA To:Cameroon  Amount:1500 USD]
4 = MoneyTransfer [id=4 From: USA To:Cameroon  Amount:800 USD]
5 = MoneyTransfer [id=5 From: USA To:Cameroon  Amount:1000 USD]

//Cache stream Map reduce operation.
TRX from US to Cameroon USD 3500.0
```

With Distributed Streams, Infinispan core organizes work and dispatches the task to nodes, and the results are then reduced and sent to the caller. Infinispan also embarks a feature where a work task can be dispatched to nodes based on the key presence on those nodes; this is included in Distributed Executors.

Distributed execution

Infinispan/JBoss Datagrid extends the JDK `ExecutorService` and `Callable` features to provide a distributable execution framework, allowing you to launch tasks on cluster nodes rather than in the local JVM. Use a `DistributedExecutorService` instance to submit various `DistributedCallable` actions on a specific and unique cache.
These `DistributableCallable` actions apply on a subset of keys; they have access to cache values and `return java.util.concurrent.Future`. When a `DistributableCallable` object is created, Infinispan identifies the nodes containing the key subset passed as a parameter and migrates the `Callable` object to this node.

Let's consider the following example. In the money transfer web app portal, the payment step can be asynchronous. When the user submits a payment request, an external call is done to a payment gateway and a status is returned to BeosBank systems with the `MoneyTransfer` ID reference for correlation. Now, let's see how to update the money transfer status in the cache using `DistributableExecutor`.

Upon receiving a notification from the payment gateway, we should submit a `DistributableCallable` task to the node containing the correlation key to update the `MoneyTransfer` status.

We create a `StatusUpdateDistributedCallable` action class to hold the status update business logic:

```
public class StatusUpdateDistributedCallable implements
DistributedCallable<Long,MoneyTransfer,List<MoneyTransfer>>, Serializable {
  private static final long serialVersionUID = 1L;
  Cache<Long, MoneyTransfer> cache;
  Set<Long> inputKeys;
  @Override
  public List<MoneyTransfer> call() throws Exception {
   List<MoneyTransfer> mts = Lists.newArrayList();
   for (Long key : inputKeys) {
    MoneyTransfer mt = cache.get(key);
     if(mt!=null &&  MoneyTransferStatus.DRAFT.equals(mt.getStatus())){
      mt.setStatus(MoneyTransferStatus.PAID);
      mts.add(mt);
     } }
   return mts;
  }
  @Override
  public void setEnvironment(Cache<Long, MoneyTransfer> cache, Set<Long>
inputKeys) {
   this.cache=cache;
   this.inputKeys=inputKeys;
   System.out.println("StatusUpdateDistributedCallable.setEnvironment()");
  }
```

The `setEnvironment` method is called by Infinispan to pass a cache reference and key subset to the task when it is submitted using `des.submitEverywhere`:

```
DistributedExecutorService des = new DefaultExecutorService((Cache<?, ?>)
cache);   DistributedTaskBuilder<List<MoneyTransfer>> taskBuilder =
des.createDistributedTaskBuilder(new StatusUpdateDistributedCallable());
taskBuilder.timeout(5,TimeUnit.SECONDS);
   DistributedTask<List<MoneyTransfer>> distributedTask =
taskBuilder.build();
    List<CompletableFuture<List<MoneyTransfer>>> futures =
des.submitEverywhere(distributedTask,1l,2l);
    List<MoneyTransfer> paidMts = futures.get(0).get();
```

The task is submitted with two keys of type long: `1l` and `2l`. A description of the money transfer request associated with these keys is printed before and after the task execution:

```
INFO: ISPN000128: Infinispan version: Infinispan 'Chakra' 8.3.0.Final-
redhat-1Created 1
Created 2
Created 3
Created 4
Created 5
Cache inspection to check status before task
MoneyTransfer [id=1 From: France To:Cameroon  Amount:100 EUR Status=DRAFT]
MoneyTransfer [id=2 From: USA To:Cameroon  Amount:200 USD Status=DRAFT]
StatusUpdateDistributedCallable.setEnvironment()
Cache inspection to check Task status updates
MoneyTransfer [id=1 From: France To:Cameroon  Amount:100 EUR Status=PAID]
MoneyTransfer [id=2 From: USA To:Cameroon  Amount:200 USD Status=PAID]
```

The full code for Distributed Executor is in the `beosank-datagrid-cluster` project. From what we have seen in this section, Infinispan is not only a memory cache, but can also act as a grid computing engine. In this specific context, depending on your environment, there may be specific requirements to access specific Infinispan features; how to manage authorizations with Infinispan is the purpose of the next section, which is dedicated to cache security.

Cache security

In the real world, some applications such as `MoneyTransferAgency`, used in different offices to check money transfer status and validate remittances, will only have read-only access to predefined JBoss datagrid caches. On the other hand, the ESB flow that pushed money transfer objects into the cache will at least have write access to the cache to be able to insert new transactions. Infinispan/JBoss datagrid leverages Java standards, such as JAAS and Security Manager, to protect access to caches and cache manager.

Different mechanisms can be used depending on your topologies: While using REST API to put/get entries, you can enable security on the REST connector using a custom security-domain and authentication method:

```
<rest-connector socket-binding="rest" cache-container="clustered" security-
domain="other" auth-method="BASIC"/>
```

Using programmatic/XML configuration, we can rely on custom authorizations to restrict access to specific cache features. Infinispan/JBoss Datagrid has a built-in set of permissions associated to specific cache and cache manager functions:

Permission	**Description**
`READ`	Grant access to read data from caches: function get, contains
`WRITE`	Grant access to write: put method and its derivates: `putIfAbsent`, `evict`, `remove` and `replace`.
`LISTEN`	Add listener to caches/cache manager operations
`EXEC`	Grant access to perform calculations on the cache
`BULK_READ/BULK_WRITE`	Grant access to bulk read/bulk write operations on the cache
`ADMIN`	Cache management and monitoring + AdvancedCache API methods such as `getStats`
`ALL`	Grant access to all features
`CONFIGURATION`	Grant access to define cache manager configuration
`LIFECYCLE`	Grant access to manage cache/cache manager life cycle operations: start/stop

Configuring security can be performed through the following steps:

1. Global security configuration: In your Infinispan XML configuration file, you can define security mapping between your application role and internal permissions. The `moneytransfer_writer` roles has the `READ`, `WRITE`, `BULK_READ`, and `BULK_WRITE` permissions in the following configuration sample, while `moneytransfer_reader` only has access to read and bulk read. The `moneytransfer_admin` role has all the permissions; this includes LIFECYCLE to create cache/cache manager, start/stop the cache, and LISTEN permission to add a cache listener to a cache instance. This mapping should be defined in the cache container security tag:

```
<infinispan>
  <cache-container default-cache="local">
     <transport cluster="beosbank-cluster"/>
     <security>
 <authorization>
  <identity-role-mapper/>
  <role name="moneytransfer_writer" permissions="READ WRITE
BULK_READ BULK_WRITE" />
```

```
    <role name="moneytransfer_reader" permissions="READ BULK_READ"
  />
    <role name="moneytransfer_admin"  permissions="ALL" />
   </authorization>
   </security>
       <distributed-cache name="beosbank-dist" mode="SYNC">
        <security>
    <authorization roles="moneytransfer_writer moneytransfer_reader
  moneytransfer_admin" />
   </security>
       </distributed-cache>
    </cache-container>
  </infinispan>
```

2. Defining role mapper: Role mapper defines how Infinispan will associate roles to users once they get authenticated; there are various options, such as the following:

- `identity-role-mapper`: Principal names are converted as is into role names
- `common-name-role-mapper`: Use distinguished name notation for principals and extract CN as user roles
- `cluster-role-mapper`: Use a cluster registry to store user roles
- `custom-role-mapper`: Use your custom class as role mapper

3. Define specific roles that can access your application: Once the roles are defined in the global configuration, you must specify which ones are available for each cache by activating the `<security>` tag in the cache definition. For the `beosbank-dist` cache, users with roles.
4. Use `Security.doAs` to run protected action on caches: There are various techniques to authenticate a user, and `PicketBox` is a nice candidate to perform authentication and create a `subject`:

```
public class CacheSecurityDemo {
...
BeosBankAuthenticationRealm auth = new BeosBankAuthenticationRealm();
  PicketBoxProcessor processor = new PicketBoxProcessor();
  processor.setSecurityInfo("moneytransfer_admin", "admin01#");
  processor.process(auth);
  Subject adminSubject = processor.getCallerSubject();
  Cache<Long, MoneyTransfer> cache = Security.doAs(adminSubject,
  new PrivilegedAction<Cache<Long, MoneyTransfer>>() {
     @Override
     public Cache<Long, MoneyTransfer> run() {
      DefaultCacheManager cacheManager;
```

```
        try {
         cacheManager = new DefaultCacheManager("config/beosbank-infinispan-
secure.xml");
         Cache<Long, MoneyTransfer> cache = cacheManager.getCache("beosbank-
dist");
         cache.addListener(new DatagridListener());
         BeosBankCacheUtils.loadEntries(cache, inputFileNames);
         System.out.println("Cache created by user=" + adminSubject + "
Size=" + cache.size());
         return cache;
        } catch (IOException e) {
         e.printStackTrace();
        }
        return null;
       }
      });

processor.setSecurityInfo("moneytransfer_reader", "jb0ss!");
  processor.process(auth);
  Subject readerSubject = processor.getCallerSubject();
  Security.doAs(readerSubject, new PrivilegedAction<String>() {
   @Override
   public String run() {
    System.out.println("Cache content cache displayed by user=" +
readerSubject);
    printCacheContent(cache);
    return null;
   }
  });
  // Stop the cache !!! no security context
  cache.stop();
..
```

While running the preceding code extracted from the `ch4/beosbank-datagrid-cluster/CacheSecurityDemo` main class with the `moneytransfer_reader` user in the context, the following log statements are printed on the console:

```
INFO: ISPN000128: Infinispan version: Infinispan 'Chakra' 8.3.0.Final-
redhat-1
Created 1
Created 2
Created 3
Created 4
Created 5
Cache created by user=Objet :
 Principal : moneytransfer_admin
 Principal : Roles(members)
 Principal : CallerPrincipal(members:moneytransfer_admin)
```

```
Size=5
Cache content cache displayed by user=Objet :
 Principal : moneytransfer_reader
 Principal : Roles(members)
 Principal : CallerPrincipal(members:moneytransfer_reader)
1 = MoneyTransfer [id=1 From: France To:Cameroon  Amount:100 EUR]
2 = MoneyTransfer [id=2 From: USA To:Cameroon  Amount:200 USD]
3 = MoneyTransfer [id=3 From: USA To:Cameroon  Amount:1500 USD]
4 = MoneyTransfer [id=4 From: USA To:Cameroon  Amount:800 USD]
5 = MoneyTransfer [id=5 From: USA To:Cameroon  Amount:1000 USD]
Exception in thread "main" java.lang.SecurityException: ISPN000287:
Unauthorized access: subject 'null' lacks 'LIFECYCLE' permission
 at
org.infinispan.security.impl.AuthorizationHelper.checkPermission(Authorizat
ionHelper.java:86)
 at
org.infinispan.security.impl.AuthorizationManagerImpl.checkPermission(Autho
rizationManagerImpl.java:42)
 at
org.infinispan.security.impl.SecureCacheImpl.stop(SecureCacheImpl.java:95)
 at
com.beosbank.jbdevg.jbdatagrid.security.CacheSecurityDemo.main(CacheSecurit
yDemo.java:72)
```

While running this sample (`CacheSecurityDemo.java`), the admin user creates the cache manager and cache instance and populates the data into the cache. `moneytransfer_reader/jb0ss!` displays the cache content, but since there's no security context associated to the `cache.stop` instruction, the operation fails. PicketBox is set up with two configuration files: `users.properties` with the following content:

```
moneytransfer_admin=admin01#
moneytransfer_reader=jb0ss!
moneytransfer_writer=jb8sS@
```

The `roles.properties` file is useless since we are using `identity-role-mapper` in the global cache container configuration. With this configuration, `moneytransfer_admin` has the `moneytransfer_admin` role with all (`ALL`) permissions.

Security is handled in various ways, depending on how the cache interfaces are exposed. A REST interface is secured through the security domain, while Hot Rod and Memcached access can be protected by specific authorization policies based on custom groups and Infinispan internal permissions.

Summary

Caches play an important role in modern applications and systems architecture. They are mostly used to improve applications' response times, but also as highly available grids and distributed computing engines. Infinispan/JBoss Datagrid provides a powerful architecture on which an application can rely for caching data easily. Interconnections with the existing and new systems are facilitated by a variety of protocols: `REST`, `HotRod`, and `MemCached`. Applications can embark cache instances in `Library` mode or consume data exposed by remote caches in a secure manner. Developers have access to a full XML configuration and advanced programmatic API to leverage infinispan/Jboss Datagrid features, while cache content can be monitored using `Infinispan-visualizer`.

With JBoss DataGrid, client applications willing to consume cached data must at least know the physical address of the remote cache server; they also need to know the key and value types and the structure of the stored data. These constraints are not specific to JBoss datagrid, and can also be found in most enterprise applications dealing with databases. With data source diversity, applications relying on direct interfacing with data providers would be subject to many modifications if one data source were to change. The issue of how to weakly couple applications and data sources is addressed by data virtualization paradigms that we will cover in `Chapter 5`, *Exposing Data as a Service*.

5
Exposing Data as a Service

This chapter introduces data virtualization and is centered around the paradigm of exposing data as a service with **JBoss Data Virtualization** (**JDV**). Through illustrated examples, you will progressively master the terminology used in this area and discover what data virtualization is. You will also learn how to create aggregated, unified, and virtualized views from disparate data sources, how to create source models, virtual models, and virtual databases, how to query join data from various sources, and finally, how to expose data views as a service. Throughout the chapter, we will work on practical use cases from the BeosBank sample. The BeosBank core management team wants to build a federated view for the EMEA region from various datasets in various databases and locations.

In the subsequent sections, we will cover the following items:

- Introduction to data virtualization
- JBoss Data Virtualization architecture and installation
- Building virtual databases from multiple heterogeneous data sources
- Interacting with a virtual database

Introduction to data virtualization

Data virtualization is both a data management approach and an enterprise pattern, allowing client applications to access enterprise data without requiring its technical details: format, physical storage, or geographical locations. The main objective of data virtualization is to provide a real-time single view of enterprise data. It differs from various data management paradigms, such as the following ones:

- **ETL** (**Extract Transform Load**): With data virtualization, original data source content is not extracted to feed the target client application repository. On the contrary, data sources are kept in place, and only the required data is accessed on demand and in real time. Caching can be used here to improve performances but it is not mandatory requirement.
- **Data Federation**: Data federation is a type of data virtualization; however, it tends to impose a single data model from heterogeneous data sources, while data virtualization doesn't. Data virtualization uses various mapping and transformation techniques to build federated data views.
- **Data Warehouse**: Data warehouses are prebuilt sets of data that attempt to reduce access time to data sources and keep data sources where they are. A data warehouse must constantly be powered to be up to date, unlike data virtualization, which works on live data sources.

With data virtualization, users can connect to heterogeneous data stores, pick only the required data, and combine it with various transformations and mappings to build virtual databases without copying or moving any data from its original source.

Client applications can then consume data from virtual databases using standard interfaces such as the `ODBC`, `JDBC`,protocols or a `REST` API.

JBoss data virtualization architecture

JBoss data virtualization is a platform provided by Red Hat and built on top of the `JBoss Teiid project` community. JBoss data virtualization supports relational sources, NoSQL data sources, big data sources such as Hadoop, and files:

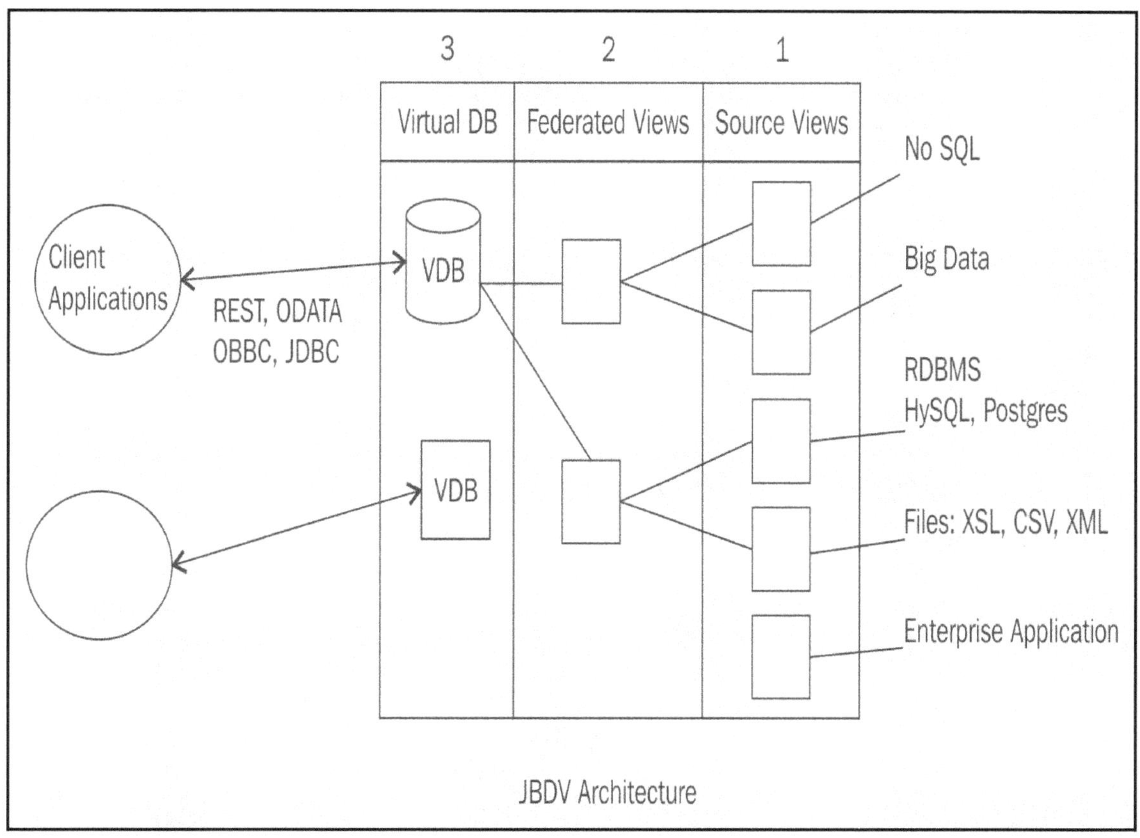

JBDV Architecture

JBoss data virtualization (JDV) has a Plug and Play architecture: users can plug new data sources as well as new client applications gradually. JDV relies on three main layers to deliver information to consumers:

- **Source view layer**: The source view layer is the lowest layer of the JBoss Data virtualization architecture. This layer uses translators to connect to various heterogeneous data sources. JDV uses a source model paradigm to represent the physical data model. There is one-to-one mapping between this model and the existing data source models; any modification on the physical model will have an impact on this model.
- **Federated view or virtual base layer**: The virtual base layer is an abstraction layer used by JBoss data virtualization to access source models and provide data to client applications. Using an intermediate model, JBoss data virtualization can perform some internal optimizations/caching operations. It can also reduce refactoring when the source model changes.

- **Virtual database layer**: The virtual database layer is the data gateway on which a client application consumes data and interacts with the data sources behind source views. Virtual database layer models are exposed to one or more virtual DBs to make them available to consumers.

All these components are supported by a JBoss Application Server, on top of which the platform runs. JBoss data virtualization also includes a high-performance query engine that processes relational, XML data, XQuery, and procedural queries from federated data sources. To build virtual databases, JBoss Developer Studio includes a specific plugin for JBoss data virtualization. This plugin includes the Teiid Designer perspective and ModeShape to store metadata. All these components will be discovered in the following section dedicated to JBoss data virtualization installation.

JBoss Data Virtualization installation

JBoss data virtualization is packaged as a standalone JAR installer available at `https://developers.redhat.com/products/datavirt/download/`. Either run the installer on top of an existing JBoss Application Server, or run it in a new directory. With the second option, it will install both the JBoss Application Server and the JDV extensions. the JDV extensions contains virtualization modules and components to run JDV on top of JBoss Server. To keep it simple, we will install the full package in a new directory. This approach has the advantage of installing JBoss Application Server patches during the installation process. In order to have a fully working JDV environment for the next lab, a user should install both the JDV server and JBoss data virtualization development plugins for JBoss Developer studio.

Installing JDV Server

All time of writing this book, the latest JDV installer is `jboss-dv-6.3.0-1-installer.jar`.

In order to have a running JDV installation, follow the given instructions:

1. Download the `jboss-dv-6.3.0-1-installer.jar` JAR file and save it on your computer, `$HOME/books/jbdevg/BeosBankDataVirtLab/install`, for example.
2. Create an empty installation directory, for example, `$HOME/books/jbdevg/BeosBankDataVirtLab/install/dv63`.
3. Start the installer with your favorite `java-jar jboss-dv-6.3.0-1-installer.jar` command-line tool.

4. The installer opens a Graphical User Interface to complete the process. Accept the license agreement and select the newly created `dv63` subfolder as the installation directory, as shown in this screenshot:

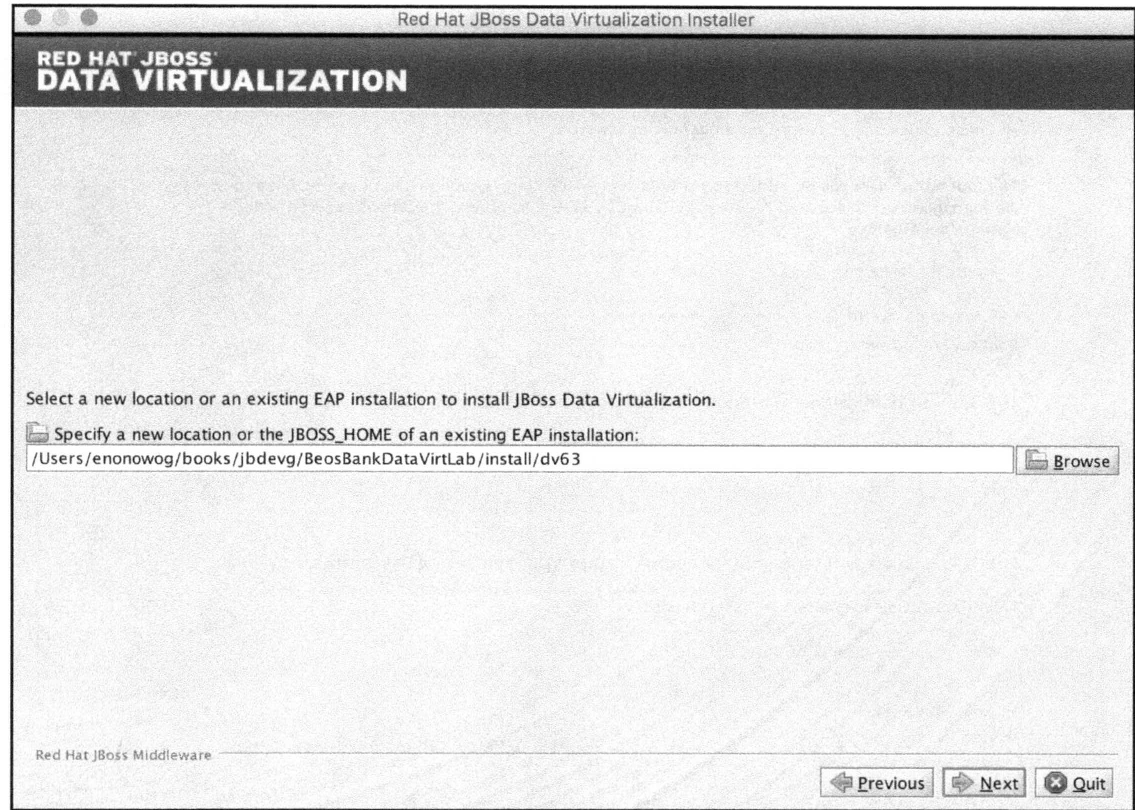

5. Review the installation details and click on **Next**. You will arrive at a page where you have to specify authentication details for various users.
6. Check the box labelled **Check to use one password for all default passwords** to use a default password for these users: `admin`, `dashboardAdmin`, `teiidUser`, and `modeshapeUser`. In production, it is better to keep these box unchecked and therefore use different passwords to increase security.
7. Enter a valid password for all these users, for example, `Admin01#`.

8. Check the **Add OData Role** and **Add Logging role** checkboxes for **TeiidUser**. **OData role** is required to be able to access virtual databases using the `OData` protocol:

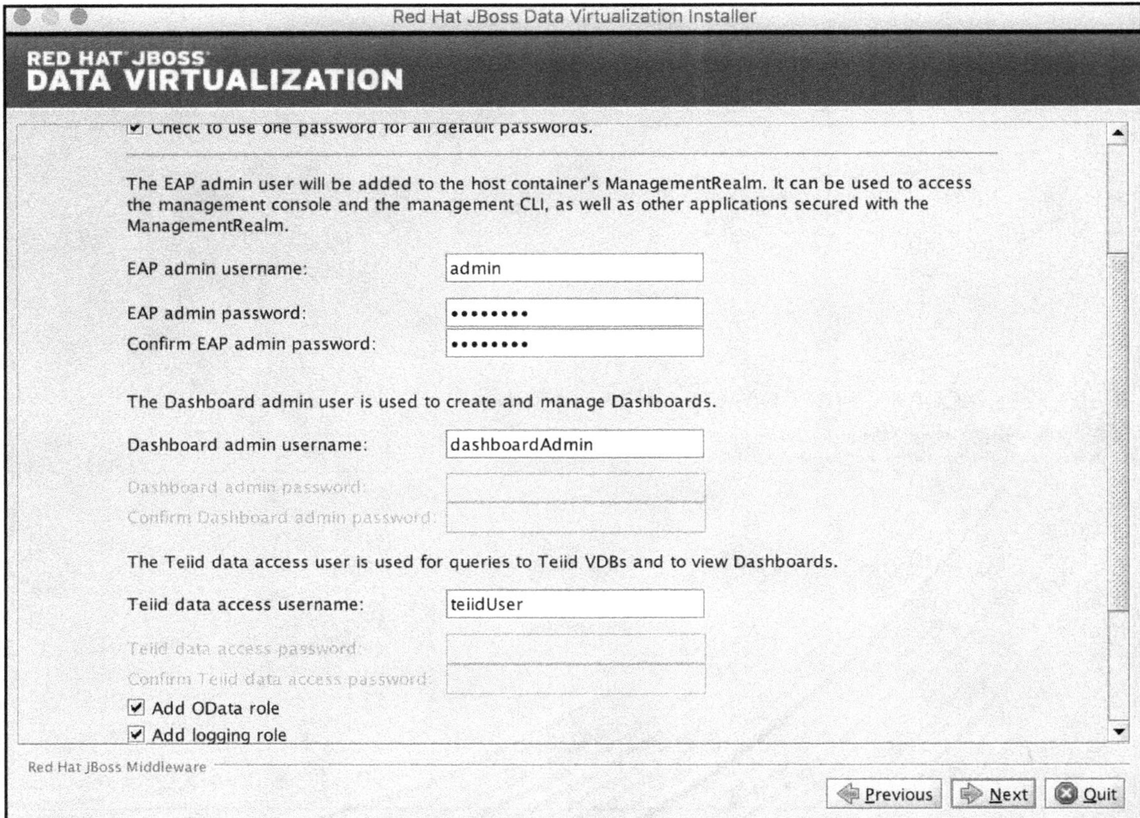

9. Perform the following steps and select **Perform default configuration.** Once the installation is complete, certain useful links are printed on the last screen to access the administration console and data virtualization dashboard, which are shown in the following screenshot:

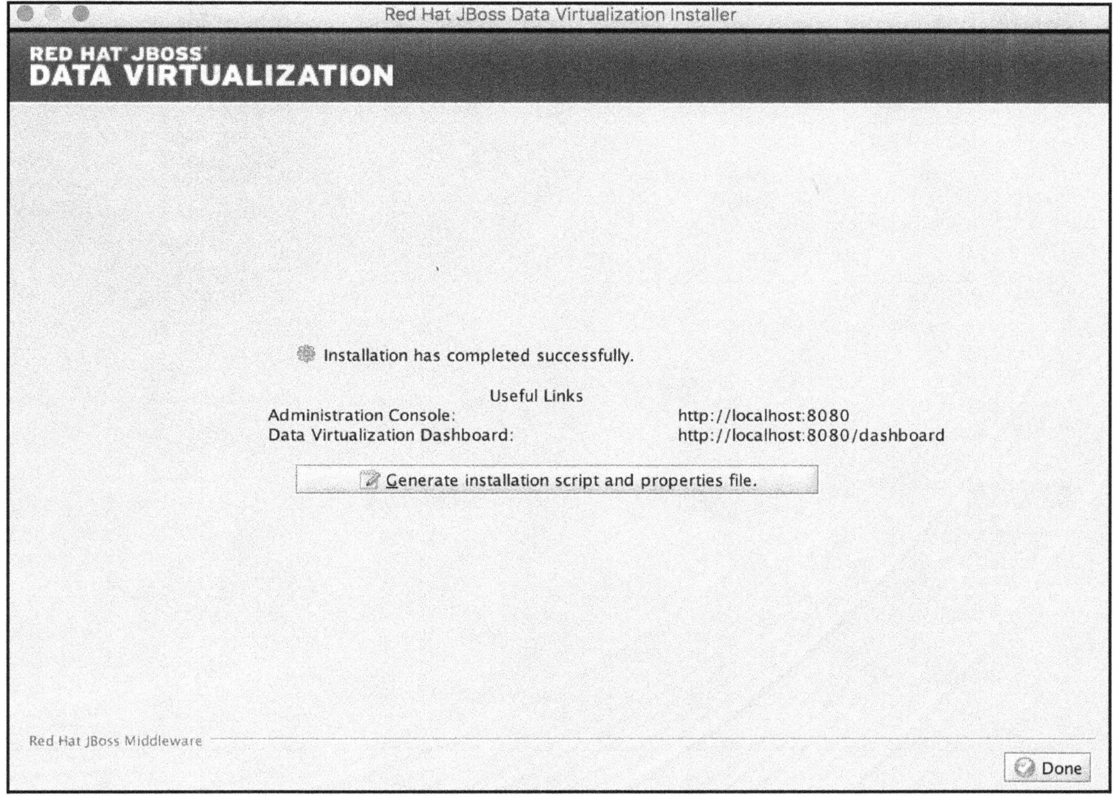

10. Click on **Done** to complete the server installation. Before reaching these URLs, the server must be started. To start the server, run the given command lines:

```
$ cd dv63/bin
$./standalone.sh
```

The administration console now responds at `http://localhost:8080` with the user--`admin/Admin01#`. You can see the console in the illustrated screenshot:

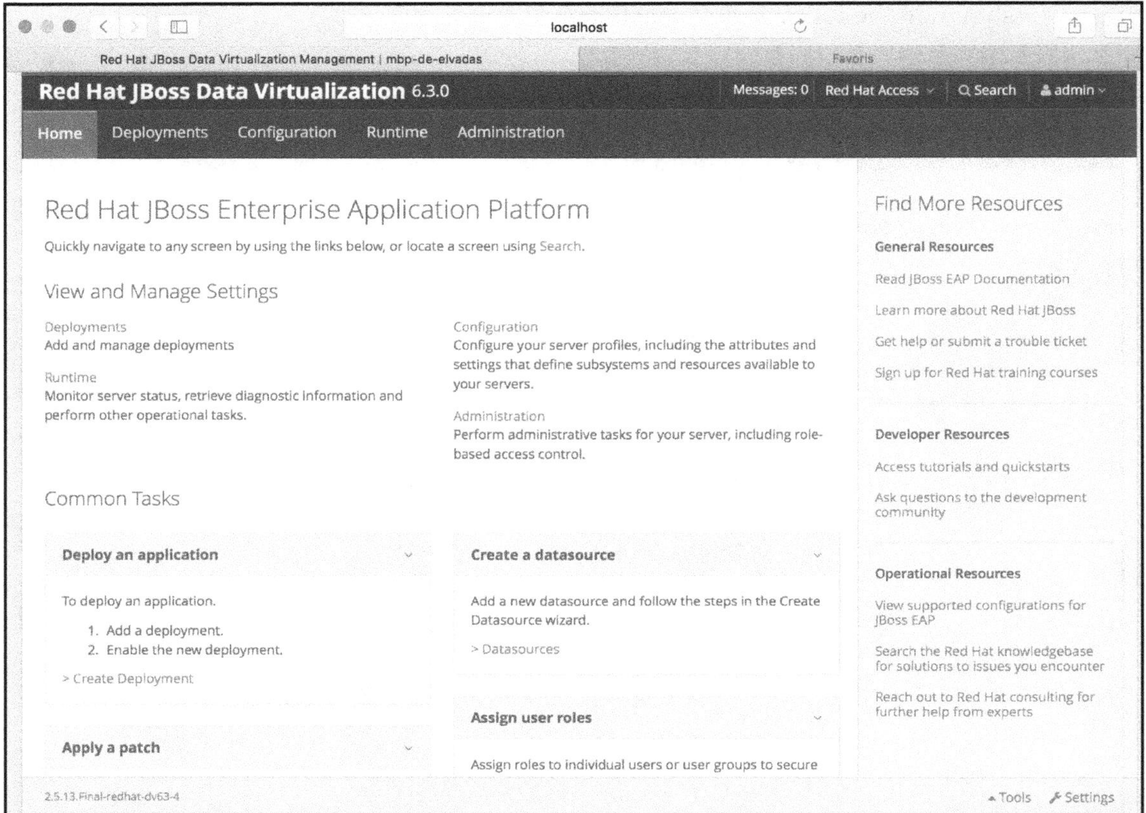

For now, we do not have much to look at on the console, but it will not be long. We still have to cleanly set up our development environment to be able to build and deploy virtual databases on this JDV server.

Setting up JDV features in JBoss Developer Studio

JBoss data virtualization plugins are included in the JBoss Developer Studio Integration Stack. JDV Plugin was installed in `Chapter 1`, *Introduction to the JBoss Ecosystem*, along with Integration Stack installation. If the plugin is not yet installed on your IDE, install it from the Red Hat Central view. Refer to the following screenshot to install the plugins:

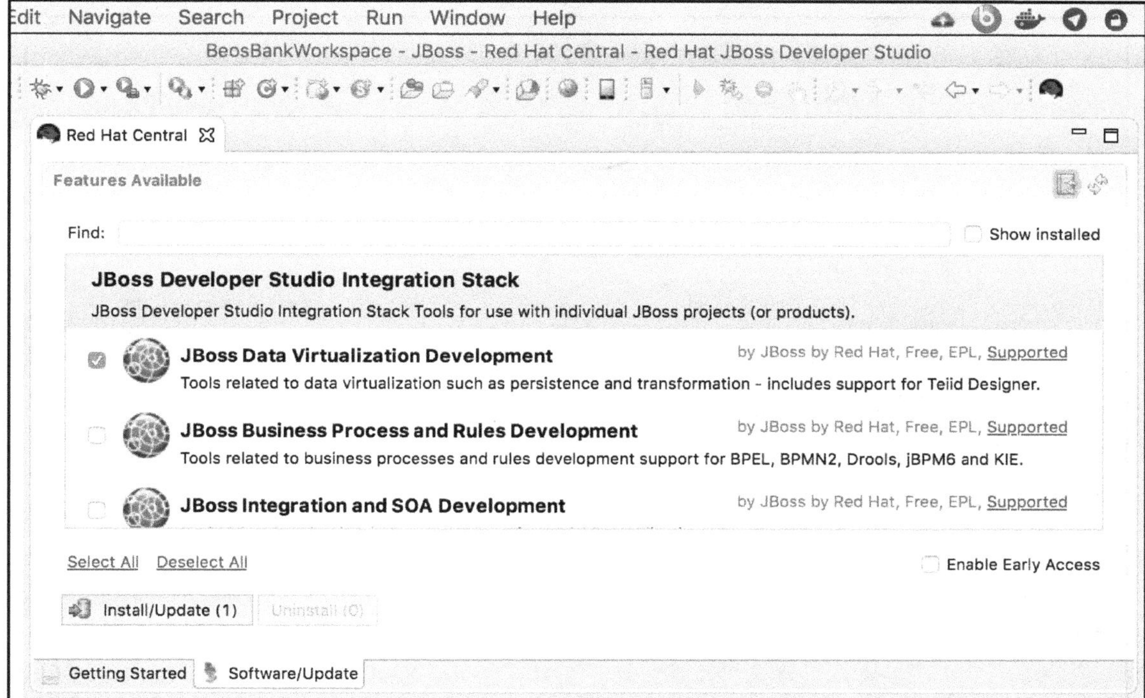

Search/select JBoss data virtualization development and click on the **Install/Update** button. This plugin brings a set of features, such as the Teiid Designer perspective, Teiid Execution plan, and Teiid Model Classes views.

In order to be able to deploy virtual databases from JBoss Developer Studio on the previous JDV server we started, we need to add the JDV63 server in the server view.

On the JBoss Developer Studio Server view, perform the following steps:

- Create a new server form with the name **JDV63**
- Select JBoss EAP 6.1+ Category
- Select your **JDV63** installation directory-- `$HOME/books/jbdevg/BeosBankDataVirtLab/install/dv63`:

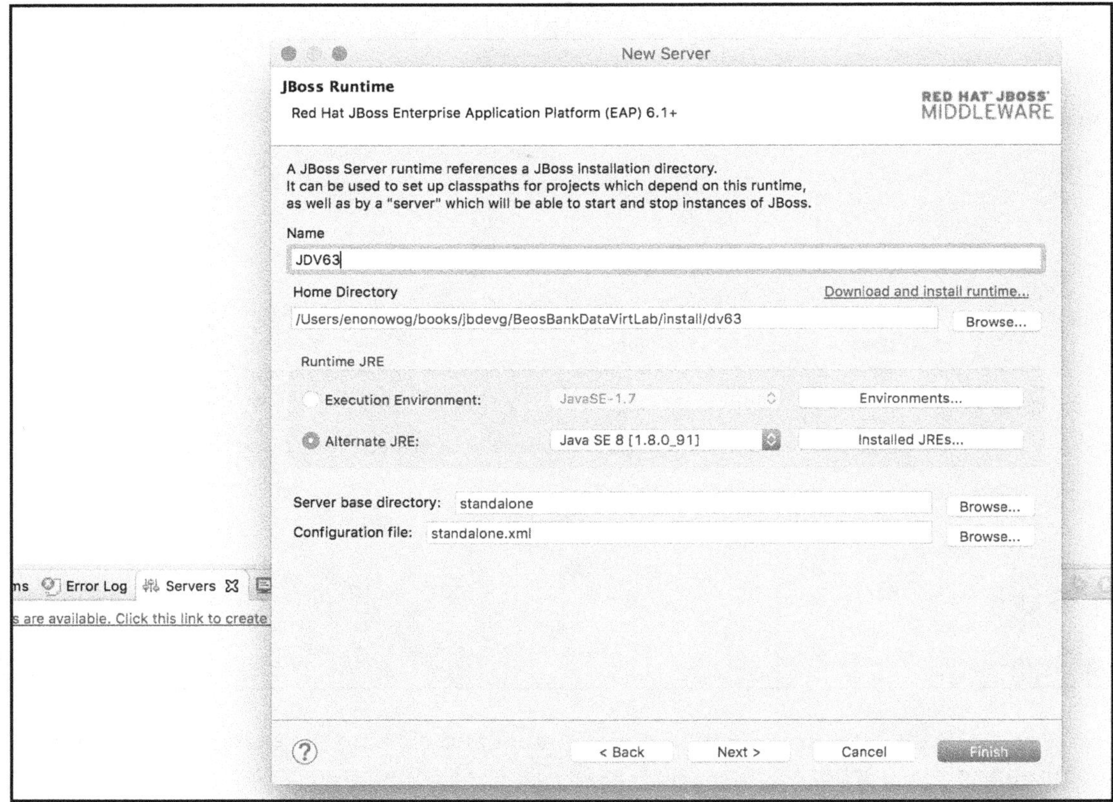

A new server is created and is available in your server view; it is referenced as the default server in your IDE. When you start/synchronize the server, the Teiid Version is detected as 8.12.5. You will need this default server to perform various operations during your virtual database development experience.

In order to be able to access the virtual database from Eclipse, you need to set up the JDBC credentials for `teiidInstance`. Follow these instructions to set up your JDBC credentials:

- Double-click on the **JDV63 Server** and select the **Teiid Instance Tab**
- Test the administration connection; you should see **OK**
- Enter **teiidUser**/`Admin01#` as the JDBC username/password
- Test the JDBC connection it should be **OK** as well; otherwise, you will not be able to query virtual databases from JBoss Developer studio:

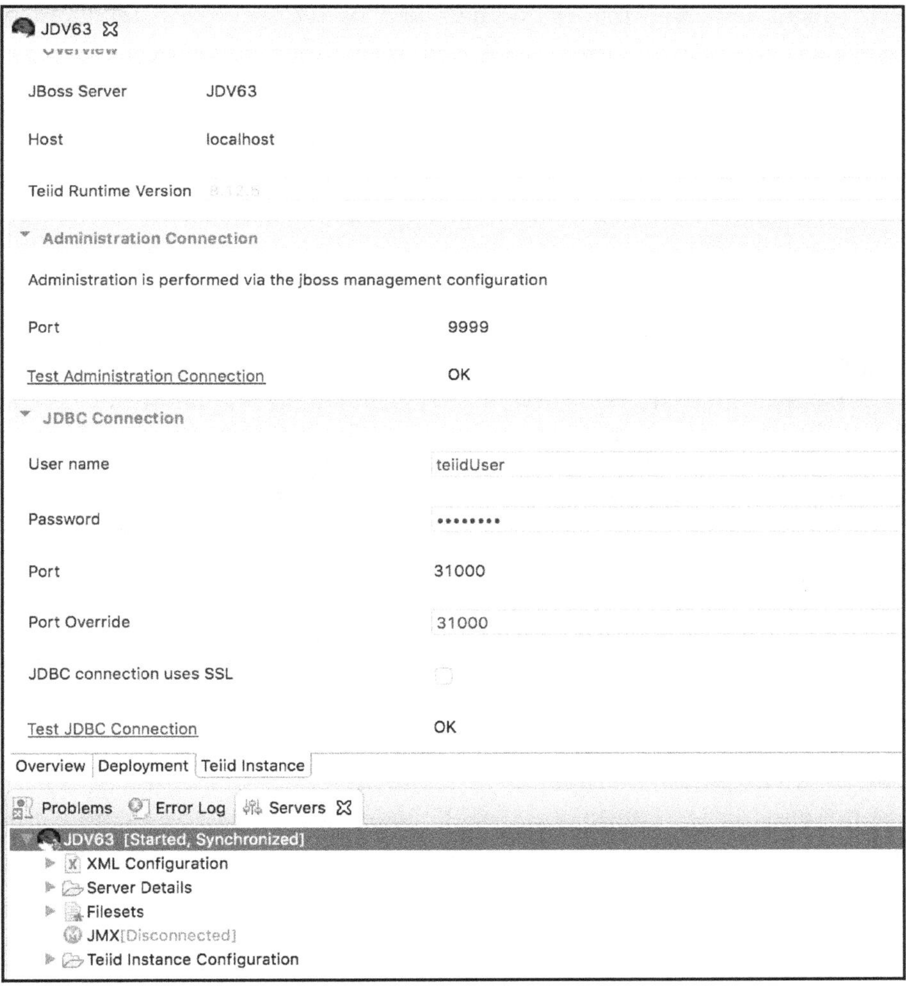

This step completes the configuration phase; the JDV63 server is up and running in standalone mode, JBoss developer studio has the JDV plugin and references the server, Teiid Runtime is 8.12.5, and JDBC connectivity working. The development environment is now ready; in the next section, we will explore the different steps required to create, build, deploy, and test virtual databases from various heterogenous data sources in detail.

Developing virtual databases

The data virtualization journey comes down to developing a set of virtual databases and interconnecting them to client applications. In this section, we will cover both creation of and connection to a virtual database thrown from a practical business use case.

Business case

Client: Hello JBoss Doctor, regarding the Beosbank money transfer database, following connectivity issues from some countries, high loads, and various regulatory and business needs, we decided to have two separate databases for the EMEA regions. The `beosbank-africa` database is used for all our customers in Africa; this database runs on a cluster. MySQL is in South Africa and holds all the transactions sent from Africa. On the other hand, for European customers, due to European Union regulations on customer data privacy and backup policies, management decided to keep this database in Europe. This database runs on Postgres and only keeps the details of transactions sent by customers from a European country. In the verification system deployed in African agencies, the details of the physical Postgres European DB are mentioned; indeed, they need to check the money transfer status for transactions sent from Europe; this is a security risk for the overall system and a limitation for our upgrades. We also have a corporate NoSQL MongoDB database serving as a company tax referential, accessible by all applications of the money transfer scope. From what you previously said, we can leverage data virtualization to improve this data management and hide the details of the corporate and European DB to other entities, right?

JBoss Doctor: You are absolutely right, dear customer. JBoss Data Virtualization can help you manage not only these RDBMS and NoSQL heterogenous databases more efficiently, but also data sources to access other third parties.

Client: How can I provide a single customer view of the EMEA region from this legacy using JBoss DataVirtualization? How can I maintain the differences between data schemas? How can I use my MongoDB instance to automatically compute taxes in various regions?

The customer really wants to see how Data Virtualization can improve his business processes and enterprise architecture. To answer these questions, let's first prepare the dataset on top of which we will build virtual databases.

Data preparation

In order to complete the next workshop, you need to have the Beosbank data legacy on your computer; to facilitate this, the book's material includes a docker folder (`https://github.com/nelvadas/jbdevg/tree/master/jbdatavirt/docker`), from which you can easily recreate the Beosbank data environment in Docker containers.

First, install the docker and `docker-compose` utils on your computer by following the official `Docker Documentation`.

If you are not familiar with Docker, you can still continue with the lab, install MySQL, Postgres, and MongoDB binaries on your computer, and then use appropriate tools to create the databases by importing the following SQL and JSON files into your instances:

Server	**Host**	**Port**	**DatabaseName**	**User**	**Password**	**Initialization File location**
postgres	`127.0.0.1`	`6432`	`beosbank-europa`	`root`	*`Europa01#`*	`docker/beosbank-pgsqldb-europa/beosbank-europa.sql`
mysql	`127.0.0.1`	`3406`	`beosbank-africa`	`root`	*`Africa01#`*	`docker/beosbank-mysqldb-africa/beosbank-africa.sql`
MongoDB	`127.0.0.1`	`28001`	`beosbank-emea-ref`	-	-	`docker/beosbank-mongodb-emea/init.json`

On the contrary, if you are familiar with Docker, just clone the `https://github.com/jbossdevguidebook/chapters/tree/master/ch5` repository and move into the `docker` project subfolder; then, build the entire database using the `docker-compose` command. While writing this book, the docker and `docker-compose` version used is 1.11.2:

```
$docker-compose --version
docker-compose version 1.11.2, build dfed245$

$ cd ch5/docker/
$ docker-compose up --build --force-recreate
```

After running this command, you have three containers running the different databases:

```
enonowog — -bash — 172×40
MacBook-Pro-de-elvadas:~ enonowog$ docker ps
CONTAINER ID    IMAGE                      COMMAND                   CREATED          STATUS          PORTS                        NAMES
12508858b07c    docker_posgres_db_europa   "docker-entrypoint..."    3 minutes ago    Up 3 minutes    0.0.0.0:6432->5432/tcp       docker_posgres_db_europa_1
3b6af150c0da    docker_mysql_db_africa     "docker-entrypoint..."    3 minutes ago    Up 3 minutes    0.0.0.0:3406->3306/tcp       docker_mysql_db_africa_1
5a3ea060fb8e    mongo:3.4.4                "docker-entrypoint..."    3 minutes ago    Up 3 minutes    0.0.0.0:28001->27017/tcp     docker_mongo_db_emea_1
MacBook-Pro-de-elvadas:~ enonowog$
```

These three containers use various techniques to initialize the database content with SQL (MySQL+PostgreSQL) and JSON (MongoDB) files. Let's connect to the servers using the command-line interface to ensure that everything is properly set up:

```
$ mongo --port=28001
MongoDB shell version v3.4.4
connecting to: mongodb://127.0.0.1:28001/
MongoDB server version: 3.4.4
> show databases;
admin                0.000GB
beosbank-emea-ref    0.000GB
local                0.000GB
> use beosbank-emea-ref
switched to db beosbank-emea-ref
> show collections
countries
>
```

The MongoDB is up and running; you can see that the `countries` collection is present in the `beosbank-emea-ref` database:

```
$  mysql -h 127.0.0.1 -P 3406 -u root --password=Africa01#
mysql> show databases;
+--------------------+
| Database           |
+--------------------+
| information_schema |
| beosbank-africa    |
| mysql              |
| performance_schema |
| sys                |
+--------------------+
5 rows in set (0,00 sec)
mysql> use beosbank-africa
mysql> show tables;
+---------------------------+
| Tables_in_beosbank-africa |
+---------------------------+
| AF_CUSTOMER               |
```

```
| AF_MONEYTRANSFER             |
+------------------------------+
2 rows in set (0,01 sec)
```

The `beosbank-africa` has two tables: `AF_CUSTOMER` and `AF_MONEYTRANSFER`; you can do the same for the Europa Postgres DB using `pgsql`:

```
$ psql -h 127.0.0.1 -p 6432 -d beosbank-europa -U root
---Password for user root: Enter the password Europa01#
psql (9.6.2)
beosbank-europa=# \d
             List of relations
 Schema |        Name        | Type  | Owner
--------+--------------------+-------+-------
 public | eu_customer        | table | root
 public | eu_moneytransfer   | table | root
(2 rows)
beosbank-europa=# select * from eu_customer  where ID=1;
 id |  city   | country |       street        |  zip  | birthdate   | firstname
| lastname
----+---------+---------+---------------------+-------+-------------+----------
-+----------
  1 | Berlin | Germany | brand burgStrasse | 10115 | 1985-06-20 | Yanick
| Modjo
(1 row)
beosbank-europa=#
```

The Postgres DB, on the contrary, has the same money transfer and customer schema as the MySQL instance, except for the prefix EU instead of AF to designate European data. We now have a fully working database environment; how do we virtualize this dataset to build a single customer view? This is the main question we will answer in the subsequent sections.

Modeling data sources with JBoss data virtualization

The first step to model a data source is to create a Teiid Model project in JBoss developer studio. In the following lines, we will create a `beosbank-datavirt` project first, and then add a source model to reference transactions from MySQL, Postgres, and MongoDB.

Creating the beosbank-datavirt Teiid Model project

Follow these steps and actions to create a Teiid Model project:

1. Start JBoss Developer Studio.
2. Open the Teiid Designer Perspective: **Menu Windows>Perspective>Open Perspective** > **Others...> Teiid Designer**.
3. The Teiid Designer perspective opens and a set of actions are available through the guides panel:

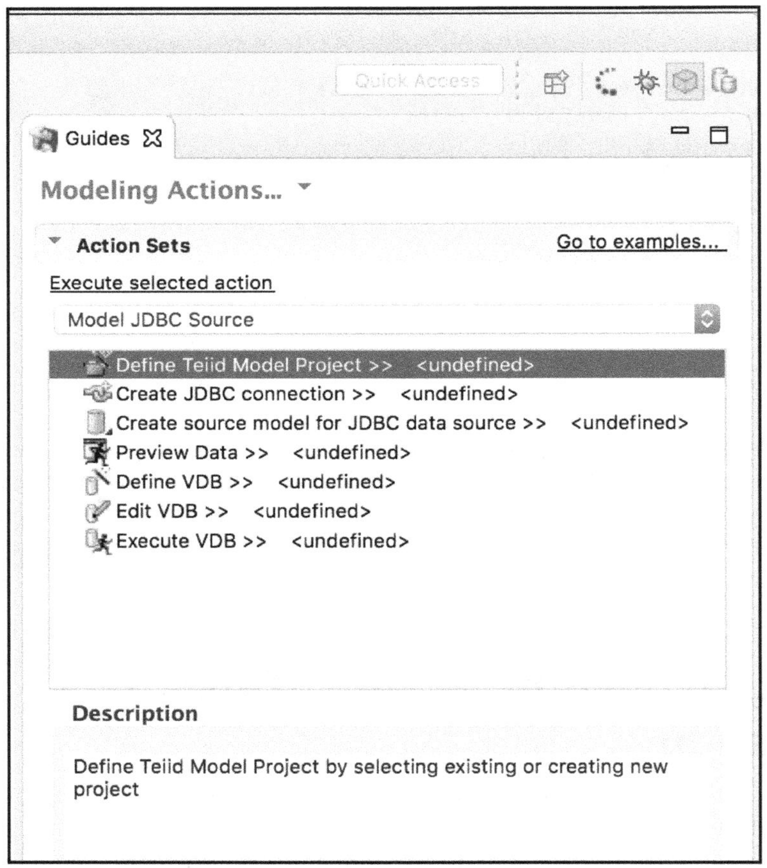

4. Select the first option--**Define Teiid Model Project**--to create the `beosbank-datavirt` project:

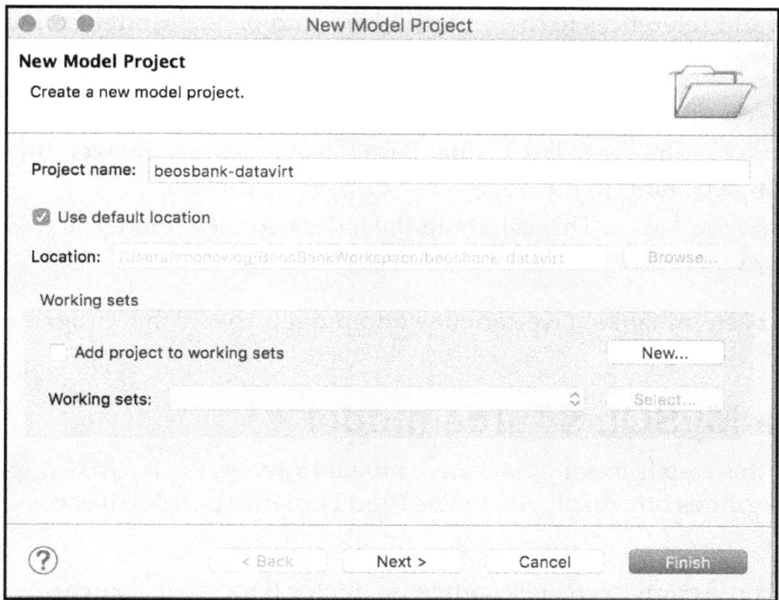

5. Click on the **Next** button after entering the project name:

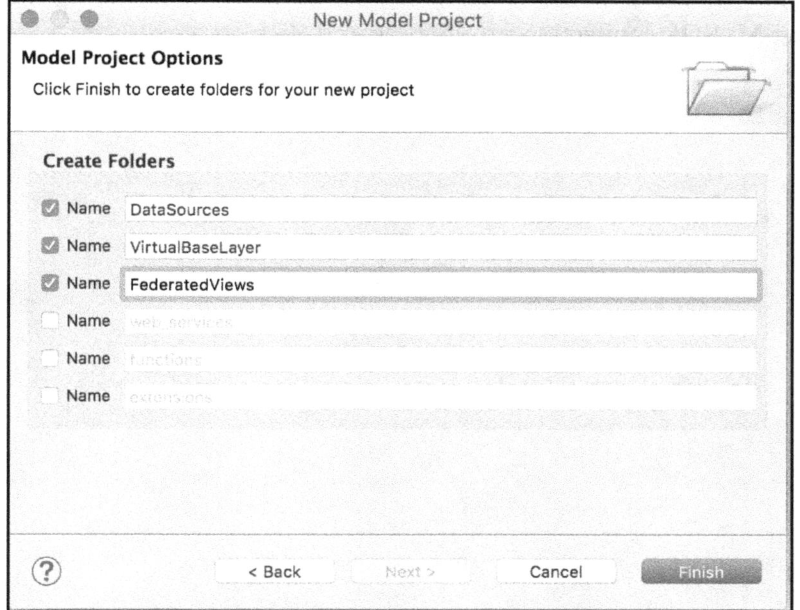

Skip the step to add references to the project, if any, and on the **Model Project Options** screen, only create three folders:

- `Datasources`: This folder will hold the source model for JDBC data sources
- `VirtualBaseLayer`: For Virtual Base Layer: abstraction layer, on which business logic will be built in the `beosbank-datavirt` project
- `FederatedViews`: This is to hold the federated view models we will expose as services

The project has been initialized; we can now add models to enrich it progressively.

Creating a MySQL source model

The purpose of this step is to set up a source model to access the `Beosbank-Mysql` Africa database; in the guides box displayed in the Teiid Designer perspective, click on the following:

1. Click on **Action** to create a source model for JDBC data source--`<undefined>`.
2. A dialog box will appear, asking you to set up your JDBC configuration; we will create a JDBC connection profile to reach the MySQL database.
3. Click on the **New** button.
4. Select **MySQL** connection profile type and click on **Next:**

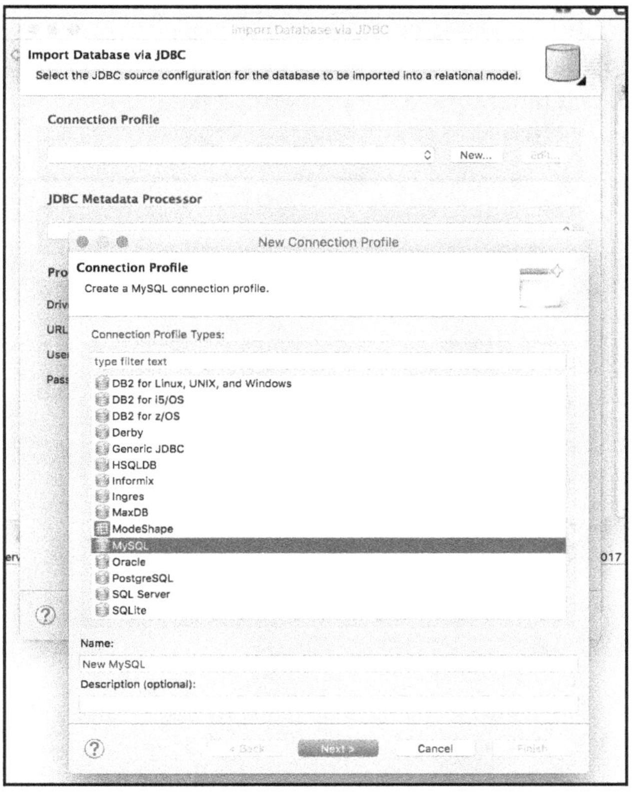

5. Rename your profile `beosbank-mysql-africa`:

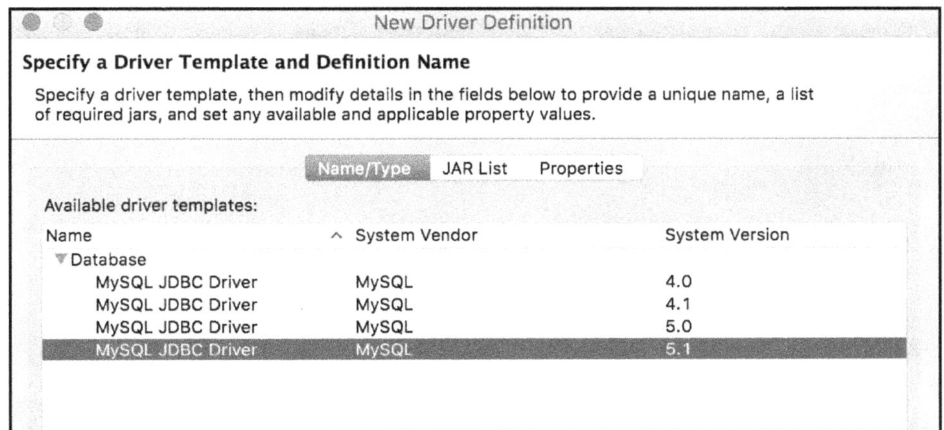

6. Click on the green cross after the driver type to create a new **MySQL 5.1** driver.
7. On the **Name/Type** tab, select **MySQL 5.1**:
8. On the **JAR List** tab, remove the predefined jar and download and add the `mysql-connector-java-5.1.42.jar`:

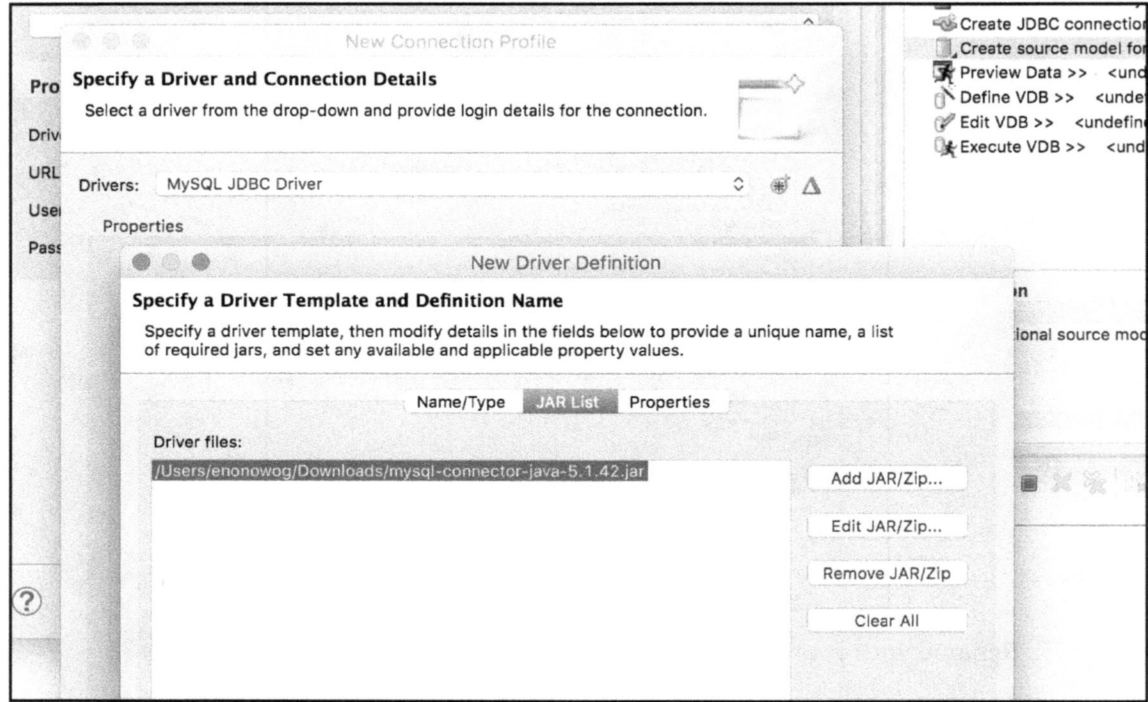

9. Fill the **Properties** tab with the `beosbank-mysql-africa` DB settings and ping the connection:

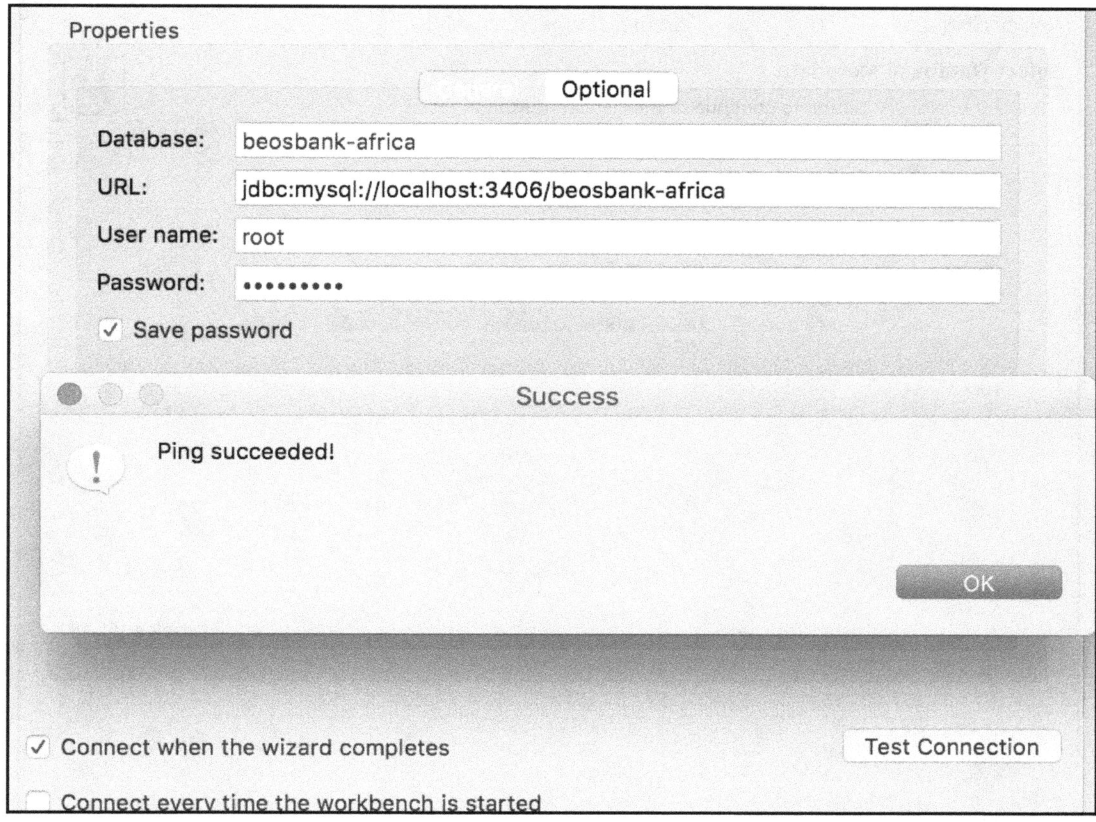

10. Click on OK to close the ping dialog box.

11. Click on **Finish**. The driver is properly registered, and a connection will be performed to fetch database metadata:

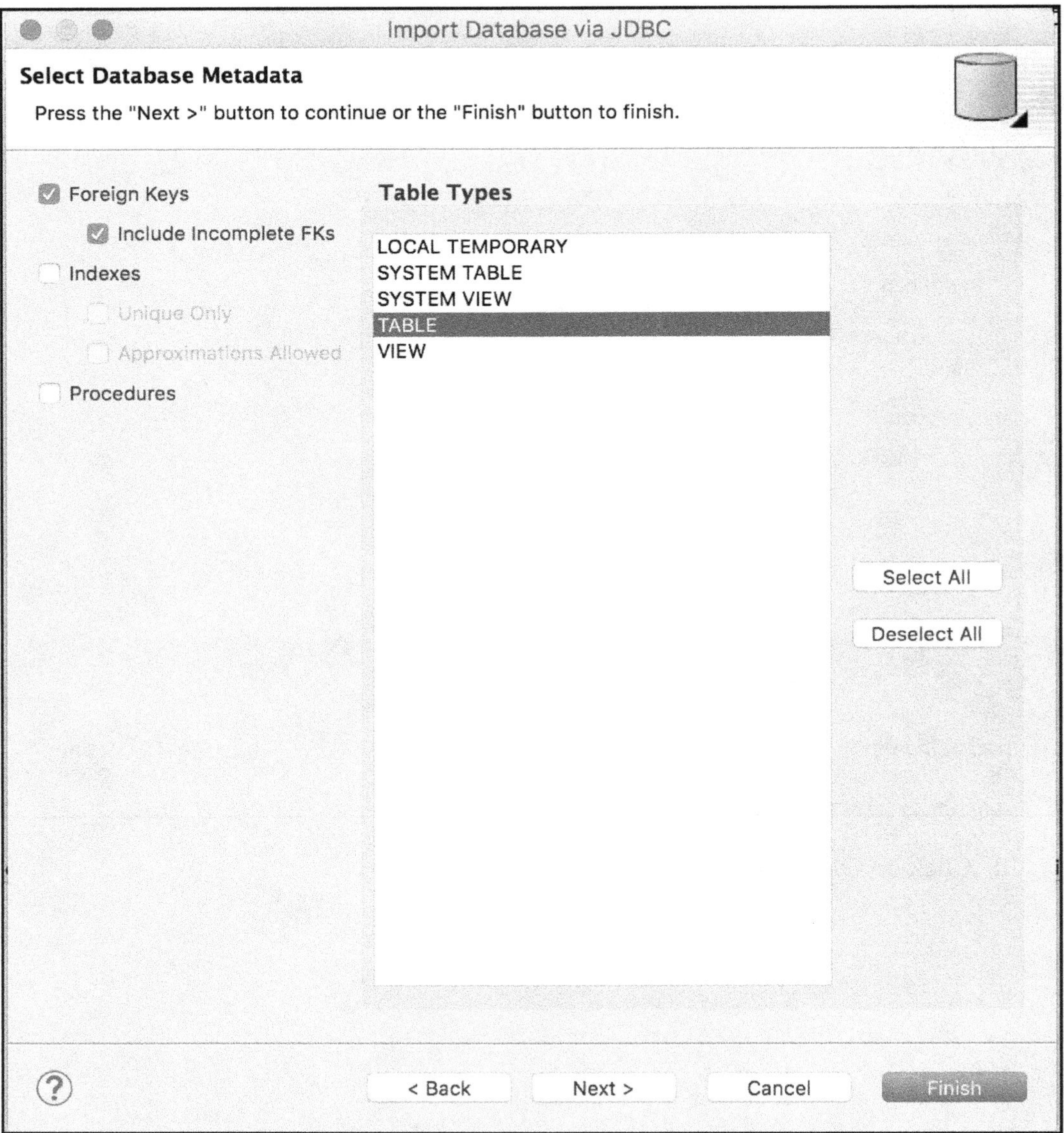

12. We are interested in getting table metadata only, so check **TABLE** and click on **Next:**

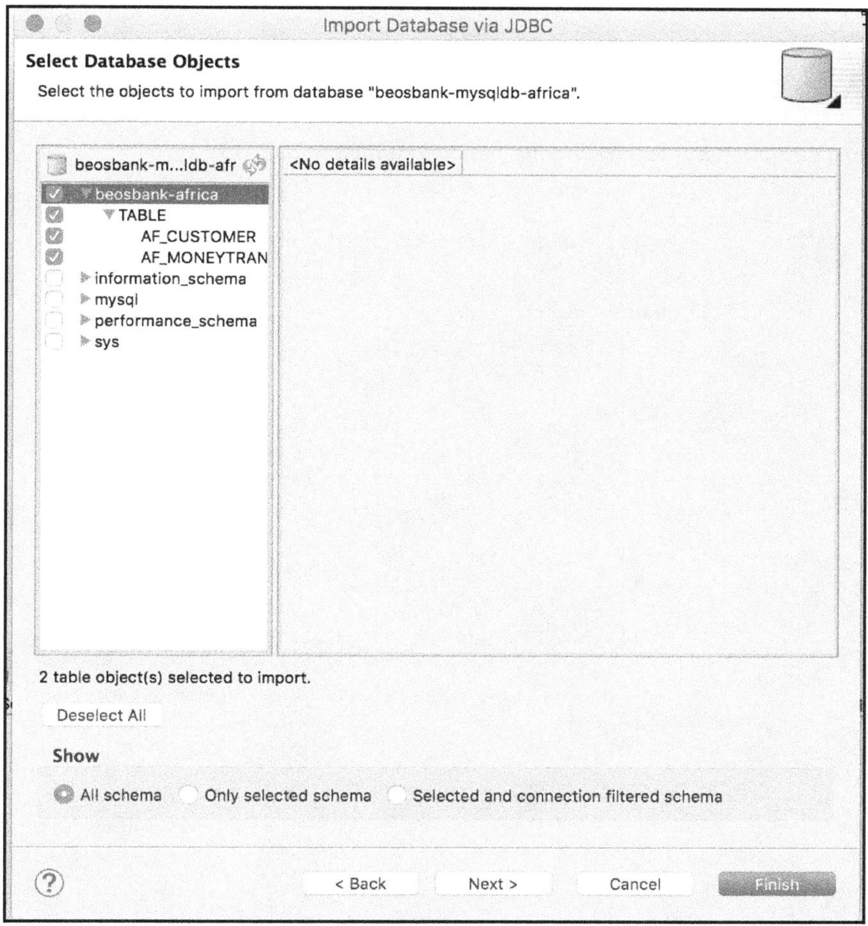

13. Select `AF_CUSTOMER` and `AF_MONEYTRANSFER` and click on **Next**.
14. The next step is to deal with the source model creation:
    - The model will be named `AF_Transactions.xmi`
    - Place your model into the project `DataSources` subfolder
    - Uncheck the **Include Catalog For fully qualified Names** option
    - Enter a JNDI name for the data source to be created--**Beosbank_MySQL_DS**, for example

- Check **Auto-create Data Source**, JDV will automatically create a data source for this connection and deploy it on the default Teiid server instance:

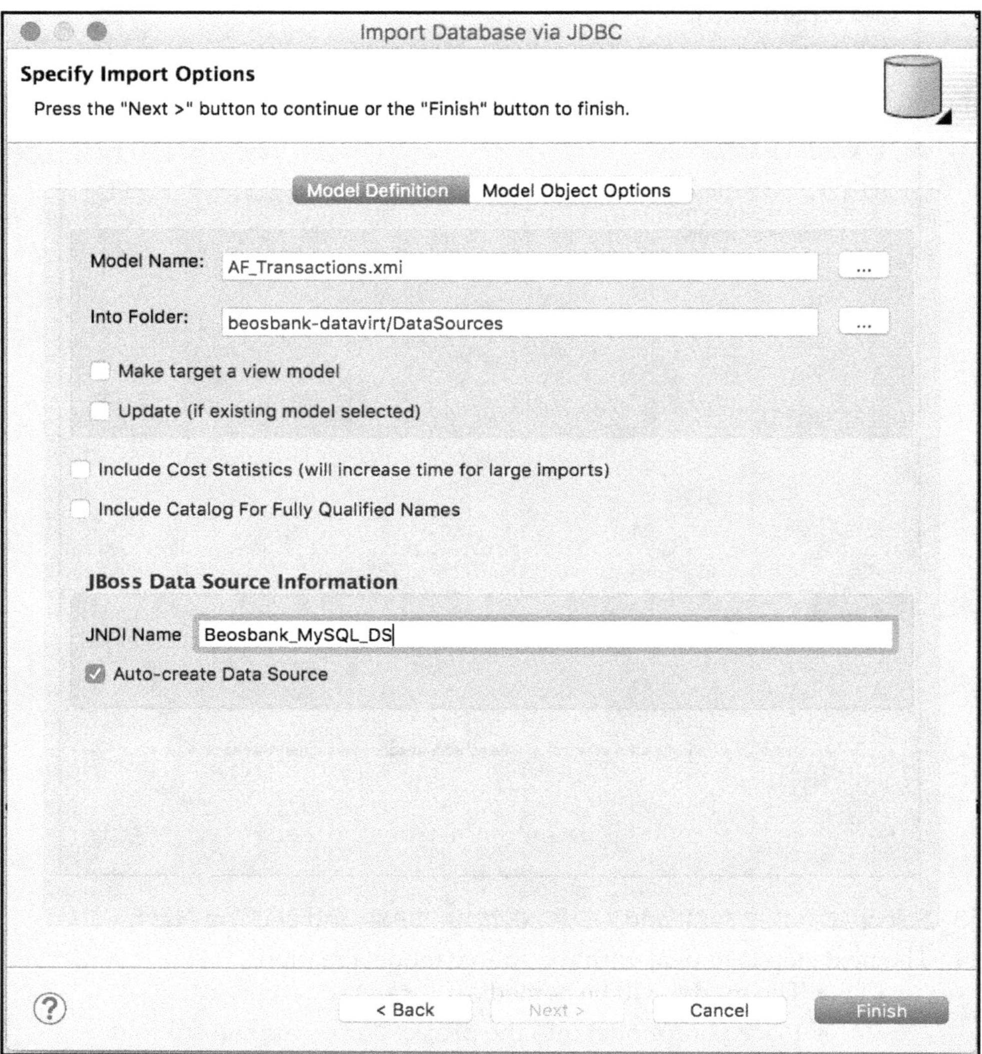

The `AF_Transactions` source model is created, and its tables are displayed with their respective fields and relations:

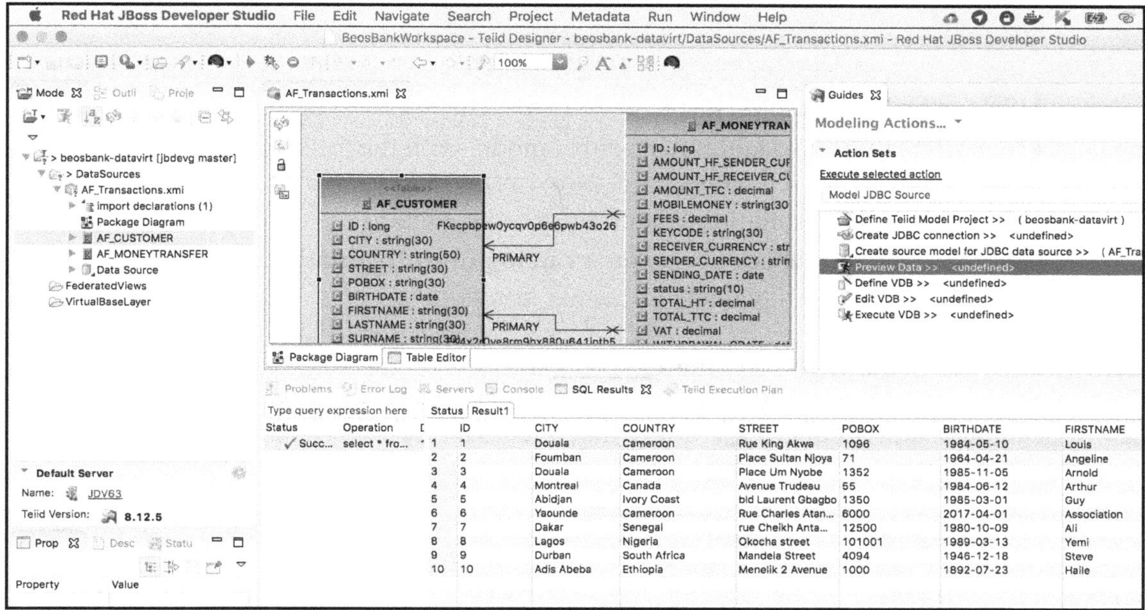

	ID	CITY	COUNTRY	STREET	POBOX	BIRTHDATE	FIRSTNAME
1	1	Douala	Cameroon	Rue King Akwa	1096	1984-05-10	Louis
2	2	Foumban	Cameroon	Place Sultan Njoya	71	1964-04-21	Angeline
3	3	Douala	Cameroon	Place Um Nyobe	1352	1985-11-05	Arnold
4	4	Montreal	Canada	Avenue Trudeau	55	1984-06-12	Arthur
5	5	Abidjan	Ivory Coast	bld Laurent Gbagbo	1350	1985-03-01	Guy
6	6	Yaounde	Cameroon	Rue Charles Atan...	6000	2017-04-01	Association
7	7	Dakar	Senegal	rue Cheikh Anta...	12500	1980-10-09	Ali
8	8	Lagos	Nigeria	Okocha street	101001	1989-03-13	Yemi
9	9	Durban	South Africa	Mandela Street	4094	1946-12-18	Steve
10	10	Adis Abeba	Ethiopia	Menelik 2 Avenue	1000	1892-07-23	Haile

Using the `Preview Data >>` action, you can view the data stored in a source model. Select the `AF_Transactions.xmi` model and then select the `AF_Customer` table; Teiid deploys a data source and runs SQL to return data. This is the final step to register a MySQL source model in JBoss data virtualization; in the following sections, we will cover steps to add the Postgres Europa database.

Creating a Postgres source model

The steps to reference the Europa database are very similar to what was done with the `beosbank-mysql-africa` database:

- Create a connection profile for Postgres with the name `beosbank-posgresdb-europa`
- Create a new JDBC Driver with the dependency `postgresql-42.1.1.jar`

- Fill in the driver connection properties:
  - Database: `beosbank-europa`
  - URL: `jdbc:postgresql://localhost:6432/beosbank-europa`
  - Username: `root` and Password: `Europa01#`
- Select the Public tables: `eu_customer` and `eu_moneytransfer`
- Associate these two tables to a source model with the following configuration:
  - Model name: `EU_Transactions.xmi`
  - Destination Folder: `beosbank-datavirt/DataSources`
  - Uncheck the **Include catalog for fully qualified Names** box
  - JNDI Name: `beosbank_POSGRES_DS`

Once completed, you can preview the `keycode` attribute on the `EU_MoneyTransfer` table. To do that, right-click on the `EU_moneytransfer` table, **Modeling>Preview Data**. A dialog box appears with a predefined SQL query that fetches all the rows from the selected table. Apply a filter to select only the transaction's KeyCode:

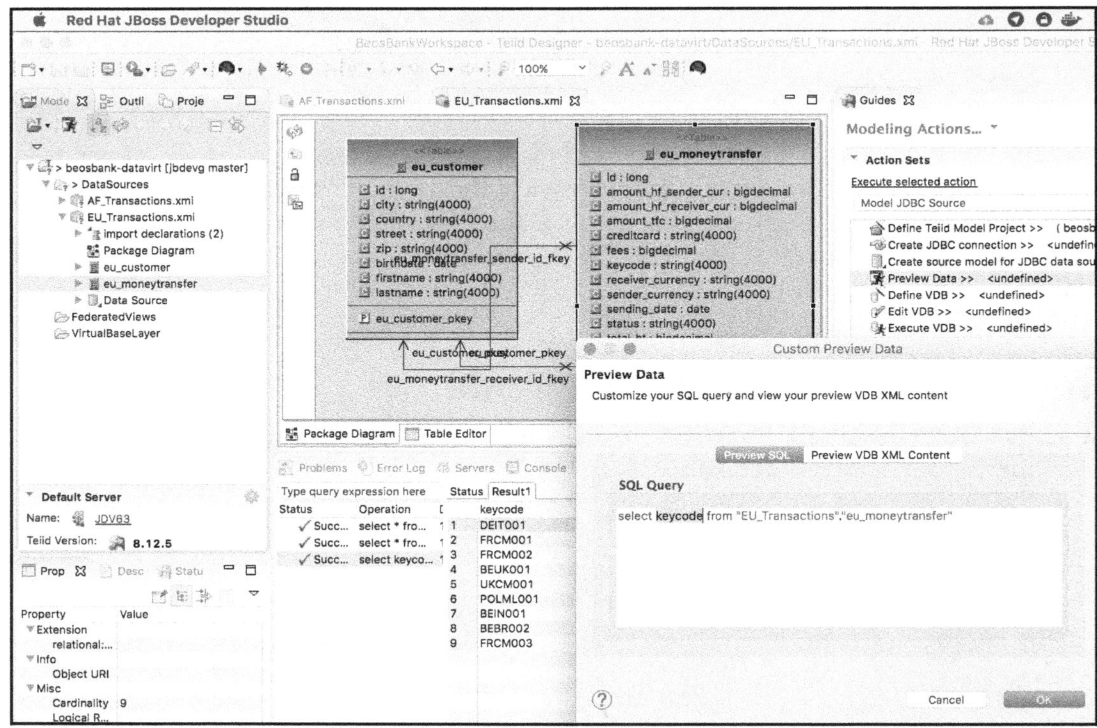

Creating a MongoDB source model

To establish a connection to the Beosbank EMEA ref MongoDB, use the Teiid connection importer. Rigth-click in your **workspace>Import Teiid Connection** >**Source Model**, and create a new data source with the following configurations:

- Name: `beosbank-MONGO-DS`
- Driver: Select the `mongodb` driver in the drop-down list
- Data source properties:
    - URL: `mongodb://127.0.0.1:28001/beosbank-emea-ref`
    - Database: `beosbank-emea-ref`

Then, use the create source model from the Teiid data source DDL action to create a model:

- Location: `beosbank-datavirt/DataSources`
- Name: `EMEA_REF`
- The tools automatically detect the `Countries` collection in the MongoStore and create a Countries Table in the `EMEA_REF` model
- Rename the default ID column `_id` in the table countries table to `countries_id`; the Mongo translator automatically uses `TABLENAME_ID` to map the `_id` attribute:

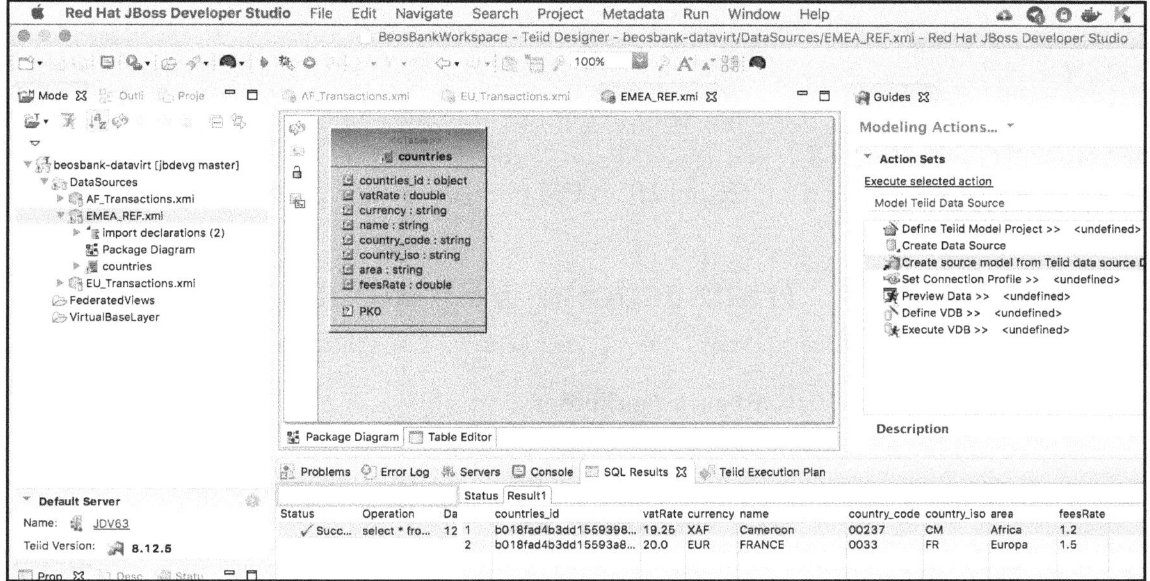

With a Mongo command line, you can check the `countries` collection, as follows, to confirm that the Datavirt component is working with live data from the Mongo Source:

```
db.countries.find()
{ "_id" : ObjectId("5915ddb3d4fa18b08bd18239"), "vatRate" : 19.25,
"currency" : "XAF", "name" : "Cameroon", "country_code" : "00237",
"country_iso" : "CM", "area" : "Africa", "feesRate" : 1.2 }
{ "_id" : ObjectId("5915ddb3d4fa18b08bd1823a"), "vatRate" : 20, "currency"
: "EUR", "name" : "FRANCE", "country_code" : "0033", "country_iso" : "FR",
"area" : "Europa", "feesRate" : 1.5 }
...
```

In this section, you learned how to create a source model from various databases: MySQL, Postgres, MongoDB. JBoss Data Virtualization relies on JDBC and can then support a lot of target platforms. What happens if the physical model is changed outside JBoss data virtualization? Any change in the original source model, undoubtedly, has an impact on the views defined in JDV; to reduce this impact, JBDV is recommended to create an abstraction stack, called Virtual Base Layer, between the source model and other views.

Building Virtual Base Layers

A Virtual Base Layer isolates higher-level view models from changes in the source model; it can be created by combining or transforming the existing source model with others. Virtual Base Layers also support a lot of features, including data mapping, data conversion, column renaming, and data type transformation. When designing a virtual database, it is a good approach to rely only on Virtual Base Layers to build high-level and presentation views. In the following section, we will create a virtual base layer for all the previously defined source models, (`AF_Transactions`, `EU_Transactions` and `EMEA_REF`). Virtual Base Layers will be stored in the `VirtualBaseLayer` project subfolder. They will be created by transforming the associated source model and be prefixed with `_VBL`.

Creating the AF_Transactions_VBL model

Apply the following actions to create the `AF_Transactions_VBL` model:

- Right-click on **VirtualBaseLayerFolder**
- New `Teiid Metadata Model`
- Select the **Relational/View** model option

- We will create `AF_Transactions_VBL` model from scratch for this first model; keep the Select model builder field mpty as on the following figure .
- Click on **Next**, then select `AF_Transactions.xmi` as the source model, and click on **Finish**:

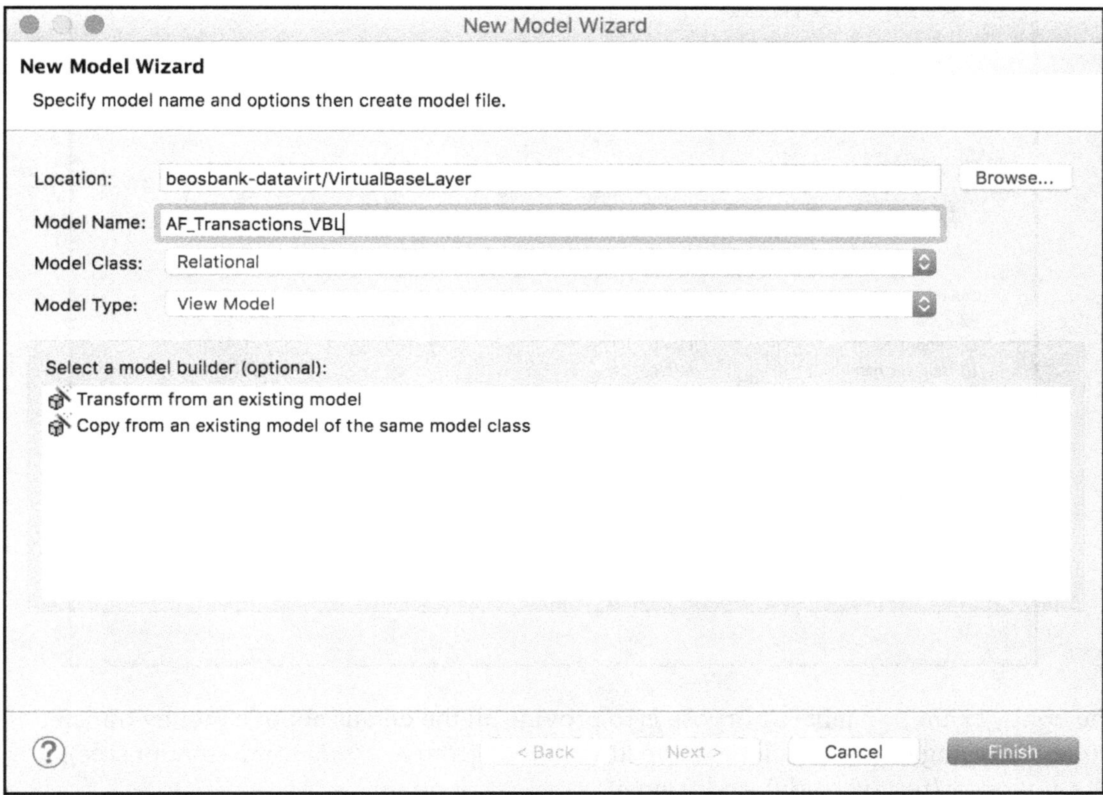

The model has been created and is empty. Now, add a new table to the VBL Model: **New Child** > **Table**:

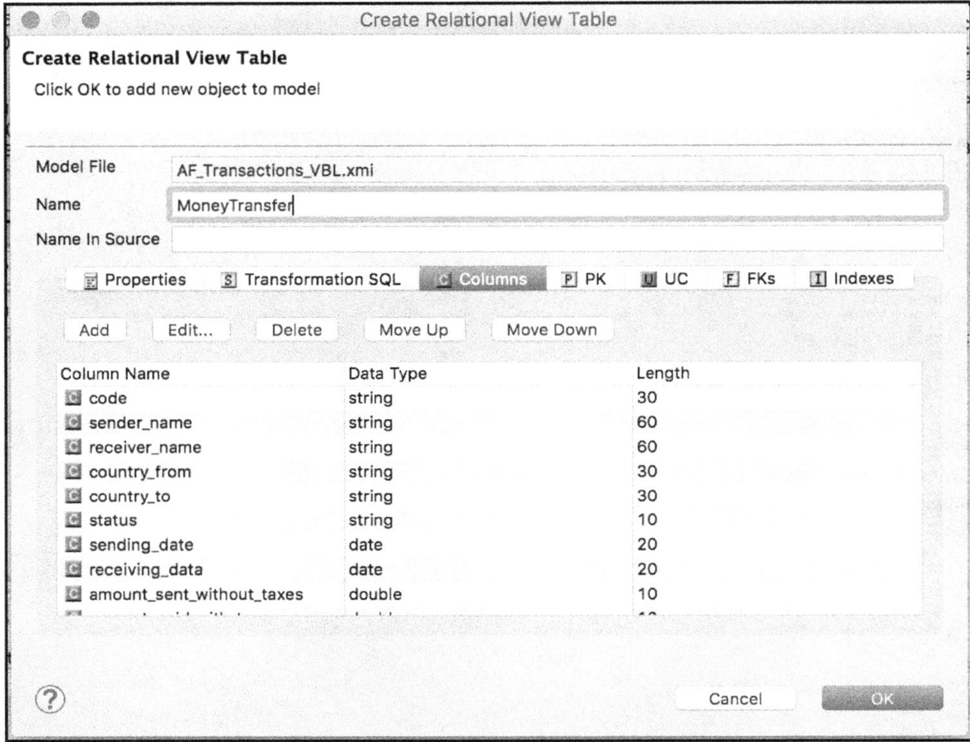

The `MoneyTransfer` table's purpose is to provide all the details about a money transfer request in a single row. It will be mapped with data from `AF_Customer` (sender side), `AF_Customer` (receiver side), and from `AF_MoneyTransfer`.

- Click on the transformation diagram link of the table
- Drag and drop the `AF_Customer` and `AF_Customer` tables (receiver link of the association with `AF_MoneyTransfer`) to the transformation diagram

- Drag and drop the `AF_Customer` table again (sender link of the association with `AF_MoneyTransfer`); an alias is required, so enter sender:

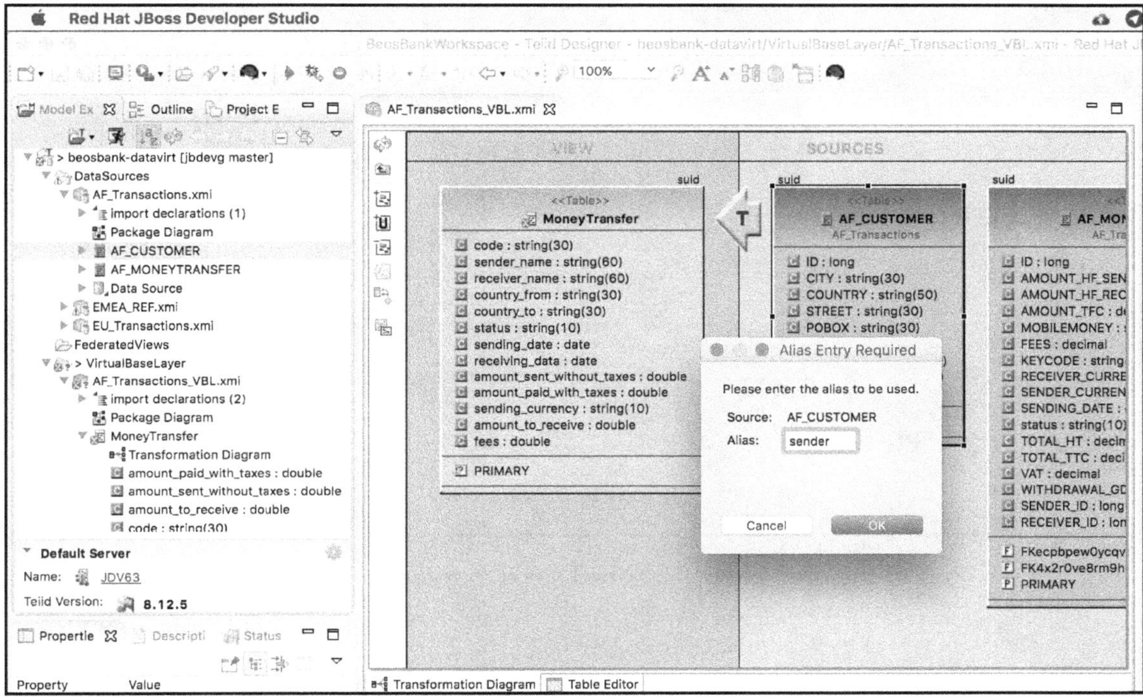

Edit the transformation symbol query to map all the output fields:

```
SELECT
money.KEYCODE AS code, CONCAT(sender.SURNAME, CONCAT('   ',
CONCAT(sender.FIRSTNAME, CONCAT(' ', sender.LASTNAME)))) AS sender_name,
CONCAT(receiver.FIRSTNAME, CONCAT(' ', receiver.LASTNAME)) AS
receiver_name, receiver.COUNTRY AS country_to, sender.COUNTRY AS
country_from, money.status AS status, money.AMOUNT_HF_SENDER_CUR AS
amount_sent_without_taxes, money.SENDER_CURRENCY AS sending_currency,
money.SENDING_DATE AS sending_date, money.AMOUNT_HF_RECEIVER_CUR AS
amount_to_receive, money.FEES AS fees, money.VAT AS vat, money.TOTAL_TTC AS
amount_paid_with_taxes, money.RECEIVER_CURRENCY AS receiving_currency,
money.WITHDRAWAL_GDATE AS receiving_date
 FROM
AF_Transactions.AF_CUSTOMER AS receiver, AF_Transactions.AF_MONEYTRANSFER
AS money, AF_Transactions.AF_CUSTOMER AS sender
 WHERE
  (receiver.ID = money.RECEIVER_ID) AND (sender.ID = money.SENDER_ID)
```

Save the model and preview the data. Data from `Customer` and `MoneyTransfer` is aggregated to produce the following results:

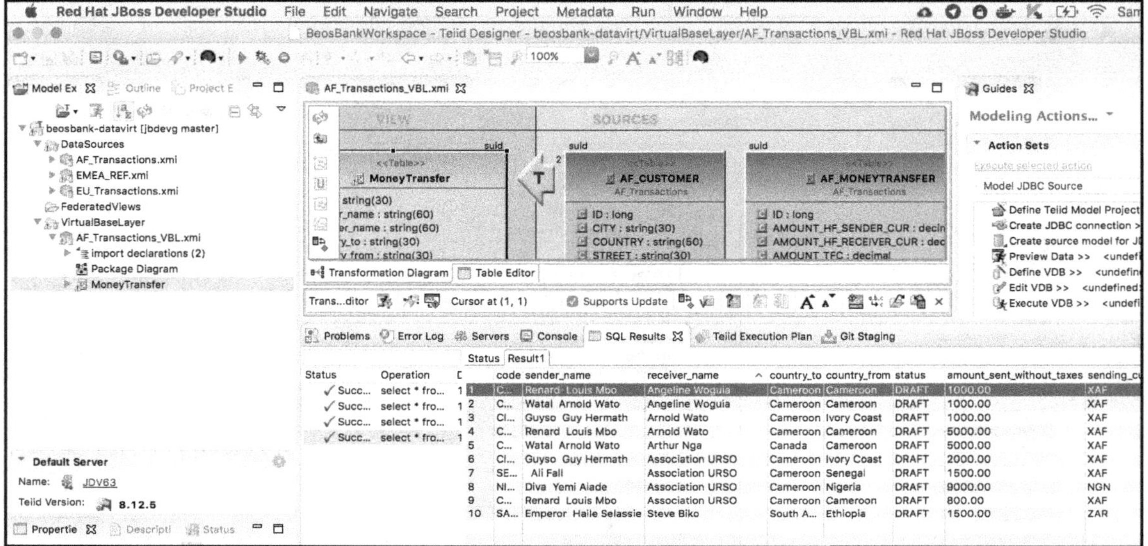

Repeat the previously described steps to create `EU_Transactions_VB.xmi` in `beosbank-datavirt/VirtualBaseLayer`.

Remember that there is no SURNAME field in the EU_Customer table, so adjust your query to match the EU fields. Once completed, the MoneyTransfer table's transformation diagram and data preview should look like this:

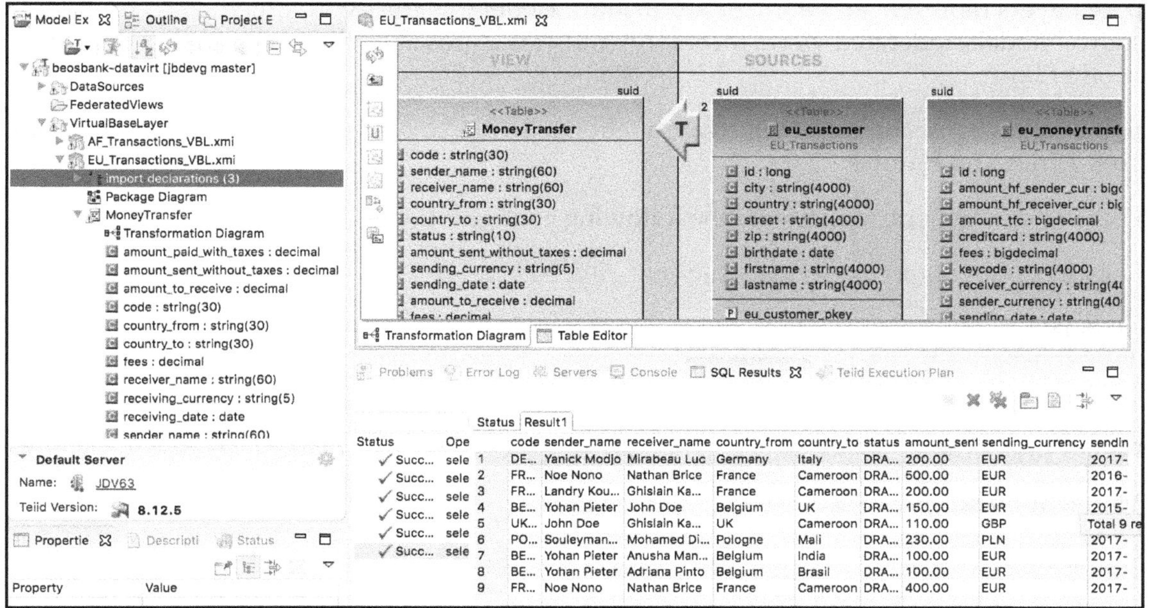

This concludes our section on Virtual Base Layer modeling. Here, we explored the purpose of a Virtual Base Layer and implemented two Virtual Base Layers for EU and AF transactions using various tables from source models; the simplest approach to create a simple VBL is to duplicate or transform the source model. A Virtual Base Layer should act as the foundation for federated views and a virtual database. The next section will explain how to create a federated view and deploy a virtual database.

Building and deploying federated data views

Depending on your organization, you can define different sets of data views or layers for your JDV projects. Federated views are built on top of Virtual Base Layers; while Virtual Base Layers represent an intermediate abstract model to reduce coupling top layers and source models, federated views mostly refer to data exposed to clients or provide data to another layer.

In the following section, we will create a federated view to consolidate all transactions from both Africa and Europe:

Create a new generic model with the following configuration:

Location: `beosbank-datavirt/FederatedViews`

ModelName: `Transactions.xmi`

ModelClass: `Relational`

Model Type: `View Model`

Model Builder: `Transfrom from an existing model`

Source model to transform: `AF_Transactions_VBL.xmi`

Now, open the MoneyTransfer table transformation diagram of the newly created model, drag and drop the `EU_Transactions_VBL.MoneyTransfer` table in sources, and update the query to perform a `UNION ALL`:

```
SELECT * FROM AF_Transactions_VBL.MoneyTransfer
UNION ALL
SELECT * FROM EU_Transactions_VBL.MoneyTransfer
```

Save the model and run a data preview. All the transactions, from both Africa and Europe, are displayed:

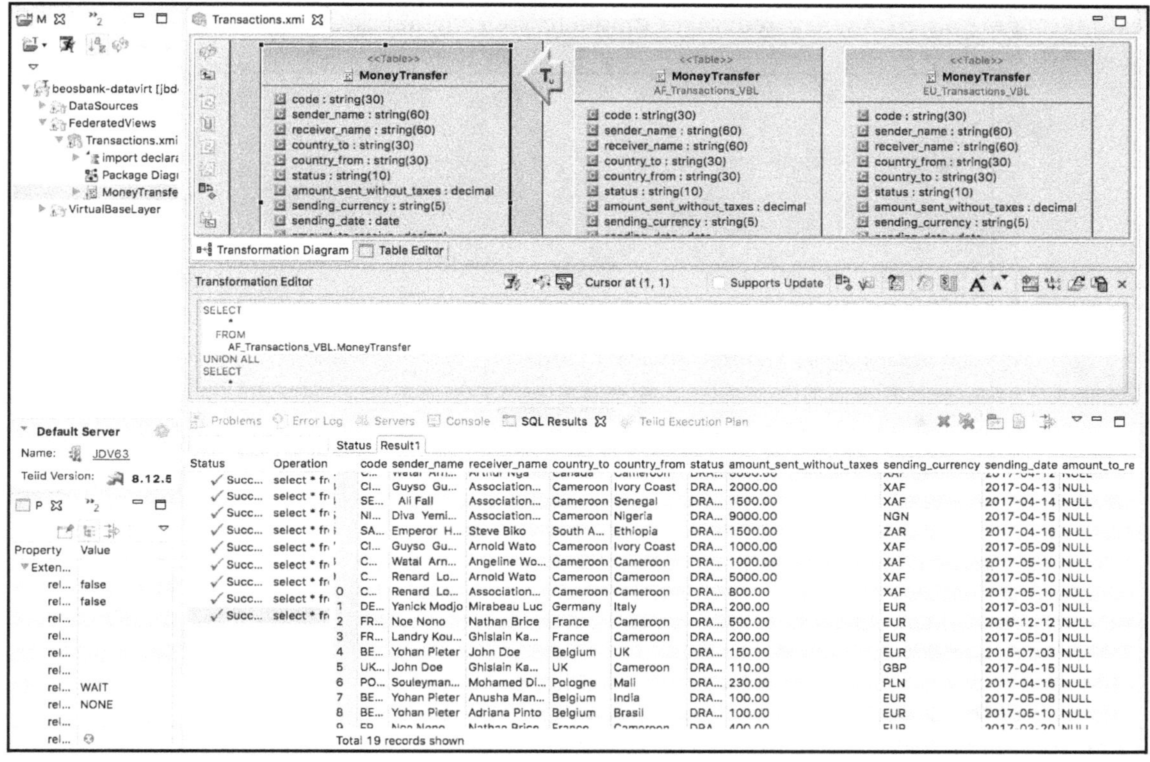

From layer to layer, we have progressively built a loosely coupled EMEA money transfer federated view that can be exposed to the company's data science department. In order to expose this model, we first need to create a virtual database.

Right-click on the `beosbank-datavirt` project and create a new Teiid VDB.

Add the `Transactions.xmi` federated model to your virtual database and click on **Finish**:

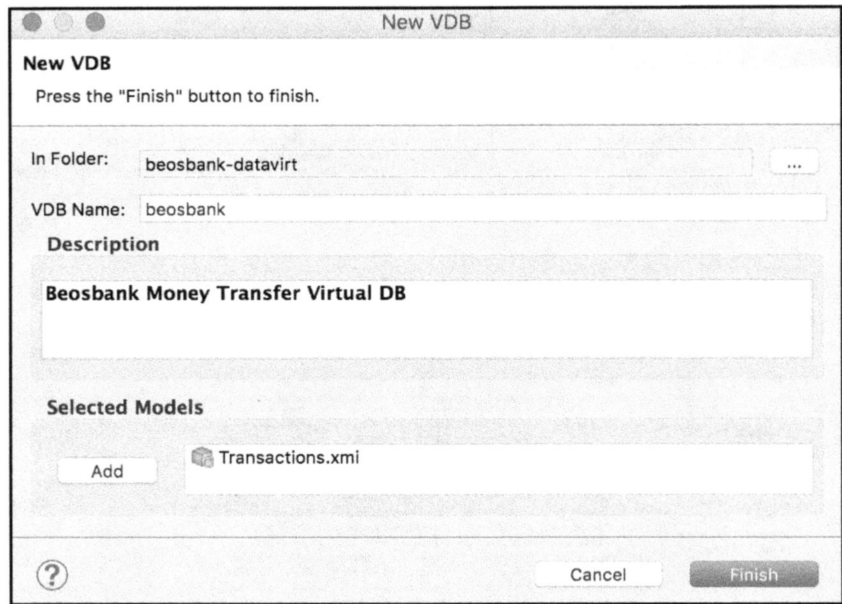

A `beosbank.vdb` file is created at the project root folder; right-click on it and launch the **Modeling>Deploy** action. A dialog box will ask to create the associated data source; answer with yes and create it. The virtual database first version is deployed with its models and their dependencies; you can see the VDB lifecycle updates in the server logs:

```
16:05:25,904 INFO  [org.teiid.RUNTIME] (teiid-async-threads - 2) TEIID50030
VDB beosbank.1 model "Transactions" metadata loaded. End Time: 13/05/17
16:0516:05:25,932 INFO  [org.teiid.RUNTIME.VDBLifeCycleListener] (teiid-
async-threads - 2) TEIID40003 VDB beosbank.1 is set to ACTIVE16:06:02,070
INFO  [org.jboss.as.connector.subsystems.datasources] (MSC service thread
1-2) JBAS010400: Source de données liée [java:/beosbank]
```

Once the VDB is deployed, there are various ways to access data: SQL Scrapbooks in JBoss Developer Studio, the OData `REST` protocol, or JDBC. We will explore the various options in the next section.

Accessing virtual databases

When developing virtual databases with JDV, the simplest option to quickly check model data is to use the data preview function. In a virtual database (VDB), a user needs to have access to a SQL Scrapbook integrated UI to query VDBs; this feature internally uses JDBC and Teiid User settings.

Right-click on your **VDB>Modeling>Execute** VDB. The VDB is first deployed on the default Teiid server instance, and an empty SQL Scrapbook--ready to use--is opened to run your queries:

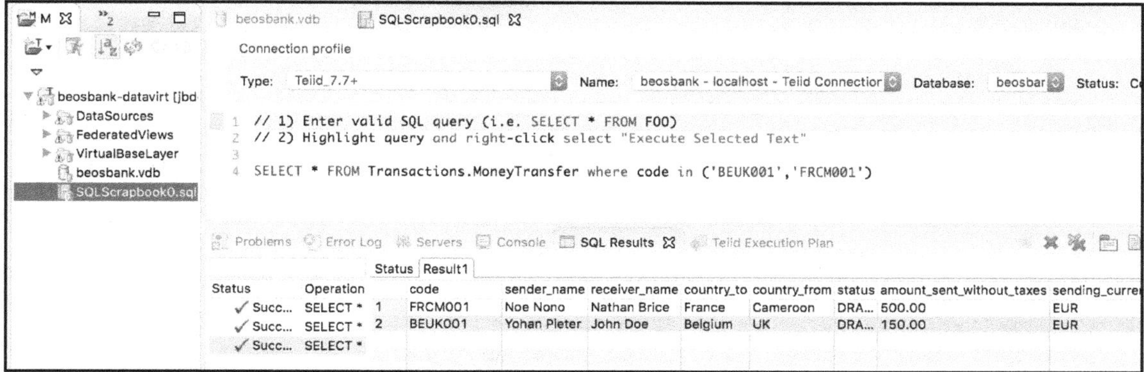

Enter various queries and execute the selected one using *Alt*+*X*.

This option is for testing purposes while setting up a VDB. Data consumers cannot rely on this approach to query VDBs in their applications; to do this, they can use the `OData/JDBC` protocol.

The ODATA application exposes every VDB as a REST resource; authorized users (`teiidUser/Admin01#`) can access `Collections` through `REST`:

- `http://localhost:8080/odata/beosbank.1/` will be the root URL to access the VDB
- `http://localhost:8080/odata/beosbank.1/Transactions.MoneyTransfer` will return the whole MoneyTransfer collection

- `http://localhost:8080/odata/beosbank.1/Transactions.MoneyTransfer('BEBR002')` will return details on MoneyTransfer with code=`BEBR002`:


```
<?xml version='1.0' encoding='utf-8'?><entry
xmlns="http://www.w3.org/2005/Atom"
xmlns:m="http://schemas.microsoft.com/ado/2007/08/dataservices/metadata"
xmlns:d="http://schemas.microsoft.com/ado/2007/08/dataservices"
xml:base="http://localhost:8080/odata/beosbank.1/"><id>http://localhost:808
0/odata/beosbank.1/Transactions.MoneyTransfer('BEBR002')</id><title
type="text"/><updated>2017-05-13T14:48:01Z</updated><author><name/></author
><link rel="edit"  href="Transactions.MoneyTransfer('BEBR002')"/><category
term="Transactions.MoneyTransfer"
scheme="http://schemas.microsoft.com/ado/2007/08/dataservices/scheme"/><con
tent
type="application/xml"><m:properties><d:code>BEBR002</d:code><d:sender_name
>Yohan Pieter</d:sender_name><d:receiver_name>Adriana
Pinto</d:receiver_name><d:country_to>Belgium</d:country_to><d:country_from>
Brasil</d:country_from><d:status>DRAFT</d:status><d:amount_sent_without_tax
es
m:type="Edm.Decimal">100.00</d:amount_sent_without_taxes><d:sending_currenc
y>EUR</d:sending_currency><d:sending_date
m:type="Edm.DateTime">2017-05-10T00:00</d:sending_date><d:amount_to_receive
m:type="Edm.Decimal" m:null="true"/><d:fees m:type="Edm.Decimal"
m:null="true"/><d:vat m:type="Edm.Decimal"
m:null="true"/><d:amount_paid_with_taxes m:type="Edm.Decimal"
m:null="true"/><d:receiving_currency>BRL</d:receiving_currency><d:receiving
_date m:type="Edm.DateTime"
m:null="true"/></m:properties></content></entry>
```


Accessing a VDB using JDBC is very similar to how you use JDBC to access a traditional RDBMS:

- Add `teiid jdbc library` to your client project, as in the `beosbank-datavirt-client` project, `mvn:org.jboss.teiid/teiid-jdbc/8.12.5.redhat-8`
- Get a SQL connection from the DriverManager with the Teiid JDBC URL as parameter

- The Teiid URL pattern is `jdbc:teiid:VDB-NAME@mm[s]://HOSTNAME:PORT;[prop-name=prop-value;]*`:

```
String url
="jdbc:teiid:beosbank.1@mm://127.0.0.1:31000;user=teiidUser;password=Admin0
1#";
Connection connection = DriverManager.getConnection(url);
Statement st = connection.createStatement();
 ResultSet rs = st.executeQuery("SELECT * FROM
Transactions.MoneyTransfer"); while(rs.next()){
 System.out.println(String.format("|%10s|%-25s|%6s|",
rs.getString("code"),rs.getString("sender_name"),rs.getDouble("amount_sent_
without_taxes")));}
#Results.
|    DEIT001|Yanick Modjo             | 200.0|
|    FRCM001|Noe Nono                 | 500.0|
|    FRCM002|Landry Kouam             | 200.0|
|    BEUK001|Yohan Pieter             | 150.0|
...
```

JBoss data virtualization provides not only a REST and JDBC transparent access to your Virtual database content, but also a lot of advanced features, such as virtual procedures.

Virtual procedures

Virtual procedures in JBoss data virtualization help in building a custom function to execute complex data processing with non-proprietary features, as in stored procedures in Rational Database Management Systems. Virtual procedures are written in a language similar to SQL, called JDV procedural language. Virtual procedures take zeros or many input parameters, and return a result set type. To create a virtual procedure on models, follow these steps:

1. Create a new procedure child on your model.

2. Add input and output columns; the virtual procedure should return a result set if any data is to be returned:

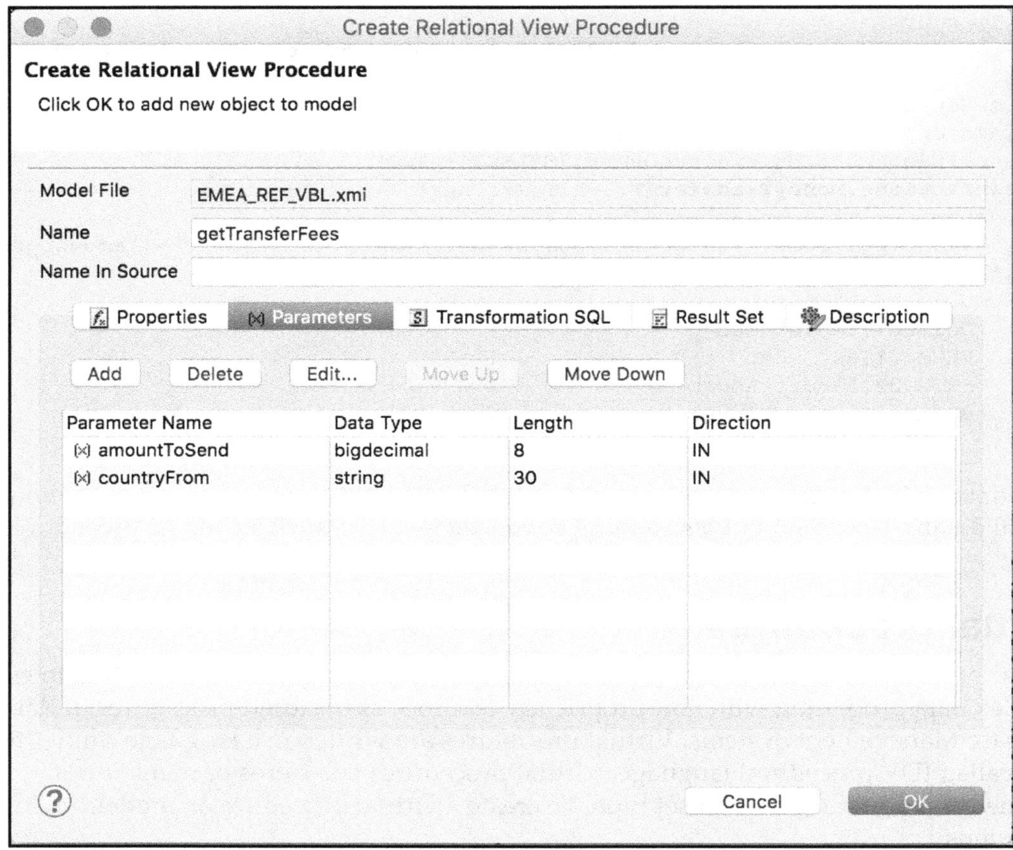

3. Customize the query to perform your business logic:

```
BEGIN
 SELECT ((EMEA_REF_VBL.countries.feesRate *
EMEA_REF_VBL.getTransferFees.amountToSend) / 100.00) AS feesToPay FROM
EMEA_REF_VBL.countries WHERE EMEA_REF_VBL.countries.name =
EMEA_REF_VBL.getTransferFees.countryFrom;
END
```

4. Test your virtual procedure; use the `EXECUTE` command in the SQL Scrapbook:

```
EXEC EMEA_REF_VBL.getTransferFees(50.00,'FRANCE');
```

The virtual procedure has been executed and the results panel displays the results, as illustrated:

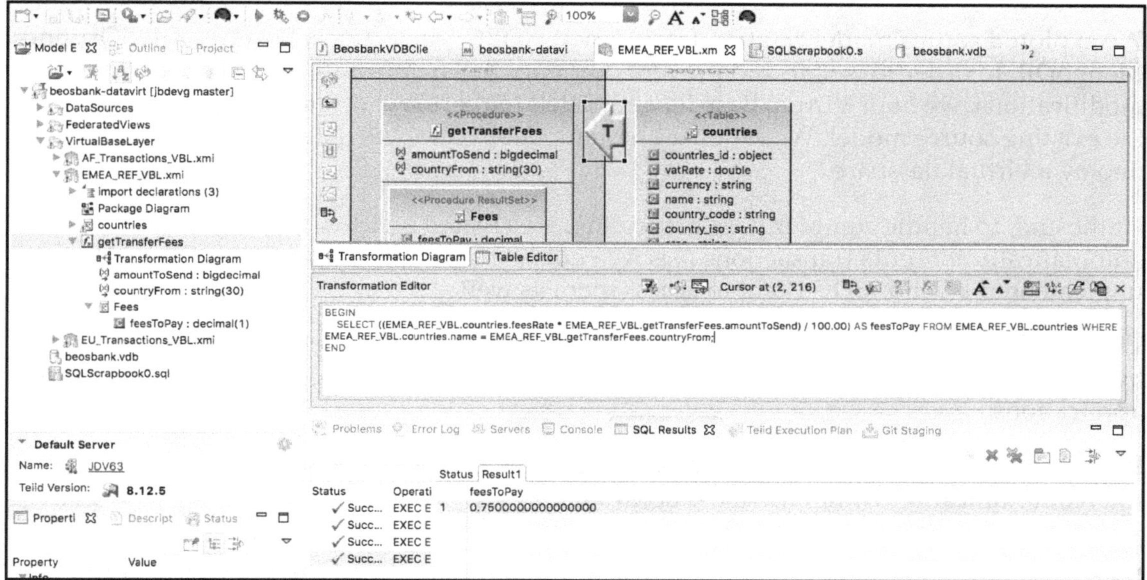

The exec can be wrapped in a `SELECT` query to return specific fields of the returned result set.

In this section, we learned how to create and execute a virtual procedure in JDV. Virtual procedures are very similar to store procedures, except that they are mainly used as functions and should return a result set.

Update the `Transactions.MoneyTransfer` transformation diagram to automatically populate the fees amount returned by the virtual procedure in the fees field.

Summary

In this chapter, we introduced the virtualization data management approach and established the main differences between ETL and data federation. We installed and set up a clean JBoss data virtualization development environment, and both Server and IDE features to build a custom virtual database step by step.

We explored source model creation from various JDBC connections: Postgres, MySQL, and MongoDB. In order to isolate and prevent our federate layer from source model modifications, we built Virtual Base Layer models, either from scratch or by transforming the existing source model. We set up a union model to combine data from two sources and deploy a virtual database.

At the end, to handle complex data processing, we created a virtual procedure to automatically compute transactions fees. We queried virtual databases with OData Rest and implemented a Teiid JBDC client to access them as well.

This concludes the data management section; now that we have caches and live data served by virtual databases, it will be interesting to see how they can be exchanged with enterprise applications.

In `Chapter 6`, *Integrating Applications with JBoss Fuse,* we will cover system intercommunication within the JBoss ecosystem.

6
Integrating Applications with JBoss Fuse

In `Chapter 5`, *Exposing Data as a Service,* we covered enterprise data integration in the data center through virtualization. Data virtualization is centered on data views and works on the principle of providing data on demand and covers both internal and external data sources. Most integration use cases with data beyond the data center are currently governed by some operational constraints that are not completely fulfilled or met by data virtualization. Among them we can list

- Complex event processing
- Messaging and interoperability
- Routing and service orchestration

To covers all these constraints and more, computer science invented the Enterprise Services Bus (ESB) to provide a reliable communication layer between two or more enterprise components. ESB defines a set of rules and principles for integrating numerous applications together over a bus-like infrastructure. The JBoss ecosystem provides a lightweight and modular service bus, called JBoss Fuse. This chapter is organized around application and system integration with JBoss Fuse. After a brief presentation of the JBoss fuse architecture, the chapter will progressively teach you how to develop, deploy, and monitor various OSGi integration scenarios on the JBoss Fuse Platform. The chapter also explores some integration patterns with Apache Camel through illustrated samples from the global integration project.

JBoss Fuse architecture

JBoss Fuse is a combination of several open source technologies, including **Apache Camel**, **Apache CXF**, **Apache ActiveMQ**, **Apache Karaf**, and **Fabric8** in a single integrated distribution:

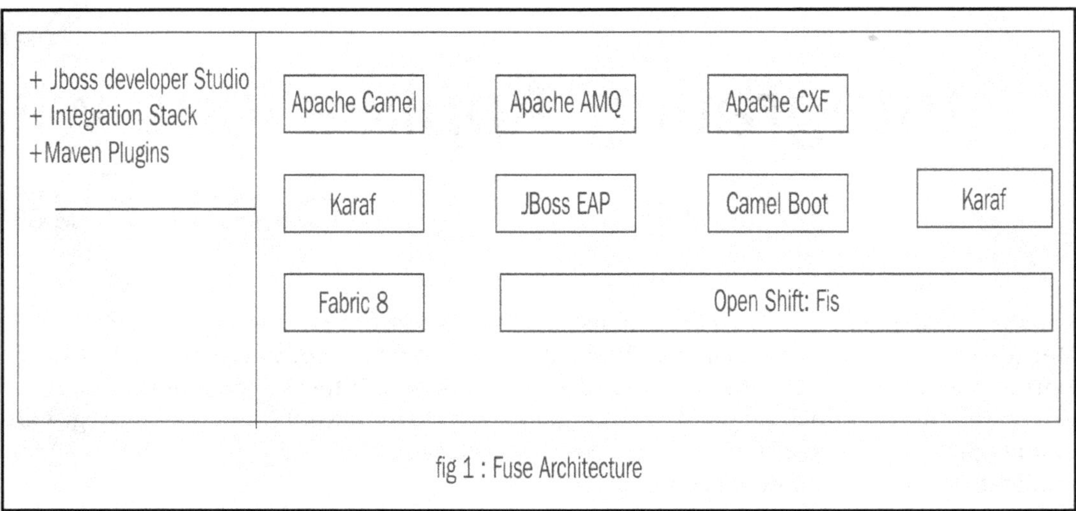

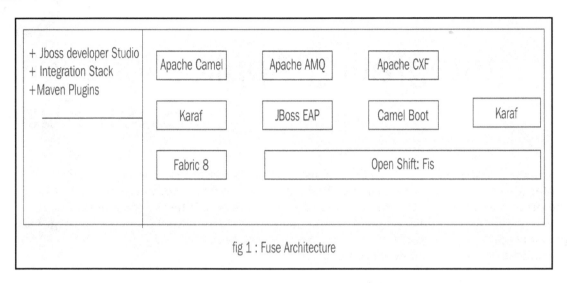

fig 1 : Fuse Architecture

Apache Camel provides a powerful routing engine, on top of which developers can build integration scenarios.

Apache CXF provides both REST and SOAP web services support, while **Apache AMQ** brings an integrated and robust messaging system to the platform. While working with JBoss Fuse, you can choose either **Apache Karaf** or **JBoss EAP** distribution. With the Karaf distribution, you can also opt for a standalone installation or a clustered environment with a container managed by **Fabric8.**

The JBoss Fuse-based integration applications can also be run on a fully certified Java EE platform, such as JBoss EAP.

Fuse Integration Services (**FIS**) extends the Fuse integration capabilities to the OpenShift Platform-as-a-Service (PaaS) solution. With FIS, users may also choose to run their fuse scenarios on **Camel Boot.**

The core integration scenario development process is basically the same--it is independent of your target deployment options (Fuse on the standalone Karaf, Fuse on the Karaf Fabric8 cluster, Fuse on the JBoss EAP, or Fuse Integration Services with Openshift). The configuration and deployment processes, on the other hand, are very specific to the target platform, including:

- Properties, placeholders, and configuration files for applications deployed on theFuseOnEAP/Fuse standalone Karaf installation
- Profiles and JVM containers for Fabric8 deployments
- Config maps, secrets, templates, and image deployments on pods for Openshift/Kubernetes installation

In the subsequent chapters, we will be working with the main Fuse distribution based on Apache Karaf.

Installing JBoss Fuse

While using Apache Karaf, Fuse can be installed as a standalone container or clustered platform using Fuse Fabric. The fabric cluster configuration comes on top of the basic standalone installation.

Basic Fuse installation

Download the Red Hat JBoss Fuse ZIP file from Redhat Developper Portal. While writing this book, the latest version is jboss-fuse-karaf-6.3.0.redhat-187.zip.

Unzip the downloaded ZIP file and use the cd command to move to the extracted directory:

```
$ unzip jboss-fuse-karaf-6.3.0.redhat-187.zip
$ cd jboss-fuse-6.3.0.redhat-187/
```

To enable remote access to the container, you must create at least one user in the ./etc/users.properties file. It is recommended that you create at least one user with the admin role by adding a line with the <Username>=<Password>, admin syntax. A default line with a default admin account exists in the file; uncomment the line to activate the default admin user:

```
 admin=admin,admin,manager,viewer,Monitor, Operator, Maintainer, Deployer,
Auditor, Administrator, SuperUser
```

The container can now be started using the `./bin/fuse` command:

```
MacBook-Pro-de-elvadas:jboss-fuse-6.3.0.redhat-187 enonowog$ ./bin/fuse
Please wait while JBoss Fuse is loading...
100% [========================================================================]

     _ ____                  ______
    | |  _ \                |  ____|
    | | |_) | ___  ___ ___  | |__ _   _ ___  ___
_   | |  _ < / _ \/ __/ __| |  __| | | / __|/ _ \
| |__| | |_) | (_) \__ \__ \ | |  | |_| \__ \  __/
\____/|____/ \___/|___/___/ |_|   \__,_|___/\___|

  JBoss Fuse (6.3.0.redhat-187)
  http://www.redhat.com/products/jbossenterprisemiddleware/fuse/

Hit '<tab>' for a list of available commands
and '[cmd] --help' for help on a specific command.

Open a browser to http://localhost:8181 to access the management console

Create a new Fabric via 'fabric:create'
or join an existing Fabric via 'fabric:join [someUrls]'

Hit '<ctrl-d>' or 'osgi:shutdown' to shutdown JBoss Fuse.

JBossFuse:karaf@root>
```

The **JBoss Fuse** server starts and provides users with a shell to run various commands. Commands can interact with both the container and/or the applications deployed on it. This method starts an interactive container; but there is also a way to start it as a daemon. To start the fuse server in the background, use the `./bin/start` script.In this folder, `./bin/status` is used to check the server status while the `./bin/client` script allows clients to connect to a running server/container or pass inline commands to the server:

```
$ ./status
Not Running ...
$ ./start
$ ./status
Running ...
$ ./client -u admin -p admin
Logging in as admin
...
JBossFuse:admin@root>
```

Apart from command lines, Fuse provides a web administration and monitoring console built from hawt.io. It is available at `http://localhost:8181/hawtio/` by default. See the following screenshot:

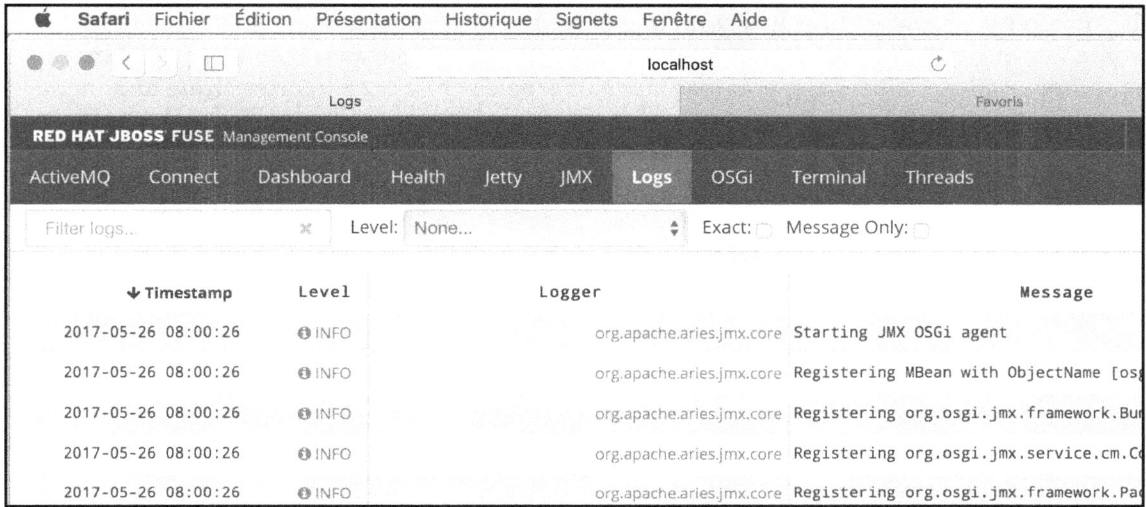

The default Fuse's karaf configuration is persisted in the `.cfg` files located in the `FUSE_HOME/etc` folder.

To access a specific configuration from the Karaf CLI, use the `config:edit config:proplist` command:

```
JBossFuse:admin@root> config:edit org.ops4j.pax.web
JBossFuse:admin@root> config:proplist
   felix.fileinstall.filename = file:.../etc/org.ops4j.pax.web.cfg
   org.ops4j.pax.web.config.file = etc/jetty.xml
   org.ops4j.pax.web.session.cookie.httpOnly = true
   org.osgi.service.http.port = 8181
   org.osgi.service.http.port.secure = 8443
   service.pid = org.ops4j.pax.web
JBossFuse:admin@root>
```

Use the `config:propset` command to change property values, as shown here:

```
JBossFuse:admin@root> config:propset org.osgi.service.http.port 8189
JBossFuse:admin@root> config:update
```

With this command, we changed the default OSGi HTTP port; the hawt.io application should now be available at `http://localhost:8189/hawtio/` instead of `http://localhost:8181/hawtio/`.

If you have a simple architecture with one or two nodes, you can manage it as a standalone container individually, but the situation becomes very complicated when you have more and more nodes. In this case, you may use Kubernetes or Fabric8 to orchestrate and manage your cluster. Fuse 6.X relies on fabric8v1 and Apache Zookeeper to manage a cluster. In the next section, we will cover simple cluster management with Fuse and fabric8v1.

Creating a Fuse cluster with Fabric8 and Apache Zookeeper

To create a clustered Fuse environment, one solution is to use the Fuse Fabric feature with Apache Karaf. Fuse Fabric is an open source integration platform for deep management of Java containers. Fuse Fabric makes it really easy to provision, automate, configure, run, manage, and maintain a Fuse platform from a central location. JBoss Fuse has been following in the footsteps of containers for quite some time; Fuse 6.X series uses Fabric8v1 for Java container orchestration, but will mainly support Docker containers in future releases:

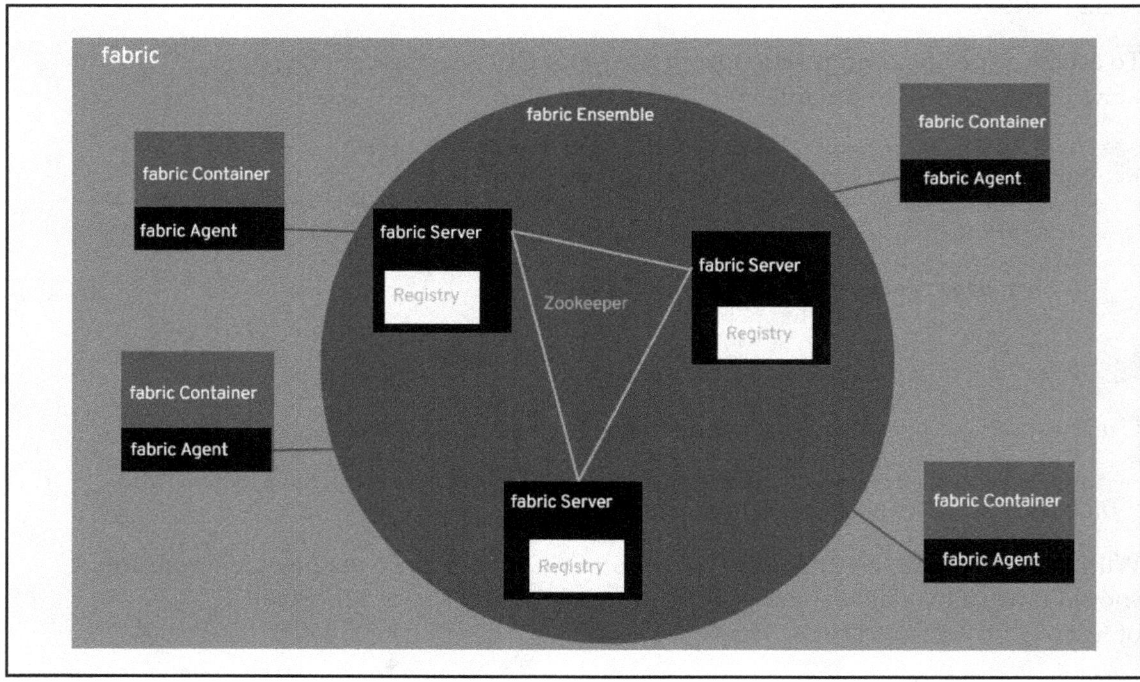

The **fabric** denotes the whole Fabric infrastructure--the fabric cluster containing a set of **fabric servers** and **fabric containers.** The fabric has access to one or more Maven repositories to pull artifacts in the cluster.
The f**abric Ensemble** is a set of **fabric servers** maintaining the fabric **registry**.

A fabric server is a member of a fabric ensemble; fabric servers exchange data using the Zookeeper protocol.
Both Fabric servers and Fabric containers can contain child containers.
The **Fabric Registry** stores configuration and runtime data; each fabric server has a registry copy.
Fuse Fabric uses **Apache ZooKeeper** (a highly reliable distributed coordination service) as its registry for storing both cluster centralized configuration and runtime metadata, such as node registration. Fabric supports discovery mechanisms, allowing client applications to locate endpoints without having to attach directly to them.

Fabric Agents interacts with the **Fabric Ensemble** to maintain the container state and configuration policies. Agents are responsible for deploying artifacts and bundles specified in the profiles attached to their parent container.

A profile is a configuration item defining a set of bundles, features, and properties available for deployment on container.

In the following section, we will create a simple fabric with one Fabric Server and three associated child containers: `node1`, `node2`, and `node3`.

A fabric can be created on top of a standalone installation using the `fabric:create` command.

Start you standalone Fuse instance and create a fabric on top of it, as follows:

```
$ cd  jboss-fuse-6.3.0.redhat-187/bin
$./fuse.sh
Please wait while JBoss Fuse is loading...
100%
[=================================================================]
...
JBossFuse:karaf@root> fabric:create --global-resolver manualip --resolver
manualip --manual-ip 127.0.0.1 --wait-for-provisioning
Waiting for container: root
Waiting for container root to provision.

JBossFuse:karaf@root> container-list
[id]   [version]  [type]  [connected]  [profiles]  [provision status]
root*  1.0        karaf   yes          fabric                  success
                                       fabric-ensemble-0000-1
```

```
jboss-fuse-full
```

In the `create fabric` command, the following options are used:

- `--global-resolver` defines the resolver policy applied to all new containers created in this fabric; its possible values are localip, localhostname, publicip, publichostname, and manualip
- The `--resolver` defines the local policy
- The `--manaual-ip` holds the IP address of the container when using the `manualip` policy
- The `--wait-for-provisioning` option returns hands to the caller only when the container provisioning operation is complete
- The `fabric:create --help` allows you to see all the possible options

The `container-list` command lists the containers in the current fabric: local or remote, and parent or child containers.

The `fabric-ensemble-0000-1` profile means that the container belongs to the fabric ensemble and therefore maintains a Zookeeper registry.

To create child containers to our root container, use the `container-create-child` command, as shown here:

```
JBossFuse:karaf@root> container-create-child root node 3
Creating new instance on SSH port 8102 and RMI ports 1100/44445 at:
/BeosBankFuse/jboss-fuse-6.3.0.redhat-187/instances/node3
Creating new instance on SSH port 8104 and RMI ports 1102/44447 at:
/BeosBankFuse/jboss-fuse-6.3.0.redhat-187/instances/node2
Creating new instance on SSH port 8103 and RMI ports 1101/44446 at:
/BeosBankFuse/jboss-fuse-6.3.0.redhat-187/instances/node1
The following containers have been created successfully:
 Container: node2.
 Container: node1.
 Container: node3.
JBossFuse:karaf@root>

JBossFuse:karaf@root> container-list
[id] [version] [type] [connected] [profiles] [provision status]
root* 1.0 karaf yes fabric success
 fabric-ensemble-0000-1
 jboss-fuse-full
 node1 1.0 karaf yes default validating baseline information
 node2 1.0 karaf yes default validating baseline information
 node3 1.0 karaf yes default success
JBossFuse:karaf@root>
```

The containers are created with the default profile. We now have a fabric cluster with one root fabric server and three child containers. All the clusters can be monitored and managed from a single hawt.io console.

After installing a Fuse infrastructure, the next natural milestone is to deploy and run applications on it. To reach this goal, we will progressively explore how to develop and deploy OSGi bundles on the Fuse platform in the next section.

Developing and deploying OSGi applications on the JBoss Fuse platform

This section handles development and deployment of OSGi bundles on Fuse cluster. To make it simple and very practical, we will implement various scenarios in the BeosBank landscape: content based router, proxying backend web services, data transformation, file processing, and messaging.

Content- and source-based routering

Content-based routing is the ability to route a message or an information to the right destination in the right format based on the message content. Source-based routing can be considered as content-based routing if the message source is stored as a message header, for example. Content-based routing plays an important role in the day-to-day activity of most businesses.

Remember that in `Chapter 2`, *Developing and Hosting Scalable Web Applications*, the BeosBank project owner raised an issue regarding the right approach to automatically synchronize newly created money transfer data in specific infinispan caches accessible to remittance applications:

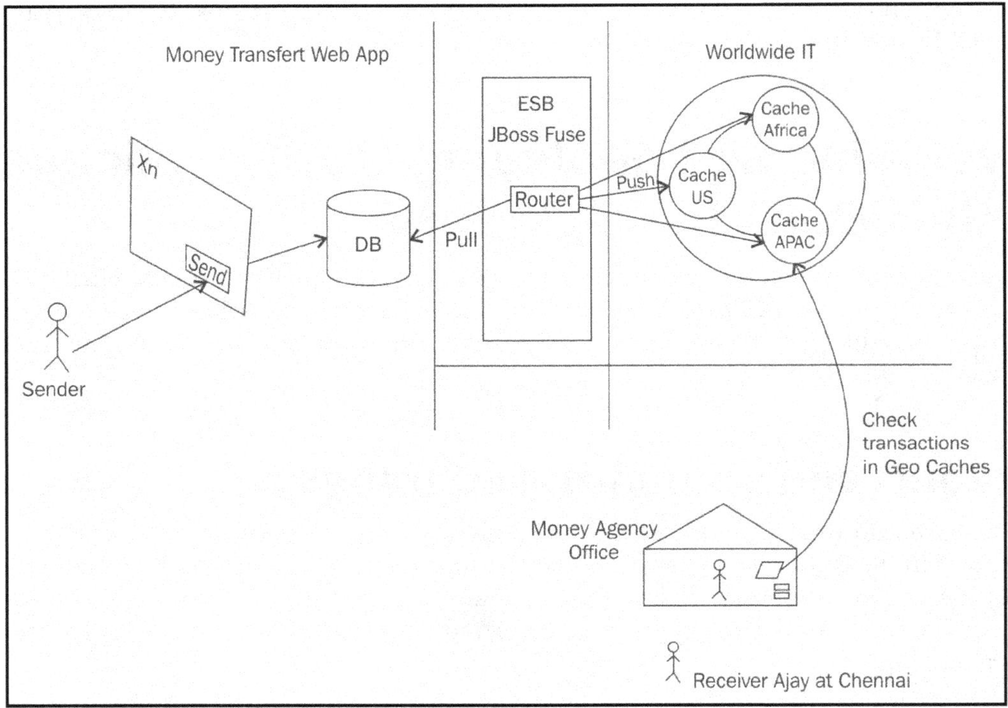

An application deployed in JBoss Fuse acts as the router. It periodically checks whether new data is available and pushes this data, if there is any, in the right caches based on some metadata and checks. How to develop and deploy the router is the purpose of the following content. Creating a Fuse project can be achieved through the project initialization and business logic implementation phases, through Apache Camel routes.

Creating a project

First of all, create the `beosbank-moneytransfert-cacheloader` Maven project with bundle packaging There are various karaf maven plugins to build and package OSGi bundles; for fuse projects, we can rely on `fuse bom` for dependency management and the maven bundle plugin:

```
<camel.version>2.17.0.redhat-630187</camel.version>
<version.maven-bundle-plugin>2.3.7</version.maven-bundle-plugin>
<jboss.fuse.bom.version>6.3.0.redhat-187</jboss.fuse.bom.version>
```

Each JBoss Fuse version is packaged and released with a specific Apache camel version and tag. Fuse 6.3.0.redhat-187 is built on top of Apache Camel 2.17.0.redhat-187, so all the camel modules for this version are, by default, included in the Fuse OSGi repository.

You need to specify all the dependencies required for the project including the following:

- `camel-jdbc`: To access the database
- `infinspan-client-hotrod`: To interact with the remote `infinispan` cache
- `mysql-connector-java`: The driver connector; we will see how to install the driver in Karaf in the next section

The Fuse project repository can be found at `https://github.com/jbossdevguidebook/chapters/ch6`.

In the first paragraph, we present some prerequisites to have a JBoss Fuse empty project; in the next section, we will focus on how to add concrete business logic to the project.

Creating the business logic

As Apache camel is the core routing engine of the Fuse platform, creating a business logic boils down to writing and configuring Apache Camel routes. Routes model dynamic interaction between various endpoints and connectors. There are various ways to write camel routes: either by Java DSL or XML DSL. Integration stacks also provide JBoss Developer Studio with a graphical tool to design camel routes:

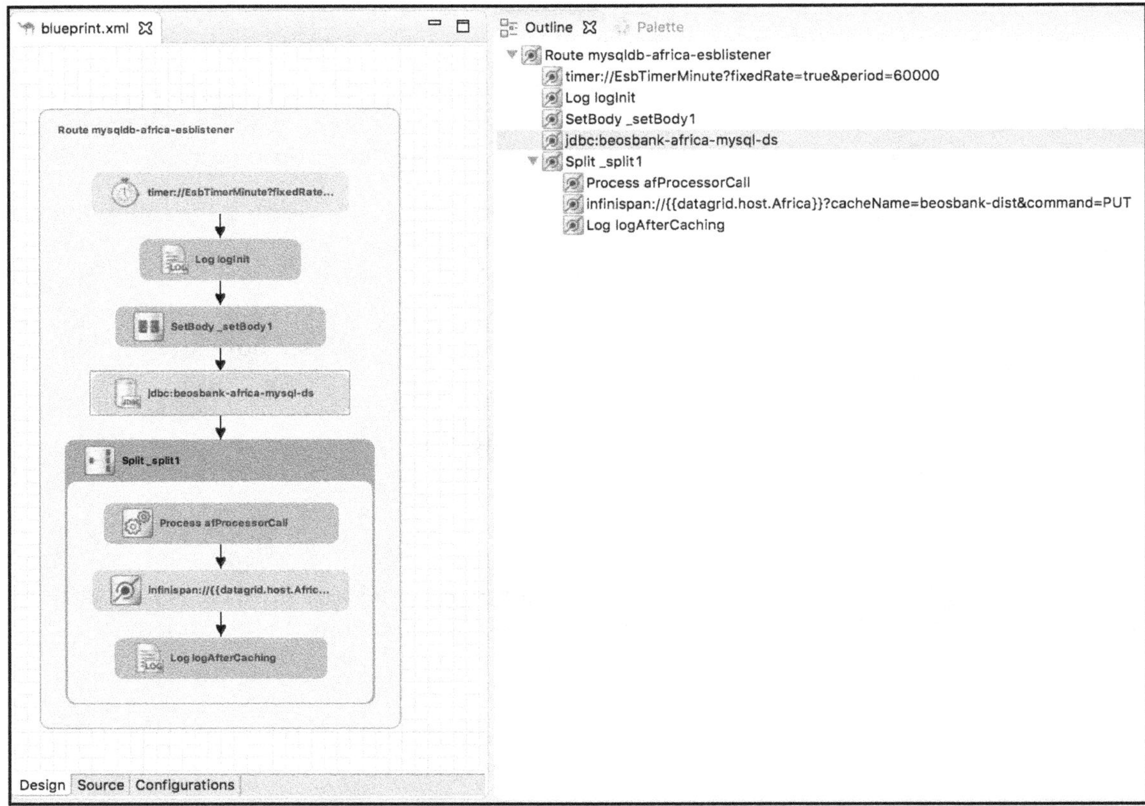

This process models the `mysqldb-africa-esblistener` camel route included in the `beosbank-moneytransfer-cacheloader` camel context. The route checks the `beosbank-africa-mysql` database periodically (every minute with `EsbTimerMinute`) to load eligible money transfer transactions using a SQL query and JDBC; Once retrieved, the transactions are sent to the infinispan cache individually, using the `HotRod` protocol. Camel contexts are modeled in the `src/main/resources/OSGI-INF/blueprint/blueprint.xml` file:

```
 <camelContext id="beosbank-moneytransfer-cacheloader"
        xmlns="http://camel.apache.org/schema/blueprint"
xmlns:order="http://fabric8.com/examples/order/v7">
        <route customId="true" id="mysqldb-africa-esblistener">
 <from id="timer1"
uri="timer://EsbTimerMinute?fixedRate=true&amp;period=60000"/>
            <log customId="true" id="logInit" message="Checking new
Transactions"/>
            <setBody id="_setBody1">
                <simple trim="false">SELECT * FROM AF_MONEYTRANSFER WHERE
status in ('DRAFT','PAID');</simple>
            </setBody>
            <to id="_to1" uri="jdbc:beosbank-africa-mysql-ds"/>
            <split id="_split1">
                <simple>${body}</simple>
                <process id="afProcessorCall" ref="afTrxProcessor"/>
                <to id="sendToBeosBankCache"
uri="infinispan://{{datagrid.host.Africa}}?cacheName=beosbank-
dist&amp;command=PUT"/>
                <log customId="true" id="logAfterCaching" message="New
Cache Entry: ${body} "/>
            </split>
        </route>
    </camelContext>
```

Every 60,000 milliseconds and at a fixed rate (`fixedRate=true`), the process is repeated. The database returns an `ArrayList` of `Map <String, object>` with one map key for each database column retrieved. `afTrxProcessor` is used to convert a SQL result to a Plain Money transfer object:

```
    <bean
class="com.beosbank.jbdevg.jbfuse.cacheloader.processor.AFProcessor"
id="afTrxProcessor"/>
```

The processor's process method is invoked for each SQL row returned from the database when reaching `<process id="afProcessorCall" ref="afTrxProcessor"/>`:

```
public void process(Exchange exchange) throws Exception {
  Message in = exchange.getIn();
  Map<String,Object> tuple= (Map<String, Object>) in.getBody();
  MoneyTransfer mt = new  MoneyTransfer();
  mt.setId((Long)tuple.get(MoneyTransfer.FIELD_ID));
  mt.setKeycode((String)tuple.get(MoneyTransfer.FIELD_KEYCODE));
mt.setPaymentMethod((String)tuple.get(MoneyTransfer.FIELD_PAYMENT_METHOD));
...
 in.setBody(mt);
 in.setHeader(InfinispanConstants.KEY, mt.getKeycode());
```

```
    }
```

Before overriding the camel in the object that will be populated as the out object, the processor also sets the key to be used for Infinispan operation after that.

Database access is provided by a JDBC data source:

```
<!-- MYSQL Data source -->
    <bean class="com.mysql.jdbc.jdbc2.optional.MysqlDataSource"
id="beosbank-africa-mysql-ds">
        <property name="databaseName" value="${db.databaseName}"/>
        <property name="url" value="${db.url}"/>
        <property name="user" value="${db.user}"/>
        <property name="password" value="${db.password}"/>
    </bean>
```

In the properties' values are injected by a blueprint placeholder. The placeholder will be persisted in `etc/com.beosbank.esb.env.cfg.properties`:

```
<cm:property-placeholder id="beosbank.placeholder" persistent-
id="com.beosbank.esb.env.cfg" update-strategy="reload">
        <cm:default-properties>
            <cm:property name="db.databaseName" value="beosbank-africa"/>
            <cm:property name="db.url"
value="jdbc:mysql://127.0.0.1:3406/beosbank-africa?relaxAutoCommit=true"/>
            <cm:property name="db.user" value="root"/>
            <cm:property name="db.password" value="Africa01#"/>
            <cm:property name="datagrid.host.Africa"
value="127.0.0.1:11322"/>
        </cm:default-properties>
    </cm:property-placeholder>
```

In the next section, we will review the different steps to set up the whole test environment and deploy the application.

Preparing the beosbank-moneytransfer-cacheloader test environment

In order to set up the whole test environment, we need the following components to be active and running: the MySQL database, the JBoss Datagrid Cluster, and the Fuse platform.

MySQL database

The `beosbank-africa-mysql-ds` data source is pointing on the `mysqldb-africa` created as the docker container in the data virtualization. Use the `docker-compose up` command to restart it if needed:

```
$ cd jbdevg/jbdatavirt/docker/
$ docker-compose up
```

```
enonowog — -bash — 166×40
MacBook-Pro-de-elvadas:~ enonowog$ docker ps
CONTAINER ID   IMAGE                      COMMAND                  CREATED       STATUS       PORTS                       NAMES
dd61e5f76826   docker_posgres_db_europa   "docker-entrypoint..."   9 hours ago   Up 9 hours   0.0.0.0:6432->5432/tcp      docker_posgres_db_europa_1
a2ad2eed90fe   mongo:3.4.4                "docker-entrypoint..."   9 hours ago   Up 9 hours   0.0.0.0:28001->27017/tcp    docker_mongo_db_emea_1
704364b467e6   docker_mysql_db_africa     "docker-entrypoint..."   9 hours ago   Up 9 hours   0.0.0.0:3406->3306/tcp      docker_mysql_db_africa_1
MacBook-Pro-de-elvadas:~ enonowog$
```

After setting up the source endpoint of the camel route, we need to ensure that the target JBoss datagrid endpoint is also up and running.

JBoss Datagrid and infinispan visualizer

Follow the steps provided in `Chapter 4`, *Storing and Accessing Distributed Data*, to start both the `BeosBankCacheAfrica` cache and `infinispan-visualizer` on an EAP7 instance:

```
$cd jboss-datagrid-7.0.0-server/bin
$ ./standalone.sh -c=clustered.xml -bmanagement=127.0.0.1 -b=127.0.0.1 -
Djboss.node.name=BeosBankCacheAfrica -Djboss.server.base.dir=Africa -
Djboss.socket.binding.port-offset=100


20:57:59,331 INFO [org.infinispan.server.endpoint] (MSC service thread 1-2)
DGENDPT10001: HotRodServer listening on 127.0.0.1:11322
```

Start the visualizer to monitor updates:

```
$./standalone.sh -b 127.0.0.1 -bmanagement=127.0.0.1 -
Dinfinispan.visualizer.jmxUser=admin -
Dinfinispan.visualizer.jmxPass=Admin01# -
Dinfinispan.visualizer.serverList='127.0.0.1:11322;127.0.0.1:11422;127.0.0.
1:11522'
```

The source and target endpoints are properly set up and ready; we must now start the integration flow and check the result every minute. To run Fuse applications, we can either start the container as a standalone or run the application in a Fabric Cluster. We will explore the two options in the following sections.

Running Fuse applications on a standalone Karaf container

Running a Fuse application on a standalone container is the simplest option when you are iterating quickly. Remember that the dependency management is very different in Karaf, and applications do not embark the JAR they need, as this is provided at runtime. Once your application dependencies are available in the container repository, you start the application by installing your bundles.

The `beosbank-moneytransfer-cacheloader` has two dependencies that are not provided by default in the Karaf containers: MyAQL driver and infinispan features. The installation process has two steps:

1. Adding the repository URL to locate the dependency: `feature:addurl`.
2. Installing the feature on the container: `features:install`:

```
JBossFuse:karaf@root> features:addurl mvn:org.infinispan/infinispan-client-hotrod/8.3.0.Final-redhat-1/xml/features
JBossFuse:karaf@root> features:install camel-infinispan
JBossFuse:karaf@root> features:install infinispan-client-hotrod
```

Pax JDBC is provided by the OPS4J community, and its main purpose is to simplify the usage of JDBC drivers in OSGi applications by extending the existing drivers according to the OSGi Enterprise JDBC Service specification:

```
JBossFuse:karaf@root> features:addurl mvn:org.ops4j.pax.jdbc/pax-jdbc-features/1.1.0/xml/features
JBossFuse:karaf@root> features:install pax-jdbc
JBossFuse:karaf@root> features:install pax-jdbc-mysql
```

After installing all the dependencies in the Karaf repositories, providing a URL to enable download, we can build the application and install the associated bundle:

1. Build the project with maven clean install phases.
2. Start your fuse instance and log in using the default admin user.
3. Install the bundle and start it (option-s) from the local maven repository using the `osgi:install` command:

```
#Build the bundle
beosbank-moneytransfer-cacheloader$ mvn clean install

#Deploy the bundle
JBossFuse:karaf@root> osgi:install -s
mvn:com.beosbank.jbdevg.jbfuse/beosbank-moneytransfer-cacheloader/1.0.0-
```

```
SNAPSHOT
Bundle ID: 342
#Check the bundle list
JBossFuse:karaf@root> osgi:list | grep BeosBank
[342] [Active] [Created] [] [80] BeosBank Datagrid transaction loader
(1.0.0.SNAPSHOT)
```

Check the log of your applications with the `log:tail` command; you will see the timer generating a top clock every minute and transactions being populated in the cache:

```
017-05-28 20:43:19,263 | INFO | //EsbTimerMinute | mysqldb-africa-
esblistener | 232 - org.apache.camel.camel-core - 2.17.0.redhat-630187 |
Checking new Transactions
2017-05-28 20:43:19,276 | INFO | //EsbTimerMinute | mysqldb-africa-
esblistener | 232 - org.apache.camel.camel-core - 2.17.0.redhat-630187 |
New Cache Entry: MoneyTransfer
[id=1;CMRCMR001;1000.00;null;0237-2222-3333-0001;null;null]
2017-05-28 20:43:19,276 | INFO | //EsbTimerMinute | mysqldb-africa-
esblistener | 232 - org.apache.camel.camel-core - 2.17.0.redhat-630187 |
New Cache Entry: MoneyTransfer
[id=2;CMRCAN001;5000.00;null;0237-2222-3333-0002;null;null]
```

You can also check the infinispan visualizer at--`http://localhost:8080/infinispan-visualizer/`. The transaction number is increased each time a new transaction is inserted in the database, and you should end up with 10 transactions with the existing test database:

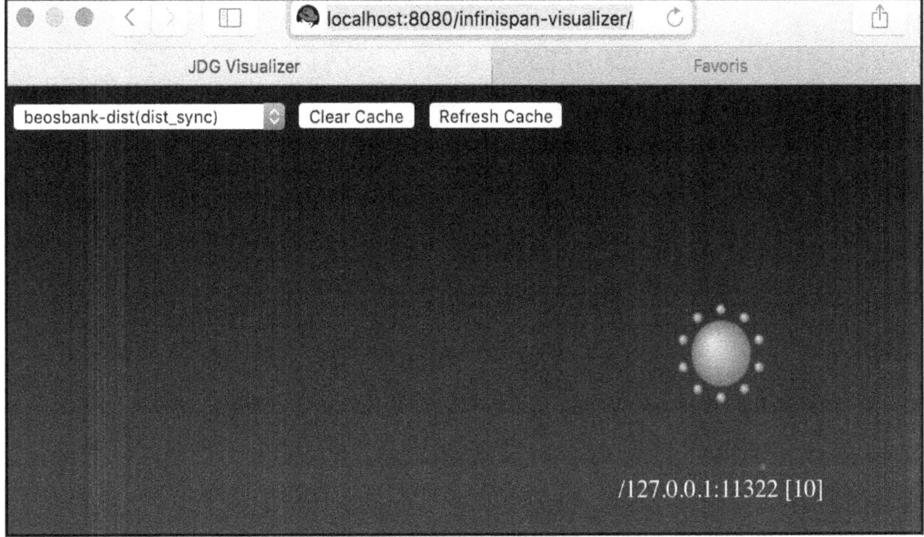

This concludes our deployment on the standalone fuse container. Now we'll see how to deploy the same application in a fabric cluster.

Running beosbank-moneytransfer-cacheloader on Fuse Fabric

In the previous section, we deployed the `beosbank-moneytransfer-cacheloader` bundle on a standalone fuse container using the `osgi:install` command. To install the same application on a fabric container, we need to make to some adjustments in the application configuration. This enhancement includes two majors steps: creating and deploying an application profile.

Creating a profile

In a standalone environment, application deployment is done from bundles using the `osgi:install` command, while in fabric, deployments are encapsulated in profiles. A profile contains a list of bundles, features, repositories, and properties. As soon as a profile is attached to a container, the agent will check for updates, download the necessary bundles, and deploy them on the container.

You can create a profile either by copying (`profile-copy`) the existing one from scratch (`profile-create`), or using the `Fabric8` maven plugin:

```
<plugin>
    <groupId>io.fabric8</groupId>
    <artifactId>fabric8-maven-plugin</artifactId>
   </plugin>
```

The `fabric8` maven plugin scans bundle `POM` files and properties to generate custom fabric8 profiles:

```
<properties>
  <fabric8.features> pax-jdbc-mysql camel-jdbc  camel-infinispan
infinispan-client-hotrod</fabric8.features>
  <fabric8.featureRepos>
    mvn:org.ops4j.pax.jdbc/pax-jdbc-features/1.1.0/xml/features
    mvn:org.infinispan/infinispan-client-hotrod/8.3.0.Final-
redhat-1/xml/features
   </fabric8.featureRepos>
 </properties>
```

- `fabric8.features` lists the feature to include in the generated profiles
- `fabric8.featuresRepos` lists the additional repositories' URLs to use while locating features

The generated profile is defaulted to the artifact name and contains one bundle (the generated artifact). The profile name can also be customized using `<fabric8.profile>myProfile</fabric8.profile>`. To invoke the `fabric8` maven plugin on the project, either run the `fabric8:zip` or `fabric8:deploy` deploy goal. The `fabric8:zip` goal creates a ZIP profile that will be stored in the Maven repository as the bundle, while `fabric8:deploy` creates and pushes the profile in the fabric using the Jolokia REST API. This option requires a fabric server to be set up in your maven settings:

```
beosbank-moneytransfer-cacheloader$ mvn fabric8:zip install
INFO] --- fabric8-maven-plugin:1.2.0.redhat-630254:zip (default-cli) @
beosbank-moneytransfer-cacheloader ---
[INFO] Found class: org.apache.camel.CamelContext so adding the parent
profile: feature-camel
...
[INFO] zipping file
com.beosbank.jbdevg.jbfuse/beosbank/moneytransfer/cacheloader.profile/com.b
eosbank.esb.env.cfg.properties[INFO] zipping file
com.beosbank.jbdevg.jbfuse/beosbank/moneytransfer/cacheloader.profile/depen
dencies/com.beosbank.jbdevg.jbfuse/beosbank-moneytransfer-cacheloader-
requirements.json
[INFO] zipping file
com.beosbank.jbdevg.jbfuse/beosbank/moneytransfer/cacheloader.profile/io.fa
bric8.agent.properties
[INFO] zipping file
com.beosbank.jbdevg.jbfuse/beosbank/moneytransfer/cacheloader.profile/READM
E.md
[INFO] zipping file
com.beosbank.jbdevg.jbfuse/beosbank/moneytransfer/cacheloader.profile/Summa
ry.md
[INFO] Created profile zip file:
/Users/enonowog/books/jbdevg/code/jbdevg/jbfuse/beosbank-moneytransfer-
cacheloader/target/profile.zip
[INFO]
..
[INFO] Installing /Users/enonowog/books/jbdevg/code/jbdevg/jbfuse/beosbank-
moneytransfer-cacheloader/target/profile.zip to
/Users/enonowog/.m2/repository/com/beosbank/jbdevg/jbfuse/beosbank-
moneytransfer-cacheloader/1.0.0-SNAPSHOT/beosbank-moneytransfer-
cacheloader-1.0.0-SNAPSHOT-profile.zip
```

The profile is assembled and pushed to the `.m2` repository in the same folder as the bundle artifact. In the next section, we will see how to deploy the generated profile in a fabric cluster and attach it to some containers.

Deploying the profile in the fabric

Once the profiles are stored in the maven repository, they can be imported in fabric using the `profile-import` command and the maven coordinates of the ZIP profile:

```
JBossFuse:karaf@root> profile-import
mvn:com.beosbank.jbdevg.jbfuse/beosbank-moneytransfer-cacheloader/1.0.0-
SNAPSHOT/zip/profile
Imported profiles into version 1.0
JBossFuse:karaf@root> Imported profiles into version 1.0

JBossFuse:karaf@root> profile-list
[id] [# containers] [parents]
acls
autoscale default
com.beosbank.jbdevg.jbfuse-beosbank-moneytransfer-cacheloader     feature-
camel
default 3 acls
fabric 1 karaf hawtio
...
```

The profile content can be reviewed using the `profile-display` command. By default, it does not show the content inherited from parent profiles. Use the overlay option to show the settings from parent profiles:

```
JBossFuse:karaf@root> profile-display com.beosbank.jbdevg.jbfuse-beosbank-
moneytransfer-cacheloader
Profile id: com.beosbank.jbdevg.jbfuse-beosbank-moneytransfer-cacheloader
Version : 1.0
Attributes:
 parents: feature-camel
Containers:

Container settings
----------------------------
Repositories :
 mvn:org.ops4j.pax.jdbc/pax-jdbc-features/1.1.0/xml/features
 mvn:org.infinispan/infinispan-client-hotrod/8.3.0.Final-
redhat-1/xml/features

Features :
 camel-jdbc
 pax-jdbc-mysql
```

```
 infinispan-client-hotrod
 camel-infinispan

Bundles :
 mvn:com.beosbank.jbdevg.jbfuse/beosbank-moneytransfer-cacheloader/1.0.0-
SNAPSHOT

Configuration details
----------------------------
PID: com.beosbank.esb.env.cfg
 db.user root
 db.password Africa01#
 datagrid.host.Africa 127.0.0.1:11322
 db.databaseName beosbank-africa
 db.url jdbc:mysql://127.0.0.1:3406/beosbank-africa?relaxAutoCommit=true

Other resources
----------------------------
Resource: dependencies/com.beosbank.jbdevg.jbfuse/beosbank-moneytransfer-
cacheloader-requirements.json
Resource: Summary.md
Resource: README.md
```

The command displays the profile parent name (`feature-camel`), the repositories added by the `fabric8.featureRepos`, and features sent by the `fabric8.features` property. The profile includes the persistence ID assigned to the `com.beosbank.esb.env.cfg` blueprint property. The profile is like a delivery note or plan; once it is imported, the profile can be assigned to a container using the `container-add-profile` command.

Let's add the profile to `node3` of our fabric cluster:

```
JBossFuse:karaf@root> container-add-profile node3
com.beosbank.jbdevg.jbfuse-beosbank-moneytransfer-cacheloader

#Check the container list
JBossFuse:karaf@root> container-list
[id] [version] [type] [connected] [profiles] [provision status]
root* 1.0 karaf    yes          fabric                          success
                                fabric-ensemble-0000-1
                                jboss-fuse-full
 node1 1.0 karaf   yes          default                         success
 node2 1.0 karaf   yes          default                         success
 node3 1.0 karaf   yes          default                         success
 com.beosbank.jbdevg.jbfuse-beosbank-moneytransfer-cacheloader
JBossFuse:karaf@root>
```

`node3` will have two profiles after the operation: `default` and `com.beosbank.jbdevg.jbfuse-beosbank-moneytransfer-cacheloader`. Once attached, the fabric agent of `node3` will download the `mvn:com.beosbank.jbdevg.jbfuse/beosbank-moneytransfer-cacheloader/1.0.0-SNAPSHOT` bundle from the fabric ensemble maven proxy and install it on the container.

You can now connect to the Fabric administration console at `http://localhost:8181/hawtio/` to inspect the logs:

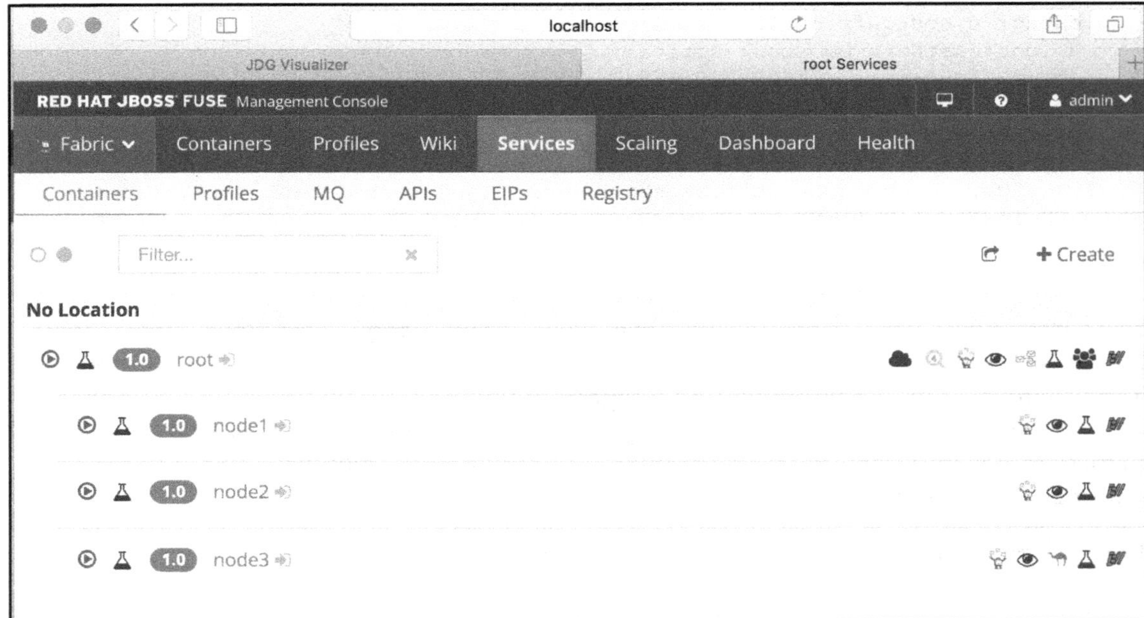

`node3` has a camel ride icon, indicating that it is currently running camel applications. Click on **node3**, and follow the open button in the top-right corner of your screen to see the logs generated by the applications on this container:

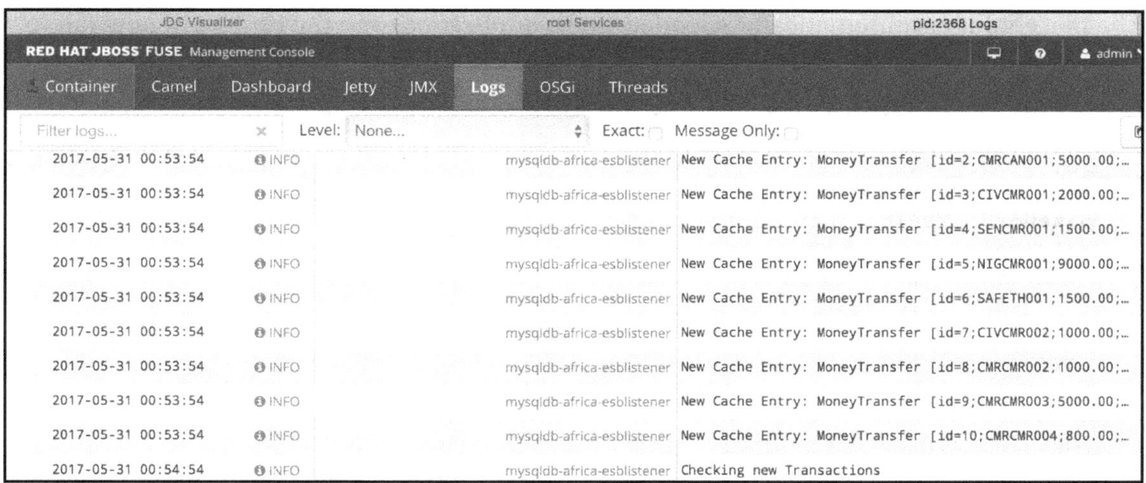

`MoneyTransfer` details are collected from the MySQL database and put in the JBoss Datagrid cache using the `Hot Rod` protocol. Application configurations are stored in profiles. Now we'll look at how to proceed if we need to change some application parameters.

Updating profiles and properties to use the encrypted password

We can use the `profile-edit` command to update the database user password. Consider the following example:

```
JBossFuse:karaf@root> profile-edit --pid
com.beosbank.esb.env.cfg/db.password=FakeClearPassword
com.beosbank.jbdevg.jbfuse-beosbank-moneytransfer-cacheloader

Setting value:FakeClearPassword key:db.password on
pid:com.beosbank.esb.env.cfg and profile:com.beosbank.jbdevg.jbfuse-
beosbank-moneytransfer-cacheloader version:1.0
```

The placeholder is automatically reloaded in the application, and the route will now fail to connect to the database:

```
Failed delivery for (MessageId: ID-MacBook-Pro-de-elvadas-
local-59392-1496295447261-6-1 on ExchangeId: ID-MacBook-Pro-de-elvadas-
local-59392-1496295447261-6-2). Exhausted after delivery attempt: 1 caught:
java.sql.SQLException: Access denied for user 'root'@'172.18.0.1' (using
password: YES)Message History
---------------------------------------------------------------------------
RouteId ProcessorId Processor Elapsed (ms)
[mysqldb-africa-esb] [mysqldb-africa-esb]
[timer://EsbTimerMinute?fixedRate=true&period=60000 ] [ 6]
[mysqldb-africa-esb] [logInit ] [log ] [ 0]
[mysqldb-africa-esb] [_setBody1 ] [setBody[simple{SELECT * FROM
AF_MONEYTRANSFER WHERE status in ('DRAFT','PAID')] [ 0]
[mysqldb-africa-esb] [_to1 ] [jdbc:beosbank-africa-mysql-ds ] [ 5]
```

To fix the application, we will now set the correct password encrypted in the profile. Use the `encrypt-message` command to encrypt your `values/messages` password. There are various algorithms that are supported; we will use the default--`PBEWithMD5AndDES`:

```
JBossFuse:karaf@root> encrypt-message Africa01#
Encrypting message Africa01#
 Using algorithm PBEWithMD5AndDES and password admin
 Result: PPZYzNdFT+c83EXr0VBOlxzycWYp8Vp7
```

The encrypted value can now be applied as the user password value using the `${crypt:EncryptedValue}` pattern:

```
JBossFuse:karaf@root> profile-edit --pid
com.beosbank.esb.env.cfg/db.password=\${crypt:PPZYzNdFT+c83EXr0VBOlxzycWYp8
Vp7} com.beosbank.jbdevg.jbfuse-beosbank-moneytransfer-cacheloader

#Check the updates by displaying the profile.
JBossFuse:karaf@root> profile-display com.beosbank.jbdevg.jbfuse-beosbank-
moneytransfer-cacheloader
Configuration details
----------------------------
PID: com.beosbank.esb.env.cfg
db.password ${crypt:PPZYzNdFT+c83EXr0VBOlxzycWYp8Vp7}
```

The database connection is automatically reestablished and transactions are again loaded from the database to the Datagrid.

In this section, we installed both a Fuse standalone and fabric cluster, and developed an application to route DB transactions to JBoss Datagrid using Apache Camel. At the end, we applied some maven configuration to automatically generate the `Fabric8` profile in the Maven repository. We imported the profile in a fabric environment and deployed the application on JVM containers. What we can learn from this, independent of the `target` platform, is that Apache Camel plays an important role in Fuse application development. It is a solid block, on top of which most of the applications will rely to set up integration scenarios very quickly. In the next section, we will cover other integration scenarios for the BeosBank context, including web services proxying and file processing.

Proxying web services

A web service proxy is a common use pattern that is frequently used in the integration landscape. For various reasons, such as security, auditing, custom transformations, and processing before reaching the final destination, a web service proxy component can be interposed between callers and the real web services they are interacting with. Let's consider the following integration use case from the BeosBank ecosystem.

Business case

In the DataVirtualization, you created the `beosbank.vdb` Virtual Database. The **Virtual Database** (**VDB**) is exposing data through JDBC and the Odata Rest interface. In this section, we will be working with the Odata service. For some reason, the bank doesn't want to grant direct access to the VDB OData URL to consumers. Beosbank would like to build a proxy on top of VDB OData using JBoss Fuse. How do we implement a proxy web service to decouple the VDB client from the backend Virtual Database Odata interface?

The following are Odata BeosBank URLs:

- `http://localhost:8080/odata/beosbank.1/` will be the root URL to access the VDB
- `http://localhost:8080/odata/beosbank.1/Transactions.MoneyTransfer` will return the whole `MoneyTransfer` collection
- `http://localhost:8080/odata/beosbank.1/Transactions.MoneyTransfer('BEBR002')` returns details on `MoneyTransfer` with `code=BEBR002`

Remember that `teiidUser/Admin01#` is authorized to access the OData interface.

Solution

Fuse and Apache camel provide various components to set up a web service proxy, including Apache CXF endpoints, Apache CXFRS, Jetty, and so on.

To build a VDB proxy on Fuse, we will create an OSGi Camel Blueprint application: `https://github.com/nelvadas/jbdevg/tree/master/jbfuse/beosbank-vdb-wsproxy:`

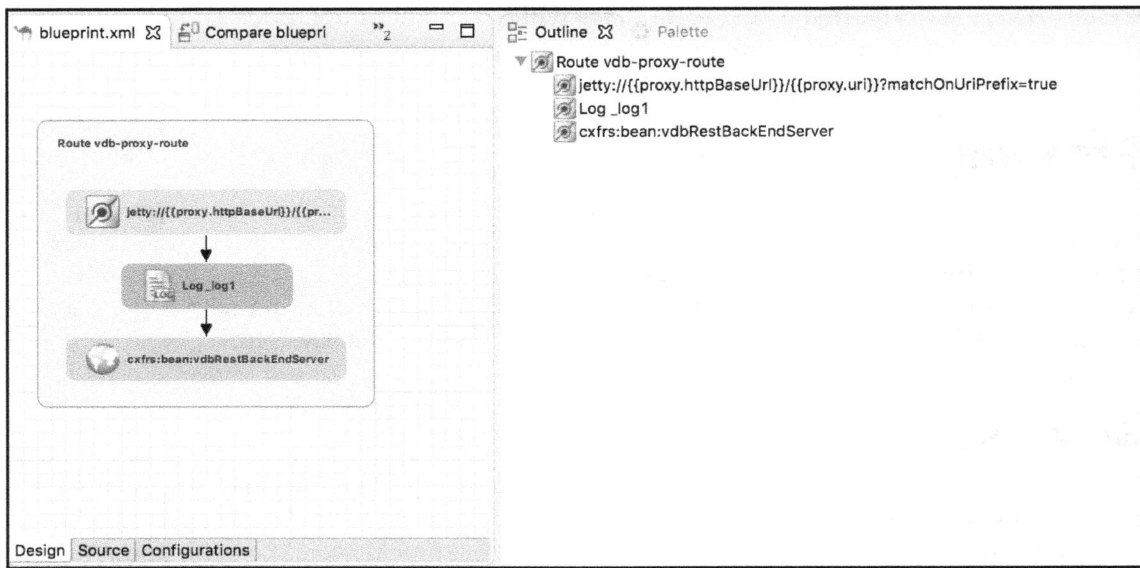

The application is using both Jetty and Apache CXFRS endpoints:

```
<camelContext id="beosbank-vdb-wsproxy">
       <route customId="true" id="vdb-proxy-route">
           <from
uri="jetty://{{proxy.httpBaseUrl}}/{{proxy.uri}}?matchOnUriPrefix=true"/>
          <log  message="Request received ${headers} body=${body}"/>
        <to uri="cxfrs:bean:vdbRestBackEndServer"/>
       </route>
   </camelContext>
```

The Jetty component acts as a frontend endpoint. By default, Jetty will only match the exact URI; the `matchOnUriPrefix=true` option is used to instruct Jetty to match prefixes or wildcard URIs.

Upon receiving a request on the `proxy.uri` address, the request is logged and forwarded to the `vdbRestBakcEndServer` camel CXF Rest Bean:

```
    <cxf:rsClient id="vdbRestBackEndServer" address="${vdb.url}"
loggingFeatureEnabled="true"/>
```

No JAX-RS resources are defined for the `rsClient` bean.

The `com.beosbank.jbdevg.jbfuse-beosbank-vdb-wsproxy` fabric8 profile is created with the `camel-jetty` and `camel-cxf` features to deploy the application in Fuse Fabric:

```
Profile id: com.beosbank.jbdevg.jbfuse-beosbank-vdb-wsproxy
Version : 1.0
Attributes:
 parents: feature-camel feature-cxf
Container settings
----------------------------
Features :
 camel-jetty  camel-cxf
Bundles :
 mvn:com.beosbank.jbdevg.jbfuse/beosbank-vdb-wsproxy/1.0.0-SNAPSHOT
Configuration details
----------------------------
PID: com.beosbank.esb.wsproxy.env.cfg
 proxy.httpBaseUrl ${container:httpurl}
 proxy.uri vdbproxy
 vdb.user teiidUser
 vdb.url http://localhost:8080/odata/beosbank.1/
 vdb.password Admin01#
```

In this profile, you should pay specific attention to the `com.beosbank.esb.wsproxy.env.cfg` persistence ID, which defines the following properties:

- `proxy.httpBaseUrl` uses the fabric features to dynamically get the container HTTP URL on which the application will be deployed
- `proxy.uri` acts as the frontend URL
- `vdb.url` is the target `beosbank.vdb` Odata URL

As the VDB access is locked by a basic authentication realm, the CXF Rest endpoint credentials can be passed through an HTTP conduit:

```
<conduit name="*.http-conduit">
    <authorization>
        <sec:UserName>${vdb.user}</sec:UserName>
        <sec:Password>${vdb.password}</sec:Password>
        <sec:AuthorizationType>Basic</sec:AuthorizationType>
    </authorization>
</conduit>
```

To test the application, first start your VDB, and then deploy the profile in your fabric cluster:

```
JBossFuse:karaf@root> profile-import
mvn:com.beosbank.jbdevg.jbfuse/beosbank-vdb-wsproxy/1.0.0-
SNAPSHOT/zip/profile

JBossFuse:karaf@root> container-add-profile wsnode1
com.beosbank.jbdevg.jbfuse-beosbank-vdb-wsproxy
```

Consequently, if the application is deployed on a container with `IP=127.0.0.1` and `httpPort=8086`, you should see the following log:

```
Route: vdb-proxy-route started and consuming from:
Endpoint[jetty:http://127.0.0.1:8186/vdbproxy?matchOnUriPrefix=true]
```

The following calls should be done to reach the whole transaction lists:

- From VDB: `http://localhost:8080/odata/beosbank.1/Transactions.MoneyTransfer`
- From proxy: `http://127.0.0.1:8186/vdbproxy/Transactions.MoneyTransfer`

With `httpie`, you can have a clearer view of the JSON result by running the `http://127.0.0.1:8186/vdbproxy/Transactions.MoneyTransfer?\$format=json` command:

```
MacBook-Pro-de-elvadas:~ enonowog$ http  http://127.0.0.1:8186/vdbproxy/Transactions.MoneyTransfer?\$format=json
HTTP/1.1 200 OK
$format: json
Accept: */*
Accept-Encoding: gzip, deflate
Content-Type: application/json;charset=utf-8
DataServiceVersion: 2.0
Expires: Thu, 01 Jan 1970 01:00:00 CET
Server: Apache-Coyote/1.1
Transfer-Encoding: chunked
User-Agent: HTTPie/0.9.8
breadcrumbId: ID-MacBook-Pro-de-elvadas-local-50391-1496445378787-0-12

{
    "d": {
        "results": [
            {
                "__metadata": {
                    "type": "Transactions.MoneyTransfer",
                    "uri": "http://localhost:8080/odata/beosbank.1/Transactions.MoneyTransfer('BEBR002')"
                },
                "amount_paid_with_taxes": null,
                "amount_sent_without_taxes": "100.00",
                "amount_to_receive": null,
                "code": "BEBR002",
                "country_from": "Brasil",
                "country_to": "Belgium",
                "fees": null,
                "receiver_name": "Adriana Pinto",
                "receiving_currency": "BRL",
                "receiving_date": null,
                "sender_name": "Yohan Pieter",
                "sending_currency": "EUR",
                "sending_date": "/Date(1494374400000)/",
                "status": "DRAFT",
                "vat": null
            },
            {
```

In this section, we created a web service proxy to access the VDB OData interface. We used Jetty for the front endpoint and a CXF Rest component to access the backend service. In the next section, we will explore another common pattern where Fuse can bring added value: file processing and data transformation.

File processing and data transformation

Apache Camel as the Fuse Router engine has a variety of components for file processing and data transformation. In the following section, we will create a fuse application to pull XML files representing `Moneytransfer` data. We will be interested in a specific business line: transactions from the USA to the Cameroons. After reading the XML file, the application should send a message into a JMS queue to a US regulatory. Then, generate a PDF bill and save it on the filesystem.

The whole project code is available at `jbossdevguidebook/chapters/ch6/beosbank-file-processor` for your reference.

Let's consider the following file as the XML representation of a mobile money transfer from the Datagrid:

```
<?xml version="1.0" encoding="UTF-8" ?>
<MoneyTransferStream>
<moneytransfer>
    <amountExcludingFees>200</amountExcludingFees>
  <creditCardNumber>1111-2222-3333-2222</creditCardNumber>
  <id>2</id>
  <receiver>
    <address>
      <country>Cameroon</country>
    </address>
    <firstName>Baba</firstName>
    <id>4</id>
    <lastName>Ahmadou</lastName>
  </receiver>
  <receiverCurrencyCode/>
  <sender>
    <address>
      <country>USA</country>
    </address>
    <firstName>John</firstName>
    <id>5</id>
    <lastName>Doe</lastName>
  </sender>
  <senderCurrencyCode>USD</senderCurrencyCode>
  <sendingDate>2017-04-11</sendingDate>
  <status>DRAFT</status>
  <vatRate/>
  <withdrawalDate/>
</moneytransfer>
</MoneyTransferStream>
```

From this chapter, XML was converted to an object using BeanIO and Java SE code. The same thing can be included in a Fuse integration scenario using the `Camel-beanio` feature. In the mapping file, we define how to create an object from the XML representation:

```
<beanio xmlns="http://www.beanio.org/2012/03"
xmlns:xsi="http://www.w3.org/2001/XMLSchema-instance"
xsi:schemaLocation="http://www.beanio.org/2012/03
http://www.beanio.org/2012/03/mapping.xsd">
 <stream name="MoneyTransferStream" format="xml">  <record
name="moneytransfer"  minOccurs="0" maxOccurs="unbounded"
class="com.beosbank.jbdevg.fuse.domain.MoneyTransfer">
        <field name="id" rid="true" />
        <field name="sendingDate" format="yyyy-MM-dd" />
        <field name="withdrawalDate" format="yyyy-MM-dd" />
```

```
        <field name="creditCardNumber" />
        <field name="keyCode" />
        <field name="amountExcludingFees" />
        <field name="fees" />
        <field name="status" />
        <field name="amountIncludingFees" />
        <field name="vatRate" />
        <field name="totalAmountExcludingVat" />
        <field name="totalAmountIncludingVat" />
        <field name="senderCurrencyCode" />
        <field name="receiverCurrencyCode" />
        <field name="amountExcludingFeesInReceiverCurrency" />
        &lt;segment name="sender"
class="com.beosbank.jbdevg.fuse.domain.Customer">
         <field name="id" />
         <field name="birthDate" format="yyyy-MM-dd" />
         <field name="firstName" />
         <field name="lastName" />
          &lt;segment name="address"
class="com.beosbank.jbdevg.fuse.domain.Address">
           <field name="street" />
           <field name="city" />
           <field name="zipcode" />
           <field name="country" />
        &lt;/segment&gt;
        &lt;/segment&gt;
        &lt;segment name="receiver"
class="com.beosbank.jbdevg.fuse.domain.Customer">
         <field name="id" />
         <field name="birthDate" format="yyyy-MM-dd" />
         <field name="firstName" />
         <field name="lastName" />
          &lt;segment name="address"
class="com.beosbank.jbdevg.fuse.domain.Address">
           <field name="street" />
           <field name="city" />
           <field name="zipcode" />
           <field name="country" />
        &lt;/segment&gt;
        &lt;/segment&gt;
      </record>
  </stream>
</beanio>
```

The mapping file defines a `moneytransfer` stream with two segments: `sender` and `receiver`. The receiver and sender segments also enclose an `address` subsegment. Each entity has a set of fields and a Java class to use for its conversion.

In a camel context, a data transformer can be created using the following `dataFormats` instruction:

```
<camelContext id="beosbank-file-processor"
xmlns="http://camel.apache.org/schema/blueprint">        <dataFormats>
            <beanio id="inputBeanio"
mapping="com/beosbank/beanio/mapping.xml"
streamName="MoneyTransferStream"/>
        </dataFormats>
 <route id="file-route">
            <from id="_from1" uri="file:work/input"/>
<setHeader headerName="beosbank.fromCountry" id="_setH1">
<xpath>/MoneyTransferStream/moneytransfer/sender/address/country/text()</xp
ath></setHeader>

 <setHeader headerName="beosbank.destinationCountry" id="_setH2">
<xpath>/MoneyTransferStream/moneytransfer/receiver/address/country/text()</
xpath></setHeader>
 <log id="_log1" message="Receiving MoneyTransfer ${file:name}
beosbank.destinationCountry=${header.beosbank.destinationCountry}"/>
            <choice id="_choice1">
                <when id="_when1">
              <simple>
                ${header.beosbank.fromCountry} == 'USA' and
                ${header.beosbank.destinationCountry} == 'Cameroon'
              </simple>
                    <log id="_log2" message="Money Transfer from
${header.beosbank.fromCountry} to  ${header.beosbank.destinationCountry}
${file:name} "/>
 <to id="_toUsaQueue" uri="activemq:queue:{{activemq.name.usVat}}"/>
 <unmarshal id="_unmarshal1" ref="inputBeanio"/>
<to id="_toPdfEngine"
uri="pdf:create?textProcessingFactory=autoFormatting"/>
 <to id="_toOutFolder" uri="file:work/output"/>
                </when>
                <otherwise id="_otherwise1">
                    <log id="_log4" message="Money Transfer to Other(
${header.beosbank.destinationCountry} )   ${file:name} "/>
                </otherwise>
            </choice>
            <log id="_log5" message="Done processing ${file:name} "/>
        </route>
    </camelContext>
```

The camel context first declares a `BeanIO dataFormat`, and a file route is created using XML DSL. The route performs the following business logic:

1. It extracts the sender country and receiver country using Xpath expressions, such as `/MoneyTransferStream/moneytransfer/sender/address/country/text()`, and creates two headers from the extracted values: `beosbank.fromCountry` and `beosbank.destinationCountry`.
2. The route then relies on the previous BeosBank headers to check whether the transaction is from the USA to the Cameroons, in which case a statement is printed in the log file. The logged line includes the filename currently being handled.
3. The XML content is then forwarded to the US JMS queue using `<to id="_toUsaQueue" uri="activemq:queue:{{activemq.name.usVat}}"/>`.
4. The XML content is unmarshalled into a Java object using the previously declared `dataFormat`: `<unmarshal id="_unmarshal1" ref="inputBeanio"/>`.
5. A PDF file is then created based on the `toString` content of the `POJO` object returned by the unmarshalling operation: `com.beosbank.jbdevg.fuse.domain.MoneyTransfer`.
6. The PDF file is saved in the `work/output` directory.

After developing the camel route, the application can be packaged and built using the following maven `mvn clean fabric8:zip install` command:

```
beosbank-file-processor$ mvn clean fabric8:zip install
```

After installing the bundle and profile in the maven repository, connect to the fabric and import the created profile, and attach it to one child container, `node1`, using the following commands:

```
JBossFuse:karaf@root> profile-import
mvn:com.beosbank.jbdevg.jbfuse/beosbank-file-processor/1.0.0-
SNAPSHOT/zip/profile

JBossFuse:karaf@root> profile-display com.beosbank.jbdevg.jbfuse-beosbank-
file-processor
Profile id: com.beosbank.jbdevg.jbfuse-beosbank-file-processor
Version : 1.0
Attributes:
 parents: feature-camel feature-cxf
Containers:
```

```
Container settings
----------------------------
Features :
 camel-beanio
 camel-pdf
 camel-cxf
 camel-amq

Bundles :
 mvn:com.beosbank.jbdevg.jbfuse/beosbank-file-processor/1.0.0-SNAPSHOT


Configuration details
----------------------------
PID: com.beosbank.esb.fileprocessor.env.cfg
 brokerURL discovery:(fabric:default)
 password admin
 userName admin

Other resources
----------------------------

#Add file processor profile to node1
JBossFuse:karaf@root> container-add-profile node1
com.beosbank.jbdevg.jbfuse-beosbank-file-processor
```

Once the profile is added to `node1`, the node's agent downloads the artifact and installs it. The container is restarted, and you can test the file processor as soon as its status is running. Copy a file in the input folder of the container `node1`:

```
$cp src/main/fabric8/data/data2.xml instances/node1/work/input/
```

The copied `data2.xml` file contains a transaction from the USA to the Cameroons with content similar to the following snippet:

```
<?xml version="1.0" encoding="UTF-8" ?>
<MoneyTransferStream>
<moneytransfer>
    <amountExcludingFees>200</amountExcludingFees>
  <creditCardNumber>1111-2222-3333-2222</creditCardNumber>
  <id>2</id>
   <receiver>
      <address>
         <country>Cameroon</country>
         </address>
       <firstName>Baba</firstName>
    <id>4</id>
    <lastName>Ahmadou</lastName>
```

```
      </receiver>
      <receiverCurrencyCode/>
      <sender>
        <address>
          <city/>
          <country>USA</country>
...
```

Once copied, the file is processed by the camel route, and you can see the messages in the **QUEUE.VAT.USA** queue by opening the **ActiveMQ** tab on the root container:

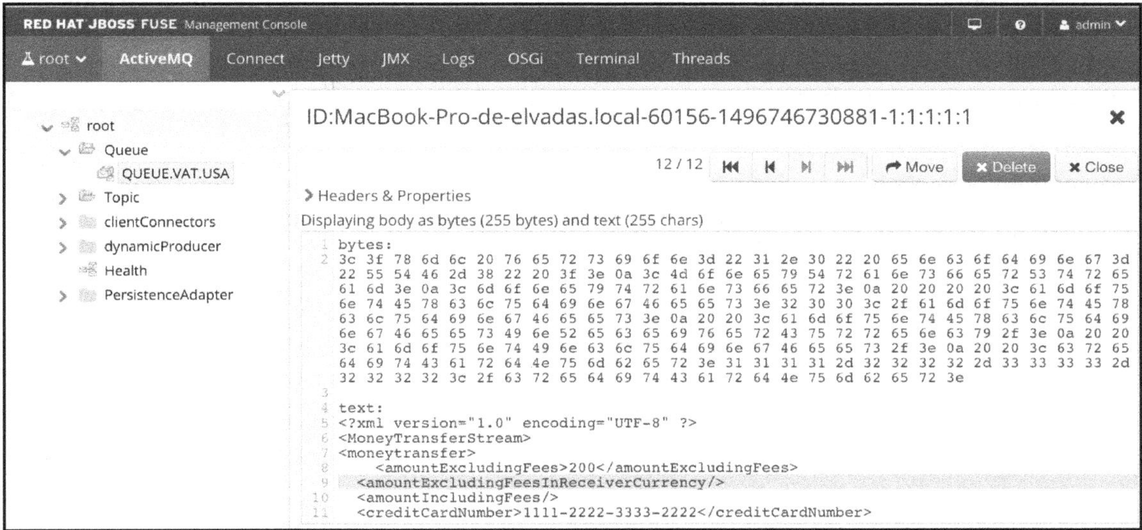

The generated output PDF files are published in the `work/output` directory of the container:

```
cd instances/node1/work/output/
output$ ls -lrt
-rw-r--r-- 1   jui  12:58 ID-xxx-local-60139-1496746608021-0-3
-rw-r--r-- 1   jui  13:17 ID-xxx-local-60139-1496746608021-0-6
```

In this section, we learned how to convert an XML file to POJO using `camel-beanio`, pull files from an input directory, and set camel headers using `xpath` expressions. We looked at the content-based routing capabilities of Apache Camel using headers to build a custom `if-else-otherwise` condition to filter transactions from the USA to the Cameroons. Also, we briefly saw how to send messages to an active MQ queue. A PDF bill was generated and persisted on the filesystem.

Summary

At the end of this chapter, we are better equipped to build custom integration scenarios interacting with various enterprise components. We discovered the Fuse modular architecture and core components, and set up, alternately, a Fuse standalone and a Fabric8 cluster, on top of which we deployed various OSGi bundles, including a datagrid cache loader, a virtual database web service proxy, and a file processor. We customized Maven POM files to automatically generate Fabric8 profiles. After successfully building profiles in the maven repositories, we saw how to import profiles in a Fuse cluster, and attached profiles to containers in order to deploy and start bundles. We also learned how to monitor application logs using the hawt.io console. If routing and orchestration are essential features for an ESB, messaging plays an important part when it comes to loosely interconnecting heterogeneous systems. In this chapter, we wisely did not cover messaging in depth; Fuse embeds ActiveMQ as a messaging platform.

Messaging concepts and features will be covered in `Chapter 7`, *Delivers Information Safely and Connects IoT*. There, we will see how to deliver information safely to remote components and connect to IoT systems.

7

Delivers Information Safely and Connects IoT

In `Chapter 4`, *Integrating Applications with JBoss Fuse*, we set up a synchronous integration process between a MySQL database and a JBoss DataGrid server. Components in this scenario were closely tied to each other; indeed, if we have to shut down the DataGrid server in a maintenance operation, for example, the integration process will result in an error due to the unavailability of the DataGrid component.

This chapter discusses how to weakly couple distributed systems using the JBoss AMQ messaging platform. In the first section, readers will master the JBoss AMQ 7 architecture, and then through practical business cases, users will learn how to set up a JBoss AMQ infrastructure and how to build and run applications that rely on JBoss AMQ to share data in a safe, asynchronous, and reliable way with distributed systems.

JBoss AMQ architecture and installation

Based on upstream Apache ActiveMQ, Apache ActiveMQ Artemis, and Apache Qpid community projects, JBoss AMQ7 is a lightweight standards-based open source messaging platform designed to enable real-time communication between different applications, components, services, devices, and the Internet of Things (IoT).

JBoss AMQ architecture

JBoss AMQ is an integration technology to loosely couple distributed systems together; it is based on an asynchronous message-passing pattern and can be used in the following contexts:

- Asynchronously connecting distributed systems
- Connecting heterogeneous components built with different languages
- Connecting devices to backend systems
- Supporting IoT and M2M integration

JBoss AMQ 7 used the Client, Broker, and interconnect components to exchange messages between containers and blocks using various protocols, including the following:

- **AMQP**: **Advanced Message Queuing Protocol**, Open binary connection based standard messaging protocol, cross-platform, flexible, and broker model independent
- **MQTT**: **Message Queue Telemetry Transport,** Protocol lightweight publish/subscribe messaging transport for the Internet of Things
- **STOMP**: **Simple/Streaming Text Oriented Messaging Protocol** text-based messaging protocol
- **Openwire**: ActiveMQ cross-language to allow native access to ActiveMQ from a number of different languages and platforms
- **Artemis "Core"/HornetQ** for interacting with Artemis/HornetQ Jms Clients

JBoss AMQ 7.X is built on top of the `Apache ActiveMQ Artemis` project, which results from merging ActiveMQ 5.X and HornetQ. ActiveMQ Artemis is also shipped as a messaging engine for JBoss Enterprise application platform 7. Compared with the AMQ 6 Broker, JBoss AMQ 7 provides high performance and scalability, adds support for JMS 2.0, and shared-nothing high-availability.

JBoss AMQ operates with three main component categories:

- **Brokers:** Containers managing the messaging infrastructure in a non-blocking way
- **Interconnects:** Message router supporting high-performance direct messaging, which can be used to shape the traffic or build hybrid clouds
- **Clients:** Components exchanging messages through brokers and routers:

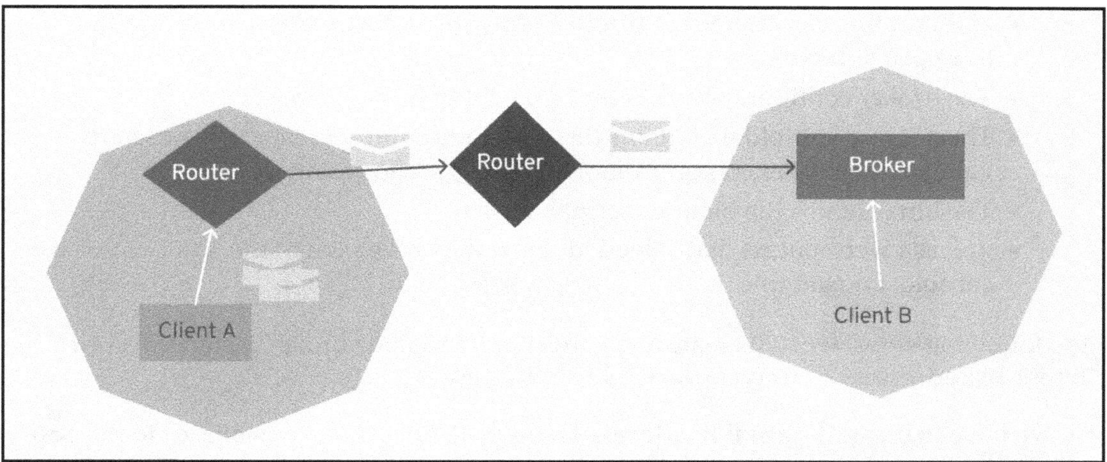

A console is also provided to manage connections, destinations, objects, and resources. In the next section, we will see how to deploy a simple AMQ infrastructure.

Clients represent applications interacting with broker resources: queues, topics, they are qualified producers when they send data to a broker and consumer whenever they are consuming data from brokers, queues or topics.

AMQ interconnects or routers act as an intermediary between clients and brokers; based on the Apache Qpid dispatch router, interconnects were influenced by Red Hat MRG use cases and are currently routing AMQP messages. Routers were primarily designed to spread the load and avoid situations where too many clients are trying to connect to a single broker.

Routers supports high-performance messaging in both one-to-one (unicast) and one-to-many (multicast) relationships. Routers can be started in standalone or interior modes; in the second case, they are interacting with other routers, and whenever a router receives a message, it automatically finds the faster routing path so that the message arrives at the destination efficiently.

JBoss AMQ insallation

Like other products, JBoss AMQ is available on the Red Hat Developer Portal; Log in with your credentials and download `jboss-amq-7.0.0.redhat-1-bin.zip`, and then unzip the file in your preferred location:

```
$ unzip jboss-amq-7.0.0.redhat-1-bin.zip -d  BeosBankAMQ/Node1
$ cd BeosBankAMQ/Node1/jboss-amq-7.0.0.redhat-1
```

- JAR and libraries needed to run the AMQ Broker are in the `installation-dir/lib` subfolder
- The broker configuration is in the `etc` subfolder
- The `schema` subfolder contains the XSD configuration schema file used to validate the broker configuration; `broker.xml`, for example
- The bin contains the binaries scripts
- `web` is a web context that is loaded when the broker starts; the `hawt.io` web console, for example

In the following steps, we will create and start two standalone broker instances on two different IP addresses of our computer: `127.0.0.2` and `127.0.0.3`.

First, we have to create a virtual IP address on the machine to add two aliases to the `lo0` interface.

On macOS systems, use the following commands:

```
sudo ifconfig lo0 alias 127.0.0.2 255.0.0.0
sudo ifconfig lo0 alias 127.0.0.3 255.0.0.0
```

On Linux systems, use the following command syntax:

```
sudo ifconfig lo0 alias 127.0.0.2 255.0.0.0 up
```

To create a broker instance, use the `bin/artemis create` command:

```
$ ./bin/artemis create  --name broker1 --user admin --password admin --host
127.0.0.2  --http-host 127.0.0.2 --allow-anonymous ../instances/broker1
Creating ActiveMQ Artemis instance at: Node1/jboss-
amq-7.0.0.redhat-1/instances/broker1
```

- `--name option` indicates the broker name
- `--user` and `--password` make a user credential to connect to the broker instance
- `--allow-anonymous` authorizes anonymous connections
- `--host` refers to the broker host
- `--http-host` is the HTTP host to use for the AMQ console and Jolokia access
- The broker data and files will be stored in `Node1/jboss-amq-7.0.0.redhat-1/instances/broker1`

You can now start the broker with the `artemis` run command:

```
$ cd  ../instances/broker1/bin
$ ./artemis run
```

The broker starts and the JBoss AMQ version is displayed:

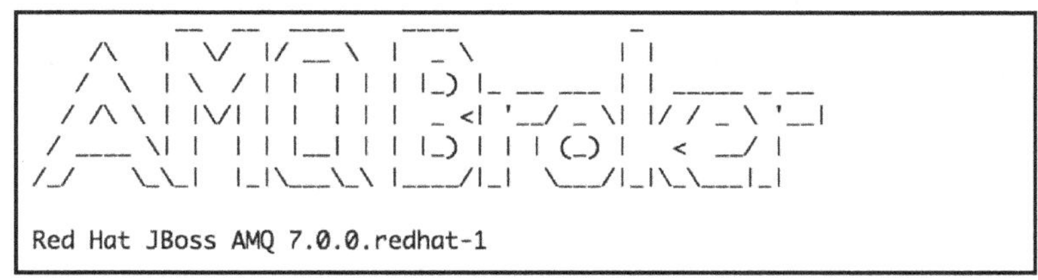


```
2:42:10,507 INFO  [] AMQ221020: Started NIO Acceptor at 127.0.0.2:61616 for
protocols [CORE,MQTT,AMQP,STOMP,HORNETQ,OPENWIRE]
12:42:10,509 INFO  [] AMQ221020: Started NIO Acceptor at 127.0.0.2:5445 for
protocols [HORNETQ,STOMP]
12:42:10,511 INFO  [] AMQ221020: Started NIO Acceptor at 127.0.0.2:5672 for
protocols [AMQP]
12:42:10,513 INFO  [] AMQ221020: Started NIO Acceptor at 127.0.0.2:1883 for
protocols [MQTT]
12:42:10,515 INFO  [] AMQ221020: Started NIO Acceptor at 127.0.0.2:61613
for protocols [STOMP]
..
12:42:13,335 INFO  [] AMQ241001: HTTP Server started at http://127.0.0.
2:8161
12:42:13,336 INFO  [] AMQ241002: Artemis Jolokia REST API available at
http://127.0.0.2:8161/jolokia
```

The various NIO interfaces on which the broker is listening are displayed in the logs with occupied ports. The `Hawt.io` console and Jolokia URL are printed at the end. Use the `admin:admin` user to connect to the `http://127.0.0.2:8161` console:

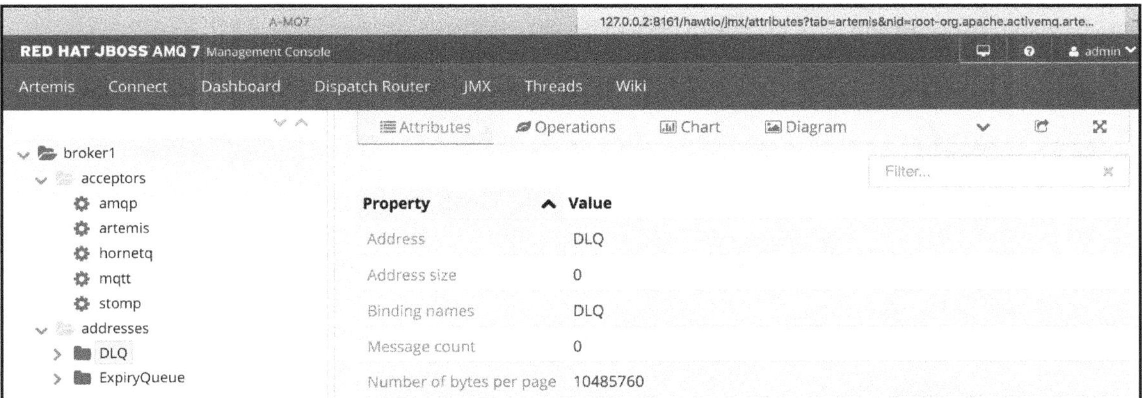

To quickly send a message in the `FIDELITYCARD.REQUEST` queue of `broker1`, use the `artemis producer` command:

```
$./artemis producer --url tcp://127.0.0.2:61616 --destination
queue://FIDELITYCARD.REQUEST --message-count 1

Producer ActiveMQQueue[FIDELITYCARD.REQUEST], thread=0 Started to calculate
elapsed time ...
Producer ActiveMQQueue[FIDELITYCARD.REQUEST],thread=0 Produced: 1 messages
Producer ActiveMQQueue[FIDELITYCARD.REQUEST],thread=0 Elapsed time in
second:0s
Producer ActiveMQQueue[FIDELITYCARD.REQUEST], thread=0 Elapsed time in
milli second : 12 milli seconds
```

The sent test message can be consumed with the `artemis consumer` command:

```
$./artemis consumer --url tcp://127.0.0.2:61616 --destination
queue://FIDELITYCARD.REQUEST --message-count 1

Consumer:: filter = null
Consumer ActiveMQQueue[FIDELITYCARD.REQUEST], thread=0 wait until 1
messages are consumed
Consumer ActiveMQQueue[FIDELITYCARD.REQUEST], thread=0 Received test
message: 0
Consumer ActiveMQQueue[FIDELITYCARD.REQUEST], thread=0 Consumed: 1 messages
Consumer ActiveMQQueue[FIDELITYCARD.REQUEST], thread=0 Consumer thread
finished
```

In this section, we discovered the AMQ main components, started broker instances, and saw how to monitor resources using the AMQ console. How to produce and consume test messages with artemis commands is a solid block on which we will rely to build applications to interact with the various AMQ routers and brokers.

Connecting clients to routers and brokers

In the following section, we will explore the various features provided by AMQ 7 through practical samples. The section is fully centered around a lab exercise to create AMQ components and interact with them from applications and monitor their states.

Lab description

In the following lab, we will learn how to connect clients with brokers and interconnects. Let's consider the following Beosbank scenario to interact with an outsource loyalty card partner called Fidelity. Beosbank signed an agreement with Fidelity company; a loyalty card should be created for all Beosbank registered users by the `FidelityAccountCreator` application of the partner. The `FidelityAccountCreator` application should also be notified whenever a user completes a transaction on the platform as the sender. The Fidelity account is bound to a counter that automatically computes user scoring based on transfer fees the user spents on the platform each day. The Fidelity counter is also used to offer discount coupons to users.

Technically, the Fidelity partner does not expose web services for account creation or transfer notification; on the other hand, it provides access to a `FIDELITY.REQUEST` JMS queue hosted by an AMQ 7 broker. Fidelity gives technical details on its broker, and it recommends following the provided roads at contrario. We will set up the components to support this architecture:

1. Create and start the Fidelity brokers
2. Create an AMQ interconnect on a RHEL 7.3 virtual machine
3. Set up the interconnect configuration to route Fidelity account creation requests to `FidelityBroker1` instances
4. Create `BeosBankFidelityApp` to send an account creation request the Fidelity partner through the router
5. Create a `FidelityAccountCreatorApp` to subscribe to the `FIDELITY.REQUEST` queue and handle the encapsulated account creation request:

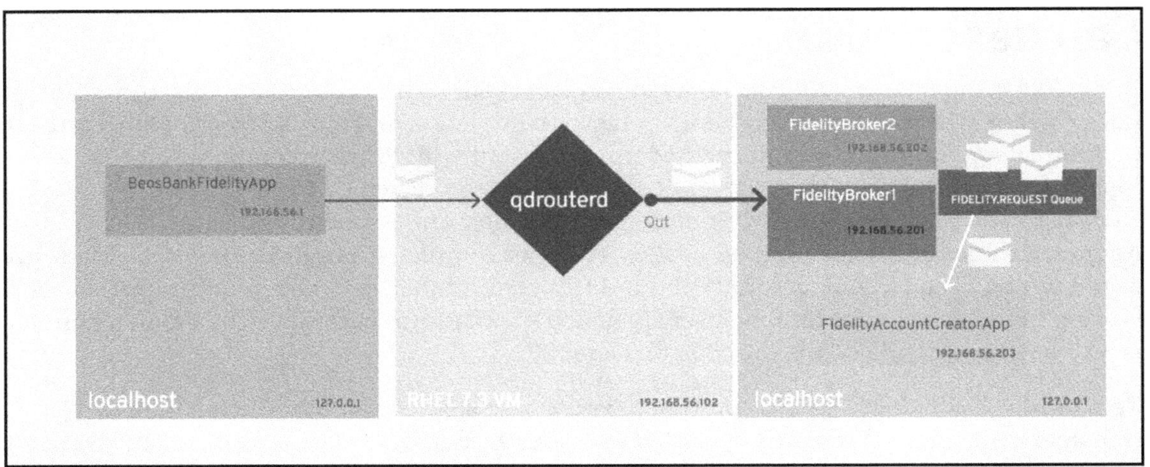

In the preceding diagram, both the `BeosbankFidelityApp` and the broker resided on the localhost machine. We will have to create a virtual IP to separate the different layers first.

Simulate the network

We will use two machines: the host (localhost) and a RHEL VM. The host provides two virtual IP ranges: `192.168.56.X/24` for Beosbank applications, and `192.168.56.20X/24` for the Fidelity landscape.

Hosts are RHEL VM from a Virtual Box Network: Host (`192.168.56.1/24`), VM (`192.168.56.102/24`).

Create a another virtual IP for Beosbank producer applications:

```
sudo ifconfig vboxnet0 alias 192.168.56.2
```

Beosbank applications will use `192.168.56.1` and `192.168.56.2`.

Create virtual IP for Fidelity brokers: `192.168.56.20X` (FidelityBrokerX):

```
sudo ifconfig vboxnet0 alias 192.168.56.201
sudo ifconfig vboxnet0 alias 192.168.56.202
```

Add gateways to the newly created virtual IP:

```
sudo route -n add  192.168.56.0.2  127.0.0.1    //Route for beosbank Apps
sudo route -n add  192.168.56.0.201  127.0.0.1  //Route for FidelityBroker1
sudo route -n add  192.168.56.0.202 127.0.0.1   //Route for FidelityBroker2
```

You can check whether all the machines are available using the `ping -S` test from various zones:

```
#extract on the vboxnet0 interface from host
$ ifconfig
vboxnet0: flags=8943<UP,BROADCAST,RUNNING,PROMISC,SIMPLEX,MULTICAST> mtu
1500 ether 0a:00:27:00:00:00
 inet 192.168.56.1 netmask 0xffffff00 broadcast 192.168.56.255
 inet 192.168.56.2 netmask 0xffffff00 broadcast 192.168.56.255
 inet 192.168.56.201 netmask 0xffffff00 broadcast 192.168.56.255
 inet 192.168.56.202 netmask 0xffffff00 broadcast 192.168.56.255
..
$ ping -S 192.168.56.202 -c 1 192.168.56.102
PING 192.168.56.102 (192.168.56.102) from 192.168.56.202: 56 data bytes
64 bytes from 192.168.56.102: icmp_seq=0 ttl=64 time=0.322 ms

--- 192.168.56.102 ping statistics ---
1 packets transmitted, 1 packets received, 0.0% packet loss
round-trip min/avg/max/stddev = 0.322/0.322/0.322/0.000 ms
```

The network is now up and running; the next step consists of creating and starting the Fidelity brokers using the `artemis create` command.

Create and start Fidelity broker instances

Create and start the brokers:

```
$./artemis create  --name FidelityBroker1 --user admin --password admin --
host 192.168.56.201  --http-host 192.168.56.201  --allow-anonymous
../instances/FidelityBroker1

$ cd ../instances/FidelityBroker1/bin/
$ ./artemis run


$./artemis create  --name FidelityBroker2 --user admin --password admin --
host 192.168.56.202  --http-host 192.168.56.202  --allow-anonymous
../instances/FidelityBroker2
$ cd ../instances/FidelityBroker2/bin/
$ ./artemis run
```

`FidelityBroker1` is waiting for an AMQ request on `192.168.56.201:5672`.

Once the broker installation is complete, the next step is to install and configure the router.

Create the router

There are two options to set up an AMQ interconnect/router. The first option is to use a RHEL virtual machine, and the second option is through a Docker container.

In this lab, we will use a RHEL virtual machine; however, you can set up the same lab using `Christian Posta`--the `ceposta/qdr` docker image available at `https://hub.docker.com/r/ceposta/qdr/`.

While using a virtual machine, you can download and install RHEL free for developers at `https://developers.redhat.com/products/rhel/download/`. Then, follow these instructions:

- Enable `EPEL RPM for RHEL 7`
- Use `yum` to install the Qpid Proton and Python dependencies, and the `qpid-dispatch-router` and `qpid-dispatch-tools` packages:

```
$sudo yum install qpid-proton-c python-qpid-proton
$sudo yum install qpid-dispatch-router qpid-dispatch-tools
```

After having installed `qdrouterd` in `/usr/sbin/qdrouterd`, the configuration file in `/etc/qpid-dispatch/qdrouterd.conf` should be customized to create the expected communication links between the router, client, and brokers.

Router configuration

In order to make the interconnect component listen to AMQP Fidelity account creation requests from `192.168.56.102:5672` and route the `FIDELITY.REQUEST` queue on `FidelityBroker1`, the following configuration can be used in `/etc/qpid-dispatch/qdrouterd.conf`:

```
router {
  mode: standalone
  id: fidelityCardRoute
  workerThreads: 4
}

listener {
    host: 0.0.0.0
    port: 5672
    authenticatePeer: no
    saslMechanisms: ANONYMOUS
}
```

```
log {
  module: DEFAULT
  enable: debug
  timestamp: true
}

connector {
    name: fidelityBroker1Connector
    host: 192.168.56.201
    port: 5672
    role: route-container
    allowRedirect: no
}

address {
    prefix: FIDELITY.REQUEST
    waypoint: yes
}

autoLink {
    addr: FIDELITY.REQUEST
    dir: out
    connection: fidelityBroker1Connector
}
```

The router configuration has a set of sections describing specific items of the configuration.

The **router** item defines the basic router configuration and has the following attributes:

- `mode`: Defines the router operating mode. **Standalone** means the router only sends messages to directly connected endpoints and does not interact with other routers in a network; this is the default value. If the router should be part of a network and collaborate with the other routers, choose the `interior` mode.
- `ID`: Defines the router unique identifier. The router will fail to start without this information; it will also be used as the AMQP container name.
- `workerThreads`: The number of threads to be created to handle message routing. The default value is four worker threads.

The **listener** component defines how clients reach the router:

- `host`: Denotes the bind address on which the router will be listening
- `port`: Port number or symbolic service name; by default, the value is `amqp`
- `authenticatePeer`: Indicates whether the router requires a client identity
- `saslMechanisms`: List of accepted SASL mechanisms

The **log** component is used to configure logging on specific router modules:

- The `DEFAULT` **module** encapsulates all the router modules: `CORE`, `AGENT`, and so on
- The **output** attribute can be used to customize log output locations

The connector component creates an outgoing connection from the router:

- `name`: An identifier for your outgoing connection; in this case, we are creating a connection to `fidelityBroker1`.
- `host`: Outgoing connection destination host: `192.168.56.201` (only broker 1).
- `port`: Service name: AQMP on `5672`; it is also possible to use the generic `61616` port here.
- `allowRedirect`: Attribute to tell whether the router should allow its peer to redirect this connection to another address. By default, it is true. This can be used to set up a bridge, for example, to another broker URL.
- `linkCapacity`: Not used here, but can be used to configure the capacity of each link of the connector (the number of messages that can be in-flight concurrently on the links)

The **address** component defines which, how, and where the router should process and send the incoming messages:

- `prefix` : Messages arriving with a destination name matching this prefix pattern will be routed according to the current address policy.
- `distribution`: How the router distributes the incoming message: `multicast/balance/closet(default). closet` => Uses the shortest path to the destination, `multicast`=> to all connected clients, and `balance`=> balance to distribution between clients.
- `waypoint`: Use the address as waypoints.

The **autolink** component is used to configure links managed by the routers:

- `addr`: The reference to the component address; here, the `FIDELITY.REQUEST` address
- `connection`: The name of the connector for this autolink-- `FidelityBroker1Connector`
- `dir`: The direction--**in** or **out**

To complete the configuration, we also need to open the AMQP port on the RHEL VM:

```
[root@localhost ~]# firewall-cmd --zone=public --add-port=5672/tcp --
permanent
[root@localhost ~]# systemctl restart firewalld.service
[root@localhost ~]# firewall-cmd --zone=public --list-ports
5672/tcp
```

Restart `qrouterd.service` to reload the updated configuration:

```
[root@localhost ~]# systemctl restart qdrouterd.service
[root@localhost qpid-dispatch]# systemctl status  qdrouterd.service
● qdrouterd.service - Qpid Dispatch router daemon
   Loaded: loaded (/usr/lib/systemd/system/qdrouterd.service; disabled;
vendor preset: disabled)
   Active: active (running) since sam. 2017-06-17 01:10:45 CEST; 6s ago
 Main PID: 4744 (qdrouterd)
   CGroup: /system.slice/qdrouterd.service
           └─4744 /usr/sbin/qdrouterd -c /etc/qpid-dispatch/qdrouterd.conf
```

To send a message to the router, we can rely on the `QPID JMS Client` Maven dependency:

```
<dependency>
        <groupId>org.apache.qpid</groupId>
        <artifactId>qpid-jms-client</artifactId>
</dependency>
```

The `loyaltycardManager` Java class should open an AMQP connection, and then a JMS session to interact with the router:

```
public class LoyaltyCardManager {
private static final String ROUTER_URL="amqp://192.168.56.102:5672";
private static final String QUEUE_NAME="FIDELITY.REQUEST";
private static final String CSVDATA="CSVDATA";
public static void main(String[] args) throws Exception {
      Connection connection = null;
      String csvData = System.getProperty(CSVDATA);
      if(CSVDATA == null || CSVDATA.equals(""))
           throw new RuntimeException("LoyaltyCardManager.main() must pass
the "+CSVDATA +" system property With format
OPERATION;USERID;FIRSTNAME;LASTNAME;TRXID;TRXFEESAMOUNT;CURRENCY");
      System.out.println("LoyaltyCardManager() will connect to router:
"+ROUTER_URL+" : at the following address: "+QUEUE_NAME);
      ConnectionFactory connectionFactory = new
JmsConnectionFactory(ROUTER_URL);
      try {
         // Step 1. Create an AMQP qpid connection
         connection = connectionFactory.createConnection();
```

```
            // Step 2. Create a JMS session
            Session session = connection.createSession(false,
Session.AUTO_ACKNOWLEDGE);
            // Step 3. Create a Producer
            Queue fidelityRequestQueue = session.createQueue(QUEUE_NAME);
            MessageProducer beosbankFidelityRequestProducer =
session.createProducer(fidelityRequestQueue);
            // Step 4. send a CSV Text Data on user transactions
beosbankFidelityRequestProducer.send(session.createTextMessage(csvData));
            System.out.println("\nmessage sent:"+ csvData+" \n");
```

The `beosbankFidelityRequest` producer sends `TextMessage` in a CSV format: `OPERATION;USERID;FIRSTNAME;LASTNAME;TRXID;TRXFEESAMOUNT;CURRENCY`.

- `CREATE/CANCEL`: The operation represents the operation code
- `USERID`: The user identifier
- `FIRSNAME` : The user's first name
- `LASTNAME`: The user's last name
- `TRXID`: Money transfer reference
- `TRXFEESAMOUNT`: The total amount of fees paid for this transaction
- `CURRENCY`: The currency of the transaction

If using OSGI bundles, the `AMQP` protocol support is provided in the `camel-amqp` component; just use `<to uri="amqp://host:port">` in the blueprint to send the message to the target router.

The full code is available at `https://github.com/nelvadas/jbdevg/tree/master/jbamq/beosbank-fidelity-app`.

Execute the `Fidelity Producer` main class with the Maven `exec` plugin:

```
beosbank-fidelity-app$ mvn clean package exec:java -
DCSVDATA="CREATE;10000;JBoss;Doctor;TRX001;4.99;EUR"
...
[INFO] --- exec-maven-plugin:1.6.0:java (default-cli) @ beosbank-fidelity-
app
LoyaltyCardManager() will connect to router: amqp://192.168.56.102:5672 :
at the following address: FIDELITY.REQUEST
SLF4J: Failed to load class "org.slf4j.impl.StaticLoggerBinder".
SLF4J: Defaulting to no-operation (NOP) logger implementation
SLF4J: See http://www.slf4j.org/codes.html#StaticLoggerBinder for further
details.
message sent:CREATE;10000;JBoss;Doctor;TRX001;4.99;EUR
[INFO] ------------------------------------------------------------------------
```

```
----
[INFO] BUILD SUCCESS
[INFO] ------------------------------------------------------------------------
----
[INFO] Total time: 3.372 s
[INFO] Finished at: 2017-06-18T06:40:31+02:00
[INFO] Final Memory: 27M/306M
[INFO] ------------------------------------------------------------------------
----
```

We can also track client (`192.168.56.1:57976`) connections in the `qdrouterd` service logs:

```
[root@localhost ]# journalctl -u qdrouterd.service -n 200 -f

juin 17 13:43:33 localhost.localdomain qdrouterd[15152]: Sat Jun 17
13:43:33 2017 SERVER (debug) Accepting incoming connection from
192.168.56.1:57976 to 0.0.0.0:5672
juin 17 13:43:34 localhost.localdomain qdrouterd[15152]: Sat Jun 17
13:43:34 2017 POLICY (debug) Connection '192.168.56.1:57976' closed with
resources n_sessions=0, n_senders=0, n_receivers=0. nConnections= 0.
```

The router process statistics are also available with the `qstat` command:

```
[nono@localhost ~]$ qdstat -l
Router Links
  type      dir  conn id  id  peer  class   addr                 phs  cap
undel  unsett  del  presett  acc  rej  rel  mod  admin    oper
========================================================================
===
  endpoint  out  1       3         mobile  FIDELITY.REQUEST       0    250
0      0       2    0       2    0    0    0    enabled  up

 endpoint  in   5       8         mobile  $management           0    250
0      0       1    0       1    0    0    0    enabled  up
  endpoint  out  5       9         local   temp.yDSytTsaDBx+PhI        250
0      0       0    0       0    0    0    0    enabled  up
```

As soon as a message is sent on the router's `amqp` interface with an address matching the `FIDELITY.REQUEST` prefix, you can see stat updates for this line.

Messages by the Fidelity application are routed to the Fidelity broker; you can browse the list at `http://192.168.56.201:8161/hawtio/`:

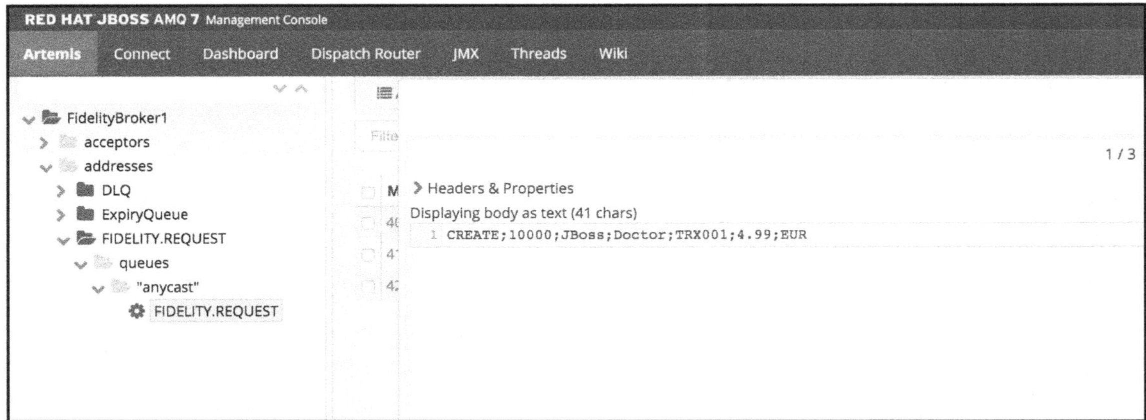

In this section, we set up an AMQ interconnect/router between a client and a broker, and exchanges were handled using the AMQP binary protocol. For some use cases where resources such as bandwidth are limited, IoT, and MQTT in general, is the recommended communication protocol. In the next section, we will connect Beosbank IoT devices to a broker using the `MQTT` protocol.

Connecting IoT devices

The JBoss AMQ broker exposed an MQTT interface that can be used to connect IoT devices. The goal of this section is to demonstrate, in a practical sample, how the MQTT lightweight protocol capabilities can be used to connect IoT devices with other systems. Let's consider the Beosbank money remittance agencies for example; each agency has special equipment (`BeosbankIOTDevice`) designed with Raspery PI to serve the following causes:

- A waiting queue manager: Each visitor in the agency should hit a button on the equipment to print a ticket. The equipment periodically (every 5 minutes) sends the total numbers of visitors in the agency to a control center.
- A screen to display some messages to visitors: Messages are designed and planned by control centers, and the screen is also used to display the partner's advertisements.

IoT devices and backend systems can interact through a set of topics hosted on the brokers. On the one hand, backend systems can publish Ad messages in the `FIDELITY.ADS` topics, while devices are registered as readers on the topic. On the other hand, devices can publish their waiting queue counter in another topic where the control centers act as consumers:

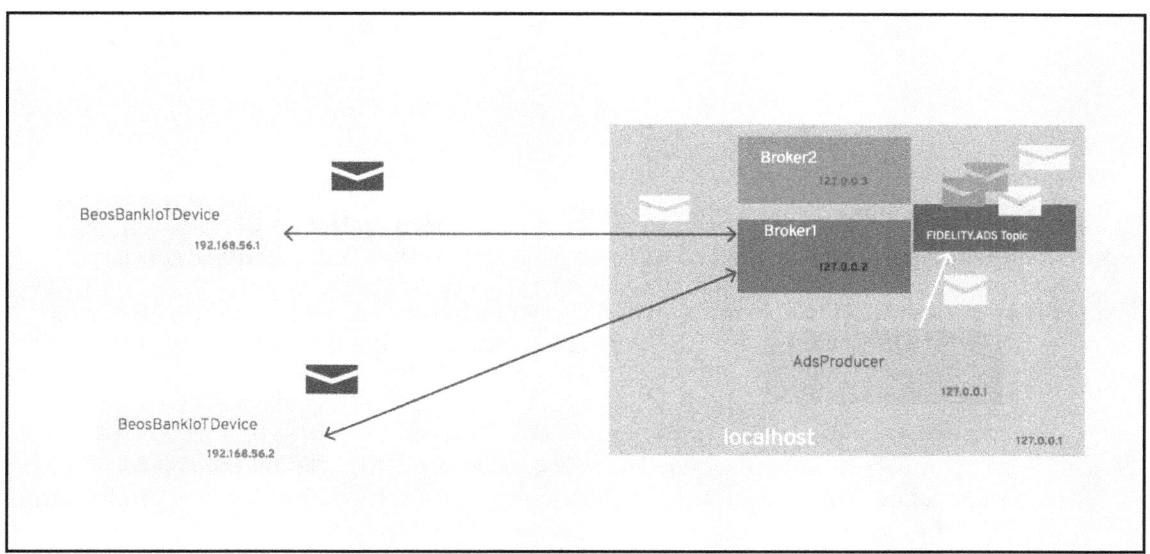

The Fuse source provides an MQTT client to interact with MQTT brokers--`org.fusesource.mqtt-client:mqtt-client:jar`:

```
public class AdsProducer {
   private static final String BROKER_URL="tcp://127.0.0.2:1883";
   private static final String FIDELITY_ADS_TOPIC="FIDELITY.ADS";

   public static void main(String[] args) throws Exception {
       System.out.println("Connecting to Broker1 using MQTT");
       MQTT mqtt = new MQTT();
       mqtt.setHost(BROKER_URL);
       BlockingConnection connection = mqtt.blockingConnection();
       connection.connect();
       System.out.println("Connected to Broker1");

       // Subscribe to  fidelityAds topic
       Topic[] topics = { new Topic(FIDELITY_ADS_TOPIC,
QoS.AT_LEAST_ONCE)};
       connection.subscribe(topics);

       // Publish Ads
```

```
        String ads1 = "Discount on transfer fees up to -50% with coupon code
JBOSSDOCTOR.  www.beosbank.com";
        int index=0;
        while(true){
         connection.publish(FIDELITY_ADS_TOPIC, (index+":"+ads1).getBytes(),
QoS.AT_LEAST_ONCE, false);
      System.out.println("Sent messages with index="+index);
         Thread.sleep(10000);
         index++;
        }
}
}
```

Devices or backend systems first need to obtain a connection on the broker hosting the topics, then try to subscribe to a set of topics with a specific needed quality of service.

The **Quality of Service** (**QoS**) level is an agreement between the sender and receiver of a message regarding the guarantee of delivering a message. There are three QoS levels in MQTT:

- At most once (0), `QoS.AT_MOST_ONCE`: A message sent with this QoS level won't be acknowledged by the receiver or stored and redelivered by the sender. This is often called "fire and forget", and provides the same guarantee as the underlying TCP protocol.
- At least once (1), `QoS.AT_LEAST_ONCE`: The message will be delivered at least once to the receiver, but the message can also be delivered more than once in some cases.
- Exactly once (2) `QoS.AT_EXACTLY_ONCE`: This guarantees that each message is received only once by the peer. It is the safest and also the slowest quality of service level; indeed, there are four exchanges between the sender and its counterpart (`Message`, `PUBREC`, `PUBREL`, `PUBCOMP`) to finalize the transaction.

Finally, the message will be delivered with the QoS defined by the client when publishing to the broker, but the QoS can be downgraded if the client subscribing to the broker defined a lower QoS expectation.

The MQTT messages are delivered asynchronously (push) through publish/subscribe architecture:

```
public class BeosBankIotDevice {
...
 // Subscribe to  fidelityAds topic
        Topic[] topics = {new Topic(FIDELITY_ADS_TOPIC, QoS.AT_LEAST_ONCE)};
        connection.subscribe(topics);
        // Get Ads Messages
```

```
        while(true){
         Message message = connection.receive(5, TimeUnit.SECONDS);
         if(message!=null){
          System.out.println("Received messages. "+new
String(message.getPayload()));
         }
      }
```

Use the `maven exec` plugin to run a producer instance:

```
$ mvn clean package exec:java -
Dexec.mainClass="com.beosbank.jbdevg.jbamq.iot.AdsProducer"
[INFO] Scanning for projects...
[INFO]
[INFO] ------------------------------------------------------------------------
----
[INFO] Building Beosbank Fidelity App Manager 1.0-SNAPSHOT
[INFO] ------------------------------------------------------------------------
----[INFO] --- exec-maven-plugin:1.6.0:java (default-cli) @ beosbank-iot-
lab ---
Connecting to Broker1 using MQTT
Connected to Broker1
Sent messages with index=0
Sent messages with index=1
Sent messages with index=2
...
```

Also, start two consumers concurrently in two tabs of your Terminal:

```
$ mvn exec:java -
Dexec.mainClass="com.beosbank.jbdevg.jbamq.iot.BeosBankIotDevice"
[INFO] Scanning for projects...
[INFO]
[INFO] ------------------------------------------------------------------------
----
[INFO] Building Beosbank Fidelity App Manager 1.0-SNAPSHOT
[INFO] ------------------------------------------------------------------------
----
[INFO]
[INFO] --- exec-maven-plugin:1.6.0:java (default-cli) @ beosbank-iot-lab --
-
Connecting to Broker1 using MQTT
Connected to Artemis
Received messages. 10:Discount on transfer fees up to -50% with coupon code
JBOSSDOCTOR. www.beosbank.com
```

Ads are delivered safely to both the consumers as soon as they establish a connection with the broker.

In this section, we created a sample IoT system with an `AdsProducer` application and various IoT devices. We connect the whole using an `AMQ` broker. In all the previous examples, the broker is a central and single point of failure; but what happens if clients cannot reach the broker or broker? In the next section, we will see which AMQ topologies can be used to improve the broker availability.

AMQ topologies

While using AMQ, one technique to avoid a single point of failure is to set up a master-slave topology. In a master-slave configuration, a set of brokers cooperate to ensure that the cluster does not go down. It is an active-passive configuration, where the master and slaves synchronize themselves using various locking mechanisms: shared filesystem, shared database, replicated stores, colocated, and so on. The master should always be active to maintain the cluster is up and running. Once the master goes down, a slave node immediately detects the breakdown and becomes the new master node. In such a configuration, clients have to adjust the calling URL with the failover URL to automatically switch to the new broker:

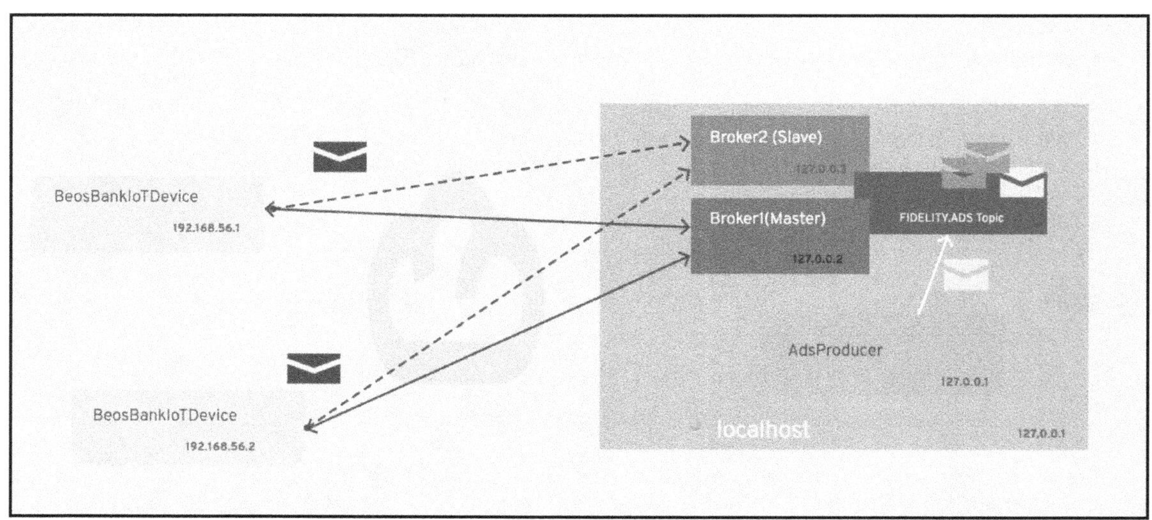

To build a master-slave configuration from the existing standalone instances--`broker1(127.0.0.2)` and `broker2(127.0.0.3)`--we need to update `broker.xml` of each instance, as follows:

- Create a shared folder, `/shared/data`
- Edit `instances/broker1/etc/broker.xml`
- Update the persistence folders:

```
<paging-directory>/shared/data/paging</paging-directory>
<bindings-directory>/shared/data/bindings</bindings-directory>
<journal-directory>/shared/data/journal</journal-directory>
<large-messages-directory>/shared/data/large-messages</large-messages-
directory>
```

These variables refer to various directories that will be used for persistence by the master and slave:

- Add the `connector` section with a connector for each broker:

```
<!--Defines connectors for broker1 and broker2 -->
<connectors>
<connector name="broker1-connector">tcp://127.0.0.2:61616</connector>
<connector name="broker2-
connector">tcp://127.0.0.3:61616</connector></connectors>
<!--Protect your cluster with a user -->
<cluster-user>cluser</cluster-user><cluster-password>cluser</cluster-
password>
<!-- Define cluster connections with a static connector on broker2 -->
<cluster-connections>
   <cluster-connection name="beosbank-cluster">
    <connector-ref>broker1-connector</connector-ref>
     <static-connectors>
      <connector-ref>broker2-connector</connector-ref>
    </static-connectors>
  </cluster-connection>
</cluster-connections>
<!-- Define the HA Policy with failover on shutdown -->
<ha-policy>
 <shared-store>
 <master> <failover-on-shutdown>true</failover-on-shutdown>   </master>
</shared-store>
</ha-policy>
```

- Protect your cluster with a cluster user/password: `cluser:cluser`
  - Create a cluster connection with the name `beosbank-cluster`
- In the cluster connection, reference the `broker1-connector` first with the `connector-ref`
- In the `beosbank-cluster`, add a static connector with a `connector-ref on broker2-connector`
- Restart the broker; you will see the lock acquisition in the `logs` file:

```
$ ./instances/broker1/bin/artemis run
...
[org.apache.activemq.artemis.core.server] AMQ221000: live Message Broker
is starting with configuration Broker Configuration
(clustered=true,journalDirectory=/shared/data/journal,bindingsDirectory=/sh
ared/data/bindings,largeMessagesDirectory=/shared/data/large-
messages,pagingDirectory=/shared/data/paging)00:05:31,626 INFO
[org.apache.activemq.artemis.core.server] AMQ221006: Waiting to obtain live
lock
```

Do the same configuration on `broker2` (slave), with the exception of the following items:

```
<cluster-connections>
<cluster-connection name="beosbank-cluster">
<connector-ref>broker2-connector</connector-ref> <!-- broker2 to broker1-
->
<static-connectors>
<connector-ref>broker1-connector</connector-ref>
</static-connectors>
</cluster-connection>
</cluster-connections>
<ha-policy>
<shared-store>
<slave> <!--not master -->
<failover-on-shutdown>true</failover-on-shutdown>
</slave>
</shared-store>
</ha-policy>
```

We create the same cluster configuration (shared folders, connectors, cluster user, cluster connections, and HA Policy), but you have to invert the `broker1-connector` and `broker2-connector` roles in the configuration. The HA Policy also refers to `salve` instead of the master component. `broker2` starts and indicates in its logs that it is a potential backup:

```
$ ./instances/broker2/bin/artemis run
...
```

```
00:25:26,463 INFO  [org.apache.activemq.artemis.core.server] AMQ221109:
Apache ActiveMQ Artemis Backup Server version 2.0.0.amq-700005-redhat-1
[694c51b2-553b-11e7-abe8-36f5725da889] started, waiting live to fail before
it gets active00:25:26,608 INFO  [org.apache.activemq.artemis.core.server]
AMQ221031: backup announced
```

With this configuration, if you stop the master node (`broker1`), the slave node automatically becomes the new master. Press *CTRL+C* to stop `broker1`; in the `Broker2` logs, you can see the following:

```
00:39:22,862 INFO  [org.apache.activemq.artemis.core.server] AMQ221020:
Started NIO Acceptor at 127.0.0.3:61613 for protocols [STOMP]00:39:22,862
INFO  [org.apache.activemq.artemis.core.server] AMQ221010: Backup Server is
now live
```

For Openwire or AMQP clients, by changing the broker URL from `tcp://127.0.0.2:61616` to `private static final String BROKER_URL="failover://(tcp://127.0.0.2:61616,tcp://127.0.0.3:61616)";`.

Client connections will be automatically switched to the new active master; on the contrary, the current version of the MQTT protocol is designed for a single connection to a single broker, so you will face an error while attempting to connect to use the failover scheme:

```
Connecting to Broker1 using MQTTConnecting to Broker1 using
MQTT[WARNING]java.lang.Exception: Unsupported URI scheme 'failover' at
org.fusesource.mqtt.client.CallbackConnection.createTransport(CallbackConne
ction.java:268) at
org.fusesource.mqtt.client.CallbackConnection.connect(CallbackConnection.ja
va:139)
```

While working with messaging platforms such as JBoss AMQ, to avoid single points of failure, master-slave topology can be used to provide high availability so that if a broker is killed, another broker can take over immediately. In this section, we set up a master-slave configuration from two standalone brokers by editing the `broker.xml` configuration. The full files are available at `https://github.com/nelvadas/jbdevg/tree/master/jbamq/configuration`.

Summary

When it comes to interconnecting and decoupling distributed systems, messaging appears to be the most elegant solution as it reduces dependencies between systems. In the producer- consumer model, if the producer application is down, the consumer simply has nothing to consume. JBoss AMQ 7, with its modular architecture and modern components, such as interconnects, and its variety of supported protocols, can be an interesting option to connect IoT and deliver information safely.

8
Making Better Decisions in Your Applications

In a traditional imperative programming model, a developer explicitly instructs the runtime engine what to do through statements, conditional structures, and loops. In this context, an application's business logic is embedded in the developer code, and any change in the business logic implies a code update and a complete release cycle. However, there are some complex problems where imperative programming cannot provide a satisfactory solution within a reasonable time. One approach to solving such kinds of problems is to rely on expert systems and constraint optimization tools. It is at this level that declarative programming takes place; instead of telling it what to do, as in imperative programming, the developer tells the system how to solve the problem through structured rules. The system then applies various pattern matching algorithms, and infers on existing rules and facts to deduce goals.

This chapter introduces artificial intelligence programming using the JBoss ecosystem. JBoss **Business Rule Management System** (**BRMS**) and **Drools Rule Language** (**DRL**) features are explored to build rule-based applications, decision tables, and complex event handlers. By the end of this chapter, the reader will be able to author, test, and run a rule-based application using the BRMS platform.

In this chapter, we will cover the following topics:

- The BRMS architecture and components
- Installing BRMS
- Rule authoring with BRMS
- **Complex Event Processing** (**CEP**) using BRMS
- Constraint optimization with the BRMS platform

JBoss BRMS components and architecture

The JBoss BRMS platform is built on top of a set of open source projects and independent components:

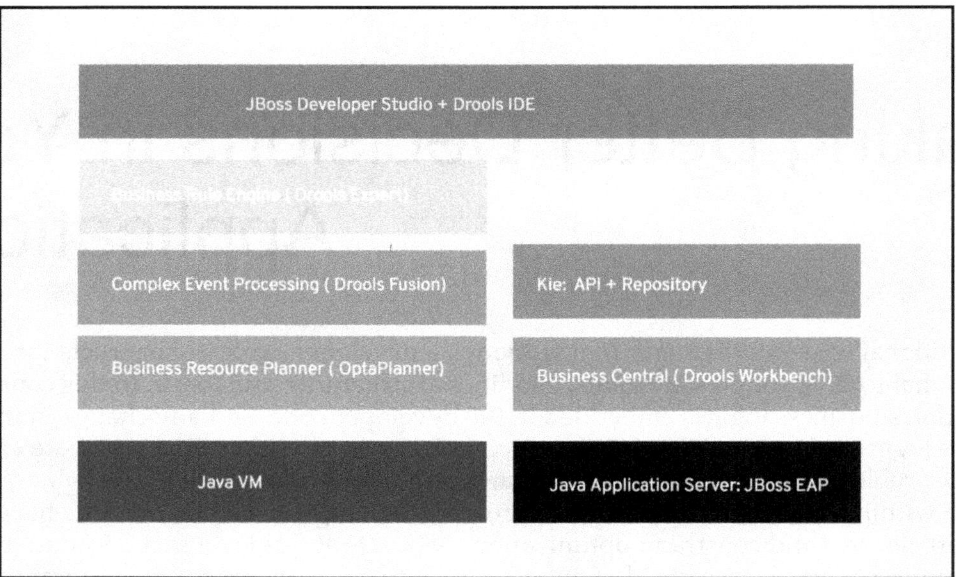

JBoss BRMS core components include the following:

- A generic UI application built from the **Drools Workbench** project to author, manage, and test business rules and decisions tables. In the BRMS platform, this module is called **Business Central.**
- BRMS includes a set of plugins shipped with Integration Stack to improve the user experience while developing business rules applications with **JBoss Developer Studio**; this set can be extended with **Drools IDE**, which is an optional Eclipse plugin that allows users to author rules within Eclipse.
- **Knowledge Is Everything** (**KIE**) provides two distinct functionalities:
    - A knowledge store where all resources are stored. The store also provides a rule and domain model artifact versioning.
    - A knowledge API that allows applications to consume rules from the knowledge store. This implements separation between applications and business rules.

- A pattern-matching **Business Rule Engine** based on the JBoss Drools Expert project. Drools Expert allows users to easily express solutions to complex problems through declarative programming. Developers express their need through rules (what to do) when some conditions are met, and the rule engine infers on facts and rules to make it happen. In traditional programming, the developer says how to do it. Drools relies on pattern-matching algorithms, such as ReteOO or PHREAK.
- The **Drools Fusion** module brings complex event processing features to the BRMS platform; the objective of complex event processing is to capture relevant and meaningful events from multiple data sources and respond as quickly as possible to them.
- **OptaPlanner** is an open source lightweight constraint optimization engine to solve planning issues.
- **Drools Expert**, **Drools Fusion**, and **OptaPlanner** are lightweight embeddable JAR engines that can be run on a Java Virtual Machine; on the contrary, Business Central and KIE web apps run on top of a Java application container such as JBoss EAP.

JBoss BRMS is a composite platform with various components that can be used individually for specific purposes. In your daily usage, you may be working with only a restricted set of components. In the next section, we will take a look at how to set up a simple BRM infrastructure for our projects.

Installing the JBoss BRMS platform

While some BRMS components, such as Drools Expert, Drools Fusion, and OptaPlanner, can be used as an individual `JAR` and be embedded in user applications, the Business Central management application, on the other hand, requires a Java application server to run. JBoss BRMS provides a package to run the suite using JBoss Application Server. Two installation methods are provided; either use the full BRMS Installer or patch an EAP Server installation with BRMS deployables. At the time of writing this chapter, the latest version of BRMS deployable is `jboss-brms-6.4.0.GA-deployable-eap7.x.zip` on the Red Hat developer portal. Unzip it on top of a JBoss EAP 7.0 to have a full BRMS platform:

```
#Install BRMS
$ unzip jboss-eap-7.0.0.zip -d brms
$ unzip -o jboss-brms-6.4.0.GA-deployable-eap7.x.zip -d brms/

#Create admin users
$ cd brms/jboss-eap-7.0/bin
$./add-user.sh -a -r ApplicationRealm -u brmsAdmin -p brmsAdmin01# -ro
```

```
analyst,admin,manager,user,kie-server,kiemgmt,rest-all —silent

$./add-user.sh -a -r ApplicationRealm -u beosbankUser -p beosbankUser01# -
ro analyst,admin,manager,user,kie-server,kiemgmt,rest-all —silent

#Stat the platform
$ ./standalone.sh

08:48:44,126 INFO [org.wildfly.extension.undertow] (ServerService Thread
Pool -- 61) WFLYUT0021: Contexte web enregistré : /kie-server

08:49:00,328 INFO [org.wildfly.extension.undertow] (ServerService Thread
Pool -- 73) WFLYUT0021: Contexte web enregistré : /business-central
```

Create two admin users-- `brmsAdmin/brmsAdmin01#` and `beosbankUser/beosbankUser01#`--and roles, such as `analyst`, `admin`, `manager`, `user`, `kie-server`, and `kiemgmt`.

Start the BRMS platform using the `bin/standalone.sh` script--you can see web context registration for `kie-server` and `business-central` from log outputs.

Business Central is available at `http://localhost:8080/business-central`:

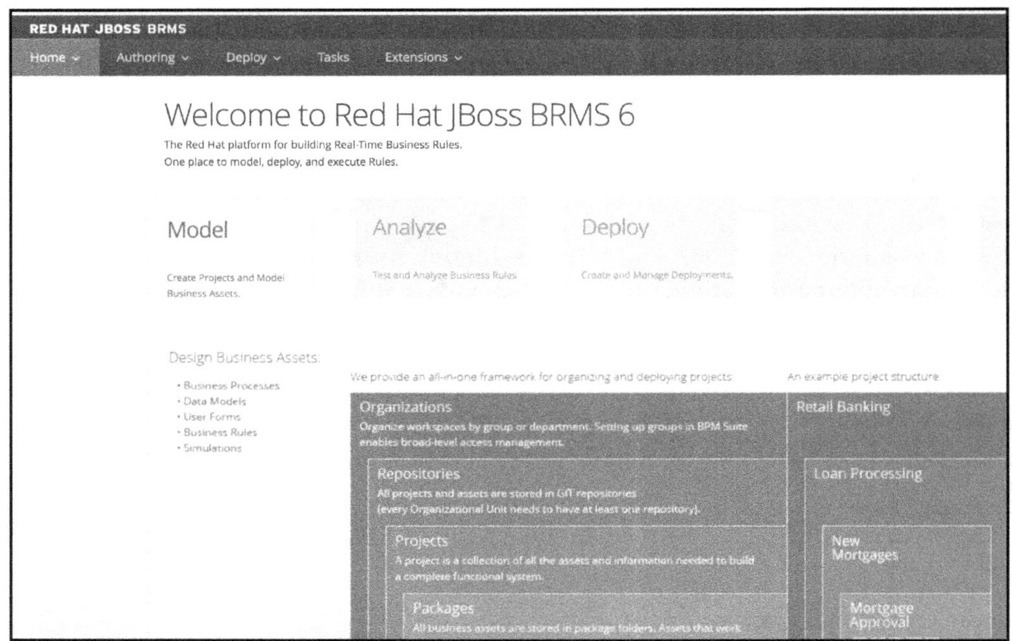

The Business Central application allows users to creating business rules projects to organize business assets into logical organizations and repositories.

The first thing that we will need is to create the Beosbank organizational unit by following the **Authoring** > **Administration** Menu, and then clicking on **Organizational Unit** > **Manage Organizational Units**:

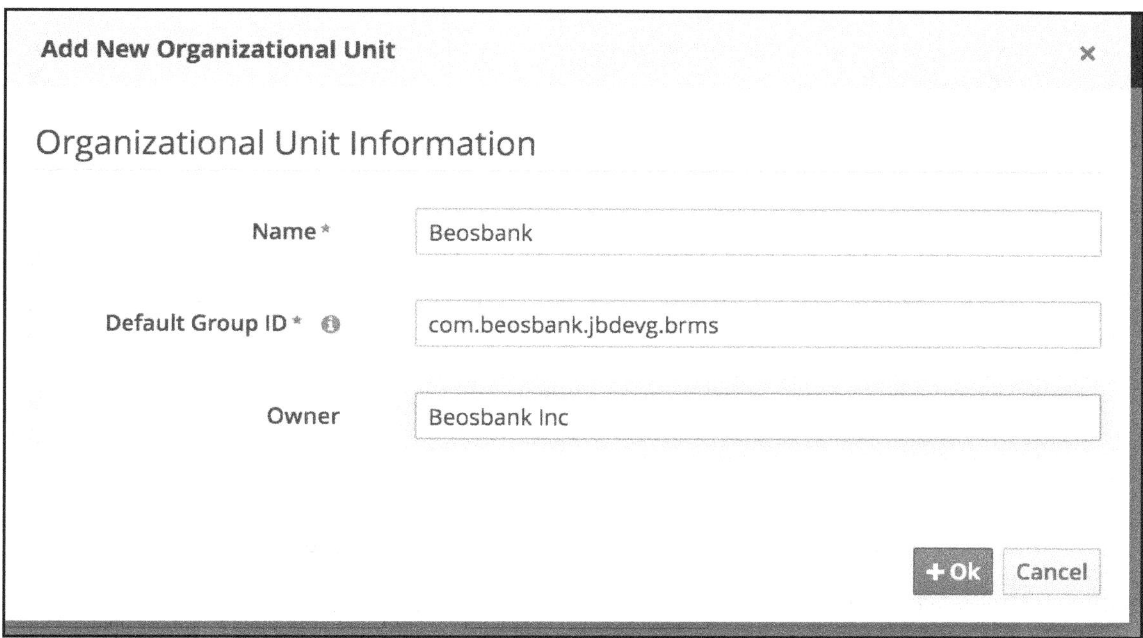

Fill in the following items as given:

- Name: **Beosbank**
- Default Group ID: **com.beosbank.jbdevg.brms**
- Owner: **Beosbank Inc**

The **Default group ID** will be used for projects of this organization. Before creating our project, we will need repositories to host them. BRMS repositories host artifacts needed to run build- and run-based rule applications; they are based on an internal Git server. BRMS allows users to manage organizational repositories through the Repositories Menu.

Create a new CRM repository to host Beosbank applications dealing with Customer Relationship Management using the `Create New Repository` action:

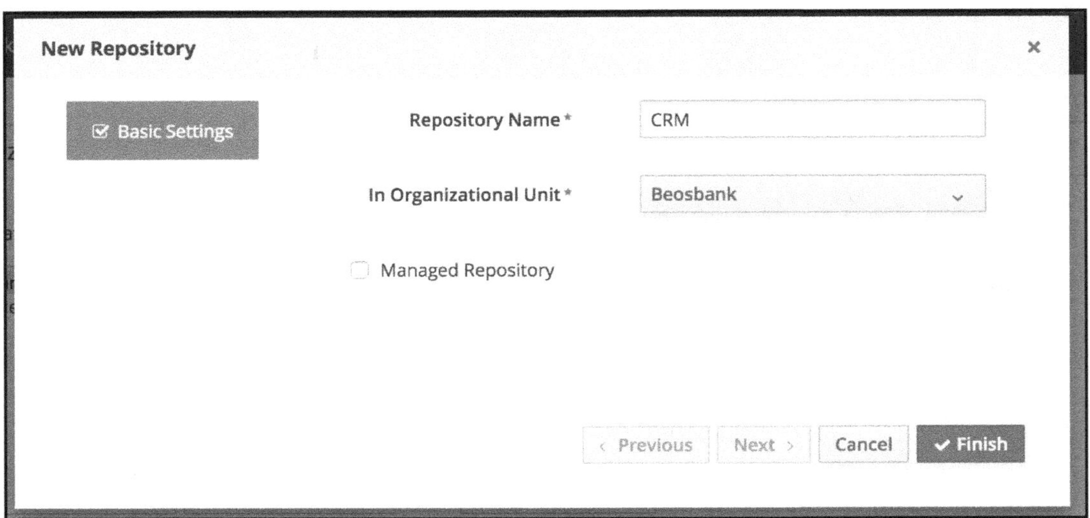

Fill in the form accordingly to create the Beosbank's CRM repository:

Repository Name: **CRM**

In Organizational Unit: Select **Beosbank**

In the next section, we will create a business rule application to apply discount codes when users send money transfers online.

Users can also clone the existing Git repository with the **Repository** > **Clone repository** features:

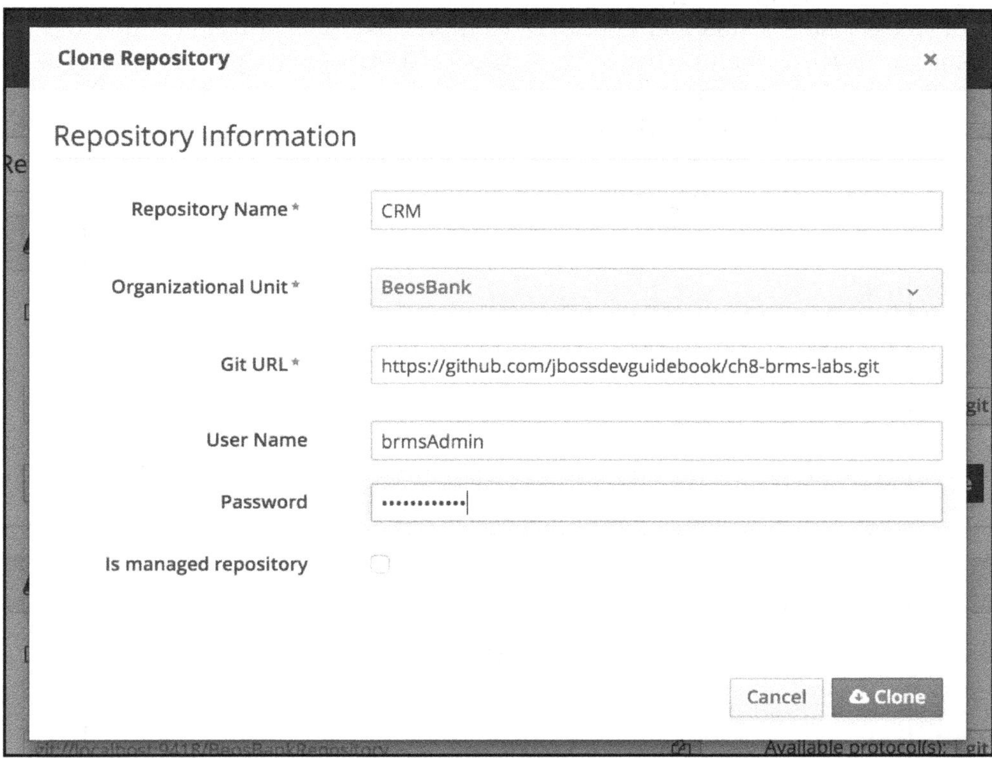

Enter the remote URL from which the repository should be imported.

Git URL: `https://github.com/jbossdevguidebook/ch8-brms-labs.git`

This repository contains a completed version of the `beosbank-brms-discounts` application. BRMS also enable users to create deployments and test business rules. In the next section, we will start authoring and testing various business rules.

Authoring business rules with JBoss BRMS

In a declarative programming style, the raw material comprises mainly business rules and facts. A business rule is a statement derived from propositional and first-order logic (for example, if <*conditions*>, then <*actions*>) to express system knowledge. The inference engine applies pattern matching algorithms on rules and data facts present in the working memory to infer conclusions that lead to actions. Facts are mainly expressed as plain Java object models:

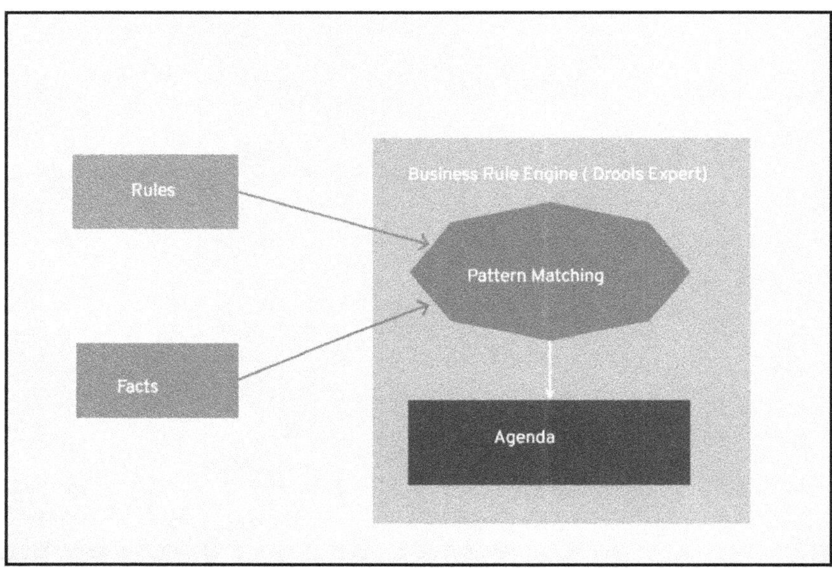

Rules reside in a space called the production memory, whereas facts are kept in the working memory. On applying pattern-matching algorithms, new facts can be generated, updated or removed from the working memory. Two rules are said to be in conflict when they both are true for the same fact assertion--an `Agenda` is important to manage execution orders in case of conflicts.

This section focuses on Business Rules Management theory; in the following section we will look at more details--how to author, test, and manage business rules using Business Central.

Authoring rules in Business Central

Periodically, the Beosbank CRM division launches marketing campaigns where a number of discount codes are released. Each code is valid during a certain period and associated to a discount rate applied to fees if used when sending a money transfer. To be eligible for a fee discount, a money transfer request should agree with the following:

- The money transfer request should include the discount coupon code value in the `discountCode` field
- The money transfer request must be created during the validity period of the associated discount coupon
- A coupon cannot be applied twice on a money transfer request
- A `PromotionFeeItem` fact should be generated for each valid match between discount and MoneyTransfer

Now, let's take a look at how to build a rule-based application with BRMS to automatically compute fee discounts.

Creating a rule-based project

To create a rule based project from Business Central, follow the following instructions.

Use the New Item menu from the project authoring view.

If you cloned the provided `https://github.com/jbossdevguidebook/ch8-brms-labs.git` repository from GitHub, just select the `beobank-brms-discount` project from it.

You can create the same project from scratch with the following instructions.

- Select the **CRM** repository, then click on **New Item** > **Project**, and fill in the Project Wizard popup with the following details:
    - Project Name: `beosbank-brms-discounts`
    - Description: Applying discount rules to Money Transfer
    - Group ID: `com.beosbank.jbdevg.brms`
    - Version: 1.0.0
- Click on the **Finish** button. A **Maven** project will be created in the repository.

Once the project is created, we need to provide valuable content: data model and rules.

Creating a data object

A data model is an abstraction for a fact. In the current scenario, we want to materialize the following items :

- The `MoneyTransfer` class to hold data from Money Transfer transactions; the `MoneyTransfer` class has a set of attributes.
- The purpose of the `Promotion` class is to store data related to the marketing campaign, such as beginning date, end date, discount code, description, and discount rate.

To create a `moneytransfer` data object class:

- use the `New Item > Data Object` action--enter the class name (`MoneyTransert`) and class package (`com.beosbank.jbdevg.brms`).
- Leave the **Persistable** box unchecked and click on **OK**. The new empty class is created under the Data Object section of the Project Editor.

You can now either edit the Java class manually or use the integrated editor to add fields:

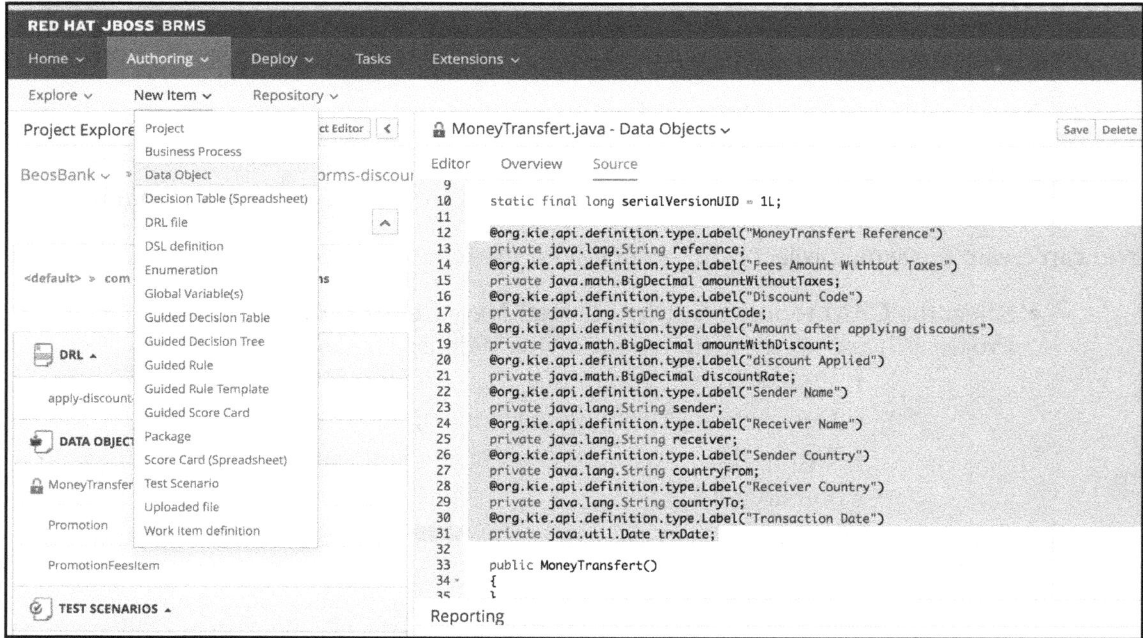

When creating a field using the editor, the source code is automatically synchronized:

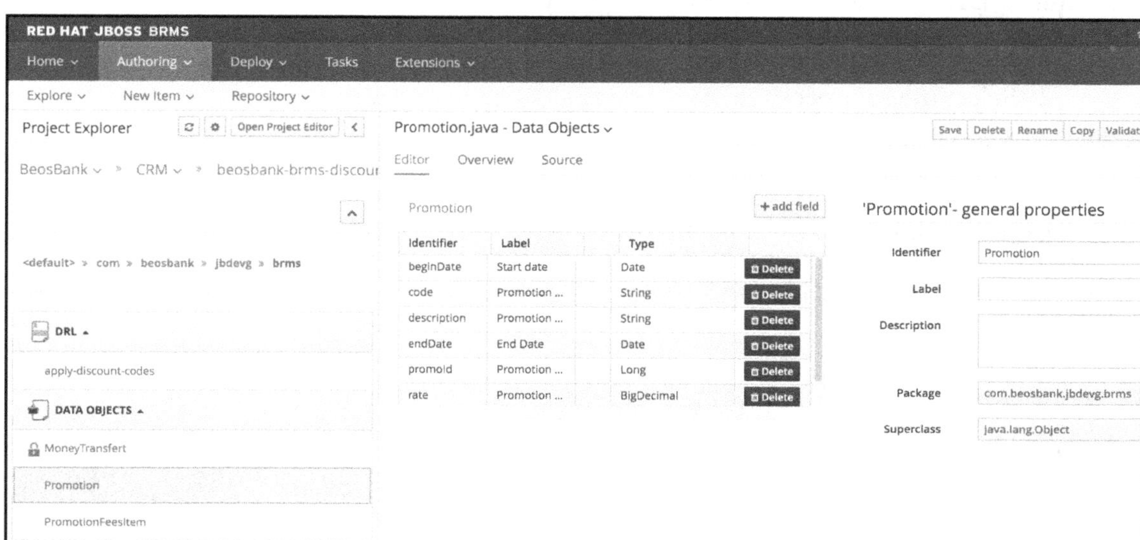

- `PromotionFeesItem` to track discount application over time. It has three fields: promotionCode, the Money Transfer identifier/reference, and the total discount amount granted when using the code on this transaction.
- Save the different model classes created by clicking on their **save** action button, Otherwise they will not be visible by rules or tests scenarios in later sections.

Creating business rules

Once facts are created, we normally have all the input to produce our business rules; BRMS rules are declarative instructions written in the **Drools Rule Language** (**DRL**) syntax. There are various options to create rules in BRMS:

- Creating DRL files from Business Central
- Using Graphical Guided Rule Editor from BRMS
- Authoring rules from JBoss Developer Studio and Drools IDE plugins
- Creating rules in a custom **Domain-Specific Language** (**DSL**)

This sample covers the first option: Authoring DRL files from Business Central using the **New Item > DRL File** through the following steps:

1. Enter the filename, `apply-discount-codes.drl`.
2. Select the root package, `com.beosbank.jbdevg.brms`.
3. Keep the Use DSL unchecked.
4. Edit the file content as follows:

```
package com.beosbank.jbdevg.brms;
import java.math.BigDecimal;
rule "Apply Discount Codes"
when
 $mt: MoneyTransfer( discountCode != null)
 $promo: Promotion ( code == $mt.getDiscountCode() && beginDate <=
$mt.getTrxDate() && $mt.getTrxDate() <= endDate)
then
 //update the mt data
 $mt.setDiscountRate( $promo.getRate());
 $mt.setAmountWithDiscount($mt.getAmountWithoutTaxes().multiply(new
BigDecimal(1.0).subtract($promo.getRate())));
 System.out.println("MoneyTransfer "+ $mt.getReference() +"
feesAmount="+$mt.getAmountWithoutTaxes()+"
priceAfterDiscount="+$mt.getAmountWithDiscount());
 //Create a promotionFeeItem Fact
 PromotionFeesItem promoFeesGranted = new PromotionFeesItem($promo, $mt);
 insertLogical(promoFeesGranted);
end;
```

A DRL File is a text file with a `.drl` extension containing a set of rule, queries, functions, imports, globals, and attributes that are used by the rules.

So, the rule name is `Apply Discount Codes`; it is located in the `src/main/resource` project folder, especially in the `com.beosbank.jbdevg.brms` package, as well as in the data objects `MoneyTransfer`, `Promotion`, and `PromotionFeesItem`.

The `ApplyDiscountCodes` rule is fired when a Money Transfer fact (referenced by the `$mt` variable) present in the working memory has a non null discount code matching an active promotion code (fact referenced by the `$promo` variable). The money transfer date should be between the promotion's beginning and end dates. When these four conditions are verified, the money transfer object is updated, a log statement is printed in the console, and a new `PromotionFeesItem` fact is inserted in the working memory using the `insertLogical` instruction. Once the rule is created, we will need to test it to make sure that facts are handled as expected. BRMS includes a graphical editor to create and run custom test scenarios. In the next section, we will create and run a test scenario to check `ApplyDiscountCodes`.

Creating test scenarios in BRMS

Test scenarios are built using a graphical editor; as with any modern tests, they provide a way to set up the test environment and validate result expectations. Use the `New Item > Test Scenario` action from the project authoring view to create the `PromotionApplicationTest` file. Test scenario is built using the graphical editor:

- Click on the **Given** action to create a `MoneyTransfer` fact
- Set the name as `mt0` and click on **Add**
- Click on the `MoneyTransfer` class to add a fact property value
    - **Fees amountWithoutTaxes**: `50`
    - **Transaction reference**: `FRCM10001`
    - Discount code submitted with this transaction: `MERRY CHRISTMAS`
    - **Transaction date**: `19-Dec-2017`
- Repeat the same operation to create a Promotion Fact for the Christmas period:
    - **Begin Date**: `01-Nov-2017`
    - **End Date**: `31-Jan-2018`
    - **Discount Code**: `MERRY CHRISTMAS`
    - **Description**: `Get 25% reduction on your Fees Transfer with code MERRY CHRISTMAS`
    - **Discount Rate**: `0.25`

The final scenario test created should look like the following image:

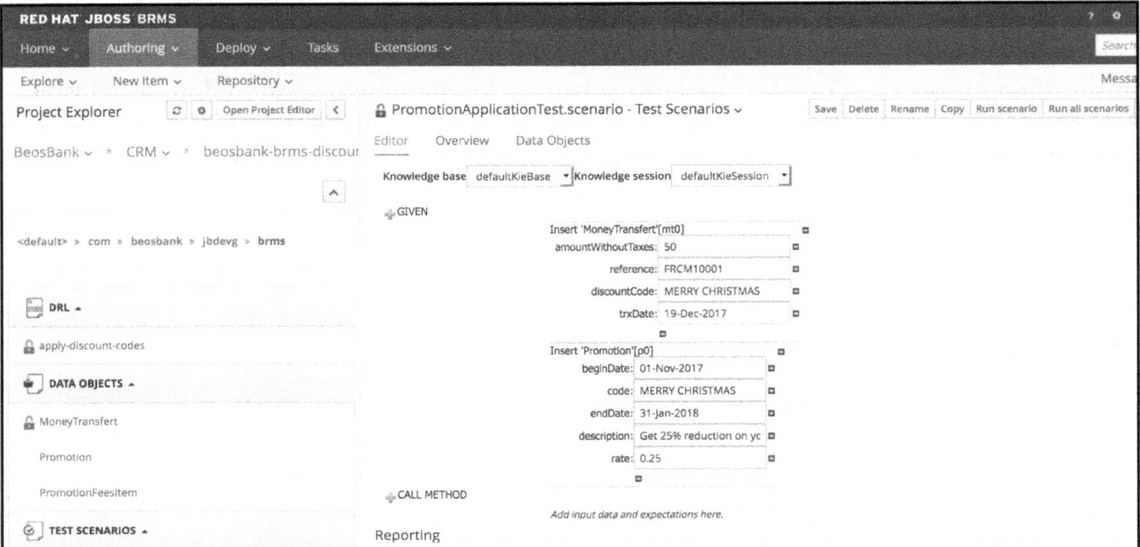

At any time, you can validate your inputs using the **Validate** button at the top-right corner of the screen. If there is an error, you will have the details to fix it.

Test scenarios include an expect section to set expected results. For this scenario, we are expecting the following:

- The `ApplyDiscountCode` rule to be fired at least once, since the `MoneyTransfer:mt0` discount code and period match the `Promotion:p0` details
- We expect a 25% discount on the final fees amount *(50*(1-0.25)=37.5)*
- We expect a new `PromotionFeesItem` to be present in the working memory with the discount and transaction details
- Click on the **Run Scenario** button to run the test case:

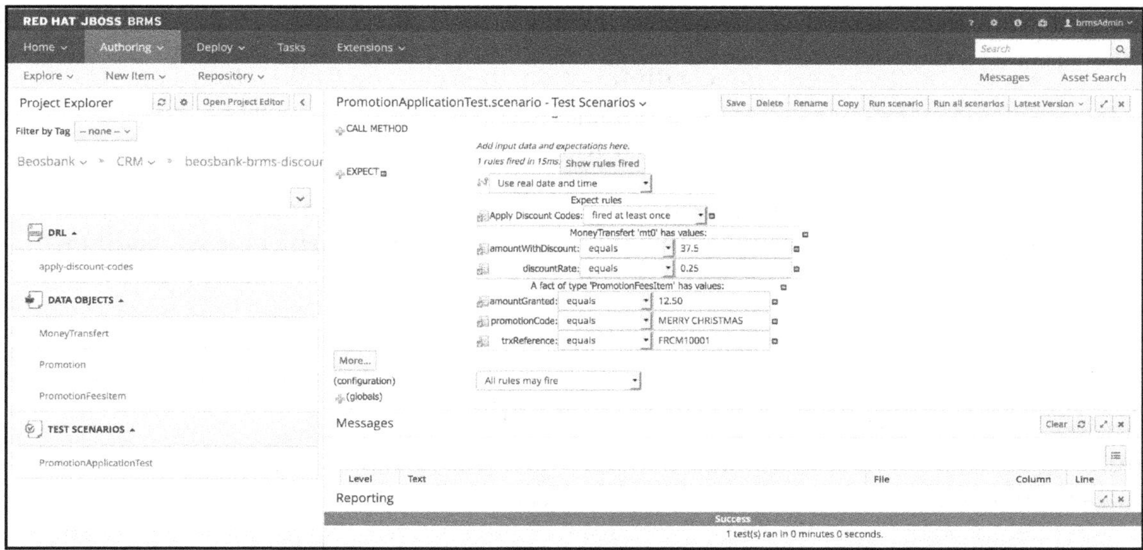

Assertions are validated and the test has been passed. Logs are also printed on the console:

```
01:47:45,995 INFO [stdout] (default task-60) MoneyTransfer FRCM10001
feesAmount=50 priceAfterDiscount=37.50
```

Try to update the expected granted amount with an invalid value and rerun the scenario. The test fails, and the actual value is presented after the failing assertion:

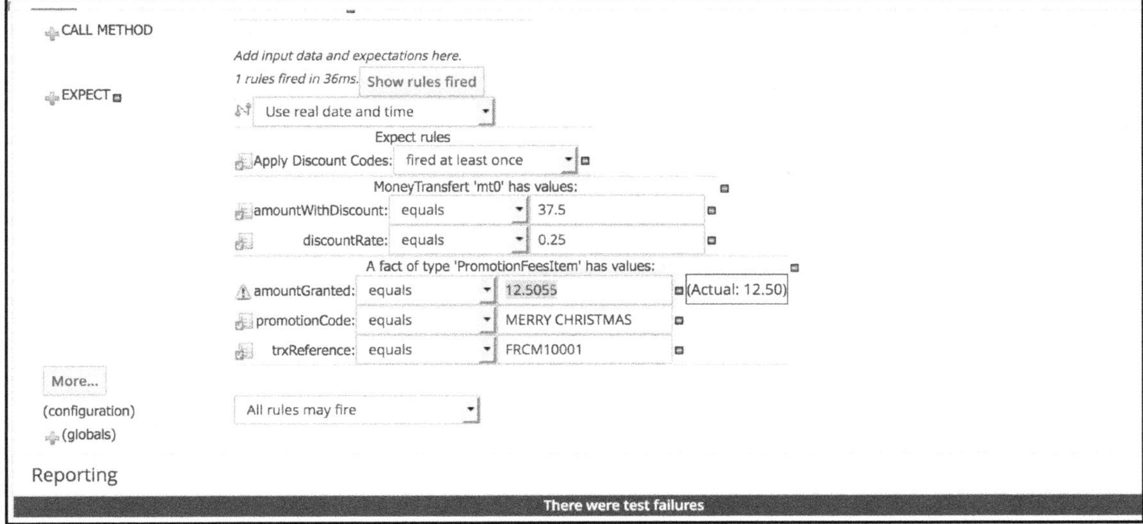

You can now build the project and deploy it in the artifact repository:

- Click on the **Open project editor** button, then click on **Build** > **Build and Deploy**
- The Maven project is built and deployed in the artifact repository; click on **Authoring** > **Artifact Repository** to browse the repository's content.

In this section, we created an if *<condition>*, then an *<action>* rule in a DRL file; in a specific workflow, you could have a long list of such rules. When the left-hand side or conditions are very similar, we are in the presence of a decision table. In the next section, we will see how to create rules from a decision table.

Implementing a decision table

JBoss BRMS provides a set of options to first create decision tables and then produce DRL rules from them: web-based and spreadsheet decision tables. Web-based decisions tables are created through a graphical user interface in Business Central by inspecting facts and fields present in the working memory, whereas spreadsheet decision tables are created by importing a custom XLS sheet. The sheet is organized by rows and columns; each row represents a rule, whereas a column can represent a condition, an action, or a rule option. Spreadsheet decision tables have the advantage of being more accessible to business users. Let's consider the following scenario:

Beosbank money transfer prices are defined periodically by a pricing division; prices may vary very frequently, depending on various criteria. The general prices are defined in relation to the sender's and receiver's countries. In business terms, they are called corridors. One could talk about the France to US Corridor to discuss money transactions by customers in France to receivers located in the US. On a corridor, there are various price lines, depending on the amount to be sent. The price can be a fixed value, a percentage of the total amount to be sent, or a combination of both schemes.

The following spreadsheet extract represents some price items for France:

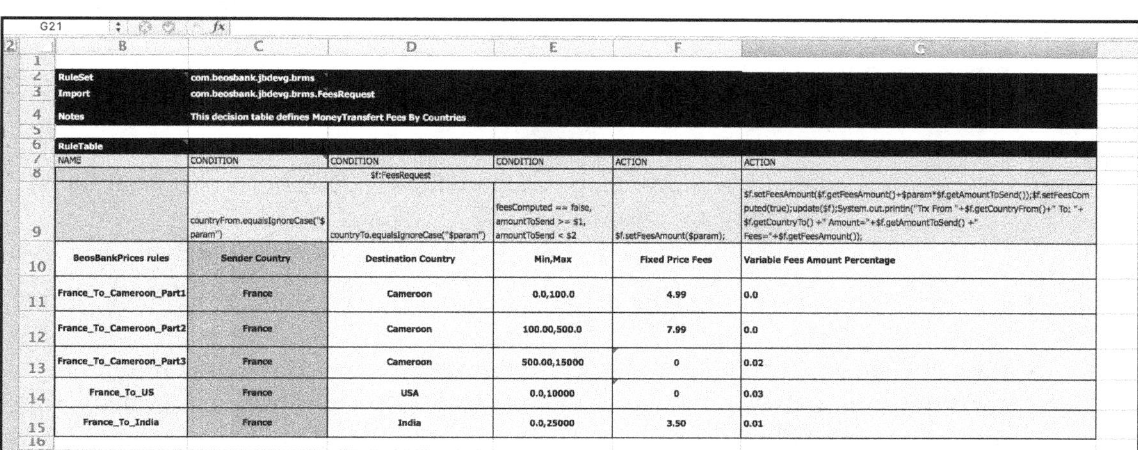

	B	C	D	E	F	G
1						
2	**RuleSet**	**com.beosbank.jbdevg.brms**				
3	**Import**	**com.beosbank.jbdevg.brms.FeesRequest**				
4	**Notes**	**This decision table defines MoneyTransfert Fees By Countries**				
5						
6	**RuleTable**					
7	NAME	CONDITION	CONDITION	CONDITION	ACTION	ACTION
8			$f:FeesRequest			
9		countryFrom.equalsIgnoreCase("$param")	countryTo.equalsIgnoreCase("$param")	feesComputed == false, amountToSend >= $1, amountToSend < $2	$f.setFeesAmount($param);	$f.setFeesAmount($f.getFeesAmount()+$param*$f.getAmountToSend());$f.setFeesComputed(true);update($f);System.out.println("Trx From "+$f.getCountryFrom()+" To: "+$f.getCountryTo() +" Amount="+$f.getAmountToSend() +" Fees="+$f.getFeesAmount());
10	**BeosBankPrices rules**	**Sender Country**	**Destination Country**	**Min,Max**	**Fixed Price Fees**	**Variable Fees Amount Percentage**
11	**France_To_Cameroon_Part1**	**France**	**Cameroon**	**0.0,100.0**	**4.99**	**0.0**
12	**France_To_Cameroon_Part2**	**France**	**Cameroon**	**100.00,500.0**	**7.99**	**0.0**
13	**France_To_Cameroon_Part3**	**France**	**Cameroon**	**500.00,15000**	**0**	**0.02**
14	**France_To_US**	**France**	**USA**	**0.0,10000**	**0**	**0.03**
15	**France_To_India**	**France**	**India**	**0.0,25000**	**3.50**	**0.01**

Each table row/column has a specific meaning:

- **Row 2:** Contains a `RuleSet` attribute, which says that this Excel file is a ruleset. The name of the ruleset is `com.beosbank.jbdevg.brms`.
- **Row 3**: Use the `Import` keyword to specify the list of Java classes referred to in rules. In this specific case, we are importing the `com.beosbank.jbdevg.brms.FeesRequest` class, which contains a set of fields:
    - `countryFrom`: The sender's country name
    - `countryTo`: The receiver's country name
    - `feesComputed`: A Boolean indicating whether fees computation has been already done for the target object
    - `amountToSend`: The amount the issuer wants to send to the receiver
    - `feesAmount`: The total fees amount computed

- **Row 6**: The `RuleTable` attribute indicates the beginning of a rule table, a spreadsheet can contain one or more rule tables. If followed by a string text; the text will serve as a prefix for the rule's name.
- **Row 7:** Defines column roles:
    - `NAME` defines a column containing rule names
    - `CONDITION` contains the left-hand side part of the DRL rule; by default, it is implicitly a conjunction (AND) of conditions if there are many conditions columns
    - `ACTION` contains the right-hand side of the rule: the then `<action>`
- **Row 8:** Defines the `$f` variable of the `FeesRequest` type to use in the remaining rules.
- **Row 9: D**efines conditions to check and the action to perform when the conditions are satisfied. `$param` refers to the dynamic attribute values defined in the yellow cells below the row referencing it (row 10 to 15 of the same).
- **Row 10:** Contains column descriptions.
    - **Row 11 to Row 15:** Define a set of rules to be generated using conditions defined in row 9. `$param` will be replaced by the cell value in the same column.
- In column E, a condition is defined to check whether the `amountToSend` is greater than $1 (the first value in the rule cell before the comma) and less than $2 (the second value in the cell after the comma).
- **Action 1 (cell F9)**: Initialises the `feesAmount` with the fixed part, then makes a computation to add the variable commission drawn from the amount to be sent:

```
//Action 1
$f.setFeesAmount($param);

//Action 2
$f.setFeesAmount($f.getFeesAmount()+$param*$f.getAmountToSend());
$f.setFeesComputed(true);
update($f);
System.out.println("Trx From "+$f.getCountryFrom()+" To: "+
$f.getCountryTo() +" Amount="+$f.getAmountToSend() +"
Fees="+$f.getFeesAmount());
```

`$f.setFeesComputed(true)` makes sure that the `$f` fact will no longer be eligible for fees computation and avoid loops.

To test the current decision table, create a new project, `beosbank-brms-pricing`, then add a new item (spreadsheet decision table).

The full `beosbank-brms-pricing` project is available at `https://github.com/jbossdevguidebook/ch8-brms-labs.git`.

Rules are generated from the decision table; let's take a look at the second rule (`France_To_Cameroon_Part2`):

```
package com.beosbank.jbdevg.brms;
//generated from Decision Table
import com.beosbank.jbdevg.brms.FeesRequest;

// rule values at B12, header at B6
rule "France_To_Cameroon_Part2"
when
    $f:FeesRequest(  countryFrom.equalsIgnoreCase("France"),
                     countryTo.equalsIgnoreCase("Cameroon"),
                    feesComputed == false,
                    amountToSend >= 100.00,
                    amountToSend < 500.0
                  )
then
   $f.setFeesAmount(7.99);
   $f.setFeesAmount($f.getFeesAmount()+0.0*$f.getAmountToSend());
   $f.setFeesComputed(true);
   update($f);
   System.out.println("Trx From "+$f.getCountryFrom()+" To: "+
$f.getCountryTo() +" Amount="+$f.getAmountToSend() +"
Fees="+$f.getFeesAmount());end
```

To test the rule, create a test scenario item with given facts matching the corridor. **feesAmount** is expected to be a linear combination of the `amountToSend`:

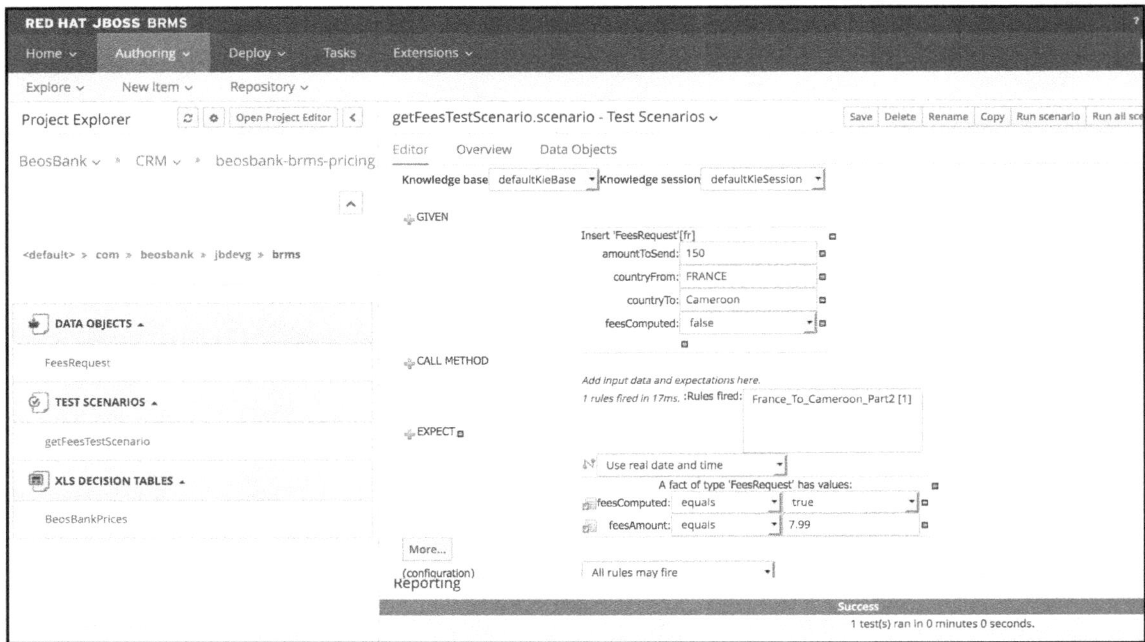

With the amount to send being equal to 150 Euros, we fall in the second price line (amount<500, and amount>=100), where the fees formula is *Fees=7.99+0.0*amountToSend= 7.99 Euros*:

```
00:47:54,921 INFO [stdout] (default task-128) Trx From France To: Cameroon
Amount=100.0 Fees=7.99
```

Change the destination country to India and relaunch the test. We have an error, since the expected price should be computed using the `France_To_India` rule (*Expected Fees=3.5+Amount*0.01=5*). The failed test result show the unverified assertion with a red background:

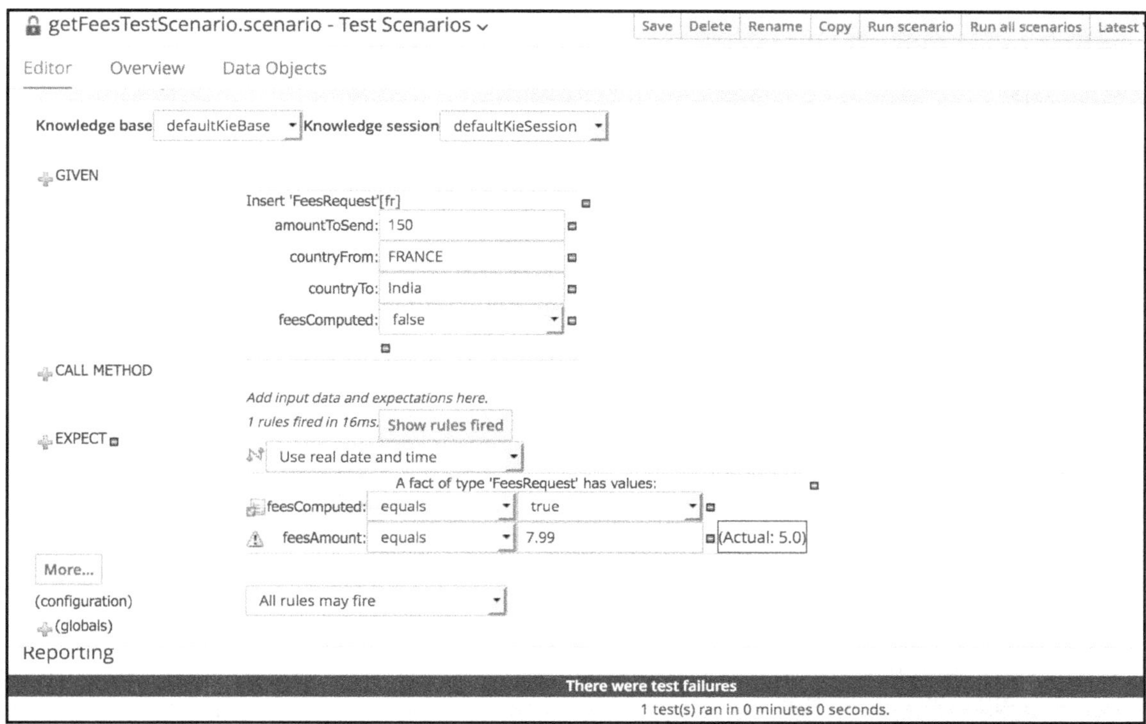


```
01:22:41,718 INFO [stdout] (default task-32) Trx From FRANCE To: India
Amount=150.0 Fees=5.0
```

With spreadsheet decision tables, a large set of rules can be imported in a single operation in the working memory. In this section, we covered how to author tests and deploy rules using the DRL and decision tables. We created various items such as data objects, DRL files, spreadsheet decision tables, and test scenarios. After completing this section, we will have a working memory (facts) and a production memory (rules). How external applications to BRMS interact with the system? This is the purpose of the KIE API.

Real-time decisions with BRMS

The standard deployment scenario for a BRMS application includes the following steps:

1. Create POJO fact classes.
2. Creating business rules.
3. Use the KIE API to create a `KieContainer` or the production memory, which is a repository holding the whole knowledge of the application.
4. Create a `KieSession` object to maintain a conversation state with the Business Engine.
5. Insert POJO Facts in the session.
6. Fire rules.
7. Handle Facts.

For an external application, there are various mechanisms to interact with a business rule:

- The fat jar approach: This is the possibility given to developers to incorporate rules in their applications, code and provide a single deployment unit. Once a rule or code changes, the whole package needs to be redelivered. This option relies on the `KieService` API provided to load business rules from the application classpath.
- The second option is to connect remote Maven repositories; in this case, the KieScanner pulls artifact releases periodically, and the `KieServices` uses the downloaded artifact to start a container.
- BRMS also leverages service-oriented architecture to enable communications with remote applications through a `REST/SOAP` web service. This is called a real-time decision server. The application acts as a client and the rule engine as the server. This approach is the most recommended for cloud- and web-based services.

Now, we will set up a real-time decision server to compute Beosbank money transfer fees according to the decision table rules implemented in the `beosbank-brms-pricing` project. Operations should be available as a REST interface to retrieve a transaction price in real time.

The decision server's features are provided by the `kie-server` WAR application; it is shipped by default with your BRMS installation, but it is not always fully activated. To make the embedded `kie-server` manage Business Central, the following configuration should be activated.

Set up the link between Business Central and the `default-kieserver` in BRM configuration file: `BRMS_HOME/standalone/configuration/standalone.xml`:

```
<property name="org.kie.server.location"
value="http://localhost:8080/kie-server/services/rest/server"/>
  <property name="org.kie.server.controller"
value="http://localhost:8080/business-central/rest/controller"/>
  <property name="org.kie.server.controller.user" value="controllerUser"/>
  <property name="org.kie.server.controller.pwd"
value="controllerUser1234"/>
  <property name="org.kie.server.user" value="controllerUser"/>
  <property name="org.kie.server.pwd" value="controllerUser1234"/>
 <property name="org.kie.server.id" value="default-kieserver"/>
```

Create the internal `controllerUser` to secure communications between Business Central and `kie-server`:

```
./add-user.sh -a -r ApplicationRealm -u controllerUser -p
controllerUser1234 -ro kie-server—silent


# restart your BRMS server, you should see the following logs items
0:23:21,715 INFO [org.kie.server.controller.impl.KieServerControllerImpl]
(default task-11) Server
http://localhost:8080/kie-server/services/rest/server connected to
controller
20:23:21,717 INFO
[org.kie.server.controller.rest.RestKieServerControllerImpl] (default
task-11) Server with id 'default-kieserver' connected
```

Now, log in to Business Central to deploy a new version 1.0.1 of the **beosbank-brms-pricing** decision table with the following instructions.

- Click on the **Open Project Editor Button**
- Change the project **version to 1.0.1**
- Click on the **Save** button
- Enter a comment and commit the modification when prompted
- Then click on the **Build > Build & Deploy**

The screen should look like the following image:

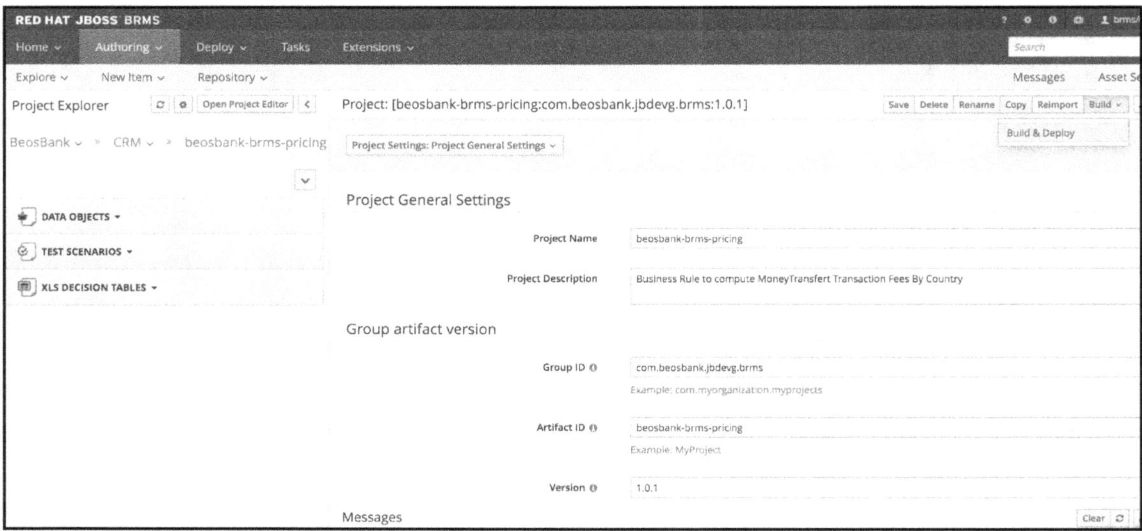

You should see the default-kieserver in the **Deploy** > **Execuction Servers** view.

Select the **default-kieserver** folder and follow the **Add Container** action to create a container with the **beosbank-brms-pricing-container** name:

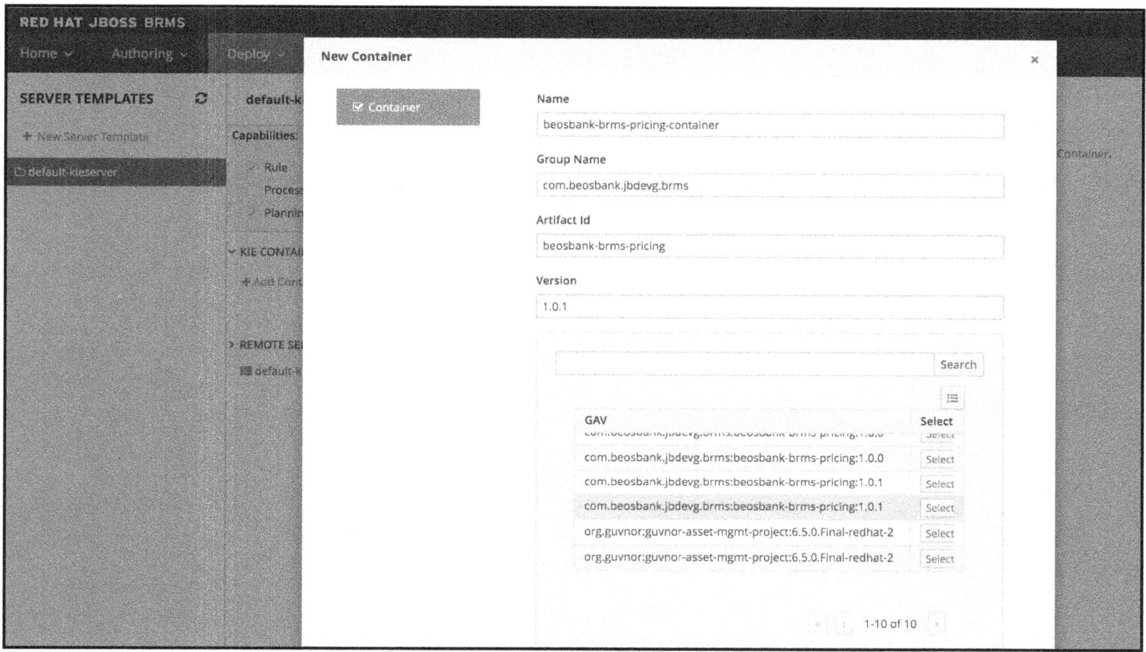

Select the **com.beosbank.jbdevg.brms:beosbank-brms-pricing:1.0.1** Maven artifact to provision your container. This is the application that will be run by your container:

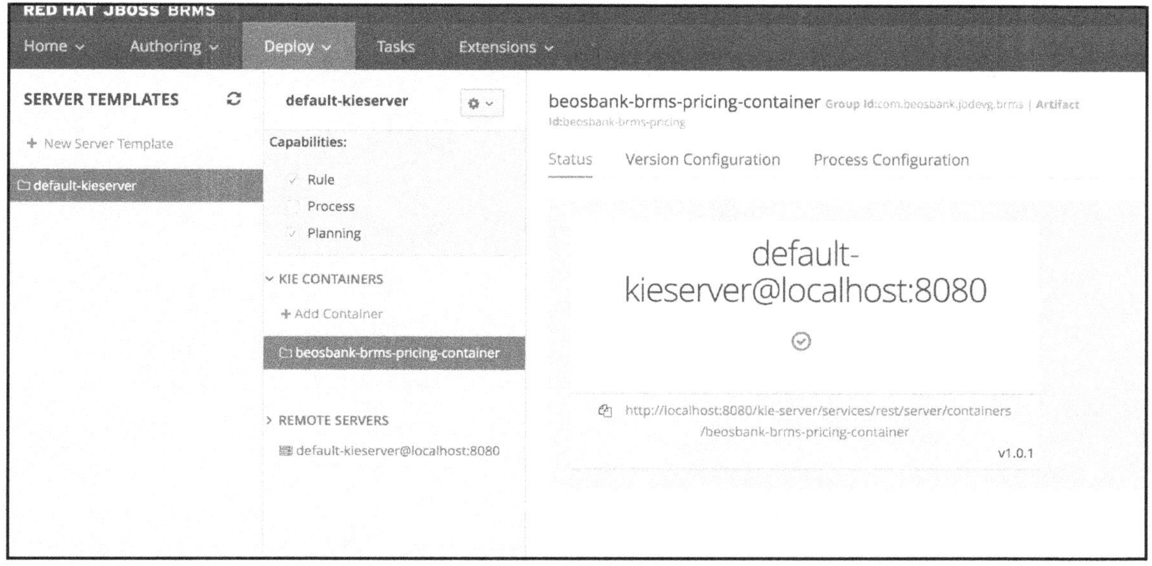

Click on the **Start** button after the creation operation to start the container. Once started, the container status screen displays the URL on which you can have the container information at `http://localhost:8080/kie-server/services/rest/server/containers/beosbank-brms-pricing-container`.

All the URLs and HTTP methods exposed by the a container are documented at `http://localhost:8080/kie-server/docs`.

From the following document, we can interact with a specific container using a `POST`:

```
http://localhost:8080/kie-server/services/rest/server/containers/instances/{id}
```

Let's try to have fire rules using the `HTTP POST` request with the following parameters:

- URL:
  `POST http://localhost:8080/kie-server/services/rest/server/containers/instances/beosbank-brms-pricing-container`
- The HTTP headers:
    - Content-Type: `application/xml`
    - Accept: `application/xml`
    - `X-KIE-ContentType`: `xtream`
    - Authorization: Basic `Authen` with `brmsAdmin` user credentials
- Request body:

```
<batch-execution>
 <insert out-identifier="feeRequest01">
 <com.beosbank.jbdevg.brms.FeesRequest>
 <requestId>1000</requestId>
 <amountToSend>150</amountToSend>
 <countryFrom>FRANCE</countryFrom>
 <countryTo>CAMEROON</countryTo>
 <feesComputed>false</feesComputed>
 </com.beosbank.jbdevg.brms.FeesRequest>
 </insert>
<insert out-identifier="feeRequest02">
 <com.beosbank.jbdevg.brms.FeesRequest>
 <requestId>1001</requestId>
 <amountToSend>5000</amountToSend>
 <countryFrom>FRANCE</countryFrom>
 <countryTo>INDIA</countryTo>
 <feesComputed>false</feesComputed>
 </com.beosbank.jbdevg.brms.FeesRequest>
 </insert>
```

```
    <fire-all-rules />
  </batch-execution>
```

For example, when sending this request with a REST client, we have the following `ServiceResponse` from the KIE Server API:

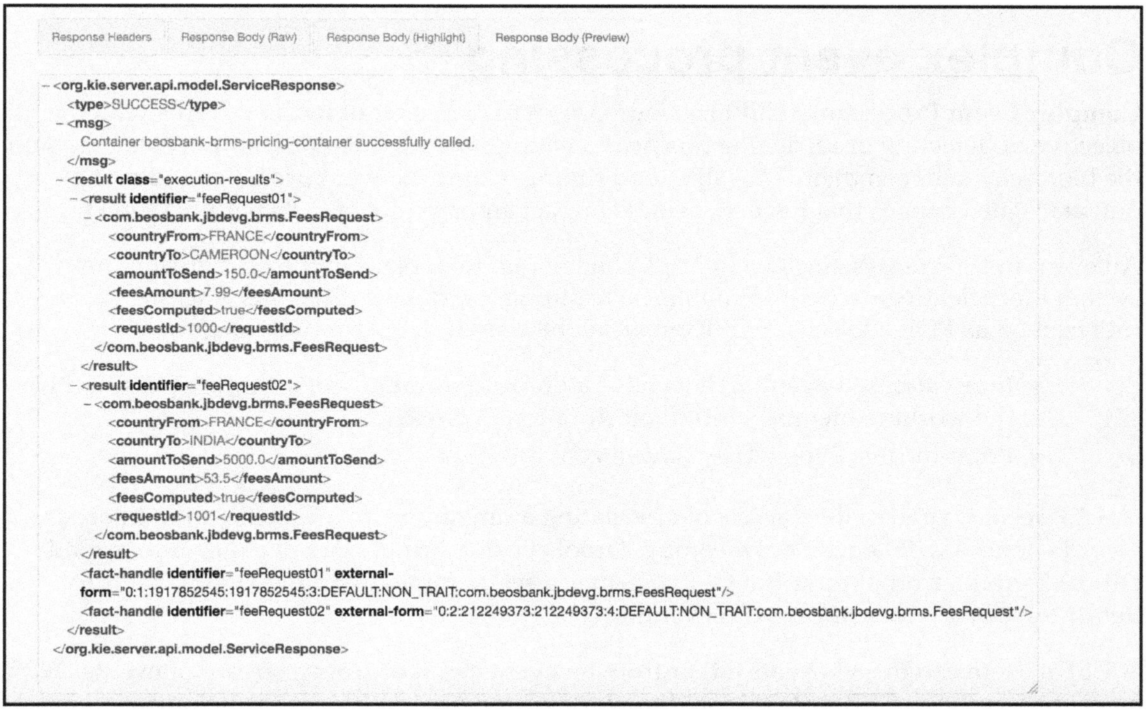

Response Headers | Response Body (Raw) | Response Body (Highlight) | Response Body (Preview)


```
- <org.kie.server.api.model.ServiceResponse>
    <type>SUCCESS</type>
  - <msg>
      Container beosbank-brms-pricing-container successfully called.
    </msg>
  - <result class="execution-results">
    - <result identifier="feeRequest01">
      - <com.beosbank.jbdevg.brms.FeesRequest>
          <countryFrom>FRANCE</countryFrom>
          <countryTo>CAMEROON</countryTo>
          <amountToSend>150.0</amountToSend>
          <feesAmount>7.99</feesAmount>
          <feesComputed>true</feesComputed>
          <requestId>1000</requestId>
        </com.beosbank.jbdevg.brms.FeesRequest>
      </result>
    - <result identifier="feeRequest02">
      - <com.beosbank.jbdevg.brms.FeesRequest>
          <countryFrom>FRANCE</countryFrom>
          <countryTo>INDIA</countryTo>
          <amountToSend>5000.0</amountToSend>
          <feesAmount>53.5</feesAmount>
          <feesComputed>true</feesComputed>
          <requestId>1001</requestId>
        </com.beosbank.jbdevg.brms.FeesRequest>
      </result>
      <fact-handle identifier="feeRequest01" external-
      form="0:1:1917852545:1917852545:3:DEFAULT:NON_TRAIT:com.beosbank.jbdevg.brms.FeesRequest"/>
      <fact-handle identifier="feeRequest02" external-form="0:2:212249373:212249373:4:DEFAULT:NON_TRAIT:com.beosbank.jbdevg.brms.FeesRequest"/>
    </result>
  </org.kie.server.api.model.ServiceResponse>
```


Rules are fired and the resulted facts are sent to the caller in real time:

```
09:49:09,147 INFO [stdout] (default task-15) Trx From FRANCE To: CAMEROON
Amount=150.0 Fees=7.99
09:49:09,150 INFO [stdout] (default task-15) Trx From FRANCE To: INDIA
Amount=5000.0 Fees=53.5
```

One optimization to improve response time is to create a more simple result data object and update the decision table actions to insert lightweight objects in the working memory.

Applications can rely on the real-time decision `REST` interface to cloudify their business rules. First, set up your application business projects, then provision the container to expose the decision process with `kie-server` features.

In this section, the engines replies in real time, but there are some uses cases where the business engine needs more time to detect or find expected results, not because of its performances, but due to the complexity of the problem to be solved. Here comes complex event processing.

Complex event processing

Complex Event Processing (**CEP**) is a mechanism to scan a set of facts or events with the objective of detecting or retrieving business meaningful events inside input events based on the hierarchy between them, causality, and timing. Complex event processing identifies unusual state changes that have a business impact among a set of facts within a time frame.

An event in CEP represents a record of a change that took place in the past during the system lifecycle. Events are immutable, have strong temporal constraints, and are represented as POJO objects. A CEP event can be classified in into two categories:

- Interval-based event: Events have a nonzero duration, and they are persisted in the working memory until their duration expires
- Point-in-time event: They have a zero duration

A CEP scenario generally consists of associating a time frame to a specific event in order to record changes with a business meaning. Drools Fusion brings a set of features to extend Droosl Language for supporting CEP; it brings a set of annotations and syntax items to define temporal relations between events.

A CEP system can detect events either from an event cloud or from a stream of events. With an event cloud, the CEP system is said to work in cloud mode (this is the default working mode); In this mode, the CEP handles all the facts and events in the same way; there is no temporal or timing notion. On the contrary, while working in stream mode, events must be ordered in a chronological order; therefore, in order to maintain the system coherence, a session clock is maintained by system. The session clock is the reference for all calculations requiring timestamps.

CEP uses various temporal operators to evaluate the distance between events and establish correlations:

- `after`: Checks whether one event occurs after another
- `before`: Checks whether an event occurs before another

- `includes`: Checks whether one event starts and ends during the lifecycle of another
- `coincides`: Checks whether two events have the same start and end dates

All these events accept a margin interval parameter to explicitly set time boundaries.

Let's consider the following use case: Beosbank would like to detect in real time transactions sent by a single user from two different locations in the last 48 hours.

A Drools application is implemented in `https://github.com/nelvadas/jbdevg/tree/master/jbbrms/beosbank-brms-ceplab` to solve the case:

```
package com.beosbank.jbdevg
import com.beosbank.jbdevg.brms.model.MoneyTransferEvent
no-loop
declare MoneyTransferEvent
    @role(event)
end
rule "Detect Potential Fraud In consecutive transfers"
    when
        $trx1: MoneyTransferEvent($ref1:reference, $s1: sender,
$c1:countryFrom)
        $trx2: MoneyTransferEvent( this after[1ms,48h] $trx1,
$ref2:reference,$s2:sender, $c2:countryFrom,$s1==$s2,$c1!=$c2)
    then
       System.out.println("Transactions sent from  two countries in 48h ("+
$ref1 +","+$c1+") ("+ $ref2 +","+$c2+")");
end
```

The rule file is a standard DRL file with temporal operators to check whether the second transaction should come after the first one and whether the two transactions should have been completed in the last 48 hours, in which case, the two transactions, details (reference and country) are printed to the standard output. To be considered as an event, the `MoneyTransferEvent` class should be declared with the role event instead of fact (the default).

To push data in the working memory, we will need to use the `KieServices` API to do the following:

- Create a container.
- Set up a specific configuration to use stream processing mode instead of the default cloud event processing.

- Set up a specific configuration to use the pseudo clock. By default, the engine will rely on its own clock; however, since we want to simulate behaviors on more than two days (48 hours), it may be a good idea to rely on a pseudo-clock instead of the default real-time clock. With the default clock, the user has the opportunity to advance the clock manually and insert a specific fact at a specific time.
- Remember that the CEP lab uses the following `MoneyTransferEvent` attributes: reference, sender name, and country from where the transaction was initiated.

The previous described steps can be implemented with the following code:

```
KieServices ks = KieServices.Factory.get();
KieContainer kContainer = ks.getKieClasspathContainer();
KieSessionConfiguration config = ks.newKieSessionConfiguration();
config.setProperty("drools.eventProcessingMode","stream");
config.setProperty( "drools.clockType","pseudo");
 KieSession session = kContainer.newKieSession("ksession-rules",config);
SessionPseudoClock clock = session.getSessionClock();
MoneyTransferEvent mt1 = new MoneyTransferEvent();
            mt1.setReference("TRX001");
            mt1.setSender("JBoss Doctor");
            mt1.setAmountToSend(800);
            mt1.setCountryFrom("France");
            session.insert(mt1);
  //create trx2 after 10hours
       clock.advanceTime( 10, TimeUnit.HOURS);
MoneyTransferEvent mt2 = new MoneyTransferEvent();
           mt2.setReference("TRX002");
           mt2.setSender("JBoss Doctor");
           mt2.setAmountToSend(5000);
           mt2.setCountryFrom("Germany");
           session.insert(mt2);
 //create trx3 after 15hours( 25hours from  trx1)
        clock.advanceTime( 15, TimeUnit.HOURS);
  MoneyTransferEvent mt3 = new MoneyTransferEvent();
         mt3.setReference("TRX003");
          mt3.setSender("JBoss Doctor");
          mt3.setAmountToSend(10000);
          mt3.setCountryFrom("France");
          session.insert(mt3);
   session.fireAllRules();
```

While running the `BeosbankMoneyTransferEventProducer.java` as a Java application, the following items are displayed; the list of transactions sent by **John Doe** from different locations in 48 hours:

```
Transactions sent from  two countries in 48h (TRX001,France) (TRX002,Germany)
Transactions sent from  two countries in 48h (TRX002,Germany) (TRX003,France)
```

In this section, we covered how to solve complex problems with complex event processing. Drools Fusion helped us to solve these kinds of problems by identifying meaningful business events with DRL; instead of solving the problem itself, you tell the engine how to solve it using temporal operators and all the features provided by Drools language. There are two processing modes: cloud event processing and stream; Remember that the cloud processing mode ignores timing notions and handles all facts and events the same way in the working memory, whereas stream mode makes use of the engine clock as its reference. The user can rely on a pseudo clock to simulate specific scenarios.

Summary

The JBoss BRMS application helps users to solve problems in a declarative manner with business rules. In this chapter, we presented the major differences between declarative and imperative programming. Imperative programming models define and reuse the control flow and the runtime engine is instructed step by step how to solve a problem; while in the declarative programming model users tell the runtime engine how to solve the problem. JBoss BRMS helps users organize, author, and maintain business rules. We covered a step-by-step BRMS installation, rule authoring, and testing. We implemented various business rules, including a decision table. We exposed a real-time decision server to serve money transfer fees on a `REST` interface using pricing rules defined by a decision table. We concluded the chapter by looking at complex event processing with a fraud detection example. BRMS is part of the BPMS Suite; in this chapter, we covered only the rule management part (BRMS).
In the next chapter, we will work at a business process level with BPMS.

9
Developing Workflows

In the previous chapters, we covered various ways to integrate enterprise applications:

- Declarative and imperative programming
- Traditional N-Tiers application development with JBoss EAP
- High availability and scalability with session replication and load balancers
- Microservice and serverless application development with Undertow
- Data caching using JBoss Data Grid
- Data virtualization using JBoss Data Virtualization
- Application integration with JBoss Fuse and AMQ
- Business rules application development with BRMS

All these technologies are made to respond more and more efficiently to business needs. However, despite their quality and prowess, in the application development journey, we sometimes reach situations where automation with pieces of software is no longer sufficient to respond appropriately to business requests in term of performance, visibility, and models. In such situations, we should find the answer out of the box. Why do we make these applications or integration scenarios? Behind the application and integration scenarios, there are business workflows and processes. Application development tends to speed up these business workflows and optimization levers reside in the knowledge of company processes. The **Business Process Management Initiative** (**BPMI**) developed a graphical standard representation for specifying business processes in business process models. The activity of representation helps business analysts understand and improve their processes.

This chapter discusses how to

- develop workflow applications using JBoss **Business Process Management Suite (BPMS)**.
- Processes and activities modeling with BPMN2 notation, and tasks and event handling are explained through practical use cases.
- Human interaction through forms is covered to enable users to design and test real-life advanced business processes.

BPM Suite covers both rule and process management; in `Chapter 8`, *Making Better Decisions in Your Applications,* we handled business rule management. In the current chapter, we will work with the second pillar of the Red Hat BPM suite mainly, to model business processes even if a business process includes business rules activities as well.

Process modeling with JBoss BPMS

In `Chapter 8`, *Making Better Decisions in Your Applications,* we installed JBoss BRMS. We could also have installed the full BPMS suite that covered both business rule management and business process management. In the following section, we will see how to quickly install BPM suite and start modeling business processes using the BPMN notation.

Installing JBoss BPM

As with BRMS, BPMS works on top of an application server. In the following section, we will install a BPMS 6.4 on top of JBoss EAP 7.0.0 server. There are two installation modes: a graphical installer that can handle the installation back-to-back or the second option, which consists of patching an existing EAP server with BPMS ZIP. The steps for the second option are given as follows:

- Download `jboss-eap-7.0.0.zip`
- Download `jboss-bpmsuite-6.4.0.GA-deployable-eap7.x.zip` from the Red Hat developer portal
- Unzip the ZIP in the same folder:

```
$ cd BeosBankBPMS
$ unzip jboss-eap-7.0.0.zip
$ unzip -o jboss-bpmsuite-6.4.0.GA-deployable-eap7.x.zip
```

- Create an admin user to access the platform using the `add-user.sh` script. The user is created in `ApplicationRealm` with all the roles specified after the `-ro` option. Start the server using the given code:

```
$ cd jboss-eap-7.0/bin
$ ./add-user.sh -a -r ApplicationRealm -u bpmsAdmin -p bpmsAdmin01# -ro
analyst,admin,manager,user,kie-server,kiemgmt,rest-all --silent
$ ./standalone.sh
```

- For the future labs, we will also create two business groups-- `beosbankAnalystGroup` and `beosbankAccountManagerGroup`--using the following commands:

    - `$./add-user.sh -a -r ApplicationRealm -u` **`beosbankAnalyst`** `-p beosbankAnalyst01 -ro analyst,user,rest-all`

      `$./add-user.sh -a -r ApplicationRealm -u` **`beosbankAccountManager`** `-pbeosbankAccountManager01 -ro analyst,user,rest-all`

- Try to access the BPM Suite business-central application from `http://localhost:8080/business-cenral/` using the `bpsAdmin/bpsmsAdmin01#` credentials.

Once logged in, the BPMS business central welcome screen displays as follows:

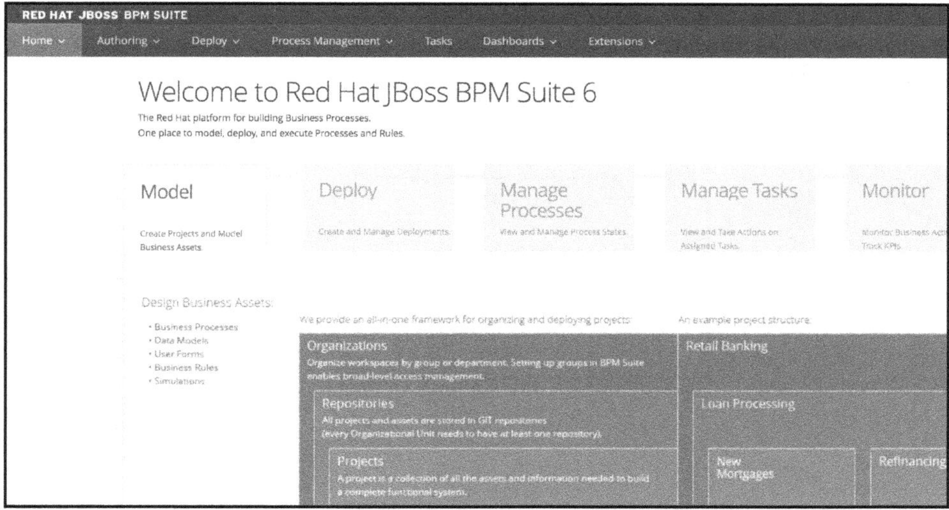

The business-central app is very similar to what we had in `Chapter 8`, *Making Better Decisions in Your Applications,* organizational units that hold repositories, repositories holding projects, projects consisting of various packages but adding stuff related to processes, project Kjar artifacts stored in a Maven repository, modifications tracked by an internal Git system. Further, BMP Suite brings process management stuff such as modeling with BPM2 notation, process and task management, and a dashboard to monitor activities on the platform. In the next section, we will cover business process modeling using the BPMN2 standard graphical notation.

The BPMN2 notation

BPMN stands for Business Process Management Notation. It combines both business process management and a graphical notation of more than 100 items representing actions and flow inside a business process. BPMN notation is a standard notation and not an executable language; however, from a BPMN representation from the model, we can generate an application to execute the process behind the notation. BPMN version 2 inherits most of the graphical charter from BPMN 1.0, but adding the XML format has the possibility of making the model executable. So, BPMN can be used to model any process in any organization, while bringing a common language around business processes. It amplifies the visibility of processes, helps identify potential improvements, and implements them all in a collaborative way. BPM notation is very large and includes the following categories:

Workflow items include activities, sequential flows, events, and gateways:

- **Activities** denote tasks that can be handled by a human, a system, or another process. They are represented by a rounded corner box:

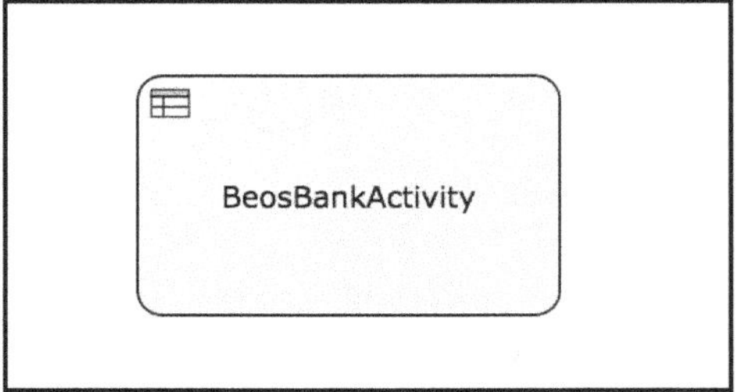

- **Sequential flow** indicates a flow progress between two activities. It is represented by an arrow link between the two items:

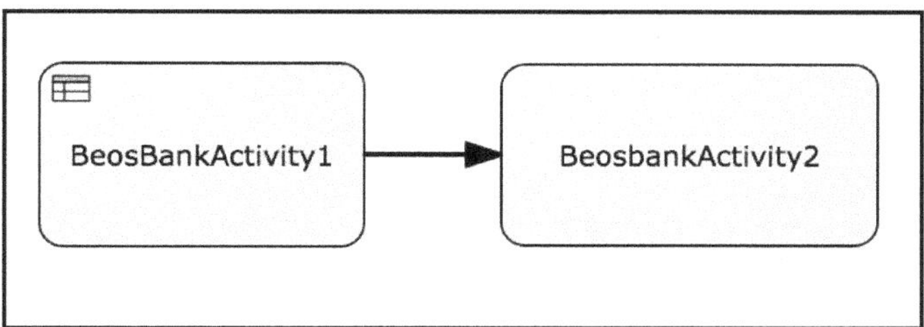

- **Events** are used to manage specific actions during the process life cycle: Start (green), end (red), or custom event happening when the process is live:

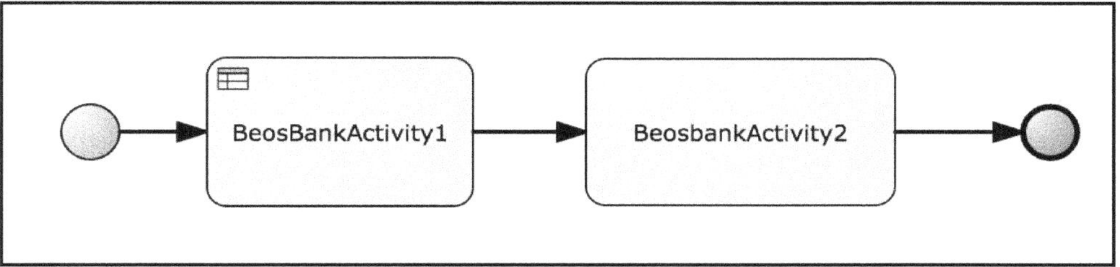

- Gateways are used to dissociate or merge flows. They can be of four types with JBPM:
    - **Event based**: In this case, they are always followed by a catching event or receive task. Sequence flow is routed to the event/task which happens first:

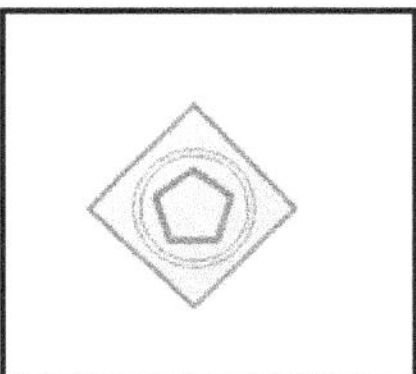

- **Parallel** (**AND**): When used to connect various input flows, it waits for all the connected input branches to complete before triggering the outgoing flows. When used to dispatch output flows, all outgoing branches are activated:

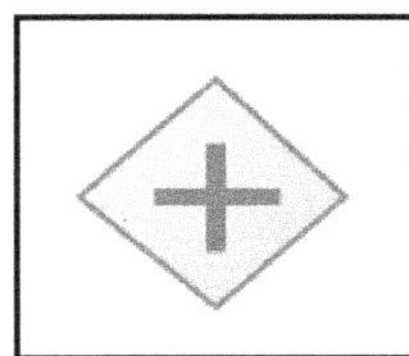

- **Inclusive** (**OR**): When splitting, one or more output flows are activated based on branching conditions, but when merging incoming flows, it waits for all branches to complete before handling outgoing flows:

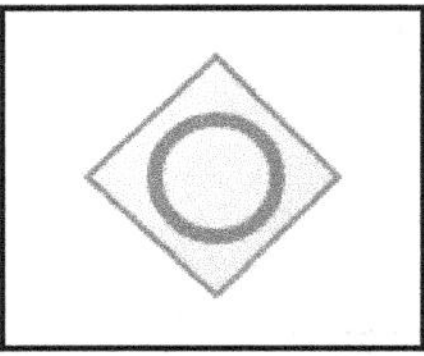

- **Data exclusive** (**XOR**): It waits for all incoming branches to complete before handling outgoing flows. Data flow will be routed to exactly one outgoing flow based on the conditions:

Workflow items plays an important part in the workflow design, but to keep it simple and readable for everyone, they can be organized through logical blocks called organizational and readability items:

- Organizational items: To organize processes such as pools, swimlanes, and groups. Swimlanes help organize the workflow when many actors are involved in a process. In this case, one swimlane is used to group actions that belong to each user or group of users.
- Readability items: Annotations and markers, and links.
- Specific events: Loops, timers, errors, and signals.

After presenting the generalities of the BPMN2 notation, we enter the practical phase in order to see how this notation is declined in JBoss BPM Suite.

The Beosbank practical sample

In this section, we will cover process modeling through a practical use case thrown from the withdrawal process of the beosbank example.

As soon as a money transfer request is sent anywhere in the world on the beosbank network, the receiver can collect the sent money from any beosbank agency. The withdrawal process in a Beosbank agency can be illustrated as follows:

1. A beneficiary comes into one of the agency offices.
2. The beneficiary passes the anti-terrorist checks with a security officer.
3. The beneficiary takes a ticket and a paper form to fill in information regarding the transaction to be collected.
4. The user takes the last position in the waiting queue if not empty.
5. When the waiting queue monitor screen displays the beneficiary ticket number, he should enter the indicated office door.
6. A home agent welcomes the user and fills in the paper notes on a computer form.
7. The welcome station validates whether the user input follows the policies defined in the BRMS rule repository.
8. At the end of the surface control validation process (step 6), if any errors occur, the form is rejected and sent back to the agent with items to fix before resending; otherwise, the form is transmitted to the financial system for business validations.

9. Business validations are implemented through a set of service tasks. To simplify, we will consider only the following two validation tasks:
    - The system checks whether there is a transaction with the requested data in the global system
    - The system checks whether the current agency global balance is enough to pay the user; a signal should be sent to provision the agency if not
10. If all the business requirements are met, the user is redirected to a financial controller for payment of the amount; an account manager validation is also required to collect the money.

This is a small snippet which illustrates how a business process can be complex, but a nice specimen to put various JBoss BPM features in place. In the subsequent paragraphs, we will cover the following BPMS features progressively:

1. Creating/cloning a Git repository in Red Hat JBoss BPMS Business Central
2. Creating a business process to welcome users, including various task types: manual, user, business rule, and scripts.
3. Building and deploying a BPMS project.
4. Starting and following up a process from BPM process definition and process instance views.

Creating the beosbank-bpms-withdrawal project

After starting BPMS suite, the process of creating a project is similar to what we saw in `Chapter 8`, *Making better decisions in your applications applications* ; you can either create a new repository in an organizational unit or clone an existing Git repository. Let's create the `beosbank-bpms-withdrawal` project in the Beosbank organizational unit using the **New Item** > **Project** action and fill in the following details in the **New Project** popup:

- Project Name: `beosbank-bpms-withdrawal`
- Project Description: Beosbank BPMS Withdrawal project
- Group ID: `com.beosbank.jbdevg.bpms`
- Artifact ID: `beosbank-bpms-withdrawal`
- Version: **1.0.0**

Click on the **Finish** button; the Maven project is created and available in your workspace. If you prefer to clone the complete version of this lab, the Git repository address is `https://github.com/jbossdevguidebook/ch9-bpms-labs.git`. After creating the project, the first action is probably to create data objects that will support all the workflows.

Modeling withdrawal data objects

In JBoss BPM Suite, Data objects' data denotes common and shared model objects that are used in business rules and business processes as well. To keep it simple and fluid, let's consider the following two objects:

- `WithdrawalRequest`: Keeps all information related to a withdrawal request from the initiation by a user to validation by an account manager. The welcoming agent introduces transaction data reported on the paper form into a `WithdrawalRequest` instance. Apart from this, the class also holds information of the request workflow: validation date, validator, status, and so on.
- `RequestStatus`: Stores information on the general request status. Each `withdrawalRequest` instance has a specific status during its life cycle.

Use the `New Item > Data object` action and the BPMS Editor to create these two entities in the `com.beosbank.jbdevg.bpms` package. Here's the final overview you will have, with self-explanatory labels:

```
public class WithdrawalRequest implements java.io.Serializable
{
static final long serialVersionUID = 1L;
@org.kie.api.definition.type.Label("Request Identifier")
 private java.math.BigInteger id;
 @org.kie.api.definition.type.Label("Request Date")
 private java.util.Date date;
 @org.kie.api.definition.type.Label("receiver First Name")
 private java.lang.String receiverFirstName;
 @org.kie.api.definition.type.Label("Receiver Last Name")
 private java.lang.String receiverLastName;
 @org.kie.api.definition.type.Label("Reference transaction to claim")
 private java.lang.String claimReference;
 @org.kie.api.definition.type.Label("Country from which the transaction was
sent")
 private java.lang.String senderCountry;
 @org.kie.api.definition.type.Label("Sender First Name")
 private java.lang.String senderFirstName;
 @org.kie.api.definition.type.Label("Sender Last Name ")
 private java.lang.String senderLastName;
```

```
@org.kie.api.definition.type.Label("amount to received ")
 private java.lang.Double amount;
@org.kie.api.definition.type.Label("Person who validate the transaction in
the Agency ( Frist Validation)")
 private java.lang.String validatedBy;
@org.kie.api.definition.type.Label("Person who certified the transaction in
the Agency ( Second Validation if Any)")
 private java.lang.String certifiedBy;
@org.kie.api.definition.type.Label("Date")
 private java.util.Date validationDate;
@org.kie.api.definition.type.Label("Certification Date")
 private java.util.Date certificationDate;
@org.kie.api.definition.type.Label("Transaction Status")
 @org.kie.api.definition.type.Description("Transaction Status")
 private int status;
@org.kie.api.definition.type.Label("receiver age / birth date")
 private int receiverAge;
@org.kie.api.definition.type.Label("Error list returned by the validation
process")
 private java.lang.String errors;
```

Regarding request status at this stage of the development, we want to be able to take different flows when surface controls are okay and when they're not:

```
package com.beosbank.jbdevg.bpms;
/**
 * This class was automatically generated by the data modeler tool.
 */
public class RequestStatus implements java.io.Serializable {
static final long serialVersionUID = 1L;
 public static final int MANDATORY_FIELDS_OK=0;
 public static final int MANDATORY_FIELDS_MISSING=1;
public RequestStatus() {
 }
}
```

The `@org.kie.api.definition.type.Label` annotation is automatically generated by the data modeler tool when passing through the editor to create fields. Once data objects are created, they can be referenced by process or business rules. In the next section, we will model and test `WelcomeUserProcess` described earlier.

Modeling the WelcomeUserProcess

The `WelcomeUser` business process starts with an agent welcoming the customer who has come to recover their money; after formal greetings, the user gives the paper form he previously filled in to the agent. At this step, the process should include a workflow activity where the agent has to report the data contained on the paper he received to a computer form. Once completed, the agent sends the form to the business rule engine for validation. The process can be represented by the following BPMN2 diagram:

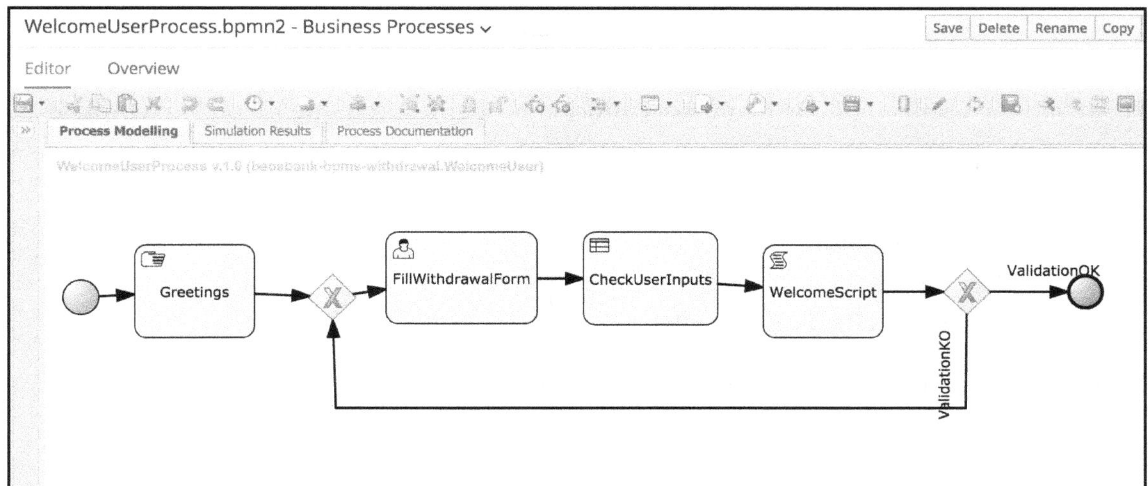

Follow the steps below to create a new process:

- Click on **New Item** > **Business Process**.
- Enter the name `WelcomeUserProcess`.
- Select the `com.beosbank.jbdevg.bpms` package and click on the **OK** button; a file with the name `WelcomeUserProcess.bpmn2` is created to store the XML representation of your process. The diagram automatically opens and contains a green box.

The green box is the BPMN2 start event symbol; it indicates the beginning of the process. You will have to create all the remaining activities with the following guidance. First of all, set up the process configuration to define variables that will be used by the process.

The process configuration

The `WelcomeUserProcess` is created with a set of default properties.

Click on the symbol in the top-right to display the properties of a process/activity:

However, the user can fill the mandatory process properties from the following template:

- **Executable**: `true`, the process will be executable
- **ID**: `beosbank-bpms-withdrawal.WelcomeUser`
- **Process Name**: `WelcomeUserProcess`
- **Version**: 1.0
- **Variable Definitions:** Empty

Variables can be used to pass a parameter to the process or return results to the external world. To pass a withdrawal request parameter to the `WelcomeUserProcess`, we have to add a process variable; let's call it `userRequest`:

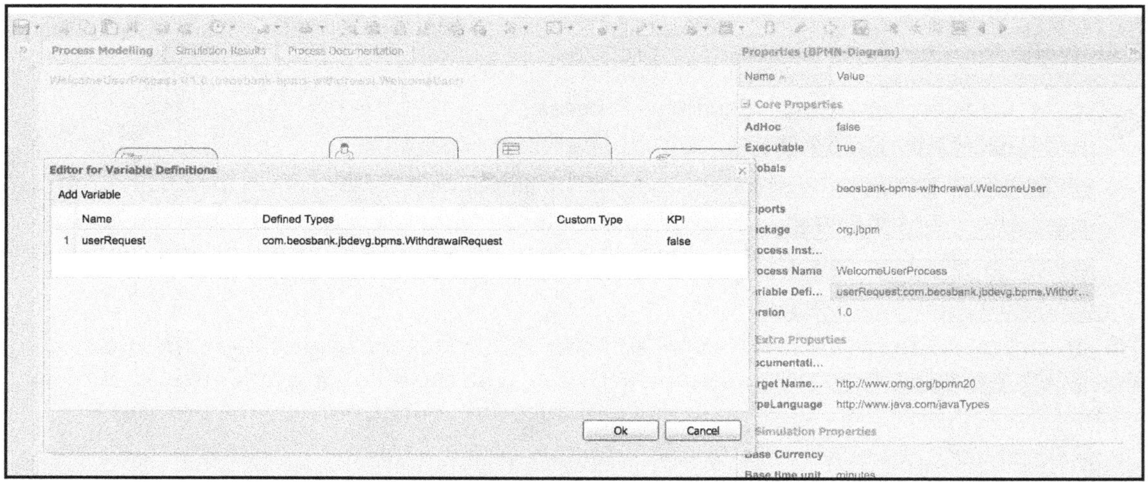

Use the following steps to add the `userRequest` Variable to the process:

- Click on the **Variable Definition** property of the process
- Click on the **Add Variable** button
- Fill in the name column with `userRequest`
- Define the `types` column with `com.beosbank.jbdevg.bpms.WithdrawalRequest`
- Click on **OK** and save your process

While starting the `WelcomeUserProcess`, a caller will be able to pass it an input using a data input and output assignments on the `userRequest` variable, as we will see in the next section dedicated to the greeting activity.

Greeting manual task

The `Greeting` activity is a manual task directly connected to the start event; manual tasks are used in JBoss BPM to indicate activities that should be handled manually. To create the greeting task, follow these steps:

- Hover your mouse over the start event box, and a set of possible next elements will appear.
- Click on the rounded rectangle to draw an activity
- Fill in the activity properties:
    - **Name**: **Greetings**
    - **Task Type**: **Manual**
    - **Script Language**: **Java** (this is the default scripting language in JBPM, but you can also opt for Javascript or MVEL scripts)
    - **onEntry Actions**: `System.out.println("GreetingsTask OnEntry ");`
    - **onExit Actions**: `System.out.println("Greetings Task onExit ");`

- Assignments: Add an input assignment to the `userRequest` process variable with the name `input` and data type `WithDrawalRequest`:

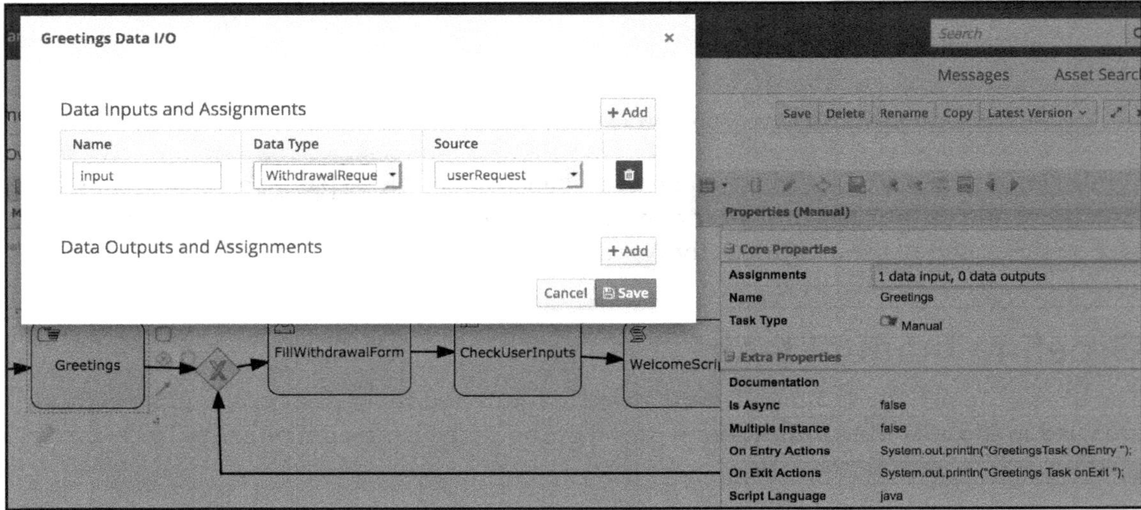

With this mapping, the `Greetings` task will receive a copy of the `userRequest` variable before running.

The `OnEntry` (`resp. OnExit`) action contains scripts that are executed before (`resp. after`) executing the activity itself. The user can use this opportunity to perform specific actions before or after triggering the associate work item handler class.

JBoss BPM leaves the work item handler implementation for manual tasks to the user, so you need to register a custom `Work` item handler for your application before running it. A specific interface is provided to implement the `org.kie.api.runtime.process.WorkItemHandler` custom work item handler.

For demonstration purposes in the greetings activity, we will reuse the core `SystemOutWorkItemHandler` class to just log the request when the process enters in greetings activity. To do so, follow the given steps:

- Click on **Open project editor** from **project authoring view**
- Click on **Project Settings**: **Project General Settings** > **Deployment descriptor**

- Add a new **Work Item handler** to your project configuration
    - **Name**: Manual Task
    - **Identifier: new org.jbpm.process.instance.impl.demo.SystemOutWorkItemHandler()**
    - **Resolver type : mvel**

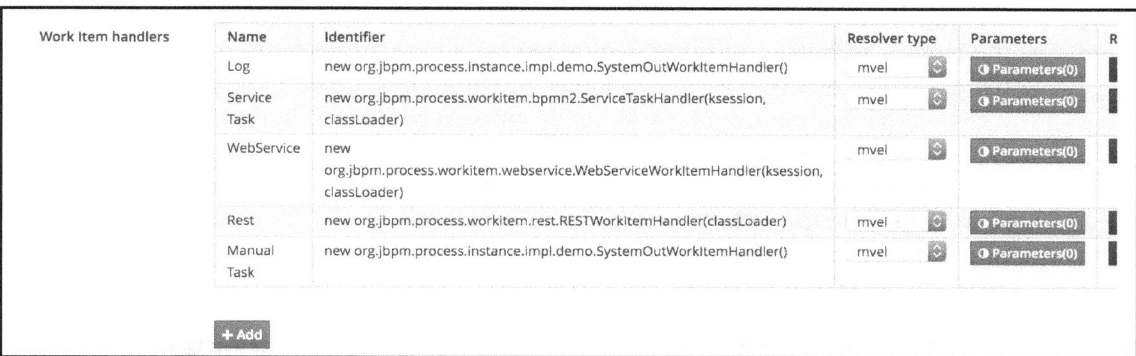

Work Item handlers
Name
Identifier
Resolver type
Parameters
R
Log
new org.jbpm.process.instance.impl.demo.SystemOutWorkItemHandler()
mvel
Parameters(0)
Service Task
new org.jbpm.process.workitem.bpmn2.ServiceTaskHandler(ksession, classLoader)
mvel
Parameters(0)
WebService
new org.jbpm.process.workitem.webservice.WebServiceWorkItemHandler(ksession, classLoader)
mvel
Parameters(0)
Rest
new org.jbpm.process.workitem.rest.RESTWorkItemHandler(classLoader)
mvel
Parameters(0)
Manual Task
new org.jbpm.process.instance.impl.demo.SystemOutWorkItemHandler()
mvel
Parameters(0)
+ Add

Save the configuration. When running this activity in the future, test results will look like this:

```
19:23:06,436 INFO [stdout] (default task-110) GreetingsTask OnEntry
19:23:06,436 INFO [stdout] (default task-110) Executing work item WorkItem
35 [name=Manual Task, state=0, processInstanceId=18,
parameters{input=com.beosbank.jbdevg.bpms.WithdrawalRequest@3fa36eb7}]
19:23:06,437 INFO [stdout] (default task-110) Greetings Task onExit
```

By using a logger as manual task work item handler, we simulated a verbal greeting conversation between the agent and the customer. Apart from manual tasks, JBoss BPM and BPMN2 define various activity types, such as user tasks and service tasks. In the next section, we will handle the second part of the welcoming process through a user task.

Filling in the withdrawal form user task

After the greetings, the customer gives their paper form to the agent who is responsible for transferring the written data into a digital form. To express this activity, a user task seems to be the perfect match; indeed, a user task node represents an atomic task that needs to be executed by a human actor:

- To specify the person or user group responsible for handling this task, use the `Actors` field or `Groups` attribute of the task. For now, we will leave this task to the `bpmsAdmin` user, but it is possible to set a user group from JBoss or LDAP using the Groups fields; so, as soon as the greetings are complete, the `bpmsAdmin` user will have a pending task in his dashboard to fill in the digital form.
- As the task needs to update the process variable at entry (if any data already exists in the process variable, copy it to initialize the digital form) and at exit (when the user quits the form, update the `userRequest` object with the data filled in this form), we need a two-way binding/assignment on the `userRequest` process variable, as shown:

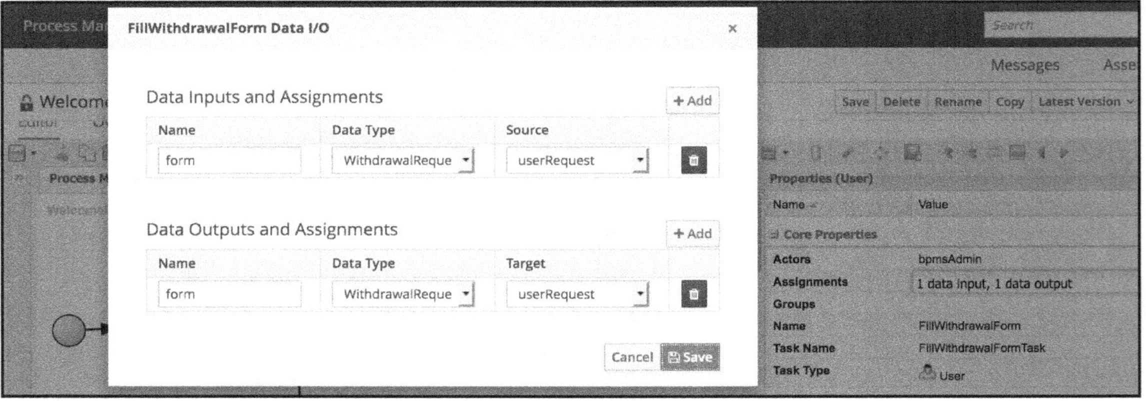

The `form` local variable is initialized from the `userRequest` process variable before starting the activity (`Data Input assignment`). At the end of the process, the values collected in the `form` variable are reversed in `userRequest` (`Data output assignment`).

Based on the assignments done, the form modeler can be solicited to generate the visual form the user will see to perform the required actions. The user can also create their own form from scratch and customize the generated forms. In this lab, we will rely on the modeler to generate the forms and perform customizations later. Click on the **Generate all forms** menu item in your process editor view:

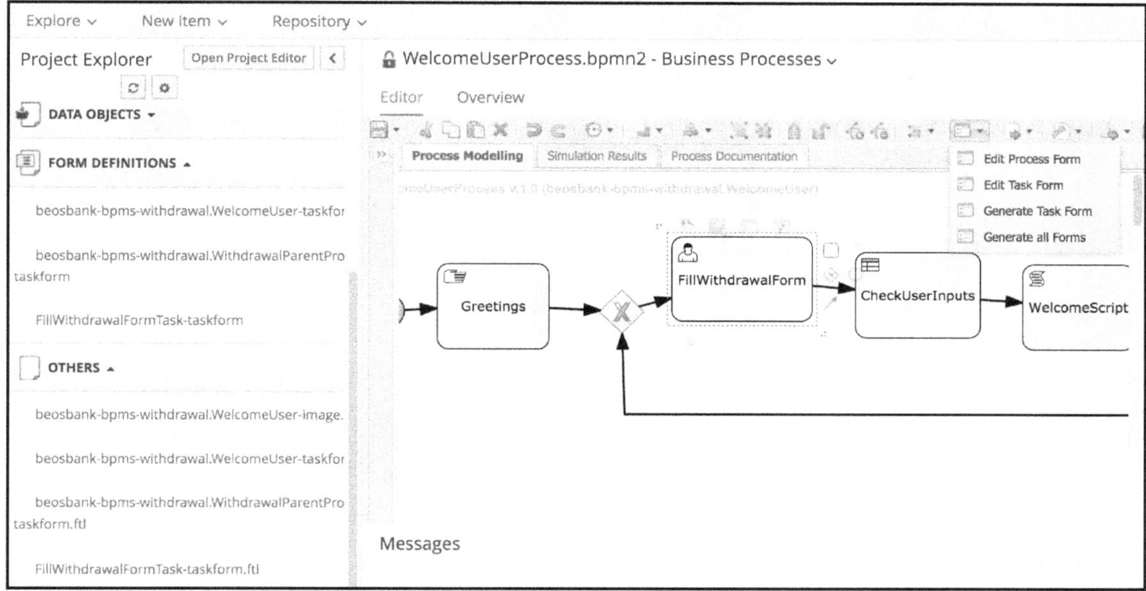

As a result, the modeler produces a form for the selected process and all its activities where forms are needed. In this specific case, the modeler generates the following output:

- `beosbank-bpms-withdrawal.WelcomeUser-taskform` in the `FROM DEFINITION` category: This is the process entry form; it is generated with all the input fields to provide a `userRequest` variable while starting the `WelcomeProcess`.

- A `FillWithdrawalFormTaks-taskform` file in the `FROM DEFINITION` category. This is the form that will be supporting the user task activity; once the user picks a task of this type in his workspace, he will have to provide all the generated fields of the withdrawal request. A built-in submit button is also provided to move to the next process activity.
- A set of `.ftl` and `.png` files associated to the previous taskform in the `OTHERS` category.

Automatically generated forms are good starting points, as they can make us save time; they may have the inconvenience of containing all the defined fields of the process `userRequest` variable:

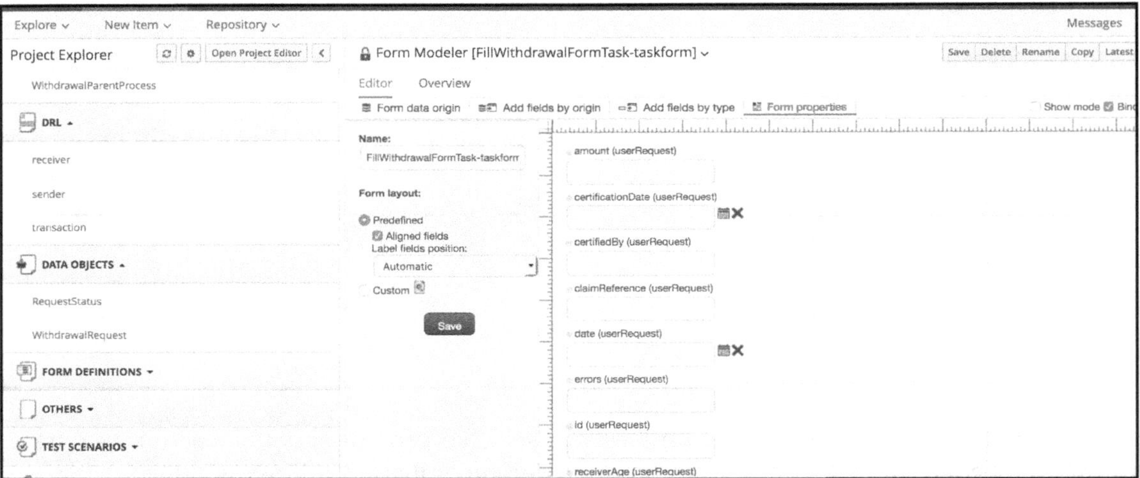

Customization is required to have a specific look and feel on one hand, and keep only the fields we want to make available on the form on the other hand. Click on each form and remove all the unnecessary fields.

On the `Welcome` process form, we will remove all the fields and keep only the Transaction Reference; consider the following example:

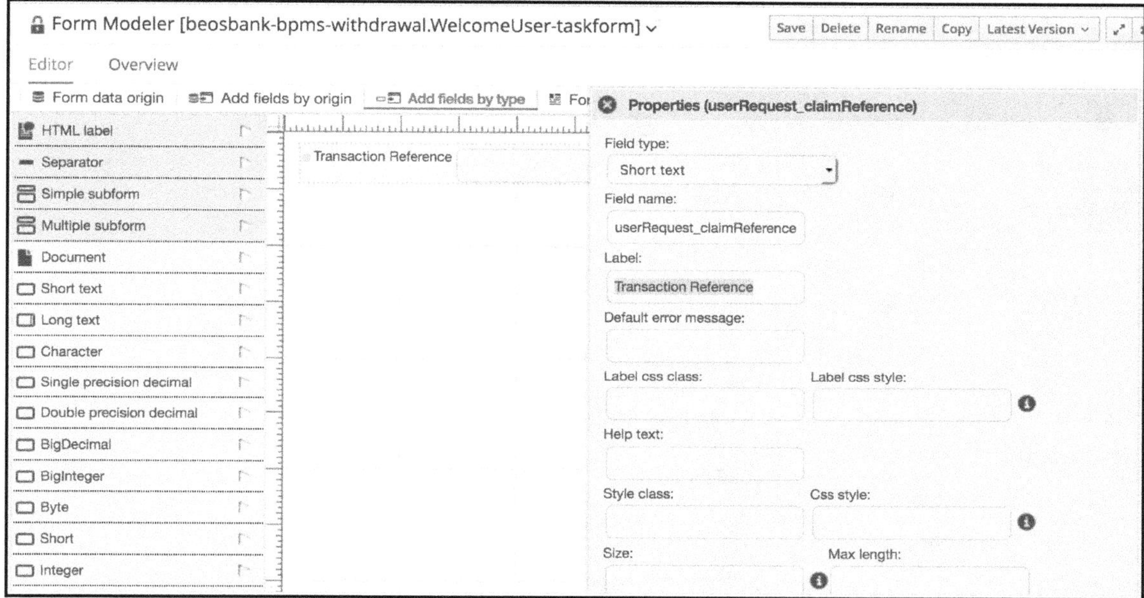

To adjust the fields, refers to the steps below.

- Click on the `Remove` icon on each field except `ClaimReference`.
- Edit the label of the remaining field from the default value of `claimReference(userRequest)` to Transaction Reference
- In the form's `Properties` tab, change the form layout to align label on the left side.

For the user task itself, we need more business fields. Repeat the operation to have a view as follows:

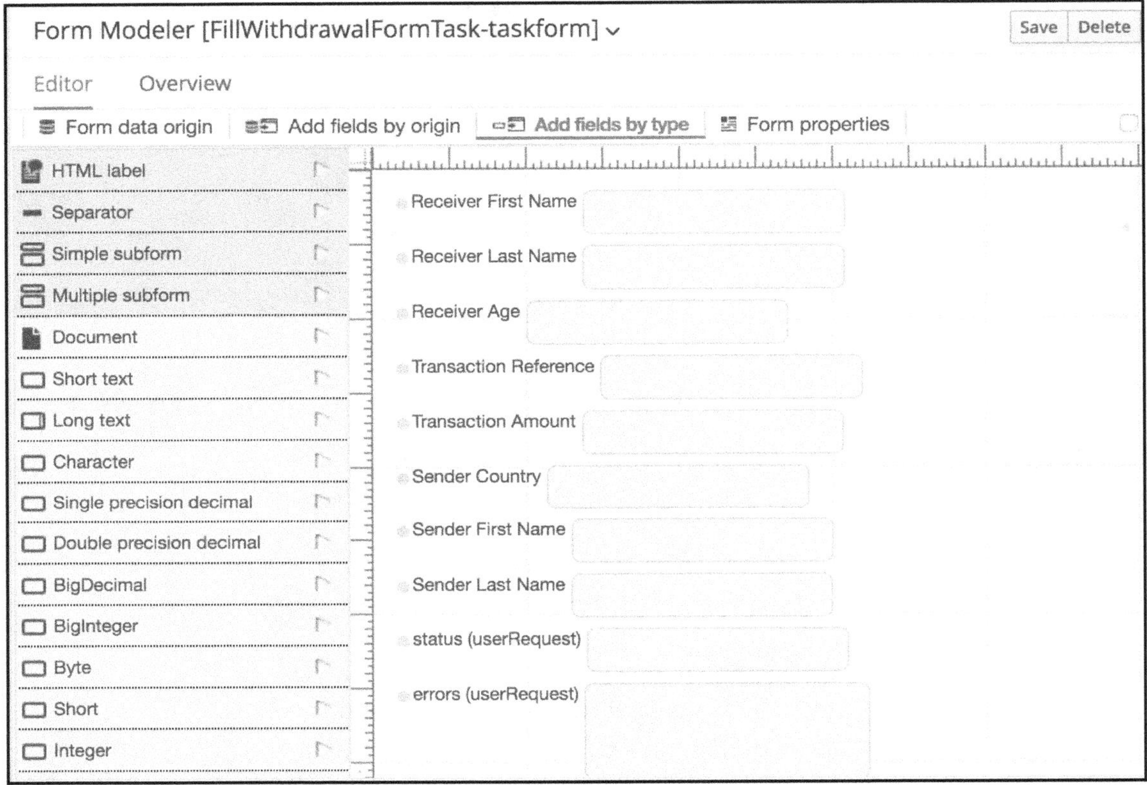

To adjust forms fields, follow these steps:

- Change field positions by clicking on their **first/move/last** icon button
- Rename the default generated labels with business labels such as **Sender Last Name** and **Transaction Reference**
- Edit the errors field; change field type from **Simple Text** to **Long Text** and check the **Read only** boxes
- Edit the status field status, and check the **Read only** box

- In the property editor, you can see the impact of the input and output data assignments; you have two expressions:
    - The `input binding` expression: form/errors: When opening the views, the `errors` field will be filled with data from the errors field of the form variable (remember that the form is mapped with the `userRequest` process variable)
    - **Output binding expression**: **form/errors**: Before leaving the form, the input errors will be copied to the form/errors and thus replicated in the `userRequest` with the data output assignment

Status and errors will only serve to pull results from the validation task.

In this paragraph, we saw how to create user tasks and assign them to specific users, how to generate and customize user task forms, and map process variables with form input/output. As soon as a `bpmsAdmin` user fills in the digital form and clicks on the **Submit** button, the form is sent to the `CheckUserInput` task. The process flow continues with form validation. In the next section, we will explore the way to integrate a set of JBoss business rules in a business process.

Modeling the checkUserInput BRMS task

BPMS Suite supports the inclusion of the `Business Rule` task in a process; in order to include a BRMS set of rules in your BPM process, you need to add a task with the type business rule. The business rule task relies on the `Ruleflow Group` attribute to determine which rule set will be available in the production memory at this stage. Use the same value as your DRL `ruleflow-group` name.

In the following screenshot, you can see the configuration to activate the `InputFieldsValidationGroup` ruleflow group:

1. Set the task attribute to **Business Rule**.
2. Define an input assignment on the `userRequest` process variable. By defining the `w` variable to be initialized with the `userRequest` process variable content, you will automatically have a fact mapped to a `_w` variable in your rules files.

3. Set the `RuleFlow` Group of the task to **InputFieldsValidadtionGroup:**

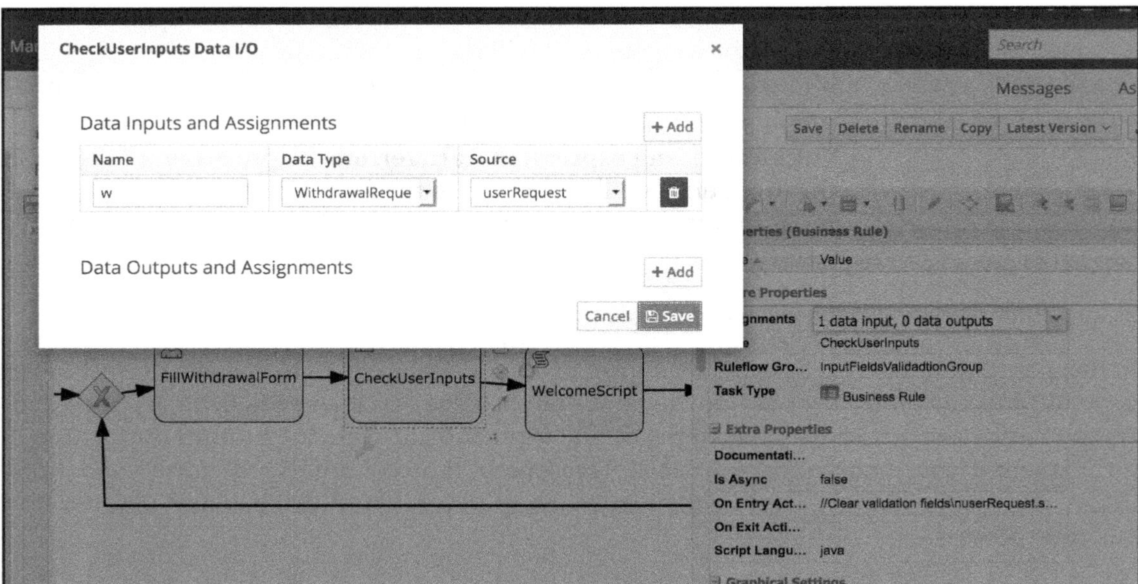

- Define an `OnEntry` action to (re)initialize the fact validation outputs: status and errors, especially before applying the rules:

```
//Clear validation fields
userRequest.setStatus(0);
userRequest.clearErrors();
```

Add a set of business rules with the `InputFieldsValidadtionGroup` rule group flow; all the rules with this `rule group flow` will be eligible to be fired when a `userRequest` fact is inserted in the session.

Regarding the current process, we can create three DRL files to encapsulate transaction, sender, and receiver validations. All the files perform basic surface controls and simple functionnal validation on the target entity (sender, moneytransfer or receiver)

Click on the **New Item** menu and select the DRL file item.

Let's explore the `receiver.drl` validation file, which ensures that the user entered their first and last name, but also ensures that the receiver is at least 18 years old:

```
package com.beosbank.jbdevg.bpms;
```

```
//Check Transaction receiver details
rule "validateReceiverDetails"
ruleflow-group "InputFieldsValidadtionGroup"
no-loop
when
 _w: WithdrawalRequest( receiverAge <18 ||
 receiverFirstName == null || receiverFirstName.trim().isEmpty()
 || receiverLastName == null || receiverLastName.trim().isEmpty()
 )
then
 System.out.println("Invalid Transaction: Check Receiver Details "
+_w.getClaimReference());
 _w.setStatus(RequestStatus.MANDATORY_FIELDS_MISSING);
 _w.addError("Receiver Names are mandatory and the person should be 18y+");

end
```

If the receiver does not provide their name or is less than 18 years old, the request status is updated to `MANDATORY_FIELDS_MISSING` and the associated error description is added to the returned error list.

In this section, we implemented a set of business rules and plugged them into a business process using a business rule task. If users had to keep two things from this section, it is certainly the way to map a process variable to fact as the first and the importance of the rule flow group attribute as the second, to make a connection between the business rule task and its eligible rules.

In the `WelcomeUser` process workflow, after the business validation task, a general script task is used to print details on the output fact. Also, depending on the request status, we can return to the form filling activity in case the rule engine invalidates the input or ends the process if all inputs are valid. In the next section, we will configure the `WelcomeScript` task and handle gateway configuration to return the form to the user if any errors occur.

Modeling the WelcomeScript task and go back gateway

Script task processing is similar to the `OnEntry/OnExit` task interceptors that we covered earlier; users have the opportunity set a language for this type of task and provide instruction in this language to the script engine (Java/Javasript/mvel). The `WelcomeScript` task acts as a logger and prints various information regarding the current `requestObject` on the console:

```
System.out.println("[Script] ***************");
System.out.println("[Script]
```

```
Errors="+userRequest.getErrors());System.out.println("[Script]
ref="+userRequest.getClaimReference());
System.out.println("[Script] sender="+userRequest.getSenderFirstName()+"
"+userRequest.getSenderLastName());
System.out.println("[Script]
receiver="+userRequest.getReceiverFirstName()+"
"+userRequest.getReceiverLastName());
System.out.println("[Script] country="+userRequest.getSenderCountry());
System.out.println("[Script] ***************");
```

Script tasks are also privileged locations where users can build powerful actions by relying on a set of runtime variables, such as `kcontext`, to perform various tasks:

- Set a process variable:

```
kcontext.setVariable(String VariableName, Object variable)
```

- Interact with the process instance:

```
ProcessInstance proc = kcontext.getProcessInstance();
proc.signalEvent(type, eventObject);
```

The current script does not change any variables; once completed, the flow continues to a gateway where the request status is scanned to determine the next outgoing branch.

To set up the branching mechanism, we have to use an `XOR` exclusive gateway component with two branches.

The first branch--`ValidationOK`--should be set up with the following properties:

- Name: `ValidationOK`
- Expression: `return userRequest.getStatus() == com.beosbank.jbdevg.bpms.RequestStatus.MANDATORY_FIELDS_OK;`; this branch will be active only if the `userRequest` status is OK. This is a Java expression including the full package name to find the `RequestStatus` class
- Probability: 50.0
- Connect the `validationOK` flow to the end process symbol

The second branch--`ValidationKO`--to handle validation failures:

- Name: `ValidationKO`
- Expression: `return userRequest.getStatus() == com.beosbank.jbdevg.bpms.RequestStatus.MANDATORY_FIELDS_MISSING ;`; this branch will be active only when validations fail in the rule engine
- Probability: 50.0
- Connect the `validationKO` flow to the `FillWithdrawalRequest` task using another gateway having a single outgoing connection with expression returned true; all the incoming flows will be directed to `FillActivityFlow`

The sum of probability for outgoing connections on a gateway should be 100 percent. With gateways and logging scripts, all the tasks are now connected, and we have a complete process. It is now time to save your modifications and move to the next section, where we will build and run the process in the Business Central.

Building and running the process

Building a BPM project in business central is exactly the same operation as building a BRMS project:

- Open the **Authoring** > **Project Authoring** view
- Click on **Project editor button**
- Click on the **Build** > **Build & Deploy** action button

The project is built and the generated artifact goes into two locations: first, the Maven repository and second, it is deployed on the execution engine.

Click on **Deploy** > **Process Deployments** to view the current process deployed artifacts:

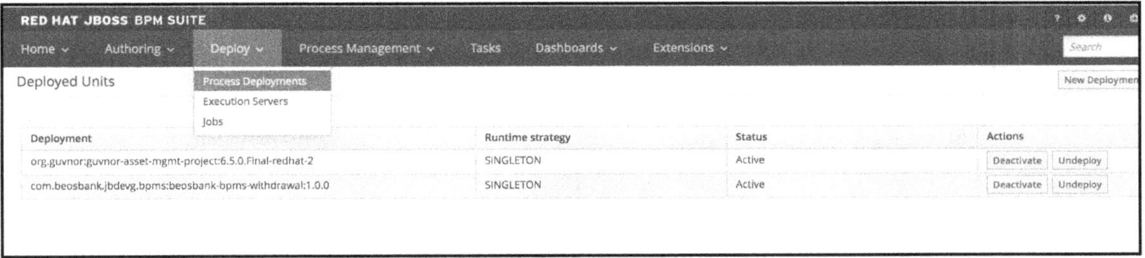

To start a specific process, follow **Process Management > Process definition** to view the process list defined.

Navigate to the `WelcomeUserProcess` and click on the **Start** button to start a process instance. The process form opens with the expected form containing only a Transaction Reference:

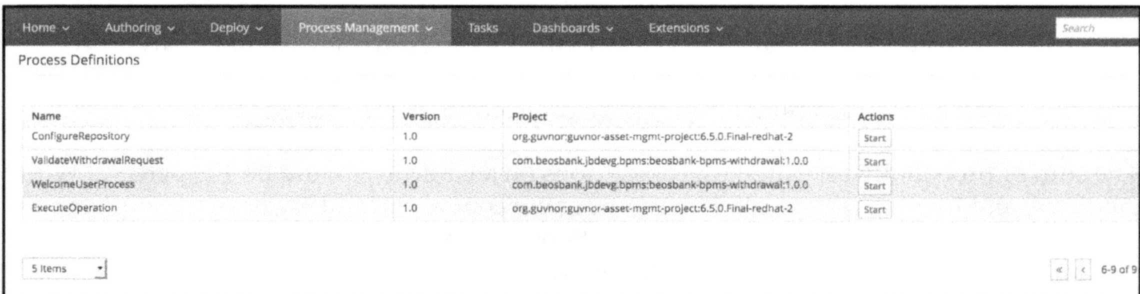

Enter a Transaction Reference, `AFCM10000` for example, and click on the **Submit** button. A message indicating a process instance is created; you can list the active process instances by clicking on **Process Management-> Process definition**:

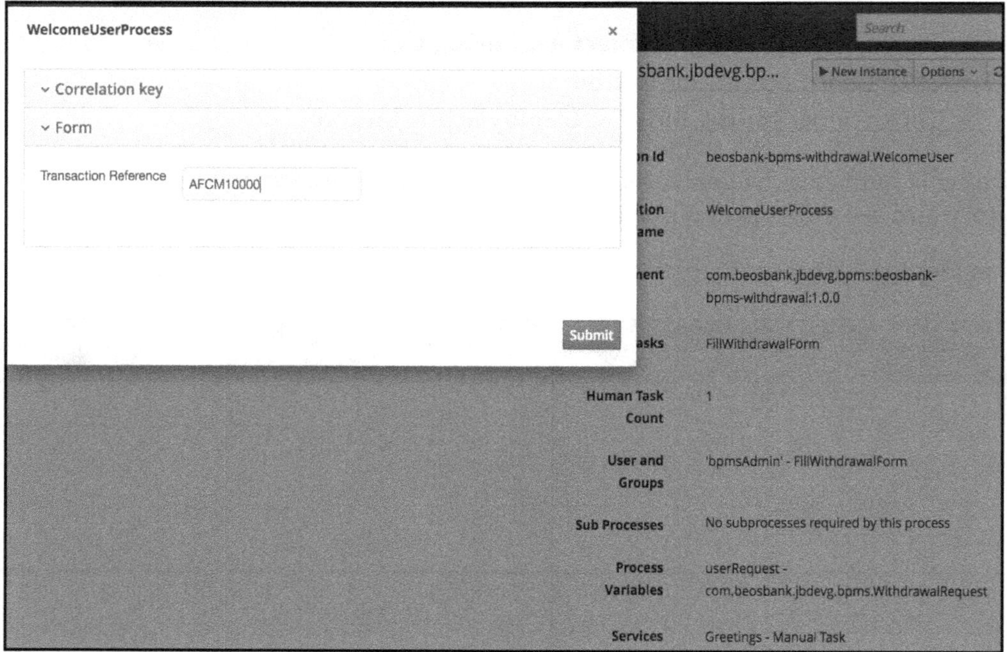

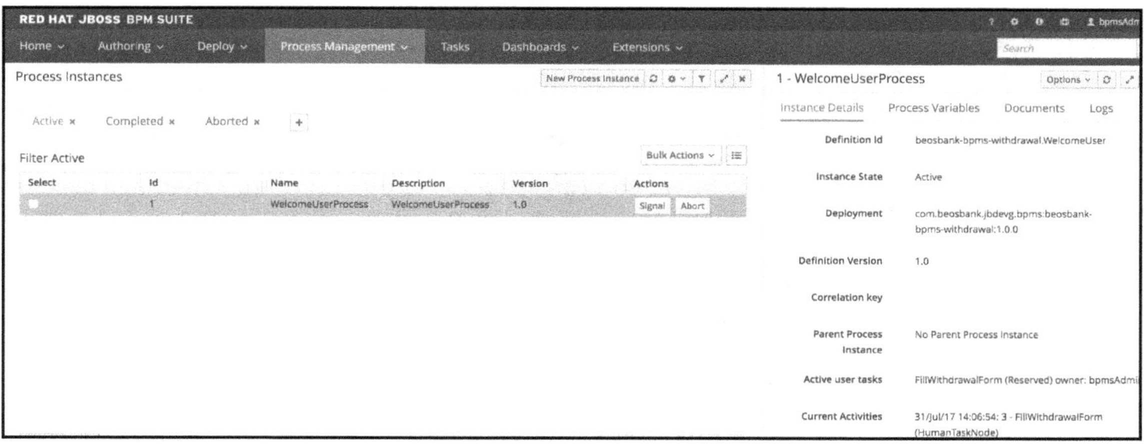

While observing these image we can see the only `WelcomeUserProcess` instance is currently **active**; to see the current instance status, click on the o**ption menu button** > **Process Model**, the following live diagram is displayed with an emphasis on `FillWithdrawalFrom`.

The already completed part of the process appears in gray, while the current project stage is emphasized in red, and the not yet completed steps have the original process color. From this image, we can conclude the greetings task already, as the log shows:

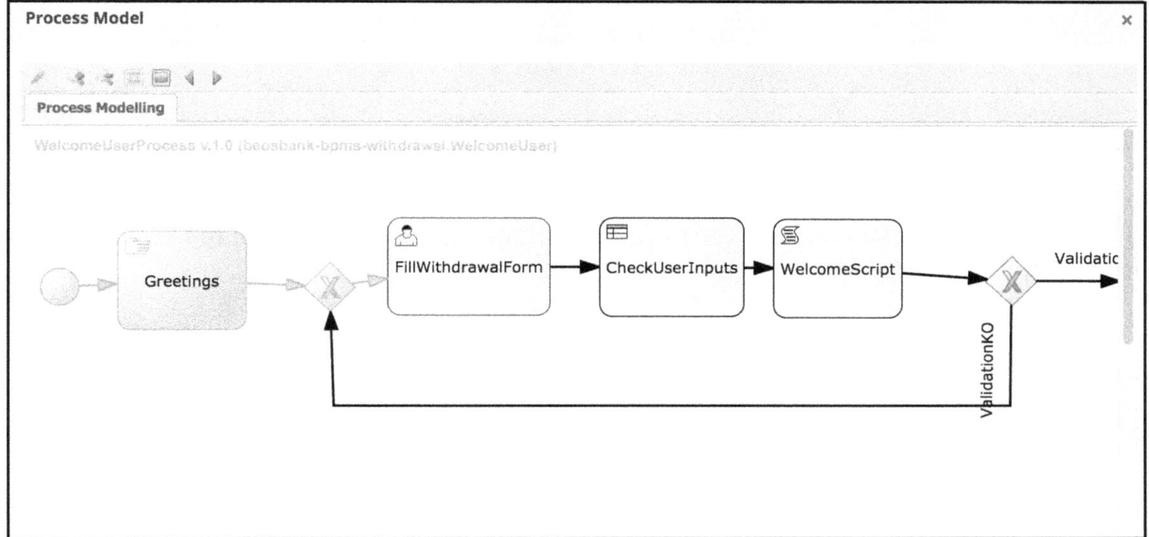

```
14:06:54,773 INFO [stdout] (default task-88) GreetingsTask OnEntry
14:06:54,776 INFO [stdout] (default task-88) Executing work item WorkItem 1
[name=Manual Task, state=0, processInstanceId=1,
parameters{input=com.beosbank.jbdevg.bpms.WithdrawalRequest@32108e30}]
14:06:54,777 INFO [stdout] (default task-88) Greetings Task onExit
```

In the console outputs displayed above, you can see the completion of the Greetings task as last items printed. No more log statement is printed as the process is currently waiting for one actor to complete the `FillWithdrawalForm` task. As we assigned the `FillWithdrawalForm` to the `bpmsAdmin` user, to continue the process, you should log in using the `bpmsAdmin` user if not using this account yet.

Click on the **Tasks** menu; the pending tasks for the user and its group are displayed in a table:

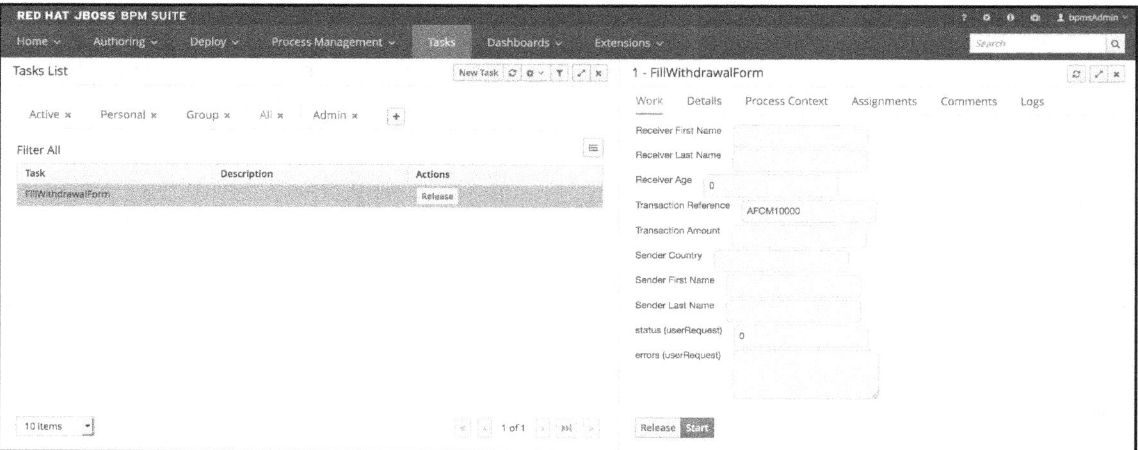

We can recognize the process instance associated with the `AFCM10000` reference when clicking on the task. To complete the task, click on the **Start** button and fill in the form accordingly.

Fill in the form as `bpmsAdmin` with only the following information:

- **Receiver First Name**: `Aditi`
- **Receiver Last Name**: `GOUR`
- **Receiver Age**: *** *Keep empty to check validations* ****
- **Transaction Reference**: `AFCM10000`
- **Transaction Amount**: `500`
- **Sender First Name**: `Larissa`
- **Sender Last Name**: `PINTO`
- Click on the **Submit** button

We can see that validation is rejected and the form comes back in the user's task list. The rule engine logs show which rules have been violated:

```
14:24:13,412 INFO [stdout] (default task-70) Exit with
userRequest=com.beosbank.jbdevg.bpms.WithdrawalRequest@fca97a2
14:24:13,413 INFO [stdout] (default task-70) [FormExit] ref=AFCM10000
14:24:13,413 INFO [stdout] (default task-70) [FormExit] sender=Larissa
PINTO
14:24:13,413 INFO [stdout] (default task-70) [FormExit] receiver=Aditi GOUR
14:24:13,413 INFO [stdout] (default task-70) [FormExit] country=
14:24:13,504 INFO [stdout] (default task-70) Invalid Transaction check
Sender details AFCM10000
14:24:13,506 INFO [stdout] (default task-70) Invalid Transaction: Check
Receiver Details AFCM10000
14:24:13,511 INFO [stdout] (default task-70) [Script] ***************
14:24:13,511 INFO [stdout] (default task-70) [Script] Errors=
14:24:13,511 INFO [stdout] (default task-70) Sender Names and country are
mandatory
14:24:13,511 INFO [stdout] (default task-70) Receiver Names are mandatory
and the person should be 18y+
14:24:13,511 INFO [stdout] (default task-70) [Script] ref=AFCM10000
14:24:13,511 INFO [stdout] (default task-70) [Script] sender=Larissa PINTO
14:24:13,511 INFO [stdout] (default task-70) [Script] receiver=Aditi GOUR
14:24:13,511 INFO [stdout] (default task-70) [Script] country=
14:24:13,511 INFO [stdout] (default task-70) [Script] ***************
```

The same errors can be seen when you reopen the task as `bpmsAdmin` in the errors field:

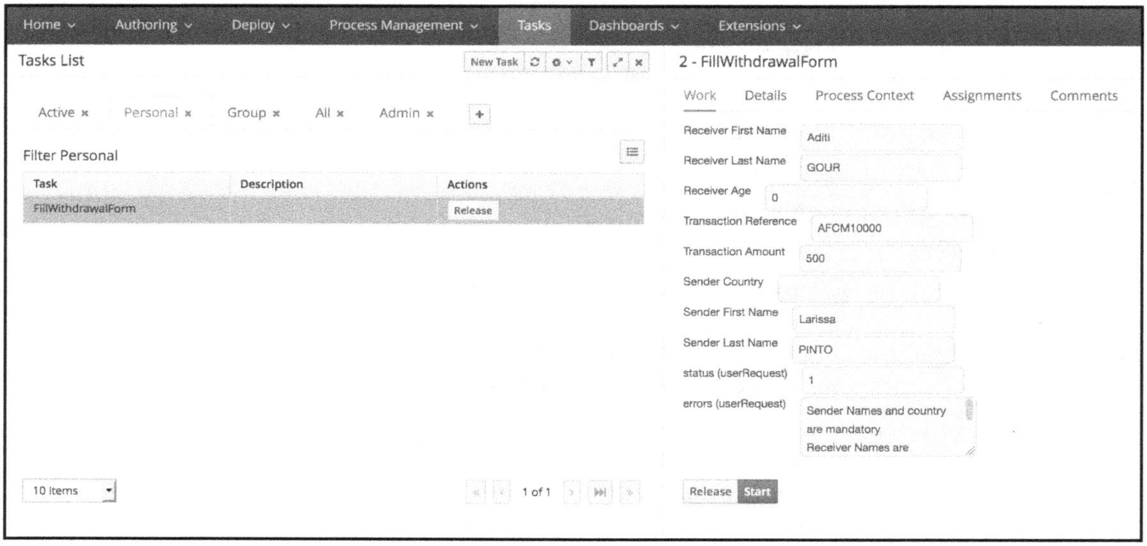

Complete the form with the two missing fields:

- Receiver Age: `20`
- Sender Country: `UK`

Now resubmit the form. The task disappears from the user's basket, and the script task logs show no more errors:

```
14:38:40,896 INFO [stdout] (default task-90) [Script] ***************
14:38:40,896 INFO [stdout] (default task-90) [Script] Errors=
14:38:40,896 INFO [stdout] (default task-90) [Script] ref=AFCM10000
14:38:40,896 INFO [stdout] (default task-90) [Script] sender=Larissa PINTO
14:38:40,896 INFO [stdout] (default task-90) [Script] receiver=Aditi GOUR
14:38:40,896 INFO [stdout] (default task-90) [Script] country=UK
14:38:40,896 INFO [stdout] (default task-90) [Script] ***************
```

While checking the process instances, the previous instance (Id=1) is now in the completed list, and the process model shows all activities in grey, as they have been executed:

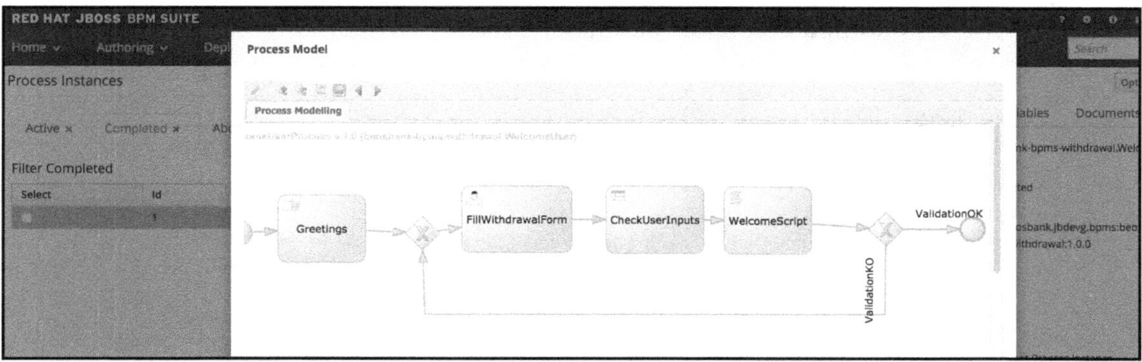

In this tutorial, we created and executed a process in business central. To be able to build readable and flexible processes, it may be interesting to check how to reference the existing processes. In the next section, we will work on process composition.

Integrating the WelcomeUser in a parent process

In general, processes are not isolated; they need to interact each other to reuse enterprise assets. An interesting feature is how to call a sub/child process from a parent process. BPMN2 and JBoss BPM provide a reusable subprocess activity to invoke another process. To create a `WithdrawalParent` process to invoke the `WelcomeUserProcess`, perform the given steps:

1. Create a new process from the `New Item` action with the name `WithdrawalParentProcess`.
2. Add a process variable to the parent process with name `withdrawalForm` and type `com.beosbank.jbdevg.bpms.WithdrawalRequest`.

3. From the object library, add a reusable subprocess activity with the following details:
    - **Name**: `WelcomeSubProcess`
    - **Called Element**: Select the `beosbank-bmps-withdrawal.WelcomeUser` process:

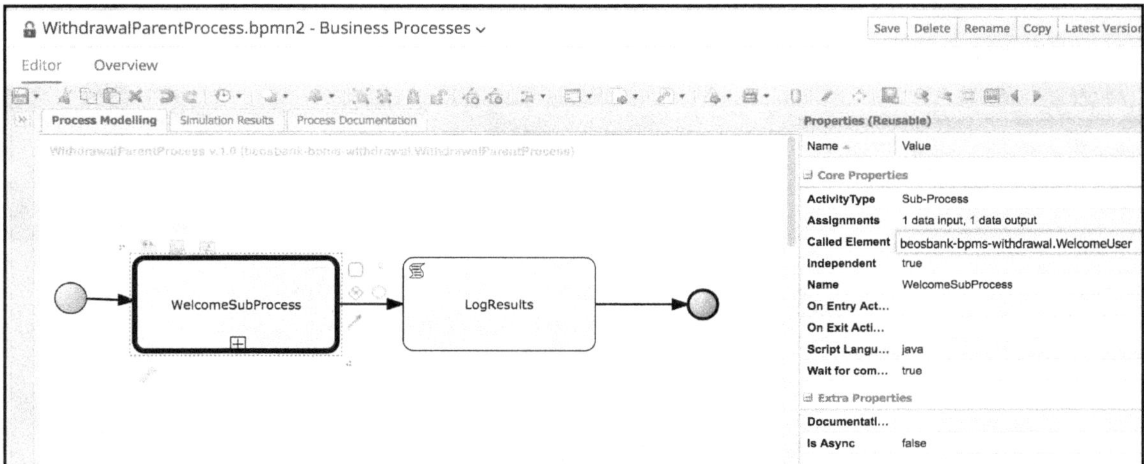

Assignments: Implements both input and output assignments:

- The input assignment should map the process `withdrawalForm` (source) variable as `userRequest` (name) input parameter for the subprocess
- The output assignment should copy the subprocess result `userRequest` (name) variable in the parent `withdrawalForm` (target) variable:

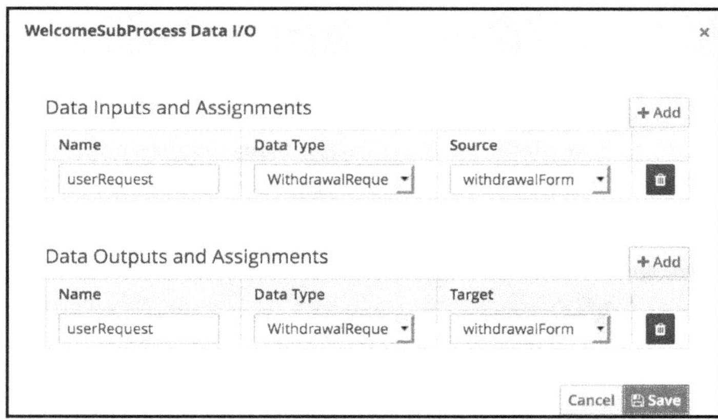

With this configuration, the parent process variable is sent as a parameter each time the subprocess is invoked; once completed, the subprocess sends the validated form back to the parent process.

BPM suite includes a set of features a chapter will not suffice to cover. Once processes are designed, users can simulate the process using a simple menu; enter the target process instances to run, and the engine takes care of the simulation activity:

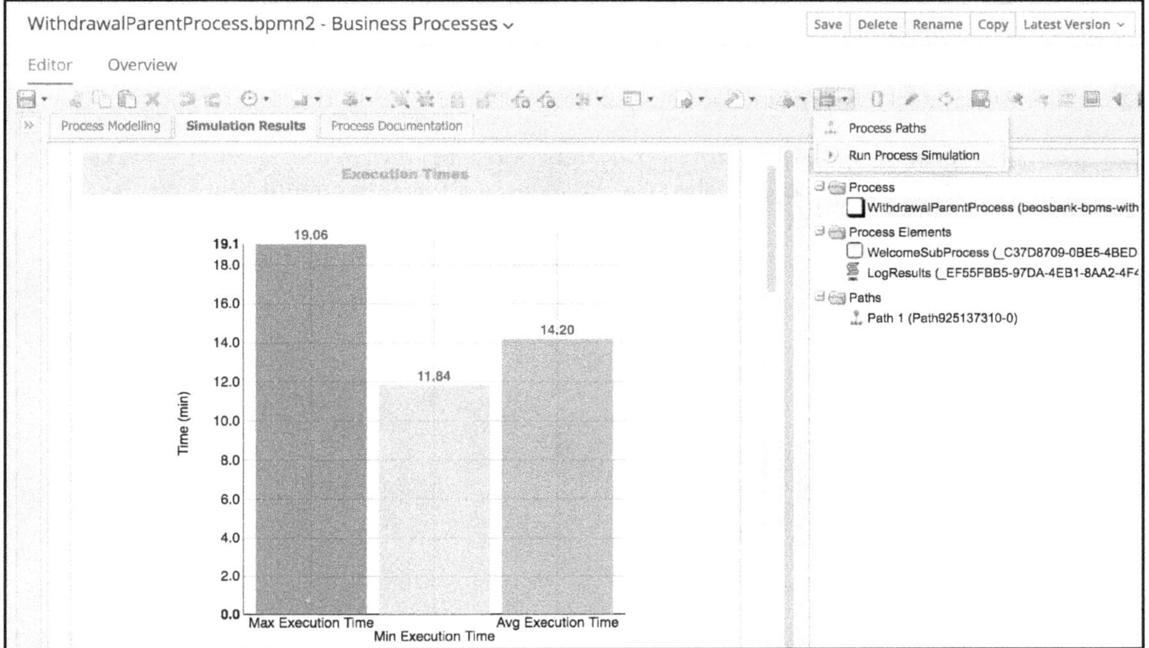

Process monitoring can help users detect bottlenecks and time-consuming tasks in their processes.

BPM Suite includes a dashboard to monitor ongoing, pending, suspended, and completed processes and tasks. Once completed, the WelcomeUserProcess instance execution completed, the dashboard should display one completed process and 2 completed tasks by `bpsAdmin` user as shown below:

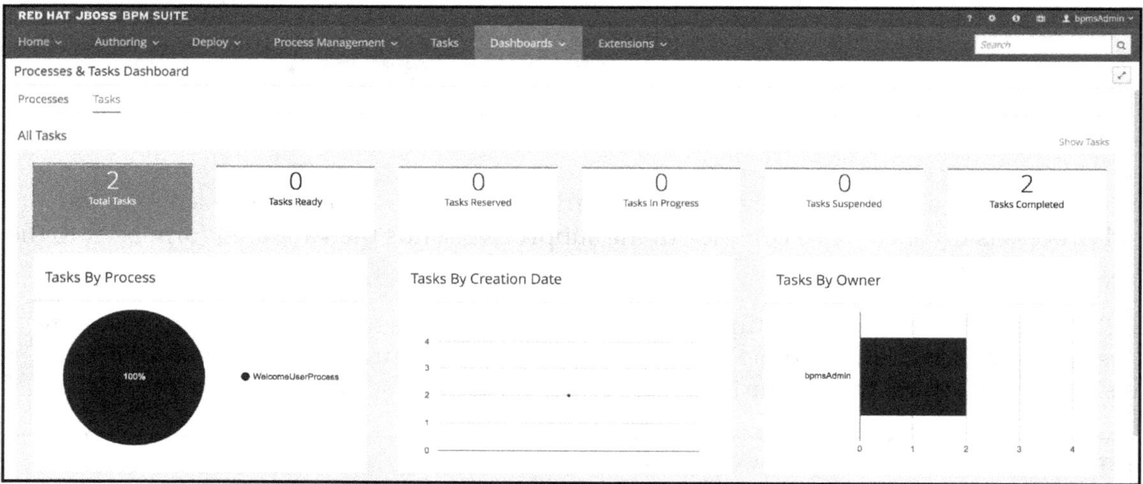

Dont forget that process simulation does not impact the dashboard indicators.

Regarding integration with other JBoss products, JBoss BPM provides a set of APIs to interact with tasks and processes. The Apache `Camel-jbpm` component relies on the `REST` API to manage JBPM assets.

Summary

Modeling business processes can help analysts detect imperfections in their daily business applications. JBoss Business Suite offers a large panel of features for process modeling, execution, monitoring, and simulation. In this chapter, we progressively modeled a subset of a withdrawal complex business process, and various objects were created: data objects to hold user inputs and data transferred objects between tasks and activities. We implemented a set of business rules to handle validations and surface controls on user inputs, assign a specific rule flow group to the Drools rules, and activate a specific set of rules in a business rule task. The validation process includes a custom manual task to welcome a customer and a human task, on which we created associated forms using the BPM suite modeler. We learned how to exchange data between process tasks, and also learned parent and subprocess communication through process variables. At the end, we executed the process in business central and monitored the generated instances and tasks on the provided dashboard.

Index

E

F

G

I

J

K

M

O

S

U

V

W

www.ingramcontent.com/pod-product-compliance
Lightning Source LLC
Chambersburg PA
CBHW080623060326
40690CB00021B/4791
9781788296199